Buying Stocks Without a Broker

Also by Charles B. Carlson

No-Load Stocks

Free Lunch on Wall Street

Buying Stocks Without a Broker

Charles B. Carlson, CFA
Editor, *DRIP Investor*

Second Edition

McGraw-Hill

New York   San Francisco   Washington, D.C.   Auckland   Bogotá
Caracas   Lisbon   London   Madrid   Mexico City   Milan
Montreal   New Delhi   San Juan   Singapore
Sydney   Tokyo   Toronto

Library of Congress Cataloging-in-Publication Data

Carlson, Charles B.
    Buying stocks without a broker / Charles B. Carlson. — 2nd ed.
       p.   cm.
    Includes index.
    ISBN 0-07-011500-1 (cloth : alk. paper). — ISBN 0-07-011501-X
(pbk. : alk. paper).
    1. Dividend reinvestment. I. Title.
HG4028.D5C37   1996
332.63'22—dc20   95-39880
                                       CIP

McGraw-Hill

A Division of The McGraw·Hill Companies

1 2 3 4 5 6 7 8 9 0 DOC/DOC 9 0 0 9 8 7 6 5 (hc)
1 2 3 4 5 6 7 8 9 0 DOC/DOC 9 0 0 9 8 7 6 5 (pbk)

ISBN 0-07-011500-1 (hc)
ISBN 0-07-011501-X (pbk)

*The sponsoring editor for this book was David J. Conti, the editing supervisor
was Stephen M. Smith, and the production supervisor was Suzanne W. B.
Rapcavage. It was set in Palatino by Terry Leaden of McGraw-Hill's
Professional Book Group composition unit and Elberta Miklusak of Horizon
Management Services, Inc.*

Printed and bound by R. R. Donnelley & Sons Company.

 This book is printed on recycled, acid-free paper containing
a minimum of 50% recycled, de-inked fiber.

To my parents, whose love and support have meant more to me than they will ever know

Contents

Preface

As you will soon discover in these pages, there are programs that permit investors to purchase stocks directly from companies, sometimes at a discount, without ever calling a broker and paying brokerage commissions. The programs are called dividend reinvestment plans (DRIPs), and they are the subject of this book.

Contrary to what you may be thinking, I have no axe to grind with brokers, who often have thankless jobs with customers taking all of the credit when things go well and dumping all of the blame on them when things go badly. I will not attempt to discuss the relative merits of brokers in this book. I trust that those brokers who have been successful for their clients have nothing to fear from these pages.

My point—and this is indisputable—is that brokers don't work for free. They cost you money in the form of commissions. And these commissions can take a toll on a portfolio's performance. Thus, if a way exists in which individual investors can hold down or eliminate commission costs, it seems to me investors have a right to know about it.

Yet, many investors are simply not aware of the commission-free investing possibilities available with DRIPs. When this subject appears as a feature in *Dow Theory Forecasts*, an investment newsletter published by my firm, it always generates many calls and letters from individuals who had never heard of the programs prior to the report. I suppose that's no surprise—it's not as though brokers beat the drums for these plans, for obvious reasons.

Hence, the reason for writing this book is to make investors aware of these plans and to provide guidance in using them. With information being everything in the investment game, you owe it to yourself to be informed about all options in stock investing. DRIPs are one option you can ill-afford not to at least consider, given their many benefits.

Acknowledgments

Putting together a book of this magnitude is by no means a one-man show. Many people deserve credit for their efforts. I'd like to thank the entire staff of *Dow Theory Forecasts* and *DRIP Investor* newsletters, especially Al Rayski, Lillian Ebert, Ethel Merkel, and Sandy Spisak, for their support and encouragement. Thanks also go to the companies that responded to our verbal and written inquiries concerning their DRIPs. And to the readers of *Dow Theory Forecasts*, whose interest in this subject was the primary impulse for this book, many thanks for your comments and suggestions.

Finally, I would be remiss if I didn't give special recognition to Avis Beitz, Elberta Miklusak, Juliann Kessey, and Monica Taylor. Without their tireless efforts, this book would still be in my head instead of in your hands.

Charles B. Carlson, CFA

Introduction

Right up front, I'm pretty sure I already know two things about you. First, your stockbroker didn't tell you about this book. Second, you probably feel like a second-class citizen when dealing with Wall Street these days.

Now, I realize I'm no clairvoyant. But, my position as editor of *Dow Theory Forecasts* and *DRIP Investor* newsletters gives me a good idea of what's on the minds of individual investors. Currently, you're a disgruntled lot. Indeed, individual investors—the "little guys," according to Wall Street—are fed up. You're fed up with insider trading scandals; fed up with computer program trading and other tactics used by the "big boys" that increase market volatility; fed up with "derivatives" and other financial alchemy that have adversely affected the performance of your mutual funds; and finally, fed up with skyrocketing brokerage commissions and service fees.

The result has been the disfranchisement of literally hundreds of thousands of investors and would-be investors. However, there is another way—and one guaranteed to save you money while keeping it out of your broker's hands. Dividend reinvestment plans (DRIPs) provide a powerful way to keep individual investors in the stock market game—and to keep them winning. Briefly, more than 900 public corporations and closed-end funds have DRIPs that allow individuals to purchase stock by reinvesting dividends in new shares. In most cases, investors may also send optional cash payments directly to the companies to purchase additional shares.

The primary appeal of these plans is that most firms charge no commissions or fees for these services. Let me say that one more time. No commissions.

DRIPs allow individuals to invest in expensive, blue-chip issues, such as General Electric and Minnesota Mining & Manufacturing, for as little as $10 at a time.

And the benefits of DRIPs don't stop with commission-free investing. DRIPs provide an ideal avenue for long-term investing—an approach that, by the end of this book, I hope you'll agree is the best way to profit in the stock market, especially during the volatile times ahead.

But perhaps the biggest benefit is that DRIPs allow any investor—even those with limited finances—to mold an investment program based solely on his or her own financial restraints.

Certainly, knowing about DRIPs and who offers them is important, and you'll learn about that inside these pages. However, to stop there without providing strategies and specific stock recommendations would shortchange the reader. Thus, this book goes several steps further:

- Just because a company offers a DRIP does not make it a worthwhile investment. This book explores which companies are best suited for investing via DRIPs—and which ones aren't—and highlights especially attractive issues.

- Investment objectives differ among individuals. Therefore, it's important to structure DRIP investments to meet these objectives. This book provides model portfolios for a variety of investors—those interested in maximum capital gains as well as those looking for safety, those who have a lot of money and those with a little.

- There are plenty of positive aspects of DRIPs, but what are the negatives? You'll find a full review of potential pitfalls of the programs as well as investor "don'ts" concerning DRIP investing.

Readers should note that this edition of *Buying Stocks Without a Broker* has made several improvements from the first edition. First, I have expanded the performance ratings in the directory to provide a greater distinction in the investment quality of companies. Second, I've added a DRIP rating to help readers compare DRIP programs. Third, many changes have occurred in the DRIP field since this book was first published at the end of 1991. Chapter 4 discusses a number of these changes and emerging trends in the DRIP world.

In short, it's all here—the nuts and bolts of DRIPs as well as various strategies, specific recommendations, and a comprehensive directory of corporate DRIPs.

Thus, whether you're a novice investor or a sophisticated stock market jockey, familiar with DRIPs or just thinking that they frequent boring dinner parties, this book has something for you. In the pages before you is a blueprint for the do-it-yourself investor—a well-marked path to building a profitable investment portfolio while saving hundreds and thousands of dollars in commissions in the process.

Author's Note

This book is a comprehensive guide to dividend reinvestment plans (DRIPs). While I have tried to give accurate and up-to-date information concerning DRIPs, readers should understand that companies frequently change aspects of these programs. It's likely that certain features of the programs discussed in the book have changed since the book's publication. A program discussed in this book may have been suspended or even eliminated. Fortunately, it's more likely that new dividend reinvestment plans have been implemented since these pages left the printer. Because of frequent plan changes, it is always best to read a company's plan prospectus, which provides all of the details of the program, before investing.

For continuous coverage of DRIPs, let me plug my monthly newsletter, *DRIP Investor*. A coupon for two free issues of the newsletter is located in the back of the book.

1
What's a DRIP?

It's probably the last remaining break for the small investor in the stock market—but don't expect to hear about it from your broker.

Though it seems too good to be true, there is a way to purchase stocks, in many cases at a discount to prevailing market prices, without paying brokerage commissions. You can bypass the broker's bite when buying stocks by using corporate dividend reinvestment plans (DRIPs). Never heard of DRIPs? That's not surprising. Even though they've been around for years, DRIPs remain a secret to many individual investors. One reason is that your broker isn't likely to speak highly of DRIPs, or comment about them at all. That's because investing via DRIPs takes commission dollars out of your broker's pocket and puts them in yours.

What's a DRIP?

What are DRIPs? They are programs, sponsored by more than 900 firms and closed-end funds, which permit current shareholders of these companies to purchase additional shares by going directly to the firms, thereby bypassing the broker and commission fees. Investors purchase the stock with cash dividends that the company reinvests for them in additional shares. In addition, most plans permit investors to make voluntary cash payments directly into the plans to purchase shares.

DRIPs have several attractive features:

- Most companies charge no commissions for purchasing stocks through their DRIPs, and those that do charge only a nominal fee.

- Approximately 10 percent of all DRIPs permit participants to purchase stock at discounts to prevailing market prices. These discounts are usually 3 to 5 percent.

- Most plans permit investors to send optional cash payments (OCPs), in many cases as little as $10 to $25, directly to the company to purchase additional shares. Thus, it's possible to purchase shares (or a fraction of one) in issues such as General Electric for as little as $10 at a crack—an especially attractive feature for small investors who otherwise might not be able to afford expensive, blue-chip issues.

- DRIPs are an excellent tool for "dollar-cost averaging," a powerful long-term investment strategy that will be explored further in subsequent chapters.

Another attractive aspect of DRIPs is that the programs are offered by many of the best companies in the world. Indeed, all but 3 of the 30 companies comprising the Dow Jones Industrial Average offer dividend reinvestment plans. Such household names as Abbott Laboratories, Coca-Cola, Exxon, Intel, Johnson & Johnson, McDonald's, Motorola, PepsiCo, and Walgreen offer DRIPs. Thus, there is no shortage of quality stocks for DRIP investors.

Read the Prospectus

Starting an investment program using DRIPs is quite simple, but it requires some homework. Not all companies offer DRIPs, so it is important to first find out if a company in which you are interested has a DRIP. Fortunately, the corporate directory in Chapter 8 lists addresses and phone numbers for approximately 900 companies offering DRIPs. Since companies drop plans periodically and others initiate them, it pays to double-check with the shareholder services department of the company you're investigating to make sure the firm offers a DRIP.

Once you find out that the firm offers a DRIP, the next step is to find out the specifics of the plan. Not all DRIPs are alike. For example:

- Although many DRIPs offer discounts on shares purchased through the plans, most do not; and those firms that do have discounts may offer them only on shares purchased through reinvested dividends and not on optional cash payments.

- Some firms permit the reinvestment of preferred dividends for common shares, while others may not.

- Some companies allow partial reinvestment of dividends, while others require that all dividends be reinvested.

- A number of firms permit optional cash payments only if the shareholder reinvests dividends, although some firms allow shareholders to receive all dividend payments and still participate only in the optional payment feature of the plan.

- Companies differ on the timing of stock purchases for shareholders. Some will enter the market only around the dividend payment dates—once every three months—while others will enter the market more frequently.

- The amount of optional cash payments that may be made into plans differs among DRIPs. For example, GE allows OCPs of $10 up to $10,000 per month, while shareholders in Motorola's DRIP may make optional cash payments of up to $5000 every three months.

- Costs of the plans differ, especially fees shareholders pay to sell stocks from the plans.

- A host of other differences may arise among plans, such as the availability of safekeeping services for shareholders' certificates and the number of shares required to enroll in the plan.

How does an investor learn about the plans? Once again, the directory in Chapter 8 provides a wealth of information concerning the individual plans. However, it still pays to obtain a plan prospectus before investing. The prospectus provides information and eligibility requirements of the DRIP.

I think that the term *prospectus* often creates anxiety in individual investors who believe they won't understand a prospectus. Not true. Sure, there are some prospectuses that require a law degree to decipher. But most DRIP prospectuses are straightforward and easy to understand. Every company that has a DRIP has a prospectus or brochure explaining the plan features.

DRIP Nuts and Bolts

Here is a summary of some of the nuts and bolts of DRIPs.

Purchasing Fees. In many cases, firms do not charge brokerage commissions or service fees for purchasing stock through the plans. However, some companies do charge participants their pro rata share of brokerage fees. These fees are usually nominal since firms can obtain favorable brokerage rates because of the large quantities they invest. Companies may also have various service charges, such as safekeeping fees. Again, these fees are usually $5 or less.

Selling Fees. DRIPs handle selling in one of two ways. Some companies permit shareholders to sell directly through the DRIP. Usually a participant must put his or her sell request in writing and submit it to the DRIP, although a growing number of DRIPs permit participants to sell via the telephone. After the DRIP receives the sell request, it may take up to 10 business days before the sale is made. While a few firms pick up selling costs for DRIP participants, the majority of companies charge brokerage fees. However, these rates are usually less than the individual would pay if going through a broker. Investors should note that not all companies will sell shares in the plan. Some firms send stock certificates to shareholders who want to sell. The participant must then go through a broker to sell shares.

Partial Dividend Reinvestment. This option, found in many DRIPs, permits participants to receive some cash dividends while having a portion of their dividends reinvested for additional shares. This feature is especially attractive for individuals who may need at least a share of their dividends to supplement other income.

Discounts. Approximately 10 percent of all DRIPs offer discounts on stocks purchased through the plans. These discounts are usually 3 to 5 percent off the prevailing market price. In most cases, the discounts apply only to shares purchased through reinvested dividends, although some companies apply the discount to stock purchased through OCPs as well. Chapter 2 discusses discounts further and provides a complete list of DRIPs with discounts.

Optional Cash Payments. Nearly every plan permits participants to make optional cash payments into the plan. The maximum and minimum amounts of these payments vary from plan to plan, as does the frequency with which these funds are invested by the firm. Also, some firms allow investors to enroll in the DRIPs to make OCPs, even if they don't reinvest their dividends. Chapter 3 goes into the OCP option in more depth.

Purchase Price. The pricing of shares differs among plans. For example, for some companies, the purchase price is the price of the stock on the last trading day prior to the investment date. In other instances, it might be the average price of all shares purchased in a five-day period preceding the investment date. Obviously, when the stock is purchased and how the purchase price is determined have a big impact on your cost basis. Make sure you check the prospectus on this one.

Safekeeping Services. Shares purchased under most DRIPs are held in the participant's plan account by the company, and certificates for these shares are not usually issued unless requested. Most companies do not charge any fee for this service, and those firms that do usually set the charge at $5 or less.

Eligibility Requirements. Most companies permit those who hold only one share to enroll in the DRIP, although a few require more shares. The corporate directory in Chapter 8 provides information on firms requiring more than one share for enrollment. Another eligibility requirement for most DRIPs is that the shares be registered in the shareholder's name, not the "street" name or brokerage name.

It is critical that investors understand the distinction between "street" name investors and registered shareholders. Stock that is registered in street name is registered in the name of the brokerage firm. Although most investors probably don't realize it, when you hold stock in street name, in most cases the company does not even know that you are a shareholder. That's why companies require investors to have the stock registered in their own name in order to enroll in a dividend reinvestment plan. Don't be surprised, however, if the broker tries to talk you out of registering the stock in your name. Brokers want investors to register shares in street name since it gives the brokerage firm control of the assets and, most likely, the commissions when the stock is sold. Nevertheless, in order to enroll in most dividend reinvestment plans, you need to have the stock registered in your name. This may require changing the registration on shares you already hold if you plan to enroll in the company's DRIP. Contact your broker on this one.

Fractional Shares. If dividends or OCPs aren't large enough to purchase whole shares, DRIPs will purchase fractional shares for plan participants. And these fractional shares participate proportionately in future dividends.

DRIP Statements. One downside of DRIPs is that they increase paperwork for participants, particularly those in several DRIPs. Companies attempt to help participants by sending regular statements, usually after every purchase of stock. The statements show amounts invested, purchase prices, shares purchased, account maintenance fees charged, if any, and other relevant information. Keep these statements, as they will come in handy at tax time.

Voting Rights.   Participants don't sacrifice their say in the company because they use DRIPs. Voting rights are granted to whole shares in a DRIP, although fractional shares may not have voting rights in all cases.

Termination of the Plan.   Terminating a DRIP is usually quite simple. Most plans require written notification stating your intention to terminate your participation. If you request it, many firms will sell your shares on the open market. Companies that do not sell shares for participants will send the stock certificates to participants along with cash for fractional shares.

Stock Splits and Stock Dividends.   Your DRIP holdings are not adversely affected by stock splits or stock dividends. New shares will be added to the participant's account reflecting the split or dividend.

Taxes.   Although DRIPs let you dodge the broker, they won't let you dodge the tax collector. Even though your dividends are reinvested, they are subject to income taxes as if you received them. This wasn't always the case. In the early 1980s, DRIPs in certain electric utilities were exempt from taxation on up to $750 ($1500 for joint filers) of dividends reinvested in the plans. However, that exemption expired midway through the decade. In addition to taxes on reinvested dividends, investors must pay taxes on the amount of commissions and service fees picked up by the firm, although these amounts are usually quite nominal. Also, these service fees may be deducted by investors who itemize. DRIPs send participants 1099 information forms, which are helpful during tax preparation time. Consult with your tax adviser concerning DRIPs so you don't get any surprises on April 15.

Getting the First Share

Okay, so you've picked out a stock you like, the company has a DRIP that meets your objectives, you've gone over the prospectus, and you're ready to take the plunge. But you need to have one share before you can enroll in the DRIP. What do you do?

Brokers offer one avenue for getting that first share, although their fees to purchase one share of stock will be quite high in percentage terms of the total investment. However, investors should realize that once the initial investment is made through the broker, they will never need a broker again to purchase stock in that company.

A frequent question I hear is, "Which is the best brokerage firm?" What the question usually means is, "Who has the cheapest commissions?" Though full-service brokers will argue that their rates are competitive with discounters—and in some instances this may be true—as a rule you'll likely pay lower brokerage costs with a discount firm if you are buying 100 shares or more. Investors who do their own research will probably choose a discount broker, while others, who feel less secure in their own investment judgments, may appreciate a full-service broker.

Since this book gives you practical guidance on DRIPs, complete with specific recommendations and model portfolios (Chapters 6 and 7), as well as performance ratings on the stocks in the company directory (Chapter 8), you probably don't need a full-service broker, unless he or she is willing to cut commission rates.

Which firm has the cheapest commission rates? It's hard to say. Some brokers will discount their commissions if they believe that the individual will throw a lot of business their way. Also, while one firm may have a lower minimum commission charge than another, the latter firm may have cheaper rates for round-lot purchases. I suggest that when you're ready to purchase stock, contact three or four brokers in order to compare rates. Below are some of the more prominent discount brokers:

Andrew Peck (800-221-5873)

K. Aufhauser (800-368-3668)

Burke, Christensen & Lewis Sec. (800-621-0392)

Charles Schwab & Co. (800-435-4000)

Fidelity Brokerage Services (800-544-7272)

Jack White & Co. (800-233-3411)

Kennedy, Cabot & Co. (800-252-0090)

Muriel Siebert & Co. (800-872-7865)

Quick & Reilly (800-221-5220)

StockCross (800-225-6196)

Vanguard Brokerage Services (800-992-8327)

Waterhouse Securities (800-934-4410)

Don't forget to try some full-service brokers as well. Depending on how desperate they are for business, you may be able to drive a bargain. Chances are most major full-service brokers have a branch in your neighborhood. I've had particularly good luck with Dean Witter and A. G. Edwards. Check the Yellow Pages.

One important thing to remember is that regardless of the brokerage firm you use, most DRIPs require that shares be held in the name of the individual investor rather than in "street" name accounts. For this reason, it is important to make sure your broker knows that the stock should be registered in your name to avoid any problems later.

Once you have purchased the stock, contact the firm concerning enrollment in the DRIP. Quite likely, the company will send you a prospectus and application form once it receives your name as a shareholder of record. Once enrolled in the DRIP, you may begin your investment program.

It's that simple—and you'll never need to call a broker again.

Commissions Matter

While we're on the subject of brokerage commissions, I think it's important to discuss how significant these fees can be in eating away at your investment dollars. I could recite a litany of academic articles emphasizing how harmful transaction costs can be on a portfolio, especially for small investors. But a personal experience may drive this point home even more.

Although I don't advise investing in stock or index options, I sometimes don't take my own advice. A few years ago I purchased a put option on the Standard & Poor's 100 index. A put option is a bet on lower stock prices.

Fortunately, the market dropped sharply, and my strategy worked, at least I thought so. I sold the put at a nice "paper" profit. Indeed, I bought the option for $350, and I sold it at $575. A profit of 64 percent. A pretty sweet gain for just a few days, right?

Not exactly. When I received my brokerage confirmation statement, I was stunned. To purchase the option, the commission and fees were $87. Likewise the commission for selling the option was $87. Thus, on an investment of $350, the round-trip commissions were a whopping $174, or roughly 50 percent of the investment value. After commissions, my profits nearly disappeared.

When I called my broker, he stated that the firm's minimum commission on options was $87 (he lowered the commission to $53 after my complaint). Of course, had I purchased five or ten options instead of one, the commissions would have represented a smaller percentage of the investment. Nevertheless, the point is that small investors, who may not have big bucks to invest, are punished disproportionately.

I admit that option commissions are generally higher than stock commissions. However, the same scenario is possible for stock investments. Of course, you might get lucky and find a broker who will buy a small number of shares in a company for $15 to $25. However, higher minimum commissions are commonplace in the brokerage industry.

Take the following example. Say you want to purchase 50 shares of a $10 stock—a $500 investment. Assuming a round-trip commission of $100—$50 to get in and $50 to get out—your investment has to rise $100, or 20 percent, just to break even after commissions. The investment game is tough enough without stacking the odds that badly against the small investor.

Now, take the same situation using a DRIP. Let's say you made an OCP of $500. Your commissions were zero. And when it comes time to sell these 50 shares, you'll pay a commission that is much lower than $50, perhaps as low as $5 to $10, if the shares are sold through the DRIP. Thus, to break even, the stock needs to increase just 2 percent. It's easy to figure out that your chances for investment success are increased greatly. Keep in mind that this is just one trade. Multiply this four or five times a year, 40 or 50 trades over the course of 10 years. That isn't a great deal of activity for an investor. But even at this modest level, the commission savings, assuming a minimum commission of $50 at your broker, are $2000. And if you're more active, your savings are greater.

For example, let's say you enroll in the DRIP for McDonald's. In addition to reinvesting dividends, you make monthly OCPs of $50. Thus, you are purchasing McDonald's stock at least 12 times a year. Let's assume a minimum commission of $50. In this scenario, your commission savings on the buy side alone are $600 annually.

Another way to look at the commission break is if you have deep pockets and make OCPs of, not $50 per month, but $5000 per month. On a $5000 investment, it's not unusual to pay commissions of $100 or more at a full-service broker. Multiply that number 12 times a year and the savings are around $1200; over 10 years, the savings are $12,000—and that doesn't take into account rising brokerage commission rates over that time period. Nor does it take into account administrative fees for things like account statements that more and more brokers are charging customers.

As you can see, we're not talking about saving a few dollars through DRIPs, but about some serious cash. The bottom line is that commissions matter, and they matter a lot in terms of portfolio performance and real out-of-pocket dollars.

The Buddy System

Investors may also obtain the first share via what I call the "buddy system." For example, let's say that someone you know has stock in Coca-Cola. You can go through Coca-Cola's transfer agent to have your friend transfer one of his or her shares into your name. After the transfer, you are now a shareholder of record and able to participate in the DRIP.

A variation of the buddy system is getting perhaps five investors together to purchase a total of five shares in a company. Splitting up the brokerage commission on a five-share investment makes each investor's commission relatively small. Following the purchase, go through the transfer agent and have the five shares transferred into the individual names of the five members of the group. Once this is done, each investor may enroll in the DRIP and begin making investments with reinvested dividends and optional cash payments.

Other "First Share" Sources

A cottage industry has developed over the last few years to help customers bypass the brokerage community to buy stocks for DRIP enrollment. The best known is run by the National Association of Investors Corporation (NAIC). For NAIC members ($35 annual membership fee), the organization will buy one share of stock in over 100 companies for a one-time charge of $5 per company. For further information, contact the organization at (810) 583-6242.

No-Load Stocks™

The easiest way to obtain the first share is by going directly to the company to make your initial purchase. The number of these *No-Load Stock*™ programs, as I call them, is small relative to the total number of DRIPs. Fortunately, due to SEC regulations handed down at the end of 1994, it is now easier for companies to implement such programs. Since the beginning of 1995, there has been a miniboom in the number of companies that are allowing investors to buy their first share and every subsequent share directly from the company. Firms that currently offer no-load stock programs include Barnett Banks, Bob Evans Farms, Dial, Exxon, Morton International, Tenneco, Texaco, and U S West. More on no-load stocks, as well as a complete list of all no-load stock programs, is discussed in Chapter 4.

Downside to DRIPs

We've discussed the many pluses of DRIPs:

- Commission-free investing in high-quality stocks
- Moderate commissions for selling in many instances
- Modest capital requirements because of small minimums in most OCP plans
- Discounts on shares purchased
- Full investment of funds due to purchase of fractional shares
- Safekeeping of shares

However, there are some minuses associated with DRIPs. A minor headache is the increased paperwork associated with the plans. True, companies do their best to simplify things by issuing regular statements. Still, if you're in 25 or 30 DRIPs, the record keeping could become a bit onerous. Thus, DRIPs do require some discipline in terms of record keeping. Therefore, it's probably not worth it to join more than 25 DRIPs. You'll achieve adequate portfolio diversification with 13 to 25 DRIPs.

A related record-keeping headache is created when you sell shares from a DRIP. Keep in mind that when you invest regularly in dividend reinvestment plans, you are buying shares at least four times a year and perhaps even on a monthly basis over an extended period of time. If you do not keep good track of your cost basis of the shares purchased, you may have a difficult time determining the cost basis on shares when you sell stock from your DRIP. Again, companies do their best to provide you with information on the cost basis of shares when you make purchases. However, it is up to you to maintain these records so you can determine a cost basis for tax purposes.

I think it is important to note that mutual-fund investors have the same problem as DRIP investors since mutual funds oftentimes reinvest dividends for investors. Thus, investors should not ignore DRIPs because of the tax implications, as these same tax implications would possibly be encountered when investing in mutual funds. Rather, DRIP investors merely need to realize that they will have to keep a closer eye on their record keeping, especially for tax purposes.

The biggest downside to DRIPs is the lack of control over the price at which shares are bought and sold. For example, let's say that you are in the DRIP for Hershey Foods. The stock has recently fallen and you want to purchase shares. However, in order to invest in the stock via the DRIP, you'll have to wait until the next investment date, which may be two weeks or more away, before you can buy. By the time you send in your OCP and the stock is purchased by the company, the issue has jumped up three points. Likewise, on the sell side, you decide to sell a stock at $50. You inform the DRIP that you would like to sell 50 shares. However, as is the case with many DRIPs, the sale doesn't take place until 10 business days after your request to sell, and the stock has fallen to $45.

As you can see, the time lag between buy and sell decisions could have an impact on your portfolio. However, investing via DRIPs is a long-term strategy and not geared toward frequent trading. Over time, this lack of control of exact buy and sell executions should wash and have a minimal impact on a portfolio. However, on a short-term basis, the impact might be large. Thus, traders need not apply when it comes to DRIPs.

There are some ways to improve on this situation. One is to focus investments on companies in which optional cash payments are invested weekly or twice a month, as in the case of Exxon and McDonald's, respectively. How do you find out when companies invest OCPs? Each directory listing in Chapter 8 includes the frequency with which OCPs are invested.

Another strategy is to have possession of a portion of your shares in certificate form. This way, once you've decided to sell, you can move quickly by going through a discount broker.

What's in It for the Companies?

You may be wondering at this point what's in it for the companies which offer DRIPs. First, many investors who have come to love the commission-free investing aspects of DRIPs buy stock only in firms that offer DRIPs. So companies that feel it is important to have individual investors represented among their shareholders will offer the plans.

Companies usually like having individual investors owning their shares. As a group, small investors are more loyal than institutional holders and generally invest for the long term. Individual investors aren't likely to be actively trading the issue and increasing the stock's volatility. Also, a large representation of individual investors makes it more difficult for a corporate raider or unfriendly suitor to accumulate shares for a proxy battle or hostile takeover.

Companies realize that individual investors also represent potential customers of the company. Exxon, for example, knows that if you are a shareholder in Exxon, you are more likely to buy Exxon gasoline. Likewise, McDonald's understands that its shareholders are more likely to buy Big Macs than they are Whoppers. Companies, especially retailers and consumer-oriented companies, like to have individual investors in their shareholder base because it can translate into increased sales of the company's products and services.

Another reason firms offer the plans is that DRIPs provide a potential source of equity capital. Some companies purchase shares for DRIP participants on the open market. Purchases in this manner do not add to the firm's capital base. Rather, the company acts merely as an intermediary for shareholders. However, many companies issue to shareholders in the DRIP "original issue shares." Proceeds from shares purchased in this way expand the firm's capital base and may be used for such corporate purposes as research and development spending or capital improvements. This method of raising capital carries little cost to the company relative to the large fees and administrative costs of making a public offering of stock through an investment bank. Raising equity capital via DRIPs does not increase the firm's debt burden and interest expense. The implications of raising equity capital via DRIPs are explored further in Chapter 2.

2

Free Lunch

Buying Stocks
at a Discount

When I first learned about DRIPs, it was hard for me to believe that in some DRIPs it was possible to buy stocks at discounts to the prevailing market price. In other words, you were guaranteed an instant profit on your holdings. A sham, I thought. No way can you actually buy stocks more cheaply than in the market. However, as I discovered, this feature is the closest thing to a free lunch that you can get in the stock market.

More than 100 companies offer discounts on stock purchased through their DRIPs. Most of the discounts apply only to shares purchased through reinvested dividends. Some firms also permit optional cash payments (OCPs) to receive the discount.

Most discounts are in the 3 to 5 percent range. Think about that for a moment. That means, in a DRIP with a 5 percent discount, you can buy $100 worth of stock for just $95. And because of the way the math works, your "instant profit" is actually greater than the 5 percent discount—more like 5.3 percent (profit of $5 divided by your cost of $95). Your actual profit may be a bit less after taxes. Nevertheless, you are still getting "free" money. Sure, you could lose this profit if the stock falls below your discounted purchase price. But your losses aren't nearly as great as are someone's who purchased the stock at the market price.

Why Do Companies Offer a Discount?

One reason for my initial skepticism concerning discounts was that I couldn't see what companies got out of the deal. After all, weren't they losing money?

Not really. As the list at the end of this chapter indicates, many of the firms offering discounts are in capital-intensive industries—primarily banks, utilities, and real estate investment trusts (REITs). These businesses require constant cash flow to conduct business.

Companies have a number of ways to raise capital. First, they can go to a friendly banker and take out a loan. Firms can float bonds. This method is basically the same thing as taking out a loan, except the creditor isn't the bank but institutional and individual investors who purchase the bonds. A company can raise money by issuing stock. The attraction of stock is that a firm doesn't make interest payments on stock as it does on bank debt or bonds. The downside is that the firm might have to pay dividends on the stock. Also, while interest payments receive favorable tax treatment for the corporation—hence the reason many companies issue debt—dividends do not.

There are two popular ways to issue stock. The more traditional method is to sell shares to the public or institutional investors via a public offering or private placement. In most cases, the firm uses an investment banker, such as Salomon, Merrill Lynch, Morgan Stanley, or Goldman Sachs, to make the offering. The investment banker, in turn, has a syndicate of other investment houses that helps to sell the offering. For their efforts, the investment banks take a piece of the action. In addition to the investment bankers' take, substantial administrative, clerical, legal, and accounting fees may be incurred. In some cases, all of these fees can be 5 percent of the offering value and as high as 10 to 15 percent, particularly if the issuer is small and the investment bank foresees potential problems in moving the stock. As you can see, this avenue for raising equity has its share of hassles.

Another way to sell stock is via a DRIP. Herein is a major reason why so many companies offer the plans. Indeed, with DRIPs, there are no investment banking fees. Companies that offer stock at a discount are not really shorting themselves of cash. If they went through an investment bank to raise funds, they would have to pay for services that potentially would cost more than the 3 or 5 percent discounts offered in DRIPs. Therefore, these firms pass on the savings to DRIP participants. The company benefits in that the discount makes the firm's DRIP more attractive to investors.

Raising Capital Quickly

The power of a DRIP with a discount to pull in cash can be impressive. Just ask South Jersey Industries, a natural gas utility serving portions of southern New Jersey, including Atlantic City. In April 1990, the firm's board of directors amended the company's DRIP to provide for the purchase of newly issued shares at a 5 percent discount from the market price. South Jersey stipulated that, in addition to reinvested dividends, OCPs of up to $30,000 annually qualified for the discount. A generous program, to say the least.

As it turned out, investors jumped all over the new plan. In fact, in June 1990, plan participants purchased approximately 479,000 new shares of common stock for almost $8 million. While companies like to raise capital through DRIPs, there is a point where too much capital too fast isn't a good thing since the company cannot profitably use it to benefit shareholders. Such was the case with South Jersey Industries. To slow down the stream of new capital, the firm amended the DRIP again in August 1990, this time lowering the discount to 3 percent on reinvested dividends and OCPs and setting a maximum on OCPs of $1000 per quarter. Since then, South Jersey Industries has eliminated the discount altogether.

South Jersey Industries is a good example of a company that has changed its discount policy frequently in the last few years. Such changes are not unusual. Indeed, companies have become very adept at using discounts to raise money, using the discount as a faucet for turning on and off the equity flow. Interestingly, the Securities and Exchange Commission appears to be somewhat uncomfortable with the notion of companies using discounts in DRIPs to raise large amounts of money and has scrutinized DRIP discounts more closely in recent years.

Another reason companies change their DRIP discount policy is the overall cost of capital in the markets. If the cost of capital is low, that is, interest rates are down and investors' appetite for stocks and bonds is strong, companies generally can raise all the capital they need through traditional channels. Also, during such environments, companies are often cash rich and may not need to raise money. However, during environments when the financial markets are stagnant and interest rates are rising, companies turn to more novel ways to raise money such as using DRIP discounts.

There has also been a certain cyclical rotation among industries using discounts. In the '80s and early '90s, it was not uncommon for utilities and banks to use discounts rather aggressively since these

industries were in periods when they needed substantial amounts of
capital. However, a number of banks have reduced or dropped their
discounts over the last few years. This is because most banks are in
pretty good financial shape at this time and do not need to raise
money aggressively. Conversely, more real estate investment trusts are
beginning to offer discounts. DRIPs, especially with discounts, provide
REITs with a form of "equity leverage" by exploiting the market pricing differential between real estate in the private market and the public stock market. Also, with electric utilities potentially facing another
round of expansion to meet growing demand, I would not be surprised to see electric utilities over time reinstitute discounts in DRIPs.

Yield "Boost"

One of the benefits of investing in DRIPs with discounts on reinvested
dividends is that the discount, in effect, boosts the stock's yield. For
example, UtiliCorp United provides a 5 percent discount on reinvested
dividends. The stock's annual dividend at the time of this writing is
$1.72 per share. Investors outside the DRIP receive a yield of 6.1 per-
cent on their investment. However, because DRIP participants have
the dividends reinvested at a 5 percent discount, the effective yield for
them is approximately 6.5 percent. This yield "boost" from the discount, over time, can provide a nice lift to a stock's total return. In the
few cases in which the company applies the discount to reinvested
dividends and optional cash investments, such as American Water
Works and United Mobile Homes which both have 5 percent discounts
on reinvested dividends and optional cash investments, the boost is
magnified.

Below is a table of four DRIPs which offer discounts. As you can see,
the yield boost from the DRIP discount can be substantial.

	Stock price	Dividend	Yield	DRIP discount	Yield "boost"
American Water Works	$30	$1.28	4.3%	5%	4.5%
Atmos Energy	20	0.92	4.6	3	4.7
United Mobile Homes*	10	0.50	5.0	5	5.3
UtiliCorp United	28	1.72	6.1	5	6.5

*Traded on the American Stock Exchange.

Drawbacks to a Discount

If there is a drawback to the discounts, it is that issuing shares in a DRIP, especially at a discount, has a dilutive impact on shares currently outstanding.

Another drawback is when the discount is really no discount at all. This could happen under certain circumstances, depending on how the company classifies the purchase price that receives the discount. For example, let's say that a firm, which offers a 5 percent discount on reinvested dividends and optional cash payments, considers the purchase price for OCPs to be 95 percent of the average of the closing stock prices for the five consecutive business days preceding the investment date. Say the stock drops steadily during this five-day period, closing on the fifth day at $7. However, the average price for the five-day period was $8. Thus, the purchase price would be 95 percent of $8, or around $7.60—a price actually higher than the last trading price. You'd be better off purchasing the stock in the market at full price than at a 5 percent discount in the DRIP. In some DRIPs, it is possible to request the return of your funds prior to the investment date. In this instance, it would obviously be in your best interest to get your money back.

Interestingly, such a scenario, if reversed, would actually increase the amount of the discount for investors. For example, let's say that the average price for the five-day period was still $8, but the closing price on the fifth day is now $9. Your purchase price of around $7.60 (95 percent of $8) now represents a nearly 16 percent discount from the last price of $9—considerably higher than the 5 percent stated discount in the plan. Such price fluctuations may be more prevalent in the future given that many companies are going to longer pricing periods to determine the price which receives the discount. For example, there are some companies with discounts that have 10-day pricing periods or longer. With such long pricing periods, instances where discounts widen or shrink may occur more frequently.

Abusing the Benefit

A number of DRIPs have eliminated discounts over the last several years. One of the reasons appears to be the manipulation of the plans by big investors. Wall Streeters don't miss a trick, and the fact that free money was available in DRIPs with discounts sent them scurrying to take advantage of it.

The scheme works something like this: Let's say you join a DRIP that offers a 5 percent discount on stock purchased with reinvested dividends as well as OCPs. And let's say that the maximum OCP that can be made into the plan on a monthly basis is $5000. Thus, every month, you can accumulate $5000 worth of stock for $4750. Now, while you're buying the stock, you are simultaneously selling the stock for the full market price. This can be done by selling the stock short in the market on the investment date or selling shares in which you have taken possession of the certificates. By simultaneously buying stock for $4750 and selling the same stock at $5000, you lock up a risk-free return of $250. Do this each month and your risk-free gains for the year, before commissions and taxes, are roughly $3000.

Now, what some investors and brokers do is to open multiple accounts in which to take advantage of the discount. It's not too difficult to see how lucrative this strategy can be. Take this risk-free profit times 10 to 15 accounts in the names of various relatives or friends, and the gains are huge. Or, if you're an investor with access to an even larger number of accounts, the gains can be downright obscene.

An interesting study on profiting from the discounts was conducted by Myron S. Scholes, best known for his option pricing model, and Mark A. Wolfson. The two college professors wanted to determine if, in fact, exploiting the discount would yield abnormal returns. From 1984 to 1988, the individuals purchased, via DRIPs, shares in companies that offered discounts on OCPs, with 90 percent of their activity occurring in a period of less than two years.

What were the results? Staggering, to say the least. With an investment of $200,000, the two realized a profit of $421,000, consisting of $163,800 of net discount income (the sum of all gross discounts less transaction costs), $182,600 of return on investment from a general increase in stock prices, and $74,600 of abnormal return on investment beyond the net discount income. This profit was net of all costs.

Are Scholes, Wolfson, and others who capitalize on these discounts villains or savvy investors merely taking advantage of an inefficiency in the market? Both, depending on your viewpoint. What they did was perfectly legal, and the two were fortunate enough to possess enough capital to generate major gains. Still, such manipulation of the discount is one reason that a number of plans have eliminated discounts, which hurts all investors.

The abuse of the discount is one reason that there are only approximately 34 firms that offer discounts on both reinvested dividends and optional cash payments. Taking advantage of the difference between the discount price and the market price is more lucrative if done through OCPs. The sums of money are larger and the frequency of investment greater because of monthly investment of OCPs by many companies.

Because of the abuse of the discount, firms offering discounts reserve the right to terminate a shareholder account in which they believe such manipulation is taking place. Companies are also making it more difficult to arbitrage the discount by using longer pricing periods. The key factor when arbitraging the stock is knowing exactly at what price you buy the stock so you can short a similar number of shares at a higher price in the market. However, with longer pricing periods, it is more difficult to know exactly what your purchase price will be since it may be the average price over a 10- or 12-day period. Thus, this uncertainty on the purchase price makes it more difficult to implement an arbitrage strategy.

Tax Treatment of DRIP Discounts

Historically, DRIP discounts were considered the same as ordinary income. Let's say you bought a $50 stock through your DRIP and received a 5 percent discount. Your purchase price would be $47.50 per share ($50 multiplied by 0.95). Under old rules, the difference between your purchase price and the actual market price, $2.50, was considered income and taxed at your ordinary rate. Another way to look at it is if you bought $5000 worth of stock at a discount for $4750, the $250 would be considered ordinary income for tax purposes. However, the IRS appears to have changed its stance on DRIP discounts and how to account for them from a tax standpoint. An IRS ruling in 1994—a ruling sought by a partnership that specializes in buying stock at a discount via DRIPs—states that if you buy stock at a discount, the amount of the discount does not constitute income to you. Thus, in our scenario, the $2.50 per share doesn't constitute immediate income for tax purposes.

The new ruling has its biggest impact on investors who hold shares purchased at a discount for at least 12 months and then sell. Let's say that your $50 stock goes nowhere for 12 months and you sell. The $2.50 profit over your purchase price would be taxed at the long-term capital-gains rate. That potentially is a far cry from the tax rate you'd pay if the discount were taxed as ordinary income, as it was under the old way. In effect, the new ruling allows you to convert what was once considered dividend income into long-term capital gains as long as you hold the shares for at least 12 months.

Investors should keep in mind that this private ruling may have certain limitations. As the ruling states (Figure 2-1), the ruling is directed

Internal Revenue Service

Department of the Treasury

Index Number: 0305.00-00

Washington, DC 20224

9446011

Person to Contact:

Telephone Number:

Refer Reply to:
  CC:DOM:CORP:3 TR-31-464-94
Date:

AUG 1 5 1994

   This letter replies to your request dated February 4, 1994
for rulings on the federal income tax consequences of a
consummated transaction. We have received additional information
in letters dated April 14, May 10, July 14, and August 5, 1994.
The information submitted for consideration is summarized below.

   P is State Y a limited partnership with three individual
general partners and more than 25 individual limited partners. P
purchases stock of publicly traded corporations that offer stock
discount purchase plans. P purchases shares at a discount
pursuant to these plans and immediately sells the stock on the
market. P does not hold any stock for investment.

   X is a corporation with a stock discount purchase plan (the
"X Plan") that entitled employees or holders of X common stock to
purchase X stock at a discount. The X Plan permitted
shareholders to reinvest their dividends in X ("Dividend
Investment"), invest their own funds in X ("Discount Purchase"),
or both. X shareholders could participate in Discount Purchase
regardless of whether they participated in Dividend Investment.

   Under the X Plan, X shareholders who chose to participate in
Discount Purchase could invest up to $a thousand in X during each
monthly investment period. The investors received X common stock
at b percent of the average of the daily high and low prices for
the last ten trading days before the first of the month. The
amount of a cash dividend, if any, received with respect to a
share of X stock would not be affected by the shareholder's
participation in Discount Purchase. X shareholders who did not
participate in Discount Purchase did not receive any cash or
other property from X in lieu of such participation.

   Between Date 1 and Date 2, P purchased C shares of X common
stock through Discount Purchase (P purchased up to $d million of
X stock per month through the use of nominee partnerships). P
received regular cash dividends on the X shares it held on
dividend qualification dates. Except for $1.56 invested with

Figure 2-1

9 4 4 6 0 1 1

TR-31-464-94

respect to an interest in a fractional X share, P did not
reinvest any of its dividends on X stock through Dividend
Investment.

Based solely on the information submitted, and provided that
P did not reinvest more than a de minimis amount of its X
dividends in Dividend Reinvestment, we hold as follows:

P's purchase of X stock at a discount through Discount
Purchase will not be treated as a distribution of X stock
described by S 305 (b) of the Internal Revenue Code.
Therefore, P will realize no income as a result of purchases
pursuant to Discount Purchase (S 305 (a)).

We express no opinion about the tax treatment of the
proposed transaction under other provisions of the Code and
regulations or about the tax treatment of any conditions existing
at the time of, or effects resulting from, the proposed
transaction that are not specifically covered by the above
rulings.

This ruling has no effect on any earlier documents and is
directed only to the taxpayer who requested it. Section
6110 (j) (3) provides that it may not be used or cited as
precedent.

The affected taxpayers must attach a copy of this letter to
their federal income tax returns for the taxable year in which
the transaction covered by this ruling letter is consummated.

We have sent a copy of this letter to the designated
representative according to the power of attorney on file in this
office.

Sincerely Yours,

Assistant Chief Counsel (Corporate)

By
John M. Geracimos
Assistant to the Chief, Branch 3

Figure 2-1 (*Continued*)

only to the taxpayer who requested it and "may not be used or cited as precedent." Nevertheless, it does appear that the IRS has reconsidered its position on DRIP discounts. For further information on this ruling and for advice on handling the DRIP discount for tax purposes, see your tax advisor.

Summary

Here are some things to remember concerning discounts:

- The ability to purchase stock at a discount under the DRIP is truly one of the few benefits the small investor has in the market. Don't abuse it by excessive trading. This defeats the purpose of DRIPs and could cause the company to eliminate the discount.

- Don't invest in a company merely because it offers a discount. Although there are quality companies with DRIPs that offer discounts, there are also plenty of companies that offer discounts because they would otherwise have trouble drawing investors' dollars because of their poor prospects and track records. Stay with quality.

- Most of the companies that offer discounts are banks, utilities, and real estate investment trusts—three areas where extra care must be taken when making investments.

The following is a list of companies offering discounts. Be sure and check the performance ratings in Chapter 8 before investing in these or other DRIPs. Companies offering discounts on both reinvested dividends and optional cash payments are indicated by bold type. Investors should note that due to companies' frequently changing their discount policies, it pays to check with the company before investing.

ADAC Laboratories
5 percent discount on reinvested
  dividends and OCPs

Atmos Energy Corp.
3 percent discount on reinvested
  dividends

American Water Works Co., Inc.
5 percent discount on reinvested
  dividends and OCPs

Ball Corp.
5 percent discount on reinvested
  dividends

Aquarion Co.
5 percent discount on reinvested
  dividends and OCPs

Bank of Boston Corp.
3 percent discount on reinvested
  dividends

Bankers First Corp.
5 percent discount on reinvested
dividends

BanPonce Corp.
5 percent discount on reinvested
dividends

Bay View Capital Corp.
5 percent discount on reinvested
dividends

Berkshire Gas Co.
3 percent discount on reinvested
dividends and OCPs

Blount, Inc.
5 percent discount on reinvested
dividends

Bradley Real Estate Trust
3 percent discount on reinvested
dividends

Burnham Pacific Properties, Inc.
5 percent discount on reinvested
dividends

California Financial Holding
Company
3 percent discount on reinvested
dividends

Capstead Mortgage Corp.
3 percent discount on reinvested
dividends and OCPs

Carolina First Corp.
5 percent discount on reinvested
dividends

Cathay Bancorp, Inc.
5 percent discount on reinvested
dividends

Chase Manhattan Corp.
5 percent discount on reinvested
dividends; 3 percent discount on
OCPs

CNB Bancshares, Inc.
3 percent discount on reinvested
dividends

Colonial Gas Co.
5 percent discount on reinvested
dividends

Columbus Realty Trust
5 percent discount on reinvested
dividends and OCPs

Commerce Bancorp, Inc.
3 percent discount on reinvested
dividends and OCPs

Connecticut Water Service, Inc.
5 percent discount on reinvested
dividends

Countrywide Credit Industries, Inc.
4 percent discount on reinvested
dividends

Cousins Properties, Inc.
5 percent discount on reinvested
dividends

Crestar Financial Corp.
5 percent discount on reinvested
dividends

Duke Realty Investments, Inc.
5 percent discount on reinvested
dividends

E'Town Corp.
5 percent discount on reinvested
dividends and OCPs

Empire District Electric Co.
5 percent discount on reinvested
dividends (doesn't apply to shares
purchased on open market)

EnergyNorth, Inc.
5 percent discount on reinvested
dividends

Essex County Gas Company
5 percent discount on reinvested
dividends

F & M Bancorp
5 percent discount on reinvested
dividends

F & M National Corp. (VA)
5 percent discount on reinvested dividends

First American Corp. (TN)
5 percent discount on reinvested dividends

First Citizens BancShares, Inc.
5 percent discount on reinvested dividends

First Commerce Corp.
5 percent discount on reinvested dividends

First Commercial Corp.
5 percent discount on reinvested dividends

First Commonwealth Financial Corp.
5 percent discount on reinvested dividends and OCPs

First Fidelity Bancorp.
3 percent discount on reinvested dividends

First Michigan Bank Corp.
5 percent discount on reinvested dividends

First of America Bank Corp.
5 percent discount on reinvested dividends

First Union Corp.
1 percent discount on reinvested dividends and OCPs

Fleet Financial Group, Inc.
3 percent discount on reinvested dividends

Fleming Companies, Inc.
5 percent discount on reinvested dividends

Fuller (H. B.) Co.
3 percent discount on reinvested dividends

GoodMark Foods, Inc.
2 percent discount on reinvested dividends and OCPs

Great Western Financial Corp.
3 percent discount on reinvested dividends

Green Mountain Power Corp.
5 percent discount on reinvested dividends

Health Care REIT, Inc.
4 percent discount on reinvested dividends and OCPs

Hibernia Corp.
5 percent discount on reinvested dividends

Household International, Inc.
$2\frac{1}{2}$ percent discount on reinvested dividends

Huntington Bancshares, Inc.
5 percent discount on reinvested dividends

Independent Bank Corp. (MI)
5 percent discount on reinvested dividends

IRT Property Co.
5 percent discount on reinvested dividends

IWC Resources Corp.
3 percent discount on reinvested dividends and OCPs

Kennametal, Inc.
5 percent discount on reinvested dividends

Lafarge Corp.
5 percent discount on reinvested dividends

Media General, Inc.
5 percent discount on reinvested dividends

Mercantile Bankshares Corp.
5 percent discount on reinvested
dividends

Meridian Bancorp, Inc.
5 percent discount on reinvested
dividends

Merry Land & Investment Co., Inc.
5 percent discount on reinvested
dividends and OCPs

Middlesex Water Co.
5 percent discount on reinvested
dividends and OCPs

Midlantic Corp.
3 percent discount on reinvested
dividends

**Monmouth Real Estate Investment
Corp.**
5 percent discount on reinvested
dividends and OCPs

National City Corp.
3 percent discount on reinvested
dividends and OCPs

New Plan Realty Trust
5 percent discount on reinvested
dividends

NorAm Energy Corp.
3 percent discount on reinvested
dividends

North Carolina Natural Gas Corp.
5 percent discount on reinvested
dividends

Old National Bancorp (IN)
3 percent discount on reinvested
dividends; 2½ percent discount on
OCPs

Oneok, Inc.
3 percent discount on reinvested
dividends

**Petroleum Heat and Power Co.,
Inc.**
5 percent discount on reinvested
dividends; 3 percent discount on
OCPs

Philadelphia Suburban Corp.
5 percent discount on reinvested
dividends

Piccadilly Cafeterias, Inc.
5 percent discount on reinvested
dividends

Piedmont Natural Gas Co.
5 percent discount on reinvested
dividends

PMC Capital, Inc.
2 percent discount on reinvested
dividends and OCPs

PMC Commercial Trust
2 percent discount on reinvested
dividends and OCPs

Presidential Realty Corp.
5 percent discount on reinvested
dividends

Public Service Co. of North
Carolina
5 percent discount on reinvested
dividends

ReliaStar Financial Corp.
4 percent discount on reinvested
dividends; 1 percent discount on
OCPs

Shoreline Financial Corp.
5 percent discount on reinvested
dividends

Signet Banking Corp.
5 percent discount on reinvested
dividends

South West Property Trust, Inc.
5 percent discount on reinvested
dividends and OCPs

Southwest Water Co.
5 percent discount on reinvested
dividends

Suffolk Bancorp
3 percent discount on reinvested
dividends (does not apply when
purchasing on the open market)

Summit Bancorporation (NJ)
3½ percent discount on reinvested dividends and OCPs

Summit Properties, Inc.
5 percent discount on reinvested dividends

Telephone & Data Systems, Inc.
5 percent discount on reinvested dividends

Thornburg Mortgage Asset Corp.
3 percent discount on reinvested dividends and OCPs

Time Warner, Inc.
5 percent discount on reinvested dividends

Timken Co.
5 percent discount on reinvested dividends

Total Petroleum (North America) Ltd.
5 percent discount on reinvested dividends

TransCanada Pipelines Ltd.
5 percent discount on reinvested dividends

UGI Corp.
3 percent discount on reinvested dividends

Union Bank
5 percent discount on reinvested dividends

Union Planters Corp.
5 percent discount on reinvested dividends

United Cities Gas Co.
5 percent discount on reinvested dividends

United Mobile Homes, Inc.
5 percent discount on reinvested dividends and OCPs

United Water Resources, Inc.
5 percent discount on reinvested dividends; 3 percent discount on OCPs

UNITIL Corp.
5 percent discount on reinvested dividends

Unocal Corp.
3 percent discount on reinvested dividends

US BANCORP, Inc.
3 percent discount on reinvested dividends and OCPs

UST Corp.
10 percent discount on reinvested dividends and OCPs

USX Corp.—Marathon
0–3 percent discount on reinvested dividends and OCPs

USX Corp.—U.S. Steel Group
0–3 percent discount on reinvested dividends and OCPs

UtiliCorp United, Inc.
5 percent discount on reinvested dividends

Valley Resources, Inc.
5 percent discount on reinvested dividends

Walden Residential Properties, Inc.
5 percent discount on reinvested dividends and OCPs

Washington National Corp.
5 percent discount on reinvested dividends

Wells Fargo & Co.
3 percent discount on reinvested dividends

Westcoast Energy Inc.
5 percent discount on reinvested dividends

Westport Bancorp, Inc.
5 percent discount on reinvested dividends and OCPs

York Financial Corp.
10 percent discount on reinvested dividends

3

Buying GE at $10 a Crack

Optional Cash Payment Plans

A popular excuse for many individuals who don't invest in the stock market is, "I just don't have enough money, especially to buy the blue chips." That excuse doesn't hold up when you look at dividend reinvestment plans. For example, with a DRIP, you can invest as little as $10 per payment to buy such high-priced blue-chip issues as Coca-Cola, General Electric, and Minnesota Mining & Manufacturing. What makes investing in these issues possible for the average investor is the optional cash payment (OCP) plans of DRIPs.

How OCPs Work

OCPs are available with most DRIPs. Investing via OCPs is simple. Once enrolled in the DRIP, and usually after the first dividend has been reinvested, an investor is eligible to send voluntary cash payments directly to the company to accumulate additional shares.

Companies differ on the minimum and maximum optional payments permitted under the plans. For example, IBM permits OCPs of $10 to $25,000 every quarter. BellSouth has a minimum OCP of $50 with a maximum of $100,000 per year. In the case of Intel, a shareholder in the DRIP can make an optional cash payment of just $25. For those with deeper pockets, Intel permits OCPs of up to $15,000 per quarter.

Investors should note that an OCP is strictly voluntary—shareholders in DRIPs are not obligated to send in money. Nor are shareholders obligated to send in the same amount of money each time. For example, let's say you get a bonus at work and drop $1000 in OCPs one month. You don't have to make another $1000 payment in the following month. In fact, you don't necessarily have to make another payment into the plan again.

One of the beauties of OCPs is that fractional shares are purchased for investors. For example, let's say you send in $10 to purchase a stock that sells for $60 per share. Obviously, your payment isn't enough to buy a single share. However, your investment buys fractional shares. In this example, the investor would be credited with purchasing 0.167 share. Your fractional share receives a fractional portion of the dividend as well. While this may not seem like much, it can add up over a period of years.

Some other factors to consider include:

1. *When the OCP is invested.* Companies usually invest the money quarterly—at the same time that the firm reinvests the dividends—or monthly, usually around the first or last business day of the month. The more often the firm purchases stock with OCPs, the increased opportunities you have to "dollar-cost average," an investment strategy discussed in Chapter 5 which is ideal for long-term investing. Briefly, dollar-cost averaging relies on regular investments in a stock with the same dollar amount each investment period. All things equal, a firm that invests OCPs monthly or weekly is a better choice for investors who plan to use OCPs extensively in order to dollar-cost average.

Several firms make monthly OCPs hassle-free by permitting "automatic supplemental contributions" via direct electronic funds transfers from a participant's account with his or her financial institution. More on these monthly automatic investment programs is provided in Chapter 4.

2. *The applicability of discounts.* As discussed in the previous chapter, most companies that offer discounts on reinvested dividends do not offer them on OCPs. Thus, if you want to invest in an issue that offers a discount on OCPs, check first with the company.

3. *The OCP "option."* Many companies permit investors who do not want to reinvest dividends to enroll in the DRIP and make volun-

tary cash payments. This feature is especially attractive for investors who may need to receive their quarterly dividends for one reason or another but would like to make purchases of additional shares through OCPs. Again, look in the prospectus to see if this option is available.

4. *The timing of OCP payments.*   It's important not to send the money too far ahead of the investment date—the date the firm enters the market to purchase stock. That's because companies do not pay interest on funds awaiting reinvestment. Therefore, funds should be sent as close to the investment date as possible prior to it (the date is given in the prospectus). Many companies provide a window of opportunity for investors to have OCPs returned prior to investment. For example, let's say you sent $2000 to purchase stock via a company's OCP option, with the money arriving 10 days prior to the investment date. However, immediately after sending the cash, your refrigerator goes on the blink and you have to replace it. In some cases, as long as you notify the plan a few days before the investment date, you can have the money returned to you.

5. *Fees charged for purchasing stock with OCPs.*   Although most companies don't charge any brokerage fees or service charges when purchasing stocks with reinvested dividends or OCPs, there are those companies that charge a nominal brokerage fee. Brokerage commissions are based, to some extent, on the size of the purchase, and big orders will usually command substantial discounts in brokerage fees. In order to keep down any pro rata brokerage fees you'll have to pay in certain plans, you should plan to send your money at times when the company is making its biggest purchases. This is usually at the dividend payment date, when the firm is reinvesting dividends.

"Rich Person's" Portfolio

As mentioned, the OCP is one of the best friends an individual investor, particularly one working with limited resources, has in the market. Through OCPs, investors need not necessarily eliminate any issue from their investment program, regardless of price. As an example, an investor can purchase stock in each of the high-priced issues in the following "rich person's portfolio" for a total minimum monthly payment of $50:

	Stock price	Min. OCP
Atlantic Richfield Co.	$112	$10
The Coca-Cola Company	69	10
General Electric Co.	62	10
International Business Machines Corp.	96	10
Philip Morris Companies, Inc.	81	10
Monthly OCP payment		$50

Here's a sampling of some issues that permit minimum OCP investments of $25 or less per payment:

AAR Corp.

Abbott Laboratories

Acme-Cleveland Corp.

AFLAC, Inc.

Albany International Corp.

AMCORE Financial, Inc.

American Business Products, Inc.

American Recreation Centers, Inc.

AmSouth Bancorp.

Aquarion Co.

ARCO Chemical Co.

Ashland, Inc.

Atlantic Richfield Co.

Atmos Energy Corp.

Avnet, Inc.

Avon Products, Inc.

Baker Hughes, Inc.

Baltimore Gas & Electric Co.

Banc One Corp.

Banta Corp.

Bard (C. R.), Inc.

Barnes Group, Inc.

Bay State Gas Co.

BayBanks, Inc.

Beneficial Corp.

Bethlehem Steel Corp.

Bindley Western Industries, Inc.

Birmingham Steel Corp.

Black & Decker Corp.

Block (H & R), Inc.

Blount, Inc.

Boise Cascade Corp.

British Airways PLC

British Petroleum Co. PLC

Brooklyn Union Gas Co.

Browning-Ferris Industries, Inc.

Brunswick Corp.

Brush Wellman, Inc.

Cabot Corp.

Carlisle Companies, Inc.

Carpenter Technology Corp.

Caterpillar, Inc.

CCB Financial Corp.

Centerior Energy Corp.

Central & South West Corp.

Central Maine Power Co.

Champion International Corp.

Charter One Financial, Inc.

Chemical Financial Corp.

Chesapeake Corp.

Chubb Corp.

CIGNA Corp.

Cincinnati Bell, Inc.
CIPSCO, Inc.
Cleveland-Cliffs, Inc.
Clorox Co.
Coca-Cola Bottling Co. Consolidated
Coca-Cola Co. (The)
Coca-Cola Enterprises, Inc.
Colonial BancGroup, Inc.
Colonial Gas Co.
Columbia Gas System, Inc.
Comerica, Inc.
Commonwealth Energy System
Computer Associates International, Inc.
Consumers Water Co.
Corning, Inc.
CPC International, Inc.
Crane Co.
Crestar Financial Corp.
Cummins Engine Co., Inc.
Dana Corp.
Dayton Hudson Corp.
Dial Corp. (The)
Diebold, Inc.
Donaldson Co., Inc.
Donnelley (R. R.) & Sons Co.
Dow Chemical Co.
DQE
DuPont (E. I.) de Nemours & Co.
Eastern Enterprises
Ecolab, Inc.
EG&G, Inc.
Engelhard Corp.
Enron Corp.
Enserch Corp.
Equifax, Inc.
Equitable Resources, Inc.

Federal-Mogul Corp.
Federal National Mortgage Assn.
Federal Paper Board Co., Inc.
FINA, Inc.
Florida Progress Corp.
Foster Wheeler Corp.
Frontier Corp.
Fuller (H. B.) Co.
Gannett Co., Inc.
GenCorp, Inc.
General Electric Co.
General Housewares Corp.
General Mills, Inc.
General Re Corp.
Genuine Parts Co.
Giant Food, Inc.
Gillette Co.
GoodMark Foods, Inc.
Goodyear Tire & Rubber Co.
Goulds Pumps, Inc.
GTE Corp.
Handleman Co.
Handy & Harman
Harland (John H.) Company
Harris Corp.
Harsco Corp.
Hartford Steam Boiler Inspection & Insurance Co.
Health Care REIT, Inc.
Home Depot, Inc.
Honeywell, Inc.
Idaho Power Co.
Ingersoll-Rand Co.
Inland Steel Industries, Inc.
Intel Corp.
International Business Machines Corp.
International Multifoods Corp.

Interpublic Group of Companies, Inc.

Johnson & Johnson

K N Energy, Inc.

Keithley Instruments, Inc.

Kellogg Co.

Kellwood Co.

Kennametal, Inc.

Kerr-McGee Corp.

KeyCorp

Keystone Heritage Group, Inc.

Kuhlman Corp.

Lance, Inc.

Lowe's Companies, Inc.

Manpower, Inc.

MAPCO, Inc.

Mark Twain Bancshares, Inc.

Marsh & McLennan Cos., Inc.

Mattel, Inc.

May Department Stores Co.

McGraw-Hill Companies, Inc.

MCN Corp.

Medtronic, Inc.

Mercantile Bancorp, Inc.

Meridian Bancorp, Inc.

Minnesota Mining & Manufacturing Co.

Minnesota Power & Light Co.

Mobil Corp.

Modine Manufacturing Co.

Monsanto Co.

Montana Power Co.

Motorola, Inc.

Nash-Finch Co.

National Service Industries, Inc.

National-Standard Co.

New York State Electric & Gas Corp.

New York Times Co.

Nordson Corp.

Norfolk Southern Corp.

Northwestern Public Service Co.

Nucor Corp.

NYNEX Corp.

Ohio Casualty Corp.

Ohio Edison Co.

Omnicare, Inc.

Otter Tail Power Co.

PaineWebber Group, Inc.

Parker Hannifin Corp.

Penney (J. C.) Co., Inc.

Pentair, Inc.

PepsiCo, Inc.

Pfizer, Inc.

Phelps Dodge Corp.

Philip Morris Cos., Inc.

Phillips Petroleum Co.

Pioneer-Standard Electronics, Inc.

Polaroid Corp.

PPG Industries, Inc.

Premier Industrial Corp.

Quaker Oats Co.

Quaker State Corp.

Raytheon Co.

Roadway Services, Inc.

Rockwell International Corp.

RPM, Inc.

Russell Corp.

Ryder System, Inc.

Safety-Kleen Corp.

St. Paul Companies, Inc.

Salomon, Inc.

Sara Lee Corp.

Savannah Foods & Industries, Inc.

Schering-Plough Corp.

Scientific-Atlanta, Inc.

Sherwin-Williams Co.

Signet Banking Corp.

Simpson Industries, Inc.

Sonoco Products Co.

Southwest Gas Corp.

Stanhome, Inc.

Stanley Works

State Street Boston Corp.

Stride Rite Corp.

SunTrust Banks, Inc.

SuperValu, Inc.

TECO Energy, Inc.

Telephone & Data Systems, Inc.

Tenet Healthcare Corp.

Thomas & Betts Corp.

Toro Co.

Transamerica Corp.

Trinova Corp.

TRW, Inc.

Twin Disc, Inc.

UJB Financial Corp.

Union Pacific Corp.

United Illuminating Co.

U S West, Inc.

Universal Corp.

USLIFE Corp.

VF Corp.

Vulcan Materials Co.

Walgreen Co.

Warner-Lambert Co.

Weis Markets, Inc.

Wendy's International, Inc.

Whirlpool Corp.

Whitman Corp.

Wilmington Trust Co.

Winn-Dixie Stores, Inc.

Witco Corp.

WMX Technologies, Inc.

WPL Holdings, Inc.

Xerox Corp.

Zions Bancorporation

Commission Breaks for Big Spenders

I have focused on OCPs as an avenue for the little investor to purchase stock in high-quality, big-ticket issues by taking advantage of the low minimum OCP payments. However, investors who are able to afford bigger voluntary cash payments can reap large benefits in the way of commission savings.

For example, the maximum OCP for McDonald's is $75,000 per year. Let's say that you like McDonald's stock a lot and have the cash to take a major position of $60,000 in the stock over the course of the year. Commissions on an investment of that magnitude could run well into four figures. However, if you make the purchases via OCPs, your commissions are zero.

The following "big spender" DRIPs permit OCPs of $60,000 or more per year:

Aetna Life & Casualty Co.

AFLAC, Inc.

Albany International Corp.

Albertson's, Inc.

Allied Group, Inc.

AlliedSignal, Inc.

ALLTEL Corp.

Aluminum Co. of America

American Express Co.

American Home Products Corp.

Amoco Corp.

Anheuser-Busch Companies, Inc.

Atlanta Gas Light Co.

Atlantic Richfield Co.

Atmos Energy Corp.

Avon Products, Inc.

Bank of Boston Corp.

Bank South Corp.

BankAmerica Corp.

Bankers Trust New York Corp.

Barnett Banks, Inc.

Bausch & Lomb, Inc.

Bob Evans Farms, Inc.

Bowater, Inc.

Bristol-Myers Squibb Co.

British Airways PLC

British Petroleum Co. PLC

Brooklyn Union Gas Co.

Browning-Ferris Industries, Inc.

Caterpillar, Inc.

Central Fidelity Banks, Inc.

Central Louisiana Electric Co., Inc.

Champion International Corp.

CIGNA Corp.

Citicorp

Clorox Co.

CMS Energy Corp.

Coca-Cola Co. (The)

Coca-Cola Enterprises, Inc.

Colgate-Palmolive Co.

COMSAT Corp.

Corning, Inc.

Crane Co.

Deere & Co.

Delmarva Power & Light Co.

Dominion Resources, Inc.

Dow Chemical Co.

DQE

Eastman Chemical Co.

Eastman Kodak Co.

Eaton Corp.

Ecolab, Inc.

Enserch Corp.

Exxon Corp.

Fay's, Inc.

Federal Realty Investment Trust

First Chicago Corp.

First Fidelity Bancorp.

First of America Bank Corp.

First Security Corp.

First Union Real Estate Investments

Firstar Corp.

Gannett Co., Inc.

General Electric Co.

Georgia-Pacific Corp.

Goodyear Tire & Rubber Co.

Goulds Pumps, Inc.

Handy & Harman

Idaho Power Co.

IES Industries, Inc.

Intel Corp.

International Business Machines
Corp.

International Multifoods Corp.
ITT Corp.
James River Corp.
Johnson Controls, Inc.
KeyCorp
Lukens, Inc.
Magna Group, Inc.
Maytag Corp.
McDermott International, Inc.
McDonald's Corp.
McKesson Corp.
Media General, Inc.
Mobil Corp.
Modine Manufacturing Co.
Morgan (J. P.) & Co., Inc.
Morton International, Inc.
Nalco Chemical Co.
National Fuel Gas Co.
New England Electric System
NICOR, Inc.
Northeast Utilities Service Co.
Norwest Corp.
Ohio Casualty Corp.
Olin Corp.
OM Group, Inc.
PacifiCorp
Pall Corp.
Panhandle Eastern Corp.
PepsiCo, Inc.
Pfizer, Inc.
Philip Morris Companies, Inc.
Phillips Petroleum Co.
Pioneer-Standard Electronics, Inc.

PMC Capital, Inc.
Potomac Electric Power Co.
Public Service Co. of Colorado
Public Service Enterprise Group, Inc.
Questar Corp.
Rochester Gas & Electric Corp.
Safety-Kleen Corp.
St. Paul Companies, Inc.
SBC Communications, Inc.
SCEcorp
Signet Banking Corp.
Southern Indiana Gas & Electric Co.
SouthTrust Corp.
Stanley Works
Summit Bancorporation (NJ)
SunTrust Banks
TECO Energy, Inc.
Tenneco, Inc.
Texaco, Inc.
Transamerica Corp.
Union Electric Co.
Union Pacific Corp.
United Carolina Bancshares Corp.
U S West, Inc.
UtiliCorp United, Inc.
Valley Resources, Inc.
Weingarten Realty Investors
Whitman Corp.
Woolworth Corp.
Wrigley (William) Jr. Co.
Xerox Corp.
Zero Corp.

Conclusion

In my opinion, the greatest benefit of a dividend reinvestment program is the ability to make optional cash investments over time in quality companies. Judging from the many portfolios I see as market strategist of *Dow Theory Forecasts*, the individuals who are the most successful in the stock market are not necessarily those who started with huge sums of money but are those who stuck to a disciplined investment program, investing on a regular basis in top-notch companies over many years. The OCP feature allows even small investors to do just that—invest regularly, in amounts of money that they can afford, in blue-chip companies. Keep in mind, however, that just because a firm will allow you to invest $10 or $25 doesn't make it a good buy. Check the performance ratings in Chapter 8 before investing.

4

What the Future Holds for the DRIP Investor

Emerging Trends in the DRIP World

Dividend reinvestment plans have been around for decades—AT&T offered one of the first prominent DRIP plans in 1973—and many of today's plans still closely resemble plans of 20 years ago. However, a number of trends have emerged over the last few years that are having a profound effect on how DRIPs will operate in the future. This chapter examines these emerging trends in the DRIP world.

No-Load Stocks™

Perhaps the most noteworthy development in the DRIP world is the emergence of what I call *No-Load Stocks™*.

No-load stocks are those firms that allow investors to buy their initial shares directly from the company. No-load stocks represent a radical departure from typical DRIPs, which require investors to be shareholders already in order to participate.

No-load stock programs work in much the same way as no-load mutual funds:

- Investors call the company, usually via a toll-free number, to request an application form and a plan prospectus.

- The company mails the materials directly to the investor.

- Once the investor receives the materials and completes the application, he or she makes the initial investment directly by returning the application and a check to the company. The minimum initial investment for most no-load stocks is under $500, with some minimums as low as $20. In most cases, your initial investment will automatically enroll you in the company's dividend reinvestment plan and/or stock purchase plan.

Although no-load stocks have been around since the early 1980s, their numbers, prior to 1994, were rather small. However, the growth in the number of no-load stocks has accelerated rapidly due to an event that occurred on December 1, 1994. On that day, unbeknownst to most investors and members of the business media, the Securities and Exchange Commission issued rulings that made it much easier for companies to implement no-load stock programs. Prior to December 1, 1994, it would take a company anywhere from nine months, if the firm was lucky, to two years to get a proposed no-load stock program through the regulatory process. However, on December 1, the SEC, in effect, approved two "model" no-load stock programs. The significance of the rulings was that any company that now wanted to implement a no-load stock program would have a "blueprint" plan, already preapproved by the SEC, that it could adopt. The upshot is that it now takes maybe three to five weeks to get a no-load stock plan up and running compared to the lengthy delays before December 1, 1994.

From a company perspective, the dramatic reduction in regulatory hassle and the associated reduction in fees to navigate the regulatory process mean that major hurdles to offering a no-load stock plan have been lowered. The number of no-load stock plans has jumped sharply since the beginning of 1995, and more are on the way. In fact, some industry insiders believe that no-load stocks could number 500 or more over the next couple of years.

Obviously, from an investor's standpoint, the emergence of no-load stocks is a long time in coming. The skyrocketing growth of no-load mutual funds over the last couple of decades has shown that investors want to deal directly with the market, without a broker and brokerage commissions. Fortunately, investors now have the opportunity to do so in the stock world via no-load stocks.

One final note: Companies are "complaint driven." In other words, change is often considered only after enough people have complained about the status quo. If you would like to see a certain company implement a no-load stock program, your best move would be to write a letter to the CEO or chairman stating why you would like such a program, possible ways the company would benefit (no-load stocks offer a cheap source of equity capital, diversification of the shareholder base to reduce the control of institutional and "street"-name investors, and a way to reach a wider consumer audience for the firm's goods and services), and perhaps ideas on how to hold down the costs of operating the program. Also, I've found a company to be more interested in offering a no-load stock plan if its competitors offer such a plan. If you contact a company about a no-load stock program—and one of its competitors already offers a program—make sure you let the CEO know what his or her competitors are doing.

The following is a list of all no-load stocks, including those that limit the ability to purchase initial shares to customers and/or residents of the state(s) in which the company operates. The minimum initial investment is in parentheses.

Firms That Permit Initial Stock Purchases Directly:

American Recreation Centers, Inc. ($100)

Arrow Financial Corp. ($300)

Atlantic Energy Corp. ($250)

Atmos Energy Corp. ($200)

Barnett Banks, Inc. ($250)

Bob Evans Farms, Inc. ($50)

Capstead Mortgage Corp. ($250)

Central Vermont Public Service Corp. ($50) (permitted in less than half the states)

COMSAT Corp. ($250)

Dean Witter, Discover & Co. ($1000)

DeBartolo Realty Corp. ($500)

Dial Corp. ($100)

DQE ($105)

Exxon Corp. ($250)

Houston Industries, Inc. ($250)

Interchange Financial Services Corp. ($100)

Johnson Controls, Inc. ($50)

Kellwood Co. ($100)

Kerr-McGee Corp. ($750)

Mobil Corp. ($250)

Montana Power Co. ($100) (permitted in 17 states)

Morton International, Inc. ($1000)

NorAm Energy Corp. ($200)

Oneok, Inc. ($100)

Pinnacle West Capital Corp. ($50)

Portland General Corp. ($250)

Procter & Gamble Co. ($100)

Regions Financial Corp. ($500)

SCANA Corp. ($250)

Tenneco, Inc. ($500)

Texaco, Inc. ($250)

U S West, Inc. ($300)

UtiliCorp United, Inc. ($250)

Western Resources, Inc. ($250)

Wisconsin Energy Corp. ($50)

Firms That Offer Initial Purchase Only for Residents of the State(s) in Which the Company Operates:

Bancorp Hawaii, Inc. ($250)

BanPonce Corp. (Puerto Rico) ($25)

Central & South West Corp. (AR, LA, OK, TX) ($100)

Central Fidelity Banks, Inc. (MD, NC, VA) ($100)

Central Maine Power Co. ($25)

Delta Natural Gas Co., Inc. (KY) ($100)

Duke Power Co. (considering availability for all investors) (NC, SC) ($25)

Florida Progress Corp. ($100)

Green Mountain Power Corp. (VT) ($50)

Hawaiian Electric Industries, Inc. ($100)

Northern States Power Co. (MN, MI, ND, SD, WI) ($10)

NUI Corp. (FL, MD, NJ, NC, NY, PA) ($125)

Puget Sound P&L Co. (WA) ($25)

WICOR, Inc. (WI) ($100)

Firms That Offer Initial Purchase Only for Their Utility Customers:

American Water Works Company, Inc. ($100)

Boston Edison Co. ($500)

Brooklyn Union Gas Co. ($250)

Carolina Power & Light Co. ($20)

Cascade Natural Gas Corp. ($250)

Centerior Energy Corp. ($10)

Central Hudson Gas & Electric Corp. ($100)

Connecticut Energy Corp. ($250)

Connecticut Water Service, Inc. ($100)

Dominion Resources, Inc. ($20)

Idaho Power Co. ($10)

IES Industries, Inc. ($50)

Interstate Power Co. ($50)

IWC Resources Corp. ($100)

Minnesota Power & Light Co. ($10)

National Fuel Gas Co. ($200)

Nevada Power Co. ($25)

New Jersey Resources Corp. ($25)

Northwestern Public Service Co. ($10)

Oklahoma Gas & Electric Co. ($25)

Philadelphia Suburban Corp. ($250)

San Diego Gas & Electric Co. ($25)

Southwest Gas Corp. ($100)

Union Electric Co. (no minimum)

United Cities Gas Co. ($250)

United Water Resources, Inc. ($25)

Another interesting "limited" no-load stock program is offered by Yankee Energy System, a natural gas distribution company in Connecticut. The firm allows family members of current shareholders to buy their initial shares directly from the company (minimum $500 initial investment).

Because of my work in this area, I maintain a list of no-load stocks that is updated continuously. As a service to readers, this updated list of all no-load stocks and their telephone numbers is available free of charge by writing *DRIP Investor*, 7412 Calumet Avenue, Hammond, Indiana 46324-2692. Use the code words "No-Load Stocks" when making requests. Please include a business-size, self-addressed, stamped envelope. For investors who desire a fuller explanation of no-load stocks, including two-page reports on more than 50 no-load stocks, let me plug my book, *No-Load Stocks* (McGraw-Hill), which is available in bookstores or by calling (219) 931-6480.

Expanded Services

Another emerging trend in the DRIP field is the addition of ancillary services that enhance the appeal of a DRIP program. The following are new, user-friendly features being incorporated into more and more DRIPs and no-load stock programs.

Frequent Purchases

One complaint investors have about DRIPs is that they permit only infrequent purchases of stocks, either monthly or, in some cases, once every three months. Fortunately, a number of DRIPs are now investing for participants on a weekly or biweekly basis. The ability to buy stock more frequently in a DRIP is a plus for investors since it provides greater control over the purchase price. For example, say you like the current price of a company's stock and you want to purchase shares through its DRIP. Since the DRIP may invest funds only on the last business day of the month, the stock price could fluctuate between the time you want to invest and the time the investment is actually made. If the DRIP buys stock weekly instead of quarterly, chances are greater that you'll be able to buy the stock closer to your desired "buy" price. More frequent investments of optional cash investments also increase the opportunities to "dollar-cost average" in a plan. Dollar-cost averaging, which is discussed in great detail in Chapter 5, is an investment strategy whereby investors buy stock on a regular basis. The aim of dollar-cost averaging is to space out buying over time so that you are not always buying stock at the peak. For long-term investors, dollar-cost averaging is an excellent strategy for building a profitable portfolio, and being able to buy stock weekly instead of monthly or quarterly enhances the power of a dollar-cost averaging program. DRIPs that offer weekly investment options include Atmos Energy and Exxon.

IRA Options

DRIPs, because of their long-term nature, are excellent vehicles for retirement. Unfortunately, including DRIPs in an Individual Retirement Account (IRA) is not easy. In order to have stocks in a self-directed IRA, you must have a custodian for the account. Brokerage firms are the usual custodians for IRAs that hold individual stocks. The problem with this arrangement is that investors incur large commission costs any time they buy or sell stock in the IRA. Thus, it makes a lot of sense to put DRIPs in an IRA since this eliminates those pesky brokerage fees. However, if you plan to hold DRIPs in an IRA, good luck in finding a custodian. Don't expect your broker to provide custodial services since the shares are held in your name, not "street" name.

Because it is so difficult to find a custodian to service an IRA holding DRIPs, DRIP programs with IRA options are very appealing. In these plans, DRIP participants may make investments in the plan, and these investments go into the individual's IRA plan. The company or an agent of the company provides the custodial services.

Readers should note that most DRIPs charge fees to administer IRAs. While these fees are not onerous, usually $20 to $50 per year, they can add up over time, especially if you are investing in more than one DRIP IRA. However, I would expect over time, as the IRA feature becomes more popular and firms have a larger number of accounts in them, economies of scale will help to lower the annual fees. Already, Atmos Energy offers a "no-fee" IRA option in its DRIP. I wouldn't be surprised to see firms lower or eliminate the annual administrative fees once an investor's IRA exceeds some minimum amount, which is similar to mutual funds. The following is a list of companies whose DRIPs offer IRAs:

Atmos Energy Corp.	Mobil Corp.
Barnett Banks, Inc.	Morton International, Inc.
Centerior Energy Corp.	Portland General Corp.
Connecticut Energy Corp.	SBC Communications, Inc.
Connecticut Water Service, Inc.	UtiliCorp United, Inc.
Exxon Corp.	

Automatic Investment Services

Mutual-fund investors are quite familiar with automatic investment services. These are services in which the mutual fund, with permission from the fund investor, withdraws electronically a predetermined amount of money each month from the investor's savings or checking account to make investments in the mutual fund. Investors like these programs because they simplify the investment process, save time, reduce postage costs, and ensure regular deposits in their mutual fund. Fortunately, several DRIPs are following the mutual-fund lead and implementing automatic investment programs for DRIP partici- pants. The minimum investment using this service is usually $25 to $50. The following is a partial list of companies that offer automatic investment services:

American Electric Power Co., Inc.	DQE
Ameritech Corp.	Duke Power Co.
Atlantic Energy, Inc.	Exxon Corp.
Atmos Energy Corp.	Hawaiian Electric Industries, Inc.
Banta Corp.	Montana Power Co.
Barnett Banks, Inc.	Morton International, Inc.
Bell Atlantic Corp.	Nevada Power Co.
Bob Evans Farms, Inc.	NUI Corp.
Carolina Power & Light Co.	Philip Morris Companies, Inc.
Central & South West Corp.	Portland General Corp.
Central Fidelity Banks, Inc.	Procter & Gamble Co.
Central Maine Power Co.	Public Service Co. of North
Clorox Co.	Carolina
CMS Energy Corp.	Tenneco, Inc.
Coca-Cola Co. (The)	U S West, Inc.
Colonial Gas Co.	UtiliCorp United, Inc.
Connecticut Energy Corp.	Wisconsin Energy Corp.
Dayton Hudson Corp.	WPL Holdings, Inc.

Telephone Redemptions

A frequent criticism of DRIPs is their apparent lack of liquidity. Indeed, if you want to sell your DRIP holdings through the company, in many cases you'll have to submit sell instructions in writing, which takes time, and wait for the firm to execute the sell order, which could take 5 to 10 business days. Companies are well aware of the lag on the sell side, and some firms have implemented ways to streamline the sell process by offering telephone redemption services. Dial, for example, allows DRIP participants to sell their holdings with just a telephone call, and Dial picks up all of the commissions when selling shares.

First Chicago Trust Company of New York, one of the largest administrators of DRIPs for corporations, has been a leader in implementing telephone redemption services in DRIPs. The following is a partial listing of names of prominent First Chicago Trust Company clients offering First Chicago Trust's "automated sales request line":

Atlantic Richfield Co.	Georgia-Pacific Corp.
Beckman Instruments, Inc.	Indiana Energy, Inc.
Becton Dickinson and Company	Johnson & Johnson
Black & Decker Corp.	Liz Claiborne, Inc.
Brown-Forman Corp.	Morgan (J. P.) & Co., Inc.
Browning-Ferris Industries, Inc.	Morton International, Inc.
Chrysler Corp.	Nalco Chemical Co.
CIGNA Corp.	Safety-Kleen Corp.
Coca-Cola Co. (The)	Tenneco, Inc.
Dayton Hudson Corp.	Thomas & Betts Corp.
Delta Air Lines, Inc.	Tribune Company
Eastman Chemical Co.	Union Pacific Corp.
Eastman Kodak Co.	Warner-Lambert Co.
Enron Corp.	

If you own stock in a company whose DRIP administrator is First Chicago Trust, contact the transfer agent to see if your company offers the "automated sales request line." If you own DRIPs whose transfer agents do not offer telephone redemption, notify the company that you would like to see the service available in the DRIP.

International Investing with DRIPs

One of the more popular investment themes of recent years has been international investing. There are a number of good reasons to have international exposure in a portfolio. Many overseas economies, especially those in emerging countries, are growing at rapid rates. Also, international exposure increases portfolio diversification.

DRIP investors have a variety of ways to invest overseas. One approach is to focus on DRIPs of U.S. companies that have extensive overseas exposure. Another method is to participate in DRIPs offered by closed-end funds specializing in overseas investments. Closed-end funds are similar to open-end mutual funds in that the funds permit investment in a basket of stocks selected and managed by an investment company. However, closed-end funds sell only a certain number of shares at the initial public offering, just like a stock. Once the shares are sold, the fund is "closed," and new money is not accepted. Also, closed-end funds trade on the stock exchanges while open-end funds do not. A number of closed-end funds focus on the stocks of certain countries. For example, there is the Brazil Fund. There's also the Italy Fund and the Mexico Fund. For DRIP investors who want to concentrate international investments in a particular country, closed-end funds offer an interesting option. More information on closed-end funds, including a directory of closed-end funds offering DRIPs, is available in Appendix C at the back of this book.

A final way for DRIP investors to invest overseas is by buying American Depositary Receipts (ADRs). ADRs are issued by U.S. banks against the actual shares of foreign companies held in trust by a correspondent institution overseas. Oftentimes, ADRs are not issued on a share-for-share basis. Instead, one ADR may be the equivalent of 5 or 10 ordinary shares of the company.

ADRs have become popular in recent years. One reason is convenience. Investors can buy and sell ADRs just like ordinary shares, eliminating the need for currency translations. Commissions to purchase ADRs are smaller than would be charged if the securities were purchased on foreign markets.

Although ADRs offer plenty of pluses for investors, there are some things to consider before investing. Currency fluctuations will impact ADRs. When local currencies strengthen versus the dollar, the return on the ADR is boosted. Thus, if you own shares in a country whose stock market is rising and whose currency is strengthening against the dollar, you're getting a double-powered boost to your portfolio. Conversely, if the dollar is strengthening against the nation's currency of your ADR, returns will suffer. Another consideration is that accounting norms differ between countries. Thus, interpreting financial data may be difficult.

The good news for DRIP investors is that there are a growing number of foreign companies with ADRs that have DRIPs available to U.S. investors. This growth is being spurred by increases in the number of foreign companies seeking listing on U.S. stock exchanges. Also, with competition increasing on a global scale, especially in various consumer-products markets, foreign companies are seeking greater name recognition with U.S. investors in order to build brand awareness.

The following is a list of ADRs, representing several countries, that offer DRIPs:

British Airways PLC, (800) 428-4237 (airlines)

British Petroleum Co. PLC, (800) 428-4237 (energy)

Broken Hill Proprietary Co. Ltd., (212) 648-3143 (natural resources)

Coles Myer Ltd., (212) 657-9522 (retailing)

Glaxo Wellcome PLC, (800) 524-4458 (drugs)

Grand Metropolitan PLC, (800) 428-4237 (conglomerate)

Hanson PLC, (800) 422-2066 (conglomerate)

HSBC Holdings PLC, (800) 428-4237 (banking)

Marks & Spencer, (800) 428-4237 (retailing)

National Australia Bank Ltd., (212) 648-3143 (banking)

Nestle S.A., (617) 774-4237 (consumer products)

News Corp. Ltd., (212) 657-7387 (media/entertainment)

Novo-Nordisk A/S, (212) 867-0131 (drugs)

SmithKline Beecham PLC, (800) 882-3359 (drugs)

Total, (212) 969-2810 (oil)

Volvo AB, (212) 754-3300 (automobiles)

Willis Corroon Group PLC, (800) 428-4237 (insurance)

In addition to these firms, several Canadian-based companies, including BCE, Inc. and Moore Corp., offer DRIPs to investors living in Canada and, in some cases, the United States.

Small-Cap Stocks and NASDAQ Issues Offering DRIPs

A common misconception concerning dividend reinvestment plans is that only big, stodgy, high-dividend-paying stocks offer DRIPs. While it is true that many companies in the DRIP universe are large, industrial concerns, a growing number of small-capitalization and NASDAQ-traded stocks are implementing DRIPs.

The emergence of smaller DRIP companies is significant for several reasons. The increased number of small-cap companies offering DRIPs enhances an investor's ability to diversify a DRIP portfolio to include small, high-growth issues. Many academic studies have shown that small-cap stocks, over time, tend to outperform their larger brethren. Also, many market watchers believe that small-cap stocks are poised to show excellent gains over the next three to five years. Thus, it is important for DRIP investors to have at least a small exposure to small-cap and NASDAQ stocks.

The following is a list of some of the more noteworthy small-cap and NASDAQ-traded stocks offering DRIPs. For telephone numbers and further information on these and other DRIPs listed in this chapter, refer to the directory in Chapter 8.

ADAC Laboratories

AMCOL International Corp.

American Greetings Corp.

American Recreation Centers, Inc.

Arnold Industries, Inc.

Banta Corp.

Bob Evans Farms, Inc.

Brady (W. H.) Co.

Cincinnati Financial Corp.

Coca-Cola Bottling Co. Consolidated

Cracker Barrel Old Country Store, Inc.

Food Lion, Inc.

Fuller (H. B.) Co.

Giddings & Lewis, Inc.

GoodMark Foods, Inc.

Goulds Pumps, Inc.

Intel Corp.

Justin Industries, Inc.

Kaman Corp.

Knape & Vogt Manufacturing Co.

Lancaster Colony Corp.

Lance, Inc.

Lilly Industries, Inc.

Lincoln Telecommunications Co.

Marsh Supermarkets, Inc.

McCormick & Co., Inc.

Meridian Diagnostics, Inc.

Nash-Finch Co.

Nordson Corp.

OM Group, Inc.

Paychex, Inc.

Pentair, Inc.

Pioneer Hi-Bred International, Inc.

Pioneer-Standard Electronics, Inc.

Regions Financial Corp.

Roadway Services, Inc.

Rouse Co.

RPM, Inc.

Simpson Industries, Inc.

Versa Technologies, Inc.

Worthington Industries, Inc.

Increased Costs of DRIP Investing

Up to this point, we've discussed emerging trends that are favorable to DRIP investors, such as improved access to stocks via no-load stock plans, a wider universe of DRIP offerings in small-cap and international stocks, and more user-friendly services including IRAs, telephone redemptions, and automatic investment services. However, some of the emerging trends in the DRIP world are not so positive for investors.

One of the biggest costs of DRIP investing has nothing to do with a DRIP plan but everything to do with getting started in DRIPs. As discussed throughout the book, most DRIP plans, with the exception of no-load stock programs, require that an investor already be a shareholder of record in order to participate. What is happening these days is that the cost of becoming a registered shareholder in order to enroll in a DRIP is rising. Many brokerage firms now charge $15 or more—this fee is on top of their commission—to register stock in a shareholder's name. Why? The name of the game in the brokerage business is asset management. Brokers want to have your assets under their control, which is why they push "street" name ownership and charge extra for investors who want to register stock in their own name.

Brokers have always aggressively pushed "street" name ownership, but their agenda was given a huge lift when the SEC mandated a shortened settlement period for stock transactions, which took effect June 7, 1995. Prior to that date, stock transactions in this country settled five days after the trade date. However, on June 7, the settlement shrunk to three days after the trade date—"T + 3" as it's known in industry parlance.

The SEC shortened the settlement period in order to reduce risk in the settlement process. Unfortunately, "T + 3" gave brokers a weapon to push investors into "street" name under the guise of meeting the shortened settlement period. I've heard reports where investors are told that they must hold stock in "street" name as a result of "T + 3." This is simply not the case. You do not have to change the way you register your shares as a result of "T + 3," regardless of what your broker tells you. Bottom line: The shift to "T + 3" makes it more difficult to register stock in your name since brokers have been told by their firms to push aggressively "street"-name ownership. And if the broker can't talk you into holding stock in "street" name, chances are he or she will make you pay extra.

Brokerage "DRIP" Services

Another ploy brokers will use to get you to hold stock in "street" name is to push you into the broker's own "dividend reinvestment service." Brokerage firms have capitalized on the growing popularity of the DRIP concept by offering their own versions of "dividend reinvestment plans"—versions that are very different from company-sponsored plans. The biggest difference is that in company-sponsored DRIPs, optional cash payments often can be made for as little as $10 to $25, and you usually incur no commissions when investing via optional cash payments. However, in the "dividend reinvestment services" offered by many brokerage firms, such optional cash investments are not permitted.

So next time you see one of Charles Schwab's full-page ads in *The Wall Street Journal* hyping its "no-fee dividend reinvestment plan" or you receive a brochure in the mail from a broker extolling the virtues of its "dividend reinvestment plan," remember that these plans are quite different from company-sponsored plans, especially in the ability to make optional cash payments. Don't get talked into participating in your broker's DRIP if what you really want is to invest commission-free directly with the company.

Higher Fees as DRIP Services Expand

Another emerging trend that could affect your pocketbook is the tendency for more companies to implement fees in their DRIPs as the menu of service options expands. DRIP fees is a rather controversial topic, and I usually get myself into trouble every time I broach the subject. My take on fees is that investors usually are willing to pay reasonable fees if the plan offers a variety of services, especially the ability to buy initial shares directly. Investors understand that paying a fee of a couple of dollars in a DRIP is still a much better deal than paying $35 or more to a brokerage firm for each transaction.

One reason for increases in DRIP fees is to defray the costs of operating the plans. Fees also help "qualify" an investor. Companies don't want small investors who buy a share or two of stock and are never heard from again. These investors are costly to service. By charging fees, companies hope to eliminate "tire-kickers" who have no plans of being long-term investors. Other ways companies deter small investors is by boosting initial investment minimums, implementing share requirements for participation in the DRIP (PepsiCo, for example, requires that shareholders own 5 shares in order to be eligible for the DRIP), and raising minimum optional cash payment amounts.

Another reason fees will be more prevalent in DRIPs is that securities transfer agents—the firms that administrate many DRIPs—have been rather aggressively pushing companies to implement fees. Transfer agents service registered shareholders. Thus, transfer agents want companies to offer DRIPs and no-load stock plans since these plans boost the ranks of registered shareholders, thereby boosting transfer agents' fees. If a company balks at starting a DRIP because of the costs, transfer agents are quick to point out that the costs can be defrayed by charging the participants fees. You can be sure that a fee structure, charged to participants, is part of every transfer agent's marketing pitch to companies that are considering DRIPs and no-load stocks.

The problems with DRIP fees usually occur when a firm implements fees without adding services or nickels and dimes investors with numerous fees on transactions. An example of what I think is the wrong way to implement fees is Bristol-Myers Squibb. This leading drug company charges 4 percent of the amount invested with dividends ($5 maximum) and 4 percent of amount invested with optional cash investments ($25 maximum). Thus, if you reinvest $125 or more in dividends each quarter, you'll be nicked for $5. And if you make optional cash investments each month of $625 or more, you'll pay $25 per month in fees, or $300 per year. Admittedly, the fees are still less than what you'd probably pay by going through a broker. Still, these fees come close to being onerous for small investors who populate DRIPs.

Now, I'm a shareholder and DRIP participant of Bristol-Myers Squibb, and I have remained in the plan because I believe the stock is a strong investment. However, I can't tell you how many investors have told me that they have bought Abbott Laboratories, Johnson & Johnson, or some other health-care stock because of the fees in the Bristol-Myers Squibb DRIP.

Conclusion

This chapter reviewed a number of emerging trends—most of them good, a few of them perhaps not so good—that are shaping the new DRIP world. When considering the effects these changes will have on your DRIP investment program, keep in mind that the most important factor to consider when investing in any company is the quality of the underlying stock. Just because a firm allows you to buy your initial shares directly or charges no fees in its DRIP does not necessarily make it a solid investment. Likewise, you should not avoid a DRIP merely because you'll be charged $5 to cover administrative costs. Sure, fees matter. But what truly will have the biggest impact on your DRIP portfolio over time is the total return of your holdings. Moral of the story: You should look first at the investment merit of the company and second at the quality of its individual DRIP plan. Fortunately, the directory in Chapter 8 provides ratings on both the investment merit of the stock and the quality of the DRIP plan, so you have plenty of information from which to pick the best DRIP investments.

5

What's Dollar-Cost Averaging and How Can It Make Me Rich?

Investment Strategies Using DRIPs

You've probably been inundated with a lot of horror stories concerning the stock market.

"My broker gave me a bum tip that lost me thousands."

"The game's stacked against the little guys."

"You're better off putting your money in CDs or a money-market fund."

However, it pays to know the facts so you can judge if stocks are for you. For example:

- From 1926 to 1994, stocks, as measured by the Standard & Poor's 500, achieved an average annual total return of approximately 10 percent, including appreciation and dividends. This outpaced the performance of long-term corporate bonds (average annual total return of 5.4 percent) and U.S. Treasury bills (3.7 percent). These numbers come from Ibbotson Associates, a Chicago-based research firm.

- Even more significant for long-term investors, Ibbotson Associates found that investors who held stocks for five years at a time would have lost money in only seven of the sixty-plus rolling five-year periods since 1926, and four of those seven periods encompassed the 1929 crash.

- To put it in simple terms, stocks have risen in more than two out of every three years since 1926, according to Ibbotson Associates.

- Money manager David Dreman conducted an interesting study regarding "crisis investing." He found that in 10 major crises since World War II, including the Cuban missile crisis, 1979–1980 oil crisis, and 1987 market crash (but not covering the period of the war in the Persian Gulf), stocks rallied from the market low of each crisis one year later in 9 out of the 10 crises and showed big gains in the two-year period following the crisis.

However, such impressive statistics lose something in translation. Let's look at some simple computations to show just how money can build over time, assuming a buy-and-hold strategy.

- Let's assume you invest $1000 in a stock, hold it for 10 years, and earn an average annual return of 10 percent (around the average since 1926). That $1000 would more than double to nearly $2600.

- Now, invest $1000 and hold for 20 years, earning an average 10 percent return on your stock. Your investment would grow to $6727—an increase of 572 percent.

- Finally, let's say you invest $1000 each year for 20 years—a total investment of $20,000—and you average a 10 percent return per year. Your sum at the end of 20 years would be around $63,000.

Of course, there's no assurance that you'll achieve 10 percent returns. However, there are individuals who do better than 10 percent. If you're among these investors, your results can be especially impressive. For example:

- A $1000 investment, earning an average annual rate of 12 percent for 10 years, would grow to over $3100.

- And if you keep up this pace for 20 years, your $1000 investment would grow to over $9600.

- Finally, an annual $1000 investment, earning an average of 12 percent for 20 years, would result in a sum of nearly $80,700.

Now let's look at real returns from a variety of stocks:

- According to Standard & Poor's, a $1000 investment in PepsiCo at the end of 1984 was worth $8989 on December 31, 1994, assuming reinvestment of dividends.

- Home Depot has provided huge returns for investors over the last 10 years. Indeed, a $1000 investment at the end of 1984 was worth nearly $27,000 at the end of 1994.

- Wrigley (Wm.) Jr., the chewing gum company, has given its shareholders a good taste in their mouths. Shareholders who invested $10,000 at the end of 1984 had nearly $190,000 by the end of 1994.

- Walgreen, a leading drugstore chain and one of my favorite DRIP investments, made lots of money for its shareholders in the 1980s and early 1990s. In fact, 100 shares of stock valued at $3900 on August 31, 1984, grew to 400 shares valued at $15,050 ten years later.

- Even a cyclical company such as Stanley Works, which produces tools and household accessories, can turn in impressive gains over an extended period of time. Indeed, an investment in Stanley Works has grown at a compound annual rate of 11.9 percent over the last 28 years.

- Utility stocks are often perceived as stodgy investments suited primarily for income. However, TECO Energy, an electric utility in Florida, turned in not-so-stodgy results over the decade ending December 31, 1994, providing an average annual rate of return of approximately 16 percent.

I picked these issues not because they were the most impressive. Rather, they show that all types of stocks—growth, income, cyclicals, and recession-resistant companies—can achieve fairly impressive gains over time. Granted, the last 10 years have been good for most stocks. Still, I think the examples provide a look at the possible returns available for investors with a long-term focus.

Start Early

Of course, a key to long-term investing is getting started in the first place. So often, investors are reluctant to begin an investment program because they fear that they either don't have enough money to get started or that the market is too high. However, there is really never a bad time to get started investing. In fact, studies have shown that if an investor starts early in his or her lifetime, he or she does not necessarily even have to be that smart. This notion is borne out by a study conducted by Neuberger & Berman Management, a mutual-fund firm.

Neuberger & Berman calculated the results that would have been achieved by two hypothetical investors in the stock market following different strategies. The one investor, "early bird," invested $20,000 via 10 annual $2000 purchases from 1963 to 1972, buying each time on the very day that the Dow Jones Industrial Average made its high for the year. The other investor, "late bird," put up $40,000 in 20 annual increments of $2000 each from 1973 to 1992. Late bird was a particularly astute market timer, picking the exact market bottom each year to make the investment. Thus, late bird not only had the benefit of investing twice as much as early bird, but was also much better at timing the market.

So which bird had the bigger nest egg as of June 30, 1994 (using the S&P 500 as a yardstick)? Surprisingly, early bird had a portfolio value of more than $264,200 to late bird's $256,000.

Moral of the story: It's hard to overstate the importance of time in an investment program. Indeed, even with perfect market timing each year for 20 years—an extremely unlikely event—late bird still came out on the short end because of a later start. The beauty of dividend reinvestment plans is that they provide a vehicle for small investors, especially those with limited resources, to get started early in their investing lives and to keep investing over many years.

Another example of how getting started early can pay huge dividends down the road is the following: Say you start investing $50 a month at the age of 22. If you can achieve the average annual long-term return of stocks of 10 percent a year, your $50 investment will be roughly $319,000 by the time you are 62. Now, if you wait until you are 32 to begin investing, you will have to invest almost three times as much per month ($140) in order to have a portfolio of approximately that size at the age of 62. As you can see from this example, there is incredible power in starting an investment program as soon as possible, even if you have only limited funds.

Focus on the Long Term

As I have shown, long-term investment results can be impressive. However, while stocks have been the best investments over an extended period of time, they have also been among the most volatile. In any given year, stock prices can fall sharply, as evident by the price drops shown in Figure 5-1. Thus, the temptation is great to attempt to time the market, trying to get in at the bottom and out at the top.

But such trading is difficult to do successfully for an extended period of time. For the average investor—and many academicians would argue all investors—timing the market is a losing proposition. Textbooks are filled with many research studies indicating the futility of attempting to trade the market:

- A 1991 study by two college professors, P. R. Chandy and William Reichenstein, shows that the biggest risk associated with stock investing is not being in the market at the wrong time, but being out of the market at the right time. The professors looked at monthly market returns from 1926 through 1987. What they found was that if the 50 best monthly returns were eliminated, the S&P 500's 62-year positive return disappears. In other words, if you had chosen the absolutely wrong 50 months to be out of the market but were invested in the market the remaining 93.3 percent of time, your return would have been nil. The study went on to find that if an investor missed the 26 best monthly stock returns, his or her return would have been roughly equivalent to the return on Treasury bills over the same time frame.

- T. Rowe Price, the mutual-fund company, conducted a study examining stock purchases at the exact worse time each year from 1969 to 1989. In the study, $2000 was invested each year in the S&P 500 Index at its annual peak, and dividends were reinvested quarterly. The study found that even if an individual invested at the market's high point each year, his or her account value at the end of the 20-year period would have been more than four times his or her cumulative investment during that time.

True, some investors have made fortunes being able to time the market. My firm, which was founded in 1946, has had success timing the market using the Dow Theory. Still, a buy-and-hold investment strategy is perhaps the one best suited for the widest group of investors, especially for individual investors who may not have the time nor the energy to track holdings on a day-to-day or week-to-week basis.

One of the most attractive long-term investment strategies is dollar-cost averaging. In a nutshell, dollar-cost averaging removes all of the guesswork of market timing and replaces it with an easy, disciplined approach to investing. The beauty of dollar-cost averaging, as you'll see, is that it guarantees that you buy more shares when a stock is

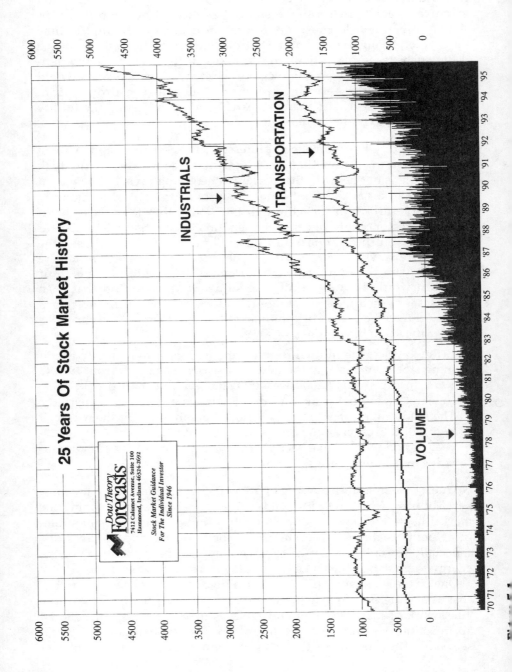

25 Years Of Stock Market History

INDUSTRIALS

TRANSPORTATION

VOLUME

Dow Theory
Forecasts
7412 Calumet Avenue, Suite 100
Hammond, Indiana 46324-2692

Stock Market Guidance
For The Individual Investor
Since 1946

cheap and fewer shares when a stock is richly valued. And best of all, dollar-cost averaging is tailor-made for investments via DRIPs.

Dollar-Cost Averaging

What if I told you that there was an investment strategy that guaranteed that your average cost of a stock would always be less than the average of the prices at the time the purchases were made? Read this last sentence one more time.

It doesn't say that your cost basis will always be less than the current market price of the stock. No market strategy guarantees this. However, what it does mean is this: Say you purchase shares in IBM on three different occasions. I can guarantee you that your average cost per share is less than the average selling price of the stock at the time of your purchases. Still interested? Read on.

Dollar-cost averaging is one of the most powerful investment strategies available to investors. It works on the principle that, instead of trying to time market purchases, you simply institute a policy of regular purchases of stock with the same cash amounts at specific intervals.

Time Diversification

All of us are familiar with the notion of diversification across investments and stocks, and this diversification is important. Fortunately, adequate portfolio diversification can be achieved with a stock portfolio of 13 to 17 stocks from a variety of industries, especially when coupled with other investments such as money-market accounts, bonds, real estate, etc. Since the capital requirements of DRIP investments are not that onerous, investors should be able to achieve a decent level of diversification over time through investment in a number of issues.

However, this is not the only diversification that can affect a portfolio's performance. Say you purchased your entire portfolio at once and hoped for the best. Perhaps you'd get lucky and buy at the bottom of a market. However, chances are just as likely that you'd buy close to the top and see your investment evaporate. Why not spread out your investments over time? That's where dollar-cost averaging is especially appropriate. In effect, it provides time diversification. Since your investments are done over time, you are assured of not always buying at the top.

Let's look at an example of dollar-cost averaging. In this example, you purchase $1000 worth of stock near the beginning of the month for a five-month period (the number of shares purchased was rounded off in this example, although fractional shares would be purchased with investments made via a DRIP):

Investment	Market price	No. of shares purchased
$1000	$25.00	40
1000	17.50	57
1000	17.50	57
1000	31.00	32
1000	25.00	40
$5000	$116.00 ÷ 5 = $23.20	226

In this scenario, the average share price at which you purchased the stock is $23.20 ($116.00 divided by 5). However, the average cost of the shares you purchased was just slightly over $22 per share ($5000 divided by 226 shares). How can this be? It's because the magic of dollar-cost averaging makes you buy more shares at the cheaper price with your fixed investment and fewer shares at the higher price. In fact, with this strategy, it pays to have the stock drop in price early in your investment program so that you accumulate more shares prior to any price rise. Also interesting is that despite the fact that the stock over this time period did not generate any capital gains ($25 per share at the beginning of the period and $25 at the end of the period), you are sitting with a profit of almost $3 per share (the current trading price of $25 minus your cost per share of just over $22) since you were dollar-cost averaging during this time frame. The key is that you invest the same dollar amount at the same time each month or each quarter. Keep in mind also that the more frequent your investments in a dollar-cost averaging program, the more opportunities to maximize your results by increasing the probability of buying at or near the bottom.

As you can see, dollar-cost averaging is a mechanical strategy that takes all of the guesswork out of market timing. How many times have you avoided investing in a stock because you thought it was too high only to see the stock race off to even higher levels? Or how many times do you wish you had bought more shares of a particular stock when it fell momentarily on some temporary bad news only to see the stock soar to higher prices?

Dollar-cost averaging takes the emotion out of investing. This is a critical point. Investing is a highly emotional activity. However, emotion can be deadly in the stock market. It causes us to make investment decisions based on the "herd mentality." We get spooked out of stocks when the market drops and everybody is selling. Yet, these instances are when we should be buying, not selling. Dollar-cost averaging helps eliminate some of these emotions. It automatically makes your buy decisions for you, and does so in a way which should help you buy low over time. It also provides a strategy for regular investments every month or quarter, not just when you get a few extra bucks or are feeling lucky.

Benefit from Market Volatility

Another plus is that dollar-cost averaging is the perfect way to beat Wall Street at its own game. I receive countless letters from investors each year deploring program trading and other antics by institutional investors which heighten market volatility. Program trading is the use of computers to generate huge numbers of transactions in a short period of time. Some program trading strategies take advantage of discrepancies between the selling prices of stock futures and options and baskets of underlying stocks, such as the S&P 500. When these discrepancies occur, institutional investors crank up their computers to perform computer-driven trading instantaneously to capture the differences. Such trading can occur at a moment's notice and have a huge impact on trading prices on a short-term basis. Obviously, for a small investor who holds a position in a company such as Motorola or GM, it's disconcerting to see the stock price jumping around, up three points one hour, only to fall two points the next. However, if you are dollar-cost averaging, you don't care about such short-term volatility. Indeed, your focus isn't the next week or next month with this strategy, but three to four years down the road at a minimum and usually much longer. Thus, it doesn't make any difference what the stock does on a day-to-day basis because of, in part, gyrations caused by program trading.

In fact, such gyrations can be a plus for investors. If a stock such as McDonald's falls because of program trading or some other institutional gimmickry but its fundamentals are still strong, the price break allows you to buy additional shares of the stock through dollar-cost averaging at a lower price. And as we've already seen, a price drop is not the worst thing in the world for an investor using dollar-cost averaging. As long as the stock eventually rebounds, you are actually better off when the stock falls when you are dollar-cost averaging.

DRIPs Perfect for Dollar-Cost Averaging

Implementing a dollar-cost averaging program is not difficult. You could do it with any stock, even in the stock of a company that doesn't have a DRIP. However, the beauty of DRIPs for dollar-cost averaging is that the programs, since they reinvest dividends quarterly for participants, assure that you will automatically dollar-cost average at least every three months. Outside of a DRIP program, you could still make quarterly investments to dollar-cost average, but you might be more apt to forget a payment or skip one because you're a little short that quarter. With a DRIP, this doesn't happen. In addition, the optional cash payment feature of most DRIPs provides an avenue to increase the frequency of your dollar-cost averaging via monthly cash payments. Best of all, DRIPs permit you to dollar-cost average without incurring the sizable commissions you otherwise would pay by dollar-cost averaging through a broker.

What Industry Groups? What Stocks?

Of course, dollar-cost averaging doesn't guarantee a profit. It does guarantee disaster if you dollar-cost average in a stock that goes from $30 to $20 to $5 and never rebounds. Thus, as in any investment strategy, a critical factor for success is proper stock selection.

What industry groups and stocks are best suited for dollar-cost averaging via DRIPs? Since DRIP investments are long-term oriented, an essential characteristic is the ability to stay in business for a long time. No kidding. Yet, how many of us insist on finding the next "Horatio Alger stock" in high-risk penny stocks or dead-end businesses where growth prospects are weak at best and competition keen? It doesn't take a genius to figure out that the prospects for failure are highest in these industries. Thus, investors should be careful when investing in certain industry groups.

REITs

Real estate investment trusts, better known as REITs, are publicly traded trusts that pool investors' funds to invest in various types of properties, from commercial retail and office space to just medical-related facilities. The cash flows from the real estate are passed to the shareholders of the REIT. Indeed, 95 percent of an REIT's net income must be passed on in the form of dividends in the year in which it is earned.

Part of the selling pitch for REITs is that they provide a low-cost way to participate in the commercial real estate market. Also, many REITs offer high yields. Sound pretty good, don't they?

Except REITs in the last several years rarely have delivered what they promised. Part of the reason is that empty commercial office space and overbuilding in many markets created cash-flow problems for REITs. The group's price appreciation has been spotty at best, and there have been some real disasters. There are a few exceptions. Washington REIT has an excellent track record of earnings and dividend growth. United Mobile Homes, an REIT which owns mobile home parks, is another interesting issue in the group. Overall, however, I don't look for great things from REITs and would suggest treading lightly in this area.

Limited Partnerships

An "evil twin" of the REIT is the publicly traded limited partnership (LP). Publicly traded LPs exist in such industries as oil, gas, real estate, and forest products. These partnerships are formed primarily as tax dodges to avoid paying higher corporate tax rates.

LPs have had their share of problems through the years. Oil and gas LPs were hit with heavy selling when oil prices fell for much of the 1980s. And certain hotel limited partnerships were hurt when overcapacity in the industry hammered profits and cash flow. Dividend cuts have been commonplace among LPs. With so many other attractive areas for DRIP investments available, don't waste your time or money investing in LPs.

Gold

Gold stocks have their ardent followers among the freeze-dried food crowd who feel that one of these days gold will have its day. Of course, they've been saying that for the last 10 years, but it hasn't happened. I suppose every dog has its day, and gold will eventually undergo a sustained rally. Nevertheless, by that time, the Dow could be long past 6000, and people who had their eye on gold stocks will look like gold fools (or is that fool's gold?).

What's with gold? One problem seems to be that gold is often seen as an inflation hedge, and inflation has been held pretty much in check over the last several years. My opinion on gold stocks is twofold: First, a small portion in a portfolio, say no more than 5 percent, is acceptable for diversification purposes, but big holdings aren't needed. Second, if you must invest in gold, consider diversified natural resources firms with gold representation rather than pure plays. Fortunately, only a couple of gold issues have DRIPs, so it's not likely you'll be tempted too greatly to jump into this group.

Other Industry Groups

The areas given above are by no means the only industries where extra care is required. Other groups that may not be appropriate for aggressive DRIP investments or require extra caution include:

- *Technology.* I know that some of the fastest-growing companies are in this area. Still, in an industry where technological obsolescence occurs weekly and where secondary players are squashed by the likes of Intel and Microsoft, it pays to be extra cautious when considering DRIPs in this group.

- *Toys.* The futures of firms in this industry depend on the whims of your average 8-year-old. Enough said.

- *Autos.* This industry is too cyclical and too exposed to foreign competition.

- *Steel.* Aside from the specialty steel producers, it's tough to get too excited about this group's long-term prospects in light of new alternative materials and perpetual labor strife.

So What Groups Are Good DRIP Investments?

We've just run through some groups that aren't good DRIP investments. Here are some that are:

Drug Companies

Dow Theory Forecasts readers are well aware of my fondness for drug firms. Indeed, several of them, including Bristol-Myers Squibb, Johnson & Johnson, Merck & Company, and Schering-Plough, are on our recommended lists. Here are some reasons why I like pharmaceutical stocks:

- *Consistent earnings growth.* Ultimately, earnings drive stock prices, and few groups match the drug sector when it comes to steady earnings gains. The recession-resistant nature of the group is a big reason for the steady performance. Further, demographics play into the industry's hands. Walgreen, the drugstore chain and major filler of prescription drugs, estimates that the median age of baby boomers will be 63 in 2020. Obviously, the graying of America has major implications for demand for drugs and health-care services.

- *Outstanding dividend growth.* A by-product of strong earnings growth is a rapidly rising dividend, and several drug companies have achieved outstanding dividend growth over the last several years. Since dividends are important in a DRIP program, drug stocks are that much more appealing for investment via DRIPs.

- *Product development.* Critics argue that one reason the United States has lost its luster in many markets is that corporations have scrimped on research and development. This criticism cannot be directed at pharmaceutical companies. It is common for these firms to have R&D outlays anywhere from 6 percent to over 10 percent of annual sales. In dollar terms, the numbers are huge. Merck alone spends well over $1 billion a year on R&D. Such dynamic product development keeps the United States on top in worldwide markets, a point that is extremely important in light of the new global economy.

- *Healthy finances.* Most pharmaceutical companies eschewed the growth-by-debt strategy that now has some companies in trouble. It's difficult to find any of the top-tier drug companies with long-term debt levels over 50 percent of capital. Such strong finances ensure that the companies will be around for a while and leave them ample flexibility to make acquisitions, fund R&D, and make capital expenditures.

If there is any downside to the group, it's that the stocks are vulnerable to government intervention. Health-care reform scares have hurt these issues in the past and could impact the stocks going forward. Still, the quality issues in the group represent attractive long-term investments in DRIP portfolios.

Food and Beverage Stocks

Another attractive area for DRIP investments is the food and beverage group. Like drug stocks, food and beverage stocks are recession resistant, and they generally post steady earnings growth. Another similarity is the steady dividend growth in the major food and beverage issues. Food and beverage companies are also poised to exploit the growing demand in Eastern Europe as well as underdeveloped nations. Finally, strong brand names provide major barriers to entry. Coca-Cola, Kellogg, PepsiCo, and Sara Lee are just four of the many attractive food and beverage issues which have DRIPs.

The Market Makers

No, I'm not talking about the people on the floors of the various financial exchanges making markets in stocks. I'm talking about marketing-driven firms in various consumer-products industries, names such as Colgate-Palmolive, Philip Morris, and Procter & Gamble, where marketing acumen has established their products as leaders and, in fact, helped define the market. Such market dominance translates into impressive earnings growth for these firms. Marketing expertise will be especially important as companies make an even bigger push in overseas markets. These companies have the ability to weather economic downturns and generally have upwardly trending earnings and dividends.

Utilities

One of the more attractive DRIP investment areas for conservative investors is the utility group. Electric and natural gas utilities generally pay decent dividends and provide moderate dividend growth over time. Also, utility stocks generally have a lower level of volatility, although there have been periods in the past when utility stocks have shown above-average volatility. Nevertheless, for conservative investors who are retired or nearing retirement, electric and natural gas utilities provide a nice complement to a well-rounded DRIP portfolio.

Despite the appeal of utilities, some pitfalls must be avoided. The biggest mistake investors make when considering an electric utility is to chase the ones with the highest yields. However, the many dividend cuts and omissions by utilities over the last several years indicate that all utilities aren't alike. How can you tell the good ones from the bad ones? One quick way is to check the yield. An electric utility that yields 2 to 4 percentage points more than the group in general is one for which Wall Street has some concerns about the safety of the dividend. Thus, an extremely high yield should be a giant red flag for investors and reason to explore more fully before buying.

Another pitfall is to eliminate from consideration electric utilities merely because of nuclear energy exposure. I'll grant you that nuclear energy doesn't have the best reputation. However, there are many quality utilities that have made this energy source work to their advantage. It would be a shame to exclude one of these quality companies because of a "no-nukes" bias.

Utility investors also need to keep in mind that the industry's competitive environment is changing. Within the next few years, there will be many "open" utility markets in this country with a number of utilities competing for the same customers. Thus, it is important to focus on those utilities with strong finances, healthy service regions, con-structive regulatory environments, and productive nonutility opera-tions.

One last word about electric utilities. I've seen a lot of portfolios in which investors have 10 or 15 utility stocks and little else. I don't care if utilities are fairly conservative. Having a lot of them in a portfolio, and little else, is not prudent portfolio allocation. Electric utilities are interest-rate sensitive; during periods of rising interest rates, they gen-erally will not behave well. A portfolio overly stocked with utilities is not the best portfolio-building strategy. Four to six quality utilities are ample for any size portfolio.

Telecommunications

It's hard to imagine an industry sector with greater long-term growth potential than the telecommunications industry. Indeed, there are ample opportunities in this country and especially abroad to upgrade and improve telecommunications, particularly with the melding of voice, data, and broadcast communications. To be sure, changing regu-latory environments will impact the issues in this sector. Nevertheless, I feel that substantial profits will be earned by investors holding the right telecommunications issues. Among the regional telephone issues, my preferences are BellSouth and SBC Communications. I am also a big fan of AT&T. Other telecommunications stock worth considering include Motorola and Scientific-Atlanta. These stocks are reviewed in greater detail in Chapters 6 and 7.

Some More Industry Groups

The groups above are not the only attractive sectors for DRIP invest-ments. The following industry groups have appeal for more aggressive investors:

- *Pollution control.* Although pollution control stocks have had their ups and downs in recent years, I continue to believe that the quality issues in this group will enjoy above-average growth over the long term. Thus, I feel it is important to have some representation in this sector in a DRIP portfolio.

- *Database and informational services.* These companies will continue to feed off our insatiable appetite for information of every kind. Clean balance sheets and healthy profit margins highlight the lead-ers in these fields.

- *Consumer and commercial services.* Companies that make life easier for individuals and corporations should find growing markets in this decade and beyond and represent attractive growth areas for DRIP investments.

Happy Hunting

Now that we've discussed the right hunting ground for DRIP investments, it's time to focus on important characteristics for DRIP investments within these favored groups. We've already mentioned many of the attributes of good DRIP investments:

- Longevity
- Market dominance, aided by strong brand names, patents, technological strength, etc.
- Strong finances, with manageable debt levels and good cash flow
- Steady earnings growth over a period of several years and at least a couple of economic cycles
- Decent growth prospects for the industry
- Attractive dividend-growth potential

Dividends Matter

This last characteristic often gets shortchanged in an investment program. However, it's tough to overstate the impact dividends can have on a portfolio, especially if you're reinvesting your dividends for additional shares as is the case with DRIPs.

The following is an excellent example that shows that dividends, indeed, matter: For the 10 years ending 1994, the S&P 500 produced a total return, including dividends reinvested, of 282 percent. But if you wash out the dividend effect, the results cool to a gain of 175 percent. To drive the point home even further, if you go back another 5 years, the S&P 500 in the 15-year period through 1994 achieved a total return, with dividends, of 665 percent. Without dividends, the gains would be reduced dramatically, to 326 percent. Clearly, dividends matter, and they matter in a big way.

Why such a big difference in investment results when dividends are considered? The magic of compounding.

Compounding is a powerful force, especially over a long period of time. For example, let's say you purchase two stocks, each priced at

$25 per share. One pays a dividend that yields 7 percent; the other pays no dividend at all. You hold each of the stocks for 10 years. At the end of the 10-year period—a period that has been brutal on stocks in general—both stocks are still the same price they were when you bought them, never budging from the $25 purchase price. A bummer, to be sure. However, your total return on each of these investments is decidedly different. On the stock that paid no dividend, your return is zilch. However, on the one that provided a 7 percent yield, your total investment (including dividends) nearly doubled, even though you had no capital gains. And if, by chance, the company increased its dividend during that time, the total return would have been even greater. Thus, dividends can be a very potent fuel for portfolio performance, especially during times when stock prices may be standing still. In addition, yields provide a cushion during price drops.

I'm not saying that all investors should focus exclusively on high-yielding, low-growth issues for DRIP investments. However, to ignore yield in portfolio selection could have long-term consequences. It's wise to combine income with growth when making investment decisions, especially in a DRIP investment. And it's especially important that the company raises its dividend on a regular basis.

The following list comprises companies—all offering DRIPs—that have raised their dividends annually for at least the last decade. Make sure to check the performance ratings before investing.

Abbott Laboratories	Bankers Trust New York Corp.
Air Products & Chemicals, Inc.	Bard (C. R.), Inc.
Albertson's, Inc.	Baxter International, Inc.
Alco Standard Corp.	Becton, Dickinson and Co.
Allegheny Power System, Inc.	Black Hills Corp.
ALLTEL Corp.	Block (H & R), Inc.
American Brands, Inc.	Boatmen's Bancshares, Inc.
American Business Products, Inc.	Bristol-Myers Squibb Co.
American Home Products Corp.	Brooklyn Union Gas Co.
American Water Works Co., Inc.	California Water Service Co.
AMP, Inc.	Campbell Soup Co.
AmSouth Bancorp.	Carlisle Companies, Inc.
Anheuser-Busch Companies, Inc.	CCB Financial Corp.
Aon Corp.	Central & South West Corp.
Banc One Corp.	Central Fidelity Banks, Inc.
BancorpSouth, Inc.	Century Telephone Enterprises, Inc.
Bandag, Inc.	Chemed Corp.

Chubb Corp.
Cincinnati Financial Corp.
Citizens Banking Corp.
Clorox Co.
Coca-Cola Co.
Colgate-Palmolive Co.
Colonial Gas Co.
Comerica, Inc.
ConAgra, Inc.
Connecticut Water Service, Inc.
Consolidated Edison Co. of New York
Consumers Water Co.
CoreStates Financial Corp.
Crompton & Knowles Corp.
Dauphin Deposit Corp.
Dayton Hudson Corp.
Dean Foods Co.
Diebold, Inc.
Dominion Resources, Inc.
Donnelley (R. R.) & Sons Co.
Duke Power Co.
Emerson Electric Co.
Energen Corp.
EnergyNorth, Inc.
Exxon Corp.
Federal Realty Investment Trust
Fifth Third Bancorp
First Empire State Corp.
First Michigan Bank Corp.
First Northern Savings Bank
First of America Bank Corp.
First Tennessee National Corp.
First Union Corp.
First Virginia Banks, Inc.
Firstar Corp.
Florida Progress Corp.

Flowers Industries, Inc.
Franklin Resources, Inc.
Fuller (H. B.) Co.
Gannett Co., Inc.
General Electric Co.
General Re Corp.
Gillette Co.
Gorman-Rupp Co.
Hannaford Brothers Co.
Harcourt General, Inc.
Harland (John H.) Company
Hartford Steam Boiler Inspection & Insurance Co.
Heilig-Meyers Co.
Heinz (H. J.) Co.
Honeywell, Inc.
Hormel Foods Corp.
Houghton Mifflin Company
Hubbell, Inc.
Huntington Bancshares, Inc.
Indiana Energy, Inc.
Jefferson-Pilot Corp.
Johnson & Johnson
Kellogg Co.
KeyCorp
Kimberly-Clark Corp.
La-Z-Boy Chair Co.
Lancaster Colony Corp.
LG&E Energy Corp.
Lilly (Eli) & Co.
Lilly Industries, Inc.
Louisiana-Pacific Corp.
Luby's Cafeterias, Inc.
Madison Gas & Electric Co.
Mark Twain Bancshares, Inc.
Marshall & Ilsley Corp.
May Department Stores Company

McDonald's Corp.

McGraw-Hill Companies, Inc.

Medtronic, Inc.

Mercantile Bankshares Corp.

Merck & Co., Inc.

Middlesex Water Co.

Millipore Corp.

Minnesota Mining & Manufacturing Co.

Minnesota Power & Light Co.

Morgan (J. P.) & Co., Inc.

National Service Industries, Inc.

NationsBank Corp.

New Plan Realty Trust

Nordson Corp.

North Carolina Natural Gas Corp.

Northern States Power Co.

Northwest Natural Gas Co.

Nucor Corp.

Ohio Casualty Corp.

Old Kent Financial Corp.

Otter Tail Power Co.

Pall Corp.

Pentair, Inc.

PepsiCo, Inc.

Pfizer, Inc.

Philip Morris Companies, Inc.

Piedmont Natural Gas Co.

Pitney Bowes, Inc.

PPG Industries, Inc.

Premier Industrial Corp.

Procter & Gamble Co.

Providian Corp.

Quaker Oats Co.

Questar Corp.

Regions Financial Corp.

Rite Aid Corp.

RLI Corp.

Rockwell International Corp.

RPM, Inc.

Rubbermaid, Inc.

St. Joseph Light & Power Co.

SCANA Corp.

Second Bancorp, Inc.

Selective Insurance Group, Inc.

ServiceMaster Limited Partnership

Sherwin-Williams Co.

Smucker (J. M.) Co.

Southern California Water Co.

Southern Indiana Gas & Electric Co.

Southern National Corp.

SouthTrust Corp.

Stanley Works

Star Banc Corp.

State Street Boston Corp.

Supervalu, Inc.

Synovus Financial Corp.

Sysco Corp.

Tambrands, Inc.

TECO Energy, Inc.

Telephone & Data Systems, Inc.

Torchmark Corp.

Union Electric Co.

Universal Corp.

USLIFE Corp.

UST, Inc.

UtiliCorp United, Inc.

VF Corp.

Wachovia Corp.

Walgreen Co.

Warner-Lambert Co.

Washington Gas Light Co.

Washington Real Estate Investment Trust

Weis Markets, Inc.   WMX Technologies, Inc.
WICOR, Inc.   Worthington Industries, Inc.
Winn-Dixie Stores, Inc.   WPL Holdings, Inc.
Wisconsin Energy Corp.   WPS Resources Corp.
Witco Corp.   Wrigley (Wm.) Jr. Co.

Selling Strategies

No discussion about investment strategy is complete without a few choice words about selling. Fortunately, in a long-term investment program such as DRIPs, selling loses some of its importance. Sure, holding onto a dog that goes into a free fall and never recovers can hurt, and we'll take a look at some ways to avoid this from happening. Perhaps the best way to approach this difficult topic is to look at reasons *not* to sell.

My Broker Made Me Do It

Countless times I have heard investors bemoaning the fact that they sold stock on their broker's advice only to see the stock rise rapidly. My rebuttal is usually the same. How does a broker make money? By performing transactions for clients. Thus, the only way the broker makes a buck is if you do something. Does this seem like a conflict of interest? Sure it is, although it's not the broker's fault. It's a problem with the system. I'm not saying that all brokers suggest frequent buying and selling just to make a living. I am saying that the temptation to do this is built into the system. Therefore, it's critical that you don't react to a broker's suggestion on blind faith. You should ask yourself some questions. What are my broker's reasons for selling, and do they make sense? How well have I done with this broker's recommendations in the past? Fortunately, if your investment program is done primarily through DRIPs, you won't be getting calls from your broker to sell.

Sell on Bad News

Wall Street's myopic tendencies dictate that a stock that is hit with bad news needs to be sold pronto to avoid further bloodshed. There are several reasons for this short-term thinking. First, the mutual-fund business has become quite competitive, and the ability to advertise excellent short-term investment results is crucial to garnering more cash from investors. Thus, investment portfolios have become more and more focused on short-term performance. That is why when bad news hits a company, institutional investors are quick to drop a stock. Related is the notion of "window dressing" which occurs in the mutual-fund field. This is the process by which portfolio managers weed out dogs and laggards prior to the end of the quarter so that they don't show a position in the stock in the quarterly reports that are sent to shareholders.

What this short-term focus does is to trash good companies that have had momentary problems. Individual investors are often tempted to follow suit and sell, but this may not be the best strategy. Indeed, shareholders who were spooked out of Johnson & Johnson during its Tylenol tampering disasters abandoned a quality company whose stock bounced back dramatically once the smoke cleared. In fact, product tamperings, particularly in industry-leading product lines, are reasons to *buy*, not sell. Other instances in which investors should probably avoid dumping stocks are strike news, lawsuits, and regulatory problems. Granted, each of these things can evolve into a long-term mess for the company. But in more cases than not, the stock discounts the problems, and the shares rise once the problems have been resolved. Thus, staying the course with your DRIP investments, particularly if the holdings are in market-leading firms, is the best strategy.

Sell on "Hot Tips" That You Read About in the Paper

Reacting to news that's in the newspapers is natural. However, by the time you see the news, it's already too late to sell in most cases. *The Wall Street Journal* and other financial newspapers and magazines frequently discuss companies that are supposedly takeover stocks. Invariably I'll receive calls from investors wishing to buy the stock. My advice is that by the time the guy on the street hears of a potential takeover deal, insiders and those close to Wall Street have already bid the stock to a level reflecting the news. This scenario works on the downside as well. By the time you see bad news about your company in the paper, the stock has already fallen and is discounting the news. Should you still sell, especially if the news has long-term ramifications? Perhaps. But it pays to do some homework to judge whether the condition is terminal. Remember, with DRIP investments and a long-term strategy, time is on your side.

Tax-Loss Selling

One common mistake is to let taxes drive sell decisions. It's understandable. The end of the year comes, you've taken some capital gains, and you want to offset them with some losses. So you sell some of your losers. Unfortunately, all too often those same stocks move up sharply in January. Why? Analysts call this the "January effect." Many reasons have been given for this phenomenon. The one that makes the most sense to me is that stocks that have been weak during the year are beaten down during December due to investors selling to establish losses for tax purposes. Thus, when January rolls around, all of the selling has been wrung out of the stocks, so any buying drives prices up sharply.

Tax selling makes sense if the stock's fundamentals have deteriorated to a point where a rebound is unlikely in any reasonable period of time. However, with a long-term investment program such as DRIPs, tax-loss selling probably does more harm than good.

So When Do I Sell?

Intuitively, it makes sense to sell stocks in which fundamentals are poor and long-term prospects are limited. Sounds pretty simple, right? But how can you tell if prospects are limited? Although selling is anything but an exact science, here are some tips that may help to discern if a stock merits dumping.

Watch Those Debt Levels

A long-term investment strategy can go up in smoke if the company goes bankrupt. Perhaps the most crucial reason to consider selling a stock is if the company's debt levels have risen rapidly. Such increases may be caused by funding an acquisition, paying out a "special" one-time dividend, or—and this can be especially disastrous—taking on debt to pay the dividend.

How much is too much debt? One important ratio is long-term debt as a percentage of total capital (total capital is shareholders' equity + long-term debt). These numbers can be found easily on the company's balance sheet. Generally speaking, any amount over 50 percent is cause for concern, and levels approaching 65 to 70 percent are downright scary. Average debt levels will vary depending on the industry. For example, capital-intensive industries will probably have higher debt levels than service firms. Further, an industry with high cash flow and inventory turnover, such as fast-food and consumer products, can support higher-than-average debt levels. Nevertheless, debt is probably the biggest factor affecting corporate livelihood, and high debt levels may be as good a reason as there is to sell a stock.

Failure to Keep Pace with Changing Industry Conditions

This reason is what makes investing in technology issues so dicey. The failure of certain mainframe computer manufacturers to respond to the increased demand for desktop power is a perfect example of the failure to change with the industry.

What companies are likely to fall victims to these developments? Those with limited R&D budgets. One sign that a firm is a candidate to fall behind is that its R&D spending fails to increase on an annual basis either in absolute dollar terms or as a percentage of annual revenues. R&D is the lifeblood of industries in fields such as drugs and computers, and scrimping on research is likely to lead to an early exit for the company.

The Stupid Acquisition or Expansion Move

In the go-go 1980s, many acquisitions took place in which you didn't have to be a rocket scientist to figure that the deals probably wouldn't work. Firms attempted to combine apples with oranges and ended up with lemons in many cases. The bottom line is that it pays to stick with what you know and do best. Academics call it a company's "core competency." If you make cars, don't buy an aerospace firm. If your position in an industry is already weak, don't hurt it even more by taking on more debt to buy an even weaker sister with a different technological strategy. *Synergy* has been one of the most overused and misused words in the investment field in the last 10 years, and many companies that have professed synergy in a merger have had nothing but problems. If a company in which you own stock never buys another company, it may not be the worst thing.

Notice I haven't said anything about falling earnings or sales as reasons to sell. These are the results of some of the things addressed above. If you address the causes and take action accordingly, you'll be ahead of the game.

6
My Favorite DRIPs

The previous chapter discussed some of the factors that make a good DRIP investment. Now it's time to look at real-life examples. This chapter features 20 of my favorite DRIP issues. Eleven of these stocks are in my own DRIP portfolio. The stocks cut across many industries and investment objectives. Thus, whether you're a growth or income investor, you should find a DRIP among these 20 that meets your objective.

Abbott Laboratories

The long-term nature of DRIPs lends itself perfectly to investments in the health-care sector. An aging population points to increased demand for health-care products over the next several years. One of the best investments in the health-care market is Abbott Laboratories.

Abbott Laboratories provides products and services in a variety of markets. Its most profitable sector is the pharmaceutical and nutritional products operation. Pharmaceuticals include Biaxin antibiotic and Hytrin antihypertensives. Nutritional products include Similac and Isomil infant formulas. Abbott's remaining operations are in hospital and laboratory products, including intravenous and irrigating fluids, anesthetics, and critical-care products. The firm has built a major position in diagnostic tests. The company is the leader in supplying diagnostic products for blood banks and was the first firm to market a diagnostic test to detect AIDS (HIV) antigens.

Several things stand out right away when you look at Abbott Laboratories. One is the fact that sales and earnings have trended higher over the last several years. Financially, the firm has always been first rate, with modest debt levels and ample cash flow. The financial position has provided ample resources for healthy research and development spending, which is now running at roughly $1 billion a year. One of the other main factors to consider for a DRIP is the dividend record, and Abbott's has been stellar. Dividends have risen each year for more than a decade and are expected to rise at an annual double-digit rate for the foreseeable future.

Any potential pitfalls in these shares? Certainly spiraling health-care costs could force more dramatic regulation of product pricing in the health-care industry, and such a development would obviously affect profit margins for Abbott. However, it's not clear, at least to me, if strict regulation is really the most efficient route to controlling costs. It could hinder the dynamic nature of the industry, especially from a product development standpoint. Even if price competition increases in the field, Abbott's efficient operations should keep it in good shape. It's hard for me to see these shares do anything but trend higher over the next 5 to 10 years and beyond.

AT&T Corp.

One of the best long-term growth industries, in my opinion, is the telecommunications sector. It is difficult to see AT&T not being a major player in nearly every telecommunications market in this country and abroad. The firm has operations in nearly every telecommunications sector, including voice and data transmissions. The firm has gotten into the cellular business in a big way via its 1994 acquisition of McCaw Cellular. The company has also been active in expanding its reach overseas. International markets are where perhaps the biggest growth in the telecommunications sector will take place.

Of course, there remains a great deal of regulatory uncertainty in the telecommunications sector, and this will periodically impact AT&T's stock. It is difficult to know for sure just how the regulatory environment will change, especially with local telephone providers being able to move into the long-distance market and cable television companies entering various telephone markets as well. Nevertheless, AT&T has the technological expertise and financial muscle to protect its primary markets while carving out major positions in emerging growth markets.

Per-share profits have good growth prospects over the next several years. I think the company's plan to split into three separate entities—telecommunications services, telecommunications equipment, and computers—is a positive move. For investors who are willing to look three to five years down the road and beyond, these shares, as well as the spin-off issues, have excellent upside potential. I am a participant in AT&T's DRIP plan, and I recommend the stock for all DRIP investors. Keep in mind that the company's DRIP requires ownership of 10 shares in order to participate.

Block (H & R), Inc.

H & R Block is probably best known for its network of more than 9000 tax-preparation offices. This business contributes the lion's share of revenues and profits. However, the fastest-growing area in the company is its CompuServe on-line services. This operation accounted for roughly one-third of sales and profits in fiscal 1994 and has been growing at a rapid rate in recent years. The steady performance of the tax business, as well as the rapid growth of the on-line service business, explains why the company's profit growth has been impressive over the last decade.

I remain optimistic that H & R Block will be able to continue its solid growth trend. However, investors should be aware of potential problems for the company. First, the computer on-line business has become very competitive. Thus, while I still feel that CompuServe will continue to grow at a healthy rate, its growth rate will likely shrink due to the increased competition. Also, the increased competition could hinder profit margins in this business. Second, there continues to be a lot of talk in this country concerning a "flat tax" system. Obviously, if a simpler tax system were implemented, it would reduce the need for Block's tax-preparation services. Of course, the call for a simpler tax system has been around for decades. Nevertheless, should the United States move toward a simpler tax structure, it could cause selling in these shares.

All the negatives notwithstanding, I continue to feel that Block offers an interesting DRIP for more aggressive investors. I am a participant in the Block DRIP plan and anticipate being well rewarded for my participation over the next three to five years and beyond. However, I also recognize that this type of stock probably carries a higher level of risk than many of the other issues reviewed in this chapter. For that reason, investors who buy these shares have to be willing to accept above-average volatility.

Bristol-Myers Squibb Co.

As you've probably noticed, I like health-care companies. Few industries have as many quality firms. One of the quality firms in the industry in which I invest is Bristol-Myers Squibb.

Chances are that even if you've never heard of Bristol-Myers Squibb, you've probably used one of their products. Its major pharmaceuticals include Capoten, one of the biggest-selling drugs in the world with over $1 billion in annual sales; Taxol anticancer medication; and BuSpar, an antianxiety drug. Over-the-counter products include Enfamil infant formula; Bufferin, Excedrin, and Nuprin analgesics; and Comtrex cough and cold remedies. Consumer products range from Clairol hair-care products to Ban deodorant.

During the 1980s—an era when mergers often made about as much sense as a Franz Kafka novel—Bristol-Myers Squibb was the exception. The firm is the result of the 1989 marriage of Bristol-Myers and Squibb. Each firm brought specific strengths to the union. Bristol-Myers had long been regarded as a marketing powerhouse. Squibb had a strong reputation in research and product development. The benefits from the merger have been substantial. Profits should post at least 10 percent annual growth over the next several years. Such growth should keep the dividend rising at a rapid rate.

New products are the lifeblood of any health-care company, so research and development is vital to continued success in the industry. But the costs of new products are high. For this reason, size matters in the drug industry. Bristol-Myers Squibb is in position to spend the dollars needed to stay on the cutting edge. Research and development outlays will probably be around $1.3 billion in 1996.

Bristol-Myers Squibb's recession-resistant businesses should allow it to post earnings gains even during slow economic periods. For this reason, the stock should hold up better than most stocks during periods of market weakness. One negative is the onerous fee structure when buying stock through the company's DRIP. Still, the issue is suitable for conservative growth investors.

Browning-Ferris Industries, Inc.

It's a dirty job, but somebody's got to do it—and Browning-Ferris Industries does it as well as any firm in the business.

This leading provider of solid-waste collection and processing services serves some 400 locations in North America and approximately 250 locations outside of the continent. In addition to residential, commercial, and industrial collection, the firm has been expanding into a variety of other waste-management markets. Recycling is a growing area for the company. Waste-to-energy is another technology the firm is exploring.

Browning-Ferris has grown rapidly over the last two decades. Revenues are expected to approach $6.5 billion in fiscal 1996. One key to Browning-Ferris' position in its industry is its ownership of landfills. Browning-Ferris' landfill acquisition program in recent years should pay hefty dividends over time. Aggressive overseas expansion is another plus.

Many opportunities exist for Browning-Ferris over the next five years and beyond, which is why I own the stock. There are some potential downsides, however. Alleged antitrust activities and problems related to waste sites periodically cause some price volatility in the group. Also, the pollution-control business can soften during economic slowdowns. Browning-Ferris Industries' risk level is higher than, say, an electric utility or a drug issue. For that reason, investors with time on their side to ride out the price swings are the best candidates for DRIP investments in Browning-Ferris Industries.

Equifax, Inc.

You don't usually hear Equifax mentioned in the same breath as IBM, GE, GM, and other well-known corporations. You may never have heard of the firm. But if you have a mortgage, life insurance, a credit card, or checking account, chances are Equifax has heard of you.

The company is a world leader in information services and systems to facilitate consumer-initiated financial transactions. Customers include banks, mortgage lenders, insurance companies, government agencies, retailers, and any firms that extend credit to consumers.

Equifax has made this information niche pay off handsomely. Per-share earnings have been rising, and the growth should be impressive for the foreseeable future. The growing demand for informational services puts the company in the right place at the right time. Equifax has not been standing still. New products have been developed, and the firm's massive database should fuel additional products. Expansion via acquisitions is another growth avenue. The 1990 acquisition of Telecredit, a provider of credit card processing, check authorization, and other payment services to retail merchants and financial institutions, meshed well with Equifax's existing businesses. Moves into health-care information markets are also a plus.

Equifax is one of the smallest firms among the 20 appraised in this chapter, and price volatility could be above average given the premium P/E ratio the issue traditionally sports. Thus, this issue may not be appropriate for an investor with a limited time horizon. However, more aggressive growth investors should score big gains with these shares via investments in the company's DRIP.

Exxon Corp.

Oil stocks have been all over the map through the years. The late 1970s saw oil issues soar as oil suppliers cried shortage and getting a tank of gas took just slightly less time than reading *War and Peace* in Russian. But the early 1980s saw the exact opposite, with a glut in the market and stock prices of oil producers and drillers dropping dramatically. The down period in the industry created problems for the poorly financed companies and opportunities for those with financial muscle. Exxon was in the latter category and used the industry slump to enhance its stature in the industry. This strengthened competitive position has allowed the firm to prosper in recent years.

It's no secret that the prospects for oil companies rise and fall with oil prices. But predicting oil prices accurately is akin to shooting skeet blindfolded—you may get lucky every now and again but you'll miss much more than you'll hit. Investors need to concentrate on quality when investing in the group. Exxon ranks high in nearly every category. Finances are top-notch, with moderate debt levels and ample cash flow. Operations are nicely divided between domestic and international markets. Such a diversified business portfolio is essential in such volatile markets. Dividend growth has been excellent, with annual payout hikes the norm.

Oil stocks present their own set of risks for investors. Obviously, the erratic history of oil prices heightens the volatility of these stocks. Environmental concerns are never far away from the group, and the Exxon *Valdez* tanker incident in 1989 reflects these risks. However, Exxon's ability to rebound following this incident reflects the quality of these shares. Given the issue's above-average yield, good dividend growth prospects, and outstanding finances, the stock is an appropriate DRIP investment for investors who are willing to accept a moderate risk level. I have my money where my mouth is, since I'm a shareholder in the company.

General Electric Co.

Ask your neighbor what GE does, and he or she will probably tell you the company makes appliances. What he or she isn't likely to tell you is that GE is also NBC, or GE is a major financial services company. And that's GE's biggest problem—investors have a hard time getting a handle on the company. Is it an appliance company? Is it a broadcasting company? Is it a financial services concern?

GE is all of these things and much more. And while many firms have attempted to duplicate GE's diversified business portfolio with little success, GE has made it work. That's because the common thread between these operations is that they all have the potential to be market leaders. Market dominance is the driving strategy behind GE. This was not always the case. The company entered the 1980s with some 350 business and product lines. The firm closed the decade with a much different look. Gone were natural resources, housewares, consumer electronics, and many more marginal operations. During the period the firm spent $17 billion in acquisitions, adding NBC, aerospace businesses, chemical operations, and medical systems—all with the potential to be one of the top two in their respective industries.

The company's bottom line benefited handsomely from the restructuring, with per-share profits and dividends more than doubling from 1980 to 1989 and rising steadily since 1990. Shareholders didn't do too badly either, with the stock providing a total return of more than 375 percent in the 10-year period ending in 1994.

The future holds more exciting opportunities for the firm. The company is poised to capitalize on the opening of overseas markets. Annual dividend growth should be in the neighborhood of at least 5 to 10 percent. The stock should find additional backers on Wall Street as more investors begin to understand and appreciate the firm's growth strategy. The stock is a suitable DRIP investment for nearly every investor.

Johnson & Johnson

If the measure of a person is his or her ability to overcome adversity, I suppose the same can be said for a corporation. And none has done it any better than Johnson & Johnson.

Twice the firm faced the ultimate in crisis management—the Tylenol tampering incidents. Both times the stock sold off immediately following the news. Both times analysts rang the death knell for Tylenol's market dominance. Both times Johnson & Johnson proved them wrong. Tylenol is still a big-selling analgesic, and Johnson & Johnson is still one of the premier companies in the health-care markets.

Johnson & Johnson is far from being a one-trick pony. In its consumer segment, which includes such popular names as Stayfree, Band-Aid, and Sure, many of its products are number one worldwide. Its stable of pharmaceuticals is just as impressive. Research and development outlays of more than $1 billion annually keep the new product pipeline well stocked.

Johnson & Johnson has been aggressive on the acquisition front in recent years. The firm acquired Neutrogena, the skin-care company, in 1994. Another 1994 deal was the purchase of Eastman Kodak's clinical diagnostics unit.

The recession-resistant nature of Johnson & Johnson's markets makes the company especially appropriate for a long-term investment strategy. The strong dividend record is just one more reason investors should take a good look at the stock. These shares are suitable for any investment portfolio.

McDonald's Corp.

Wall Street analysts love to take potshots at McDonald's. A saturated domestic market for fast-food restaurants, higher labor costs, increased emphasis on healthy eating habits, and the increasing number of dishes prepared for microwave cooking spell a slow demise for Big Mac, say the experts.

Don't believe them. True, few industries are as competitive as the fast-food industry, and McDonald's sheer size makes it difficult for the firm to maintain its growth pace in the United States. But there are other worlds to conquer for McDonald's, and overseas expansion is the real kicker behind these shares.

Not that its domestic business requires life support. Aside from the heavy discounting which pervades the industry periodically, U.S. operations are in relatively good shape. Its huge network of more than 10,000 franchised outlets provides a stable base of revenues for the firm relative to other fast-food chains. An important aspect of the franchise system is McDonald's fee structure with its franchisees, which is based on a percentage of sales, not profits. This payment scheme assures a steady stream of revenues back to McDonald's and helps shield the firm from higher food and labor costs.

McDonald's is attempting to duplicate its U.S. success throughout the world. Currently, foreign outlets number around 5500, or roughly 36 percent of all units. Concentrations have been primarily in Australia, France, Canada, Japan, West Germany, and the United Kingdom. Golden Arches have also been popping up in Russia and China. Forays abroad have been growing increasingly profitable for the firm. As economies of scale take over with a greater concentration of outlets, profitability should rise even further. The lack of any real competition overseas makes McDonald's look even more attractive.

McDonald's has all the ingredients for a DRIP investment—consistency of earnings growth, outstanding finances, a rising dividend, and market leadership. These shares have already been outstanding holdings for shareholders over the last decade, with a $10,000 investment at the end of 1984 turning into more than $56,200 by the end of 1994. There's no reason that this stock should go on a diet at this point. I own McDonald's stock and recommend these shares for conservative growth investors.

Merck & Co., Inc.

From a drug company's laboratory springs its future, and firms that make the big R&D outlays usually are at the top of the industry. Merck spends approximately $1.4 billion annually on R&D. What has Merck received for its big spending?

- Some 15 products bringing in $100 million or more on an annual basis
- Billion-dollar drugs in Vasotec, an antihypertensive drug, and Mevacor, a treatment for elevated cholesterol
- Pioneering positions in a variety of exciting long-term growth markets

R&D is not the whole story at Merck. The firm formed a joint venture with DuPont to develop and market new drugs. Another joint venture with Johnson & Johnson expands its presence in over-the-counter medications. AIDS research is a major priority, and it is hard to conceive of a breakthrough in this area not involving Merck. Any company that can afford to spend more than $1 billion in R&D annually obviously has its financial house in order. A strong financial position is also one reason the dividend has more than doubled since 1989.

Merck's strengths have not been lost on Wall Street. Such popularity may, ironically, work to the stock's disadvantage from time to time, since the rich P/E ratio leaves ample downside potential during shakeouts in the stock market. However, for investors willing to ride through intermittent volatility, these shares offer exceptional opportunities for DRIP investments.

Minnesota Mining & Manufacturing Co.

Many companies give lip service to product development. 3M mandates it. One of the firm's corporate goals is to generate at least 30 percent of annual sales from products introduced within the last four years.

One of its better-known products is the Post-it self-stick removable notes. How the Post-it was developed is one of the more popular stories in business literature and exemplifies the innovation at 3M. The idea was hatched by a 3M scientist who was frustrated by page markers that constantly fell out of his church hymnals. The scientist recalled a discovery by another 3M scientist of a barely sticky adhesive. The scientist applied the adhesive to pieces of paper, and the material worked perfectly—sticky enough to hold a piece of paper to nearly any surface, yet not so strong that the paper couldn't be removed easily. To be sure, championing the product through 3M and to the marketplace presented its own set of problems for developers, but the product eventually reached the market and was a success.

The product would never have evolved if one scientist didn't know what the other had discovered. Communication is the cornerstone of the firm's innovation.

On every count, 3M rates high marks. The company sports stellar finances; strong and growing overseas representation; a diversified business portfolio, including life sciences, consumer products, and imaging markets, that helps shield the firm from downturns in any one market; and a record of annual dividend increases spanning more than three decades. The stock has excellent total-return potential over a 5- to 10-year time horizon and would be a worthwhile DRIP investment for any investor.

Motorola, Inc.

Admittedly, I am not a huge fan of most technology stocks. Quite frankly, I'm not smart enough to keep up with this fast-changing sector. However, the one technology stock that I do feel comfortable owning is Motorola.

Motorola is a diversified manufacturer of a variety of electronic products. The firm is a major player in the semiconductor market as well as in the production of radio telephone equipment and cellular telephones. Motorola has been in the right place at the right time given the rapid growth in a number of its industries. This growth is seen in the fact that revenues have more than doubled since 1992 to nearly $30 billion in 1995. Profits have shown similar growth, increasing more than threefold since 1990. The stock has enjoyed huge price gains since bottoming at a split-adjusted price of around $11 per share in 1991. This rapid rise in price in a relatively short period of time does leave the stock vulnerable to periodic price sell-offs. However, I think that over time these shares should continue to trend higher. One important factor that gives me a high level of comfort in owning this stock is that its management team is regarded as one of the best in any industry.

Motorola is not what I would call a "cheap" stock given its premium P/E ratio. Nevertheless, with strong positions in a number of attractive growth markets, excellent management, and sound finances, I think the premium P/E is not too much to pay for this quality issue. For DRIP investors willing to ride through periodic volatility, these shares offer a top investment.

PepsiCo, Inc.

If I asked you what is the world's largest restaurant company, you'd probably say McDonald's. Good guess—but you'd be wrong. And you probably would be even more surprised to discover that the world's largest restaurant company is also the world's largest snack food company.

Still don't know who it is? Okay, last try. The largest restaurant and snack food company is also the world's second-largest soft-drink company.

By now you've probably guessed that the company is PepsiCo. Interestingly, the business it's best known for is the only one in which it is not number one in its markets. But that doesn't mean that the company runs a distant second. Just ask Coca-Cola (which, by the way, is another five-star issue). Indeed, these two powerhouses have waged aggressive campaigns for market share in recent years.

PepsiCo's restaurant operations include the Pizza Hut, Taco Bell, and KFC (Kentucky Fried Chicken) chains. Each of these chains is the leader in its respective niche in the fast-food field. Menu innovations and aggressive promotional campaigns have helped the restaurant operations.

Snack foods are under the Frito-Lay banner. This unit dominates the U.S. market for snack chips. Overseas expansion has put the firm in position to capitalize on the opportunities in this market.

Fundamentally, PepsiCo is sound. Operations throw off plenty of cash, and interest payments are easily handled. Earnings and dividends have trended higher over the years, and growth should continue for the foreseeable future. Fueling future gains will be an expanded overseas presence. PepsiCo already receives around 30 percent of total sales from foreign operations. Because of its market leadership and steady track record, the stock is rarely cheap. However, I have been pleased with my investment in PepsiCo, and I think you will be, too.

Philip Morris Companies, Inc.

Strong brand names are to consumer-products concerns what patents are to drug companies—licenses to print money. And Philip Morris Companies, with its powerful brand names in the tobacco, food, and brewing industries, has its money machine in high gear. Paced by such popular brands as Marlboro, Benson & Hedges, Miller, Lowenbrau, Oscar Mayer, Maxwell House, Jell-O, and Kraft, Philip Morris has charted an impressive growth course. The firm had 66 brands that each generated more than $100 million in 1994 operating revenues. The company's growth performance is especially impressive considering that the firm is posting such growth on top of a revenue base of some $70 billion.

Philip Morris' business profile looks much different than it did at the beginning of the 1980s. Indeed, tobacco was its primary activity, supplemented with operations in soft drinks (7-Up). However, Philip Morris embarked on an extensive restructuring program, shedding operations while moving aggressively into the food sector via acquisitions. First was the acquisition of General Foods in 1985. The firm followed up with the purchase of Kraft at the end of 1988.

Not only did these purchases bring on board a number of attractive brand names, but they also helped lessen dependence on the tobacco sector. The tobacco segment continues to be the company's major profit center. However, Philip Morris realizes the possible problems for the tobacco sector down the road—escalating excise taxes, public sentiment against smoking, and potential liability issues. True, burgeoning overseas markets should continue to keep profits rising from this sector. However, Philip Morris saw the need to diversify, and its choice of the food industry has been quite profitable.

Fundamentally, Philip Morris is sound. Dividends have increased at a healthy rate over the last decade. Long-term debt, though above 50 percent of total capital, is manageable given the firm's huge cash flow. In fact, it wouldn't be surprising to see Philip Morris add to its business portfolio via a major acquisition. Tobacco stocks may be volatile depending on liability litigation that looms over manufacturers, and Philip Morris has had some fairly wide price swings in the past.

However, the stock combines excellent capital-gains potential with healthy dividend-growth prospects and is appropriate for investment via DRIPs.

Procter & Gamble Co.

Marketing expertise will be more important than ever for the remainder of this decade and beyond, especially if U.S. firms hope to capitalize on growth in overseas markets. Few firms match the marketing muscle of Procter & Gamble. The company is often regarded as tops in brand management, and its brand managers are hotly recruited by other consumer-products companies. Procter & Gamble has managed to retain enough good managers to keep its profits growing at a healthy rate in recent years—an especially impressive performance considering the many mature markets the company serves.

A common theme among many of the companies highlighted in this chapter is strength via brand names, and Procter & Gamble certainly has its share of top names in a variety of consumer-products markets—Bounce, Ivory, Cheer, Pampers, Crest, Head & Shoulders, Pepto-Bismol, Crisco, and Old Spice. Most of these names have been home grown, although the firm has benefited from selected niche acquisitions. For example, the company has beefed up its cosmetics operations over the last six years via the acquisitions of Noxell and Revlon's Max Factor line.

With the advent of the global market, Procter & Gamble should reap sizable profits. Financially, the firm has more than enough resources to support its growth plans. Long-term debt is manageable, and its products generate large amounts of cash. Strong finances, along with steady earnings growth, have funded regular hikes in the dividend. I own Procter & Gamble, and this high-quality issue is suitable for conservative growth investors.

Regions Financial Corp.

Regions Financial may seem out of place in this chapter given the household names of many of the firms reviewed here. However, there is nothing second-rate about this regional bank. Indeed, few firms can match Regions' track record of per-share earnings growth. Net income has risen each year since the bank's inception in 1971. Dividends have expanded rapidly, rising more than threefold since 1982. I look for double-digit dividend hikes to continue on an annual basis.

A big reason for the success of the company has been its aggressive acquisition program. The firm operates offices in Alabama, Florida, Georgia, Louisiana, Mississippi, South Carolina, and Tennessee. With takeover activity expected to remain high in the banking business, Regions Financial will likely remain one of the major buyers.

Banking stocks generally are interest-rate sensitive, which causes periodic volatility in these shares. Nevertheless, Regions Financial provides a DRIP portfolio with good growth potential and reasonable income. DRIP investors should be especially attracted to the company's "no-load stock" program. Initial stock purchases may be made directly with $500. Once enrolled in the dividend reinvestment plan, optional cash payments as low as $100 allow investors with limited finances to build positions in this quality issue. Regions Financial is the only banking stock that I own, and I would recommend it for any portfolio.

SBC Communications, Inc.

SBC Communications, formerly Southwestern Bell, is one of the seven regional holding companies formerly owned by AT&T. The company provides telecommunication services in Arkansas, Kansas, Missouri, Oklahoma, and Texas. SBC Communications also has a substantial cellular business and ownership in overseas telecommunications companies, including a 10 percent equity stake in Telefonos de Mexico.

Although Wall Street has gone back and forth on the regional Bell companies, I think that over time the quality regional Bells will do exceptionally well in the changing telecommunications environment. SBC Communications has a number of factors in its favor. First, the firm is financially sound and should be able to fund the capital requirements necessary to compete in tomorrow's telephone markets. Second, the company's location in an attractive part of the country should aid growth prospects. Third, SBC Communications has excellent nonregulated businesses, especially its fast-growing cellular telephone business. This operation, in particular, should help earnings growth exceed that of the average regional Bell company.

Investors should note that SBC Communications has had an impressive dividend-growth record, with dividends rising annually since 1984. I would expect that trend to continue given the growth in per-share earnings expected over the next several years.

Of course, changes in the regulatory environment will boost the risk level of these shares going forward, as increased competition in the local-telephone markets could crimp earnings growth. However, I remain positive on the long-term prospects of SBC Communications and feel the stock is an appropriate total-return holding for any DRIP investor.

Scientific-Atlanta, Inc.

Scientific-Atlanta is not a stock for the faint of heart. The issue has demonstrated wide price swings over the years. For example, the stock went from $5 in 1992 all the way above $19 in 1993 only to fall to roughly $12 in 1994. However, if you are willing to accept such price volatility, I think that these shares should show substantial price gains over the long term.

One reason I am bullish on Scientific-Atlanta is that the firm has strong market positions in a number of attractive growth markets. The company produces equipment for satellites and data communications as well as cable TV markets. The firm is providing TV-top systems to a number of companies involved in interactive television trials. Scientific-Atlanta has emerged as one of the leaders in this attractive growth market. Indeed, with many cable television companies trying to enter a variety of telecommunications markets, Scientific-Atlanta's products are an important link in bringing cable TV companies into the telecommunications sector. Profits have jumped dramatically in recent years, and earnings should continue to move higher as demand increases for its systems. Overseas growth offers another exciting avenue for the company.

Investors should keep in mind, however, that as the markets for cable and interactive television grow, so, too, will competition. Scientific-Atlanta spends roughly 7 percent of annual sales on research and development, so the firm seems well positioned to combat increased competition with technologically advanced new products. Nevertheless, I don't want to undersell the risks involved in these shares. For that reason, while I feel that this stock has outstanding growth potential, I would not suggest it for conservative DRIP accounts. However, for investors who want to add some spice to a portfolio, Scientific-Atlanta certainly fits the bill.

Walgreen Co.

An aging population guarantees strong demand for pharmaceutical products. Attractive offshoots of the health-care sector are those firms which serve as the intermediaries between the drug companies and the customers—retail drugstores. The leader in this sector—and one of my personal DRIP holdings—is Walgreen.

Walgreen operates more than 2000 stores throughout the nation. Its stores serve nearly two million customers daily.

Walgreen's competitive strengths lie primarily in its use of technology and its focus on cost cutting. The company has been increasing its use of scanning technology, which provides such benefits as faster checkout, reduced labor costs, and better inventory control. The firm's satellite data network provides faster and more reliable communications between stores.

Another competitive advantage is its lucrative position as the nation's leading filler of prescription drugs. Walgreen fills more than 7 percent of all U.S. retail prescriptions. Pharmacy sales are around 43 percent of total revenues for the company, and that figure is likely to grow in the years ahead.

Fundamentally, Walgreen is sound. Dividends have increased fourfold since 1984. Strong finances should continue the company's aggressive growth strategy. The stock has been an excellent performer since the end of 1984, with a $10,000 investment becoming more than $45,300 by the end of 1994. Conservative growth investors may consider these shares for investment via the firm's DRIP.

7

Model Portfolios
Using DRIPs

This book attempts to construct from the ground up an investment strategy using DRIPs. Chapters 1, 2, 3, 4, and 5 lay the foundation. Chapter 6 provides the building blocks.

Now it's time to build the portfolio. But an appropriate portfolio for a single 28-year-old is not necessarily the right one for a married couple five years from retirement.

What are some factors to consider when building a portfolio?

- *Investment time horizon.* Obviously, an investor with 30 years or more has ample time to make up for a multitude of investment sins. He or she can be more aggressive than an investor who is retired and cannot afford to take a big loss in any one year.

- *Portfolio diversification.* An individual who has assets in several investments—real estate, fixed-income investments, tax-exempts, life insurance, and common stocks—will have a different portfolio objective than an individual beginning an investment program and having only a few investments. The proper number of stocks in a portfolio is a much debated topic in the financial community. Probably most academicians would agree that a portfolio of 13 to 17 stocks, representing a variety of industries, is sufficient to achieve decent diversification. Given the small financial requirements for DRIP investments, building a portfolio, over time, of 13 to 17 stocks shouldn't be too daunting for most investors.

- *Financial responsibilities and restraints.* A married couple facing college bills only five years down the road has certain financial obligations to consider when investing, unlike empty nesters whose houses are paid for and consumer debt is minimal or nonexistent. Also, a doctor making $200,000 a year will have different investment objectives than a young single parent.

- *Risk aversion.* Some investors just flat out do not like to take risks with their investments, even assuming such risk is prudent given long time horizons and ample financial assets. And then there are those investors who should be cautious, but they like the action and are comfortable with a higher level of risk.

Only after you consider these factors are you ready to build a portfolio. This chapter features model portfolios to meet a variety of investment objectives. All of the companies in these portfolios offer DRIPs.

Starter Portfolio

I'm often asked by investors what is a good portfolio to get started in dividend reinvestment programs. The following starter portfolio features four "no-load stocks"—those companies in which, as discussed in Chapter 4, you can make your initial purchase directly from the firm. That you don't need to have a broker to get your first shares makes these four issues very easy to purchase, especially with a small amount of money.

Dial Corp.	Procter & Gamble Co.
Exxon Corp.	Wisconsin Energy Corp.

Wisconsin Energy is a top electric utility. I would expect these shares to be among the leading performers in their industry group over time. Exxon is perhaps the top pick in the oil sector. The firm's geographical diversification enhances appeal. Procter & Gamble is one of the top consumer-products companies in the country. Dial, also a leading consumer-products company, has undergone a major restructuring of its operations over the last decade and is poised to show excellent growth over the long term. The major attraction of this portfolio is that investors can take positions in all four of the stocks with a total minimum initial investment of just $500. To continue investing on a monthly basis in each of the four stocks requires just $185. I personally own Exxon and Procter & Gamble and would feel very comfortable implementing a DRIP investment program with these four stocks as my initial investments.

The Golden Years Portfolio

Investors near or at retirement age have definite investment objectives, not the least of which is preservation of capital. Thus, stocks with relatively low volatility are appropriate for this portfolio. In addition, high yields are an important consideration, especially as these investors are at a point when they probably will begin to want to take at least some of their dividends in order to supplement Social Security and pension payments. It is also important not to neglect growth in a retirement portfolio. A frequent mistake investors near retirement or in retirement make is that they put all of their money in income vehicles. However, with many people living 20 years or more after the age of 62, it is important to include some growth representation in a golden years portfolio. Industry groups which are suitable hunting grounds for conservative stocks are electric and natural gas utilities and telephone issues. These areas are well represented in the portfolio below:

American Brands, Inc.	Morgan (J. P.) & Co., Inc.
Bristol-Myers Squibb Co.	Northern States Power Co.
Brooklyn Union Gas Co.	SBC Communications, Inc.
Exxon Corp.	TECO Energy, Inc.
Indiana Energy, Inc.	

Exxon and SBC Communications were reviewed in Chapter 6 and offer excellent growth-and-income selections.

Brooklyn Union Gas, Indiana Energy, Northern States Power, and TECO Energy give the portfolio a healthy representation in natural gas and electric utilities. All of these utilities have good finances, solid dividend-growth prospects, and favorable growth prospects relative to most utility issues. With the rash of dividend cuts and omissions among utilities over the last several years, investors should be able to sleep well holding these issues.

To enhance diversification as well as the growth potential of this portfolio, I have included American Brands, Bristol-Myers Squibb, and J. P. Morgan. These three issues combine healthy yields with above-average long-term capital-gains potential.

The Bluest-of-the-Blue-Chips Portfolio

Investing in corporate America's elite has its advantages. Indeed, you'd expect these stocks to be here today, tomorrow, and 20 years from now. Such longevity is critical when undertaking a long-term investment strategy such as DRIPs. Further, these industry leaders, because of pricing flexibility, large research and development programs, strong brand names, and other competitive advantages, should be able to hold up better during periods of market or economic weakness. The following portfolio contains many familiar names and would be suitable for investors who desire decent appreciation potential, steady dividend growth, and an above-average degree of safety.

AT&T Corp.	Kimberly-Clark Corp.
Coca-Cola Co.	Merck & Co., Inc.
Colgate-Palmolive Co.	Minnesota Mining &
Du Pont (E. I.) de Nemours & Co.	Manufacturing Co.
Exxon Corp.	Motorola, Inc.
General Electric Co.	Philip Morris Companies, Inc.
Johnson & Johnson	Procter & Gamble Co.
Kellogg Co.	

AT&T, Philip Morris Companies, Motorola, Johnson & Johnson, Procter & Gamble, 3M, GE, Exxon, and Merck & Co. were highlighted in Chapter 6 as some of my favorites for DRIP investments.

Kellogg's record of earnings and dividend growth over the last three decades stacks up against nearly any firm. Kellogg's stable of top brand names—Corn Flakes, Rice Krispies, Special K, Frosted Flakes, Froot Loops, and Eggo waffles—ensures strong profit margins and return on equity.

Colgate-Palmolive has its own profitable brand names—Fab, Ajax, Palmolive, Colgate, and Irish Spring. While domestic business remains decent, Colgate-Palmolive's star is hitched to international markets. The firm has been aggressive in bringing new brands to overseas markets. Overall, international operations account for roughly 68 percent of sales. Given the improved living standards in many developing countries, foreign business will no doubt expand even more. The stock's performance over the last decade has been impressive, and further capital gains are expected.

Rounding out the portfolio are Du Pont (E. I.), Kimberly-Clark, and Coca-Cola. All three of these companies are leaders in their respective industries. I expect each of these companies to post healthy earnings gains over the next three to five years. The stocks should outperform the overall market in that time.

Conservative Growth Portfolio

The title of this portfolio seems oxymoronic. However, it is possible to have a portfolio of stocks invested primarily for growth that doesn't leave you exposed to large risk levels. Granted, any growth-oriented portfolio will carry a slightly higher risk level than, say, an income portfolio. Nevertheless, the following conservative growth portfolio shouldn't turn your hair gray (unless it is already) and should pay off handsomely over a five-year time frame and beyond:

Abbott Laboratories	Gannett Co., Inc.
Block (H & R), Inc.	McDonald's Corp.
Browning-Ferris Industries, Inc.	Morton International, Inc.
Donnelley (R. R.) & Sons Co.	PepsiCo, Inc.
Emerson Electric Co.	Regions Financial Corp.
Equifax, Inc.	Walgreen Co.

Many of these issues are already familiar to you from Chapter 6—Abbott Laboratories, H & R Block, Browning-Ferris Industries, Equifax, McDonald's, PepsiCo, Regions Financial, and Walgreen. Each of these firms has a growth rate far in excess of the growth of the economy, and, with minor exceptions, has managed to post a long history of higher annual profits. Given the expected growth of some of the industries represented among these stocks—pollution control, informational services, restaurants, and health care—these stocks should continue to post healthy profits.

One could argue that Emerson Electric's operations in a variety of electrical equipment and electronics markets are anything but traditional growth markets. But nobody told Emerson Electric. Profits have risen annually for more than three decades. This record takes into account several recessionary periods and indicates the quality of these shares. Emerson Electric hasn't done it with smoke and mirrors but with old-fashioned cost controls and industry-leading products. Overseas expansion, strategic acquisitions, and over three decades of higher dividends enhance long-term appeal of this issue.

R. R. Donnelley & Sons, the world's largest commercial printer, doesn't have permission to print money. But you couldn't tell it from its bottom line. The firm has its hand in nearly every printing market—catalogs, tabloids, directories, magazines, books, and financial documents. Despite being in an industry that is sometimes cyclical and always price competitive, Donnelley's per-share profits more than tripled in the 1980s and have continued to grow in the 1990s. Strong finances have allowed the company to expand market share at the expense of poorly financed competitors. The stock's trend has been up, and investors should continue to enjoy good returns from these shares.

Most companies cannot absorb start-up costs on a new venture and continue to post strong earnings. But Gannett isn't most companies. This leading newspaper publisher showed its mettle by bringing out the first true national newspaper, *USA Today*. Although quarterly results have been erratic, *USA Today* represents an important profit center down the road. The company's network of small regional newspapers generates big profits. Its strategy is to enter small- to medium-sized towns where there is little or no competition, control the market, and hold the line on costs. This strategy plays extremely well with shareholders. Although economic downturns will limit advertising revenues and profitability from time to time, the upward trend in the bottom line and stock price is intact.

Morton International is a leader in three industry groups—salt, specialty chemicals, and automotive airbags. It is the latter area that is driving growth. With airbag usage expected to grow not only in this country but also abroad, Morton International should find its bottom line rising rapidly.

Light-Blue-Chip Portfolio

I suppose you could call the stocks in this portfolio blue-chip "wannabees." Light-blue chips are issues that lack the size and seasoning of consensus blue chips, such as GE, PepsiCo, and Johnson & Johnson, but have the potential to become tomorrow's blue-chip stocks.

What makes a light-blue chip?

- Leadership in a profitable and growing market niche
- The ability to weather economic cycles
- Strong finances, highlighted by little long-term debt and ample cash flow
- Steady earnings and dividend growth
- Annual revenues of $1 billion or less
- Outstanding shares totaling no more than 125 million, with a preference toward firms with 25 to 50 million shares outstanding

Stocks that meet these criteria usually have several things in common. First, they traditionally aren't institutional favorites because of their size and moderate number of shares outstanding. This is a plus since the stocks can generate substantial returns once they are discovered by Wall Street. Second, since the firms are working from a smaller base than larger companies, the opportunity for substantial earnings gains is greater for these issues. Since earnings surprises are a major fuel for superior stock performance, the odds improve on finding such stocks among light-blue chips. Finally, because of their size, light-blue chips may tend to be more volatile than investment-grade and conservative-growth stocks. However, investors with long time horizons or an aggressive approach to portfolio management should find the following stocks attractive:

Cracker Barrel Old Country Store, Inc.	Pall Corp.
	Paychex, Inc.
Crompton & Knowles Corp.	Rollins, Inc.
Diebold, Inc.	Rollins Truck Leasing Corp.
Loctite Corp.	RPM, Inc.

You've probably either never heard of most of these companies or know very little about them. That's okay—Wall Street doesn't know much about many of them either. But that situation won't last forever, especially as these firms grow and their track records become better publicized. Thus, investors who take positions now should be in excellent shape 5, 10, or 15 years from now when these issues are more popular—and more expensive.

Perhaps the quintessential light-blue-chip issue is Rollins. The firm meets our criteria for light-blue chips in convincing style. Rollins is the leader in extermination services under its Orkin unit. In addition, it has expanded into lawn-care and protective security services. Clean finances, rising profits and dividends, and well-defined growth prospects give this issue outstanding capital-gains potential. If there is a drawback, it's that Rollins' DRIP doesn't permit optional cash payments and a minimum of 50 shares is needed before enrolling in the DRIP. Nevertheless, investors should be pleased with the long-term performance of these shares.

Loctite, a producer of adhesives, sealants, coatings, and other specialty chemicals, generates the majority of sales and profits from overseas markets. This international reach has allowed the firm to offset some of the cyclical aspects of its domestic markets. Dividend growth has been especially attractive, with the payout increasing more than fourfold in the last 10 years.

Pall produces disposable filters and fluid-clarification equipment for health-care, aerospace, and processing industries. The company's growth record has been impressive, and a focus on fast-growing markets, such as health care, should help the bottom line accelerate.

Certain NASDAQ stocks sometimes suffer from guilt by association. True, it would be hard to classify all NASDAQ stocks as stable and steady. However, RPM has a record that stands up well against any company listed on any exchange. This manufacturer of specialty chemicals, hobby crafts, and sealants has achieved ever-higher sales and earnings for over 40 consecutive years. Acquisitions have been a major cog behind this growth. Dividend growth has been impressive as well, and further hikes are expected. Debt, because of its acquisitions, is a bit higher than I would normally like for light-blue chips. However, strong cash flow allows the firm to handle this debt load well.

Corporate restructurings often offer fertile ground for bargain hunting. Crompton & Knowles was one restructuring situation that turned into a bonanza for shareholders. In the second half of the 1980s, this producer of specialty chemicals and food ingredients sold off marginal areas to concentrate on its primary businesses. The move paid off beautifully. Profits, which had been stagnant for much of the 1970s and well into the 1980s, took off. The stock, which has taken a breather in the last two years following its strong advance from 1990 to 1993, has plenty of upside potential.

Rollins Truck Leasing is a leading provider of leasing services in the trucking industry. The firm has a solid growth record despite the cyclical nature of its industry. The stock will have its ups and downs but offers an attractive value at a favorable price.

Diebold and Paychex represent two of the more exciting stocks in this portfolio. Diebold is a leading provider of ATM machines. Growth in the ATM market is expected to be substantial, especially overseas, and Diebold is positioned to capitalize on this growth. Paychex provides computerized payroll-accounting services for small and medium-sized companies. The company's track record has been extremely strong over the years, and further profit growth is likely. Paychex stock always seems to be on the expensive side, but the stock's upward action in recent years has been extremely impressive. Both Diebold and Paychex have shown volatility through the years, but these stocks represent attractive selections for more aggressive DRIP investors.

Rounding out the portfolio is Cracker Barrel Old Country Store. This restaurant chain has experienced huge growth over the last decade. Granted, the restaurant industry is extremely competitive, and restaurant stocks have a tendency to run hot and cold on Wall Street.

However, the firm's aggressive expansion program should boost per-share profits going forward. The stock has interesting appreciation potential and could be considered by growth investors.

The Playschool Portfolio

For several reasons, not the least of which are minimal start-up dollars and a long-term focus, DRIPs have become an investment vehicle of choice for many parents saving for their children's college educations. One interesting side benefit of investing in this manner is that you can teach your children about stocks and even have them kick in a few dollars from their piggy banks each month toward their college educations.

A good case could be made that most of the portfolios we have covered up to this point would be appropriate for a program geared toward meeting college tuition bills and teaching children about money management. However, I think it's important that, in the case of a portfolio in which your son or daughter will likely have an active interest, you invest in stocks that might mean something to your child. I'm not advocating that you throw out all good stock-picking rules and choose a stock strictly because the company makes a product that's the rage with preschoolers. However, if you can find stocks in quality firms with products or services that your child knows, I think it makes for a much more enjoyable and profitable venture for child and parent. This goes for you grandparents, too.

The notion of investing in companies because you use their products or have a familiarity with the company is one of the most underrated methods of stock selection. All of us tend to make stock investing too complicated. We have to use the latest technical and fundamental indicators. We have to have the latest investment gadgets and equipment. However, I have had the most success with companies whose products I'm familiar with   and whose business I can understand. Applying this strategy to a child's portfolio is especially appropriate since your son or daughter could lose interest fast if he or she doesn't relate to the company.

The companies listed at the top of page 102 have interesting business segments or popular products that give their stocks a place in a child's portfolio. Note that these companies span the interests and needs of children of all ages. So you should be able to find an issue or two that would appeal to your child.

Abbott Laboratories	Mattel, Inc.
AT&T/Baby Bells	McDonald's Corp.
Coca-Cola Co.	PepsiCo, Inc.
Harley-Davidson, Inc.	Procter & Gamble Co.
Hershey Foods Corp.	Rubbermaid, Inc.
Intel Corp.	VF Corp.
Kimberly-Clark Corp.	Wrigley (Wm.) Jr. Co.

An obvious selection for a child's portfolio is a toy company. However, I have generally avoided this group over the years since the stocks are too volatile. Remember when demand for Cabbage Patch Dolls was driving prices so high that they were costing just slightly less than a condo? When near riots were breaking out at your local toy store to gobble up the limited supply? What happened to Coleco? It filed for bankruptcy in 1988. Nevertheless, one toy company that deserves consideration is Mattel. The company's track record of earnings growth is especially impressive considering the volatile nature of the toy industry. The stock has been an excellent performer over the last five years and has further upside potential.

It's essential to invest in toys that have stood the test of time if you plan to invest in the toy group. One popular line of toys is produced by Little Tikes, a division of Rubbermaid. Little Tikes is just one of Rubbermaid's many operating units. As with Rubbermaid's other operations, new-product development has been the key to success in its toy operations. Little Tikes is situated nicely in the market for infant, toddler, and preschool toys—a business that should continue to be strong.

It makes no difference to a baby what stocks are purchased for him or her in an investment program. But by owning shares in the companies listed above, you may not feel so bad dropping big bucks during your next shopping trip. First, it seems you can't buy enough diapers when you have a baby, even when you buy them in those packages that are about the size of Sputnik. One way to see some benefits of this spending, other than in unsoiled living room furniture, is via investment in the two leading diaper manufacturers—Procter & Gamble (Pampers) and Kimberly-Clark (Huggies). And if you have a financial interest in one end of your baby, why not have a stake in the other? Abbott Laboratories is a leading producer of infant formula (Isomil and Similac) and has excellent appreciation potential.

A number of foods and drinks are staples among our teens. For example, hanging out at McDonald's after a Friday night high school football game certainly is universal among teens. Why not own a piece of the Golden Arches? Or perhaps you never see your child without a Pepsi or Coke. Why not have some of those quarters go toward your dividends by owning some shares in those companies? Finally, who doesn't remember finding a wad of chewing gum under his or her desk in school (or, for that matter, putting one there)? Chances are, the gum was one of the brands manufactured by William Wrigley, Jr., the world's largest chewing gum producer. Apparently a lot of us still buy the firm's products since the trend of Wrigley's profits has been upward over the years. No long-term debt and double-digit profit margins reflect the quality of these shares. And what other product defined our early teens (and complexions) more than Hershey's chocolates? You could do a lot worse than buy shares in Hershey Foods for your child. Rising profits and healthy dividend growth should help propel the stock price higher.

Our childhood and teen years are defined not only by what we eat and drink but also by what we wear. Jeans remain a popular wardrobe choice for our youth, and VF Corp., through its Wrangler and Lee brands, has a strong position in this market.

Harley-Davidson, the motorcycle manufacturer, is one of the newer companies to offer a DRIP. The firm has been paying a dividend only since 1993. Profit growth has been impressive over the last four years, and the bottom line should continue to receive a boost from strong demand for the company's motorcycles. Harley-Davidson's DRIP provides an opportunity for youngsters with an interest in motorcycles to own a piece of this American legend.

While most of us still fumble around with computers, our kids seem much more at home in front of a PC. If your child is a budding Bill Gates, perhaps he or she would want to be a shareholder of Intel, the big computer-chip maker.

Finally, what would our teen years have been without the permanent attachment of a telephone to our ears? Now, when your children are following in your footsteps and churning out huge phone bills, at least you can find solace if you have investments in AT&T or the regional Bells, such as BellSouth or SBC Communications. Each of these companies has attractive long-term growth prospects and decent dividend-growth potential.

We have had some fun with this portfolio. Nevertheless, let's not forget its basic point—to achieve long-term growth via sound, high-quality stocks and to focus on those companies in which your children may be familiar or have some attraction. All of these issues have four- and five-star ratings and meet demanding criteria concerning finances, growth potential, market leadership, and rising dividends. And best of all, they all offer DRIPs.

8

Directory of Company Dividend Reinvestment Plans

You've now read the book. You buy the concept of DRIPs and the power of dollar-cost averaging. The dollar amounts to get started don't scare you. And you're fired up to get going.

But you have some questions and concerns. You wonder if McDonald's minimum optional cash payment amount fits with your investment budget of $75 a month. You'd like to find an electric utility with a DRIP that lets you reinvest some of your dividends while pocketing some of the cash. You want to know which top-rated issues offer DRIPs with discounts.

Relax. These and a thousand other questions and concerns are addressed in the following pages.

About the Directory

The directory listings provide a plethora of information—addresses, phone numbers, stock symbols, business profiles, and DRIP specifics.

Nearly all of the listings provide a performance rating to help steer you toward the best stocks and away from the worst. Each directory listing also provides a rating of the DRIP plan itself.

Here are some things to consider when using the directory:

- The performance ratings range from the highest (*****) to the lowest (*). In the case of a few firms—primarily small regional banks—I lacked sufficient corporate information and financial data on which to rate the companies. These firms were not rated (NR).

- The DRIP ratings consist of a "thumbs up" for acceptable programs or a "thumbs down" for unattractive DRIP plans.

- Each listing features the stock exchange on which the issue trades (NYSE: New York Stock Exchange; ASE: American Stock Exchange; NASDAQ: NASDAQ National Market and the Over-the-Counter Markets) and the stock symbol.

- Unless specified in the company's Plan Specifics, you can assume that a company picks up all costs and fees for purchasing stock in its DRIP.

- Many companies allow shareholders to enroll in the plans with only one share. For those few firms in which more shares are required, the number is stated in the Plan Specifics. Also, programs which permit investors to make their initial purchases directly from the company are clearly designated.

- OCP is the abbreviation used for optional cash payments—the voluntary payments that shareholders may make directly into the DRIP in order to purchase additional shares. For example, in the case of Abbott Laboratories, the OCPs allowed under the plan are a minimum of $10 to a maximum of $5000 per quarter. Each listing indicates how frequently OCPs are invested by the company. If a DRIP doesn't offer OCPs, it is indicated by "not available" in the Plan Specifics.

- Some plans permit partial dividend reinvestment. This option allows participants to receive dividends on part of the shares held in the plan while reinvesting dividends on the remainder. This option is addressed in the Plan Specifics.

- When possible, specific costs for selling shares from a DRIP are given. Plans in which investors must go through their own broker to sell stock are highlighted in the Plan Specifics.

- Often, the best source of information about a particular plan is the plan administrator. For that reason, many listings contain the address of the agent administering the plan. In addition, two phone numbers are often provided—the company's and the administrator's. If you call the company for information, ask for either the investor relations or shareholder services department.

- Each listing will indicate if a discount is available and, if so, the amount of the discount and whether it applies to just reinvested dividends or both reinvested dividends and OCPs.

- Each listing provides the monthly dividend payment dates for the stock. While most DRIP investors reinvest their dividends, many DRIP investors like to receive at least some of their dividends in cash and thus may find this listing particularly helpful in generating income from their DRIP investments. This information is especially useful for building a DRIP portfolio in which dividends are paid every month.

About the Ratings

Any ratings—I don't care if it's the weekly Associated Press college football poll, Siskel & Ebert's movie reviews, or Mr. Blackwell's List of the 10 Worst-Dressed Women—always have an element of controversy. After all, you can't please everyone. However, I can assure you that both the performance rating and the DRIP rating were not given lightly.

The performance rating resulted from examining and evaluating several factors. Financial strength was one of the major determinants of the ratings. Companies with high debt levels usually found themselves receiving one or two stars. Does that mean all companies with large debt loads are bad? Certainly not. But bankruptcy files are filled with highly leveraged firms that ran into problems when business dried up and interest payments were missed. Since investing with DRIPs is a long-term proposition, you want companies that will be able to stay in the game. Heavy debt burdens often make for an early exit. Am I painting all debt-heavy firms with too broad a brush? Perhaps. But my aim is to protect you from danger spots. If I err on the conservative side, so be it.

Earnings, sales, and dividend records were also important in assigning performance ratings. Firms with consistent sales and earnings growth were rated higher than firms where profitability has been inconsistent. Companies with records of steadily increasing dividends usually fared better in the ratings than those in which dividend growth has been erratic or where dividend cuts or omissions have occurred. Safety of the dividend was a key point.

The company's industry weighed heavily in the ratings. As you know from Chapter 5, real estate investment trusts and oil and gas limited partnerships leave a lot to be desired, in my opinion. Thus, I had a hard time giving any REITs or limited partnerships ratings higher than two stars.

Utility stocks came under close scrutiny as well. Utility stocks are often the refuge for the most conservative investors—people who depend on dividends to supplement their fixed income and who can't afford to have dividend cuts or omissions. Therefore, these issues faced a tougher test than other issues when it came to the ratings.

The long-term prospects of the industry were important. Cyclical industries, such as steel, precious metals, and autos, didn't do as well in the ratings as growth-oriented, recession-resistant sectors, such as food, drugs, and consumer products.

Finally, the performance ratings were based on the issue's overall suitability for investment via a DRIP. This analysis considered such factors as the competitive nature of the industry, the potential for technological obsolescence, and the projected volatility of the stock.

How should you use the performance ratings? Obviously, new investments should be focused on four- and five-star issues. However, because a stock you own has a two- or three-star rating doesn't automatically make it a sell. A two- or three-star rating should force you to take a closer look at the firm and its prospects. Does the stock still meet your objectives? Does it have the favorable prospects that led you to invest in it in the first place? If the answers are "yes," then maintain your position. Remember that these ratings are on the conservative side.

Each directory listing also features a DRIP rating. This rating refers to the quality of the overall DRIP program. Factors taken into account when assigning this rating include the ease of enrolling in the program; the fees, if any, of investing through the DRIP; the availability of special services, such as IRAs and automatic investment services; and the frequency of purchases with optional cash investments. While this particular rating should not necessarily deter an individual from investing in a stock, especially a five-star rated issue, it should at least give investors reason to pause to consider whether this DRIP program truly meets their needs. Fortunately, most DRIPs are attractive from cost and user-friendly standpoints, which is why the bulk of the programs received a "thumbs up" rating.

With that said about the performance and DRIP ratings, I still expect to hear from companies moaning about their ratings. As I said, you can't please everyone.

A Reminder

Although I have said this throughout the book, it bears repeating. Companies frequently change certain aspects of their plans. For example, firms might drop the discount, lower the maximum amount of OCPs, or implement a service charge for administering the plan. Thus, it is critical that investors consult with the company and obtain a prospectus before investing.

(The directory begins on page 110.)

AAR Corp. (NYSE:AIR)
1111 Nicholas Blvd.
Elk Grove Vlg., IL 60007
(708) 439-3939

Business Profile: Leading provider of services for commercial aviation markets.

Plan Specifics:

- Partial dividend reinvestment is not available.
- No Discount.
- OCP: $10 to $3000 per quarter.
- Selling costs are brokerage commissions.
- Company purchases stock quarterly with OCPs.
- Dividends are paid March, June, September, and December.

Performance Rating: ***

DRIP Rating: 👍

Abbott Laboratories (NYSE:ABT)
100 Abbott Park Rd.
Abbott Park, IL 60064-3500
(800) 730-4001   (708) 937-3923

Business Profile: Major manufacturer of health care and nutritional products for hospitals and laboratories. Maintains leading position in AIDS testing.

Plan Specifics:

- Partial dividend reinvestment is not available.
- No Discount.
- OCP: $10 to $5000 per quarter.
- Stock is purchased every 45 days with OCPs.
- Selling fees may include brokerage commissions.
- Dividends are paid February, May, August, and November.

Performance Rating: *****

DRIP Rating: 👍

Acme-Cleveland Corp.
(NYSE:AMT)
1242 E. 49th St.
Cleveland, OH 44114
(216) 813-5745

Business Profile: Provides products and services to improve telecommunication and metalworking equipment.

Plan Specifics:

- Partial dividend reinvestment is not available.
- No Discount.
- OCP: $10 to $5000 per quarter.
- Selling costs are brokerage commissions.
- Company purchases stock quarterly with OCPs.
- Dividends are paid February, May, August, and November.

Performance Rating: ***

DRIP Rating: 👍

ADAC Laboratories
(NASDAQ:ADAC)
540 Alder Dr.
Milpitas, CA 95035
(408) 321-9100

Business Profile: Designs, produces, markets, and services medical imaging and information management products throughout the world.

Plan Specifics:

- Must own at least 100 shares to enroll.
- Partial dividend reinvestment is not available.
- 5 percent discount on reinvested dividends and OCPs.

- OCP: $100 to $2500 per quarter.
- Company purchases stock quarterly with OCPs.
- Selling costs are brokerage commissions.
- Dividends are paid January, April, July, and October.

Performance Rating: **

DRIP Rating: 👎

Aetna Life and Casualty Co. (NYSE:AET)
151 Farmington Ave.
Hartford, CT 06156
(203) 273-3977

Business Profile: Largest investor-owned insurance company providing business and personal insurance.

Plan Specifics:

- Partial dividend reinvestment is not available.
- No Discount.
- OCP: $50 to $5000 per month.
- Selling costs are brokerage fees.
- Company purchases stock monthly with OCPs.
- Dividends are paid February, May, August, and November.

Performance Rating: ***

DRIP Rating: 👍

AFLAC, Inc. (NYSE:AFL)
Worldwide Headquarters
1932 Wynnton Rd.
Columbus, GA 31999
(800) 227-4756

Business Profile: Holding company with insurance and broadcasting interests.

Plan Specifics:

- Partial dividend reinvestment is available.
- No Discount.
- OCP: $20 to $5000 per month.
- Selling costs are brokerage commissions of 5 cents per share.
- Company purchases stock monthly with OCPs.
- Safekeeping services are available.
- Dividends are paid March, June, September, and December.

Performance Rating: ****

DRIP Rating: 👍

Air Products & Chemicals, Inc. (NYSE:APD)
7201 Hamilton Blvd.
Allentown, PA 18195-1501
(610) 481-4911

Business Profile: Manufactures industrial chemicals, equipment, and gases.

Plan Specifics:

- Partial dividend reinvestment is not available.
- No Discount.
- OCP: $25 to $20,000 per year.
- Company purchases stock monthly with OCPs.
- Selling fees include a $5 service charge, brokerage commissions, and applicable transfer taxes.
- Dividends are paid February, May, August, and November.

Performance Rating: *****

DRIP Rating: 👍

**Albany International Corp.
(NYSE:AIN)**
1373 Broadway
Albany, NY 12204
(518) 445-2200

Business Profile: World's largest manufacturer of engineered fabrics essential to papermaking machines.

Plan Specifics:
- Partial dividend reinvestment is available.
- No Discount.
- OCP: $10 to $5000 per month.
- Selling costs are brokerage commissions and costs of sale.
- Firm purchases stock around the 1st of the month with OCPs.
- Safekeeping services are available.
- Dividends are paid January, April, July, and October.

Performance Rating: ***
DRIP Rating: 👍

Albemarle Corp. (NYSE:ALB)
330 S. Fourth St.
Richmond, VA 23219
(312) 461-6834   (504) 388-8180

Business Profile: Makes specialty chemicals and intermediates for polymers, detergents, electronics, agricultural chemicals, and pharmaceuticals.

Plan Specifics:
- Partial dividend reinvestment is not available.
- No Discount.
- OCP: $25 to $1000 per month.
- Selling costs are brokerage commissions.
- Stock is purchased monthly with OCPs.

- Dividends are paid January, April, July, and October.

Performance Rating: ***
DRIP Rating: 👍

Albertson's, Inc. (NYSE:ABS)
c/o Chemical Trust Co. of CA
PO Box 24850, Church St. Stat.
New York, NY 10249
(800) 982-7464   (208) 385-6200

Business Profile: Fourth largest U.S. food retailer.

Plan Specifics:
- Need at least 15 shares to participate.
- Partial dividend reinvestment is available.
- No Discount.
- OCP: $30 to $30,000 per quarter.
- Purchasing fees are brokerage commissions and any other costs.
- A service charge of $5 will be charged for each optional cash payment.
- Company purchases stock quarterly with OCPs.
- Selling costs are a sales fee of $15 per transaction, brokerage commissions and any other costs of sale.
- Dividends are paid February, May, August, and November.

Performance Rating: *****
DRIP Rating: 👍

Alcan Aluminium Ltd.
(NYSE:AL)
Shareholder Services
PO Box 6077
Montreal, Quebec H3C 3A7
Canada
(514) 848-8050

Business Profile: One of the largest aluminum manufacturers in the world primarily serving the United States, Canada, Europe, and the Pacific.

Plan Specifics:
- Partial dividend reinvestment is available.
- No Discount.
- OCP: $100 to $9000 (United States) per quarter.
- Must go through own broker to sell shares.
- Stock is purchased on the 15th of the month with OCPs.
- Dividends are paid March, June, September, and December.

Performance Rating: ***
DRIP Rating: 👍

Alco Standard Corp. (NYSE:ASN)
825 Duportail Rd.
Wayne, PA 19087
(610) 296-8000

Business Profile: Manufactures paper and office products.

Plan Specifics:
- Partial dividend reinvestment is not available.
- No Discount.
- OCP: $25 to $1000 per month.
- Purchasing fees include brokerage commissions.
- Stock is purchased around the 10th of the month with OCPs.
- Selling costs are brokerage commissions and $2 charge.
- Dividends are paid March, June, September, and December.

Performance Rating: ****
DRIP Rating: 👍

Allegheny Ludlum Corp.
(NYSE:ALS)
1000 Six PPG Pl.
Pittsburgh, PA 15222
(412) 394-2800

Business Profile: Major manufacturer of stainless steel, specialty metals, and steel alloys.

Plan Specifics:
- Partial dividend reinvestment is not available.
- No Discount.
- OCP: $25 to $3000 per quarter.
- Stock is purchased 8 times per year with OCPs.
- Selling costs are $5 service charge and brokerage commissions.
- Dividends are paid January, April, July, and October.

Performance Rating: **
DRIP Rating: 👍

Allegheny Power System, Inc.
(NYSE:AYP)
12 E. 49th St.
New York, NY 10017
(212) 752-2121

Business Profile: Electric utility operating in Pennsylvania, Virginia, Ohio, West Virginia, and Maryland.

Plan Specifics:
- Partial dividend reinvestment is available.
- No Discount.

- OCP: $50 to $10,000 per quarter.
- The firm charges $3 per OCP investment and 3 percent of dividend (maximum $3) reinvested.
- Company invests stock quarterly with OCPs.
- Selling costs are brokerage commissions, transfer tax, and a $15 transaction fee for each sale of any number of whole shares.
- Safekeeping feature is available for one-time fee of $3.
- Approximately 21,000 shareholders are in the plan.
- Dividends are paid March, June, September, and December.

Performance Rating: ****

DRIP Rating: 👍

Allergan, Inc. (NYSE:AGN)
2525 Dupont Dr.
PO Box 19534
Irvine, CA 92713-9534
(714) 752-4500   (201) 324-0498

Business Profile: Provides therapeutic products for eye and skin care and neuromuscular disorders.

Plan Specifics:

- Partial dividend reinvestment is available.
- No Discount.
- OCP: $10 to $50,000 per year.
- Company purchases stock monthly with OCPs.
- Selling costs are brokerage fees, any service fee, and any other costs of sale.
- Dividends are paid March, June September, and December.

Performance Rating: ***

DRIP Rating: 👍

Allied Group, Inc.
(NASDAQ:ALGR)
701 Fifth Ave.
Des Moines, IA 50391-2000
(800) 532-1436 Ext. 4617
(312) 461-2731

Business Profile: Provides property-casualty insurance. Performs financial services for other insurance companies.

Plan Specifics:

- Partial dividend reinvestment is available.
- No Discount.
- OCP: $25 to $5000 per month.
- Fees for purchasing shares include brokerage commissions.
- Selling costs include nominal commission and any Harris Trust handling charge.
- Company purchases stock each month with OCPs.
- Dividends are paid March, June, September, and December.

Performance Rating: ***

DRIP Rating: 👍

AlliedSignal, Inc. (NYSE:ALD)
101 Columbia Rd.
Morris Township, NJ 07962
(201) 455-2127   (800) 524-4458

Business Profile: Manufactures aerospace and automotive products as well as plastics and synthetic fibers.

Plan Specifics:

- Partial dividend reinvestment is available.
- No Discount.
- OCP: $25 to $120,000 per year.
- Stock is purchased monthly with OCPs.
- Selling costs are brokerage

commissions and a bank service charge.
- Approximately 18,000 shareholders are in the plan.
- Dividends are paid March, June, September, and December.

Performance Rating: ****

DRIP Rating: 👍

Allstate Corp. (NYSE:ALL)
Allstate Plaza
2775 Sanders Rd.
Northbrook, IL 60062
(312) 461-2288   (708) 402-5000

Business Profile: Second largest property-liability insurer in the U.S. and one of the largest life insurers.

Plan Specifics:
- Partial dividend reinvestment is not available.
- No Discount.
- OCP: $25 to $3000 per month.
- Purchasing fees are a service charge and brokerage commissions.
- Company purchases stock monthly with OCPs.
- Selling costs are a $5 sales charge plus brokerage commissions.
- Dividends are paid March, June, September, and December.

Performance Rating: ***

DRIP Rating: 👍

ALLTEL Corporation (NYSE:AT)
One Allied Dr.
Little Rock, AR 72202
(501) 661-8000

Business Profile: A diversified telecommunications and information services company.

Plan Specifics:
- Partial dividend reinvestment is not available.
- No Discount.
- OCP: $500 to $25,000 per quarter.
- Stock is purchased monthly with OCPs.
- Selling costs are brokerage fees and a $5 termination fee.
- Safekeeping services are available ($5 charge for each share certificate deposited).
- Dividends are paid January, April, July, and October.

Performance Rating: ***

DRIP Rating: 👎

Aluminum Company of America (NYSE:AA)
425 Sixth Ave.
Alcoa Building
Pittsburgh, PA 15219
(412) 553-4545   (800) 446-2617

Business Profile: Largest aluminum producer in the United States.

Plan Specifics:
- Partial dividend reinvestment is available.
- No Discount.
- OCP: $25 to $5000 per month.
- Stock is purchased monthly with OCPs.
- Preferred dividends are eligible for reinvestment for additional common shares under the plan.
- Participants incur brokerage fees when selling shares.
- Dividends are paid February, May, August, and November.

Performance Rating: ***

DRIP Rating: 👍

Amax Gold, Inc. (NYSE:AU)
9100 E. Mineral Circle
Englewood, CO 80112
(303) 643-5500

Business Profile: Company explores for and produces gold in North and South America.

Plan Specifics:
- Partial dividend reinvestment is available.
- No Discount.
- OCP: not available.
- Selling costs are brokerage fees.
- Dividends are currently not being paid.

Performance Rating: *
DRIP Rating: ☜

Amcast Industrial Corp.
(NYSE:AIZ)
7887 Washington Village Dr.
Dayton, OH 45459
(513) 291-7000

Business Profile: Manufactures metal products, flow-control products, and engineered components for manufacturers of original equipment.

Plan Specifics:
- Partial dividend reinvestment is not available.
- No Discount.
- OCP: $25 to $1000 per month.
- Selling costs include brokerage fees and $1 service charge.
- Company purchases stock with OCPs at least quarterly and more often if enough funds accumulate to purchase a 100 share lot.
- Dividends are paid March, June, September, and December.

Performance Rating: **
DRIP Rating: ☝

AMCOL International Corp.
(NASDAQ:ACOL)
One N. Arlington
1500 W. Shure Dr.
Arlington Hgts., IL 60004
(708) 394-8730

Business Profile: One of the world's principal producers of bentonite, a nonmetallic clay used in many different industries and products.

Plan Specifics:
- Partial dividend reinvestment is available.
- No Discount.
- OCP: $25 to $2000 per month.
- Purchases are made monthly with OCPs.
- Purchasing fees are brokerage commissions.
- Selling costs are brokerage commissions and transfer tax.
- Dividends are paid March, June, September, and December.

Performance Rating: ***
DRIP Rating: ☝

AMCORE Financial, Inc.
(NASDAQ:AMFI)
PO Box 1537
501 7th St.
Rockford, IL 61110-0037
(815) 968-2241   (800) 637-7549

Business Profile: Multibank holding company located in Illinois.

Plan Specifics:
- Partial dividend reinvestment is available.
- No Discount.
- OCP: $10 to $3000 per quarter.

- Company purchases stock around the first business day of the month with OCPs.
- Approximately 665 shareholders are in the plan.
- Dividends are paid March, June, September, and December.

Performance Rating: ***

DRIP Rating: 👍

Amerada Hess Corp.
(NYSE:AHC)
1185 Avenue of the Americas
New York, NY 10036
(800) 851-9677

Business Profile: Explores, refines, and markets oil and natural gas.

Plan Specifics:
- Partial dividend reinvestment is available.
- No Discount.
- OCP: $50 to $5000 per quarter.
- Stock is purchased monthly with OCPs.
- Selling costs include brokerage fees and $1 service charge.
- Dividends are paid March, June, September, and December.

Performance Rating: ***

DRIP Rating: 👍

American Brands, Inc.
(NYSE:AMB)
Stockholder Relations Dept.
1700 E. Putnam Ave.
PO Box 815
Old Greenwich, CT 06870
(203) 698-5000

Business Profile: Global consumer products holding company with five core businesses — international tobacco, distilled spirits,

hardware and home improvement products, office products, and golf products.

Plan Specifics:
- Partial dividend reinvestment is available.
- No Discount.
- OCP: $50 to $15,000 per quarter.
- Selling fees are brokerage commissions.
- Stock is purchased monthly with OCPs.
- Dividends are paid March, June, September, and December.

Performance Rating: *****

DRIP Rating: 👍

American Business Products, Inc.
(NYSE:ABP)
2100 Riveredge Pkwy., Ste. 1200
Atlanta, GA 30328
(404) 953-8300

Business Profile: Important producer of business forms and printed business supplies.

Plan Specifics:
- Partial dividend reinvestment is not available.
- No Discount.
- OCP: $10 to $1000 per month.
- Stock is purchased monthly with OCPs.
- Selling costs are brokerage commissions.
- Dividends are paid March, June, September, and December.

Performance Rating: ****

DRIP Rating: 👍

American Electric Power Co., Inc.
(NYSE:AEP)
PO Box 16631
1 Riverside Plaza
Columbus, OH 43216-6631
(800) 237-2667

Business Profile: Major electric
utility holding company serving
portions of Indiana, Kentucky,
Michigan, Ohio, Tennessee,
Virginia, and West Virginia.

Plan Specifics:
- Partial dividend reinvestment is
  available.
- No Discount.
- OCP: up to $100,000 per year.
- Stock is purchased twice a
  month with OCPs.
- Selling fees include brokerage
  commissions and handling
  charges.
- Automatic investment services
  are available.
- Direct deposit of dividends is
  available.
- Shares may be sold over the
  phone by calling 800-935-9330.
- Dividends are paid March, June,
  September, and December.

Performance Rating: ***
DRIP Rating: 👍

American Express Co.
(NYSE:AXP)
American Express Tower
World Financial Center
New York, NY 10285-4775
(212) 640-5693   (800) 851-9677

Business Profile: Specializes in
travel-related services with
operations in investment services
and international banking.

Plan Specifics:
- Partial dividend reinvestment is
  available.
- No Discount.
- OCP: $50 to $5000 per month.
- Stock is purchased with OCPs
  around the 10th of every month.
- Selling costs are brokerage
  commissions and applicable
  stock transfer tax.
- Safekeeping is available.
- Dividends are paid February,
  May, August, and November.

Performance Rating: ****
DRIP Rating: 👍

American Filtrona Corp.
(NASDAQ:AFIL)
3951 Westerre Pkwy., Ste. 300
Richmond, VA 23233
(804) 346-2400

Business Profile: Manufactures
specialty bonded fiber products
and plastic products.

Plan Specifics:
- Partial dividend reinvestment is
  not available.
- No Discount.
- OCP: $25 to $1000 per month.
- Nominal broker fees for pur-
  chases.
- Selling costs include brokerage
  fees.
- Stock is purchased monthly with
  OCPs.
- Dividends are paid February,
  May, August, and November.

Performance Rating: ***
DRIP Rating: 👍

American General Corp. (NYSE:AGC)
2929 Allen Pkwy.
Houston, TX 77019
(713) 522-1111

Business Profile: A consumer financial-services organization with operations in life insurance, retirement annuities, and consumer loans.

Plan Specifics:
- Partial dividend reinvestment is available.
- No Discount.
- OCP: $25 to $6000 per quarter.
- Selling costs include brokerage fees and applicable transfer taxes.
- Purchases with OCPs are made around the 1st of each month.
- Dividends are paid March, June, September, and December.

Performance Rating: ***
DRIP Rating: 👍

American Greetings Corp. (NASDAQ:AGREA)
1 American Rd.
Cleveland, OH 44144
(216) 737-5742   (216) 252-7300

Business Profile: Leading supplier of greeting cards and gift wrap.

Plan Specifics:
- Partial dividend reinvestment is not available.
- No Discount.
- OCP: up to $10,000 per quarter.
- OCP is invested once per quarter.
- Selling costs may include any brokerage fees and $2 termination.
- Dividends are paid March, June, September, and December.

Performance Rating: ****
DRIP Rating: 👍

American Health Properties, Inc. (NYSE:AHE)
6400 S. Fiddler's Green Circle, Suite 1800
Englewood, CO 80111-4961
(303) 796-9793

Business Profile: Real estate investment trust invests in broad range of health-care-related facilities throughout the country.

Plan Specifics:
- Partial dividend reinvestment is available.
- No Discount.
- OCP: $50 to $3000 per quarter.
- Stock is purchased monthly with OCPs.
- Approximately 2000 shareholders are in the plan.
- Dividends are paid February, May, August, and November.

Performance Rating: **
DRIP Rating: 👍

American Heritage Life Investment Corp. (NYSE:AHL)
1776 Amer. Heritage Life Dr.
Jacksonville, FL 32224
(904) 992-2545   (904) 992-1776

Business Profile: Insurance-based holding firm offers life, accident, and health insurance and annuities.

Plan Specifics:
- Partial dividend reinvestment is available.
- No Discount.
- OCP: not available.
- Selling costs are brokerage commissions and any taxes.

- Dividends are paid every month.

Performance Rating: ****

DRIP Rating: ☞

American Home Products Corp. (NYSE:AHP)
5 Giralda Farms
Madison, NJ 07940
(800) 565-2067

Business Profile: Manufacturer of prescription drugs, medical supplies, diagnostic products, consumer health-care items, food products, and agricultural products.

Plan Specifics:

- Partial dividend reinvestment is available.
- No Discount.
- OCP: $50 to $10,000 per month.
- Fees for purchasing stock under the plan include proportionate brokerage fees, $1.50 service charge for each quarterly dividend reinvestment, and $5 fee for each investment of optional cash payments.
- Selling fees include brokerage costs and termination fee of $15.
- Stock is purchased monthly with OCPs.
- Dividends are paid March, June, September, and December.

Performance Rating: *****

DRIP Rating: 👍

American Industrial Properties REIT (NYSE:IND)
6220 N. Beltline, Ste. 205
Irving, TX 75063
(800) 527-7844　(214) 979-5100

Business Profile: Real estate investment trust.

Plan Specifics:

- Partial dividend reinvestment is available.
- No Discount.
- OCP: not available.
- Small service fees may be charged for purchases.
- Selling costs are approximately 3 to 5 cents per share.
- The company is not currently paying a dividend.

Performance Rating: *

DRIP Rating: ☞

American Real Estate Partners, LP (NYSE:ACP)
90 S. Bedford Rd.
Mount Kisco, NY 10549
(914) 242-7700

Business Profile: Partnership involved in management and acquisition of real estate for office, retail, and industrial properties.

Plan Specifics:

- Partial dividend reinvestment is not available.
- No Discount.
- OCP: not available.
- Purchasing fees are 5 percent on each amount invested — not less than 75 cents or more than $2.50 — plus proportionate brokerage commissions for each investment transaction.
- Selling fees are brokerage commissions plus termination fee of $2.50.
- The company is not currently paying a dividend.

Performance Rating: *

DRIP Rating: ☞

American Recreation Centers, Inc. (NASDAQ:AMRC)
11171 Sun Center Dr., Ste. 120
Rancho Cordova, CA 95670
(916) 852-8005

Business Profile: Owns bowling centers in California, Texas, Oklahoma, Missouri, and Kentucky. Owns a majority interest in The Right Start, Inc., a leading mail-order catalog merchant of children's products.

Plan Specifics:

- Initial purchases may be made directly through the company ($100 minimum).
- Partial dividend reinvestment is not available.
- No Discount.
- OCP: $25 to $5000 per month.
- Stock is purchased monthly with OCPs.
- Selling costs are brokerage commissions and other expenses.
- Dividends are paid January, April, July, and October.

Performance Rating: **

DRIP Rating: 👍

American Water Works Co., Inc. (NYSE: AWK)
1025 Laurel Oak Rd.
PO Box 1770
Voorhees, NJ 08043
(800) 736-3001

Business Profile: Utility holding company provides water services in 21 states.

Plan Specifics:

- Partial dividend reinvestment is available.
- 5 percent discount on reinvested dividends and OCPs.
- OCP: $100 to $5000 per month.
- Company purchases stock monthly with OCPs.
- Utility customers may buy initial shares directly from the company ($100 minimum).
- Selling costs include brokerage fees, transfer taxes, and a handling charge.
- Dividends are paid February, May, August, and November.

Performance Rating: ****

DRIP Rating: 👍

Ameritech Corp. (NYSE:AIT)
30 S. Wacker Dr.
Chicago, IL 60606
(312) 750-5353   (800) 233-1342

Business Profile: Major telephone holding company for upper-midwestern states.

Plan Specifics:

- Must own at least 2 shares in order to participate in the plan.
- Partial dividend reinvestment is available.
- No Discount.
- OCP: $50 to $50,000 per year.
- Fees for purchasing stock in the open market are nominal brokerage commissions; $1 fee per account, per quarter.
- Selling costs are brokerage commissions, any applicable transfer tax, and a $5 service fee.
- Purchases are made on the 25th of the month with OCPs.
- Automatic investment services are available.
- Direct deposit of dividends is available.
- Dividends are paid February, May, August, and November.

Performance Rating: *****
DRIP Rating: 👍

Amoco Corp. (NYSE:AN)
200 E. Randolph Dr.
Chicago, IL 60601
(312) 856-6111   (800) 446-2617

Business Profile: Largest holder of natural gas reserves in North America. Refines, markets, and transports crude oil and natural gas worldwide.

Plan Specifics:
- Partial dividend reinvestment is not available.
- No Discount.
- OCP: $50 to $5000 per month.
- Stock is purchased monthly with OCPs.
- Purchasing fees are 5 percent of amount invested up to a maximum of $2.50 plus brokerage commissions, which are about one-half of 1 percent of amount invested.
- Selling costs are $10 service charge plus broker commissions and transfer taxes.
- The company is planning to permit all investors to buy their initial shares directly.
- Shares can be sold via the telephone.
- Dividends are paid March, June, September, and December.

Performance Rating: *****
DRIP Rating: 👍

AMP, Inc. (NYSE:AMP)
Eisenhower Blvd.
Harrisburg, PA 17105-3608
(800) 851-9677

Business Profile: World's largest supplier of electrical and electronic connection devices.

Plan Specifics:
- Partial dividend reinvestment is not available.
- No Discount.
- OCP: $50 to $5000 per month.
- Selling costs may include brokerage fees.
- Company purchases stock monthly with OCPs.
- Dividends are paid March, June, September, and December.

Performance Rating: *****
DRIP Rating: 👍

AmSouth Bancorp. (NYSE:ASO)
PO Box 11007
Birmingham, AL 35288
(800) 284-4100   (205) 320-7151

Business Profile: Largest banking institution headquartered in Alabama. Serves customers through 311 banking offices in four southeastern states and 63 mortgage banking offices in nine southeastern states.

Plan Specifics:
- Partial dividend reinvestment is available.
- No Discount.
- OCP: $10 to $5000 per quarter.
- Company purchases stock quarterly with OCPs.
- Selling costs are brokerage commissions, an agent's fee, and transfer tax.
- Dividends are paid January, April, July, and October.

Performance Rating: ***
DRIP Rating: 👍

**AmVestors Financial Corp.
(NYSE:AMV)
415 S.W. 8th Ave.
PO Box 2039
Topeka, KS 66603
(913) 232-6945**

Business Profile: Insurance holding company selling single-premium deferred annuities and single-premium whole life insurance.
Plan Specifics:

- Partial dividend reinvestment is not available.
- No Discount.
- OCP: $25 to $2500 per quarter.
- Stock is purchased quarterly with OCPs.
- Purchasing fees are very nominal brokerage fees.
- Selling costs are very nominal brokerage commissions and $1 service fee for withdrawal.
- Dividends are paid January, April, July, October.

Performance Rating: **
DRIP Rating: 👍

**Angeles Mortgage Investment
Trust (ASE:ANM)
2049 Century Park E.
Los Angeles, CA 90067
(800) 526-0801**

Business Profile: Real estate investment trust.
Plan Specifics:

- Partial dividend reinvestment is available.
- No Discount.
- OCP: $25 to no maximum per month.
- Purchasing costs are nominal brokerage fees.
- Selling costs are brokerage

commissions plus a $5 fee.
- The company is not currently paying a dividend.

Performance Rating: *
DRIP Rating: 👍

**Angeles Participating Mortgage
Trust (ASE:APT)
2049 Century Park E.
Los Angeles, CA 90067
(800) 526-0801**

Business Profile: Real estate investment trust making participating mortgage loans on factory-direct shopping malls.
Plan Specifics:

- Partial dividend reinvestment is available.
- No Discount.
- OCP: $25 to no maximum per month.
- OCP is invested monthly.
- Purchasing fees are brokerage commissions.
- Selling fees include brokerage commissions plus $5 service fee.
- The company is not currently paying a dividend.

Performance Rating: *
DRIP Rating: 👍

**Angelica Corp. (NYSE:AGL)
424 S. Woods Mill Rd.
Chesterfield, MO 63017
(314) 231-9300**

Business Profile: Leading manufacturer and marketer of uniforms and business career apparel.
Plan Specifics:

- Partial dividend reinvestment is not available.
- No Discount.

- OCP: $10 to $3000 per quarter.
- Selling costs are brokerage commissions and a service charge.
- Company purchases stock quarterly with OCPs.
- Dividends are paid January, April, July, and October.

Performance Rating: ***

DRIP Rating: 👍

Anheuser-Busch Cos., Inc.
(NYSE:BUD)
1 Busch Pl.
St. Louis, MO 63118
(314) 446-1357   (800) 456-9852

Business Profile: Largest brewer of beer in United States. Significant operations in bakery items and theme parks.

Plan Specifics:

- Partial dividend reinvestment is not available.
- No Discount.
- OCP: $25 to $5000 per month.
- Stock is purchased around the 9th of the month with OCPs.
- Selling costs are brokerage commissions and any other costs of sale if incurred.
- Dividends are paid March, June, September, and December.

Performance Rating: *****

DRIP Rating: 👍

Aon Corp. (NYSE:AOC)
123 N. Wacker Dr.
Chicago, IL 60606
(800) 446-2617

Business Profile: Insurance holding company whose operating subsidiaries engage in commercial insurance and reinsurance broker-

age, benefits consulting, and the underwriting of accident, disability, life, and specialty property-casualty insurance.

Plan Specifics:

- Partial dividend reinvestment is not available.
- No Discount.
- OCP: $20 to $1000 per month.
- Stock is purchased monthly with OCPs.
- Selling costs are brokerage fees.
- Dividends are paid February, May, August, and November.

Performance Rating: ****

DRIP Rating: 👍

Apache Corp. (NYSE:APA)
2000 Post Oak Blvd., Ste. 100
Houston, TX 77056
(713) 296-6504   (800) 272-2434

Business Profile: Independent oil and gas company involved in exploration, production, and marketing crude oil and natural gas.

Plan Specifics:

- Partial dividend reinvestment is available.
- No Discount.
- OCP: $50 to $5000 per quarter.
- Stock is purchased monthly with OCPs.
- Selling costs are brokerage fees and a nominal withdrawal fee.
- Approximately 4000 shareholders are in the plan.
- Dividends are paid January, April, July, and October.

Performance Rating: **

DRIP Rating: 👍

Aquarion Co. (NYSE:WTR)
835 Main St.
Bridgeport, CT 06601
(800) 526-0801

Business Profile: Public water supply and environmental testing laboratories are the principal businesses.

Plan Specifics:
- Partial dividend reinvestment is not available.
- 5 percent discount on reinvested dividends and OCPs.
- OCP: $10 to $5000 per quarter.
- Selling costs are brokerage commissions and a $5 service charge.
- Company purchases stock monthly with OCPs.
- Approximately 3500 shareholders are in the plan.
- Dividends are paid January, April, July, and October.

Performance Rating: ***
DRIP Rating: 👍

ARCO Chemical Co.
(NYSE:RCM)
3801 W. Chester Pike
Newtown Square, PA 19073
(800) 446-2617   (215) 359-2000

Business Profile: Produces specialty chemicals including propylene oxide, styrene monomer and polymers, and oxygenated fuels.

Plan Specifics:
- Partial dividend reinvestment is not available.
- No Discount.
- OCP: $10 to $12,000 per year.
- Stock is purchased monthly with OCPs.

- Selling costs are a $5 handling charge, brokerage commissions, and any other costs of sale.
- Dividends are paid March, June, September, and December.

Performance Rating: ***
DRIP Rating: 👍

Armstrong World Industries, Inc.
(NYSE:ACK)
313 W. Liberty St.
PO Box 3001
Lancaster, PA 17604
(717) 396-2810

Business Profile: Leading residential and commercial manufacturer of interior furnishings, including floor coverings, building products, and furniture.

Plan Specifics:
- Partial dividend reinvestment is available.
- No Discount.
- OCP: $50 to $3000 per month.
- Stock is purchased monthly with OCPs.
- Selling costs are brokerage fees and a $5 handling fee.
- Approximately 2600 shareholders are in the plan.
- Dividends are paid March, June, September, and December.

Performance Rating: ****
DRIP Rating: 👍

Arnold Industries, Inc.
(NASDAQ:AIND)
625 S. Fifth Ave.
Lebanon, PA 17042
(717) 274-2521

Business Profile: Trucking company that provides less-than-truckload, truckload, and warehouse services mainly in the northeastern United States.

Plan Specifics:
- Partial dividend reinvestment is not available.
- No Discount.
- OCP: $25 to $3000 per quarter.
- There are no costs for selling shares from the plan.
- Company purchases stock quarterly with OCPs.
- Dividends are paid March, June, September, and December.

Performance Rating: ****
DRIP Rating: 👍

Arrow Financial Corp.
 (NASDAQ:AROW)
250 Glen St.
PO Box 2161
Glen Falls, NY 12801
(518) 745-1000   (518) 793-4121

Business Profile: Regional banking company with offices in New York and Vermont.

Plan Specifics:
- Initial purchase of stock may be made directly from the company ($300 minimum).
- Partial dividend reinvestment is not available.
- No Discount.
- OCP: $50 to $10,000 per quarter.
- Selling costs are brokerage commission.
- Company purchases stock monthly with OCPs.
- Dividends are paid March, June, September, and December.

Performance Rating: ***
DRIP Rating: 👍

Arvin Industries, Inc.
 (NYSE:ARV)
1 Noblitt Plaza
Box 3000
Columbus, IN 47202
(812) 379-3000   (312) 461-3310

Business Profile: Manufacturer of automotive parts to original equipment and replacement markets.

Plan Specifics:
- Partial dividend reinvestment is not available.
- No Discount.
- OCP: $25 to $1000 per month.
- Purchasing fees include 5 percent service charge for each amount invested up to a maximum $2.50 plus pro rata brokerage fees.
- Selling fees are brokerage commissions.
- Dividends are paid March, June, September, and December.

Performance Rating: ***
DRIP Rating: 👍

ASARCO, Inc. (NYSE:AR)
180 Maiden Ln.
New York, NY 10038
(800) 524-4458   (212) 510-2000

Business Profile: Operations in copper, silver, and other metals, as well as specialty chemicals.

Plan Specifics:
- Partial dividend reinvestment is available.
- No Discount.
- OCP: $25 to $1000 per month.
- Stock is purchased monthly with OCPs.
- Selling costs are brokerage

commissions and any other costs of sale.

- Dividends are paid March, June, September, and December.

Performance Rating: ***

DRIP Rating: 👍

Ashland Coal, Inc. (NYSE:ACI)
2205 5th St. Rd.
Huntington, WV 25701
(800) 446-2617   (304) 526-3333

Business Profile: Producer of low sulfur bituminous coal in the central Appalachian region of the United States.

Plan Specifics:

- Partial dividend reinvestment is not available.
- No Discount.
- OCP: $10 to $20,000 per year.
- Selling costs are brokerage commissions, a $5 handling fee, and other costs of sale.
- Company purchases stock monthly with OCPs.
- Dividends are paid March, June, September, and December.

Performance Rating: ***

DRIP Rating: 👍

Ashland, Inc. (NYSE:ASH)
PO Box 391
Ashland, KY 41114
(606) 329-3333   (312) 461-2288

Business Profile: Leading petroleum refiner providing motor oil and chemicals.

Plan Specifics:

- Partial dividend reinvestment is not available.
- No Discount.
- OCP: $10 to $5000 per quarter.

- Stock is purchased quarterly with OCPs.
- Selling costs are brokerage commissions.
- Approximately 10,500 shareholders in plan.
- Dividends are paid March, June, September, and December.

Performance Rating: ***

DRIP Rating: 👍

ASR Investments Corp. (ASE:ASR)
335 N. Wilmot, Ste. 250
Tucson, AZ 85711
(800) 851-9677

Business Profile: Real estate investment trust.

Plan Specifics:

- Partial dividend reinvestment is available.
- No Discount.
- OCP: $250 to $100,000 per quarter.
- Stock is purchased quarterly with OCPs.
- Selling costs are brokerage commissions and $15 fee.
- $5 fee for issuing certificates.
- $3 certificate safekeeping fee.
- Dividends are paid March, June, September, and December.

Performance Rating: **

DRIP Rating: 👎

Asset Investors Corp. (NYSE:AIC)
3600 S. Yosemite, Ste. 900
Denver, CO 80237
(303) 793-2703

Business Profile: Real estate investment trust.

Plan Specifics:

- Partial dividend reinvestment is

not available.
- No Discount.
- OCP: $50 to $10,000 per quarter.
- Selling costs are brokerage commissions and a $5 termination charge.
- Company will reinvest OCPs within 30 days of receipt.
- Dividends are usually paid January, April, July, and October.

Performance Rating: *

DRIP Rating: 👍

Associated Banc-Corp.
(NASDAQ:ASBC)
112 N. Adams St.
Green Bay, WI 54301
(312) 461-5545   (414) 433-3166
(800) 236-2722

Business Profile: Third largest commercial bank holding company in Wisconsin with banks in Illinois and Wisconsin.

Plan Specifics:
- Partial dividend reinvestment is available.
- No Discount.
- OCP: not available.
- Dividends are paid February, May, August, and November.

Performance Rating: ****

DRIP Rating: 👎

AT&T Corp. (NYSE:T)
32 Avenue of the Americas
New York, NY 10013
(800) 348-8288

Business Profile: Major services include long-distance calling, data communications, and international telecommunications with operations in manufacturing and

marketing telecommunications equipment.

Plan Specifics:
- Need 10 shares to participate in the plan.
- Partial dividend reinvestment is available.
- No Discount.
- OCP: $100 to $50,000 per year.
- Purchases stock with OCPs every month.
- An account activity fee of the lesser of $1 or 10 percent of the amount invested during the month will be charged for each month during which a plan investment is made.
- Selling costs are brokerage commissions.
- Dividends are paid February, May, August, and November.

Performance Rating: *****

DRIP Rating: 👍

Atlanta Gas Light Co.
(NYSE:ATG)
303 Peachtree St., NE
PO Box 4569
Atlanta, GA 30302
(800) 633-4236

Business Profile: Largest natural gas utility in the southeastern portion of the United States.

Plan Specifics:
- Partial dividend reinvestment is available.
- No Discount.
- OCP: $25 to $5000 per month.
- Stock is purchased monthly with OCPs, generally on the first business day of the month.
- Selling costs include brokerage fees and transfer taxes.

- Dividends are paid March, June, September, and December.

Performance Rating: ****

DRIP Rating: 👍

Atlantic Energy, Inc. (NYSE:ATE)
6801 Black Horse Pike
PO Box 1334
Pleasantville, NJ 08232
(609) 645-4506

Business Profile: Public utility holding company located in New Jersey.

Plan Specifics:

- Initial purchases of stock may be made directly from the company (minimum $250).
- Partial dividend reinvestment is available.
- No Discount.
- OCP: no minimum to $100,000 per year.
- Fees include small brokerage commissions when stock is purchased on open market.
- Stock is purchased monthly with OCPs.
- Selling costs are brokerage fees if sold on open market but not for shares sold to other participants in plan.
- Automatic investment services are available.
- Direct deposit of dividends is available.
- Safekeeping services are available.
- Approximately 23,400 shareholders are in the plan.
- Dividends are paid January, April, July, and October.

Performance Rating: ***

DRIP Rating: 👍

Atlantic Richfield Co.
(NYSE:ARC)
515 S. Flower St.
Los Angeles, CA 90071
(800) 446-2617   (213) 486-3593

Business Profile: Refines, produces, and markets crude oil and natural gas.

Plan Specifics:

- Partial dividend reinvestment is available.
- No Discount.
- OCP: $10 to $60,000 per year.
- Stock is purchased monthly with OCPs.
- Selling costs are brokerage commission, transfer taxes, and any other costs of sale.
- Preferred stock dividends are eligible for reinvestment for additional common under the plan.
- Shares can be sold via the telephone.
- Dividends are paid March, June, September, and December.

Performance Rating: ****

DRIP Rating: 👍

Atmos Energy Corp. (NYSE:ATO)
PO Box 650205
Dallas, TX 75265-0205
(800) 382-8667   (800) 543-3038

Business Profile: Supplies natural gas to residential, industrial, agricultural, and commercial users in parts of Kentucky, Louisiana, Texas, Colorado, Kansas, and Missouri.

Plan Specifics:

- Initial purchases may be made from the company (minimum $200).

- Partial dividend reinvestment is available.
- 3 percent discount on reinvested dividends.
- OCP: $25 to $100,000 per year.
- Stock is purchased every Monday with OCPs.
- Selling costs are brokerage commissions, a $5 fee, and any other costs of sale.
- Automatic investment services are available.
- IRA option is available.
- Safekeeping services are available.
- Dividends are paid March, June, September, and December.

Performance Rating: ****
DRIP Rating: 👍

Avery Dennison Corp. (NYSE:AVY)
150 N. Orange Grove Blvd.
Pasadena, CA 91103
(800) 522-6645

Business Profile: Worldwide leader in self-adhesive base materials, labels, and office products.
Plan Specifics:

- Partial dividend reinvestment is not available.
- No Discount.
- OCP: $25 to $3000 per month.
- Company purchases stock monthly with OCPs.
- No selling costs.
- Dividends are paid March, June, September, and December.

Performance Rating: ****
DRIP Rating: 👍

Avnet, Inc. (NYSE:AVT)
80 Cutter Mill Rd.
Great Neck, NY 11021
(516) 466-7000   (800) 524-4458

Business Profile: Distributes electronic components, computers, and computer parts. Manufactures and distributes satellite television antennae and electrical motors.
Plan Specifics:

- Partial dividend reinvestment is available.
- No Discount.
- OCP: $10 to no maximum, in increments of $10 per payment.
- Stock is purchased eight times a year with OCPs.
- Selling costs are $1 handling charge, brokerage commission, and any other costs of sale.
- Dividends are paid January, April, July, and October.

Performance Rating: ****
DRIP Rating: 👍

Avon Products, Inc. (NYSE:AVP)
9 W. 57th St.
New York, NY 10019
(201) 324-0498

Business Profile: Direct seller of beauty and related products.
Plan Specifics:

- Partial dividend reinvestment is not available.
- No Discount.
- OCP: $10 to $5000 per month.
- Stock is purchased on the 1st business day of the month with OCPs.
- Selling costs are brokerage commissions and any other costs of sale.

- Dividends are paid March, June, September, and December.

Performance Rating: ***

DRIP Rating: 👍

Baker Hughes, Inc. (NYSE:BHI)
3900 Essex Ln.
Houston, TX 77027-5177
(800) 446-2617   (713) 439-8668

Business Profile: Manufactures equipment used in drilling oil and gas wells. Produces equipment for pumping and treating liquids.

Plan Specifics:
- Partial dividend reinvestment is not available.
- No Discount.
- OCP: $10 to $1000 per quarter.
- Stock is purchased quarterly with OCPs.
- Selling costs are approximately 10 cents per share plus a $5 service charge.
- Dividends are paid February, May, August, and November.

Performance Rating: ****

DRIP Rating: 👍

Baldwin Technology Company, Inc. (ASE:BLD)
65 Rowayton Ave.
Rowayton, CT 06853
(203) 838-7470   (617) 575-2900

Business Profile: Leading multinational manufacturer of material handling, accessory, control, and pre-press equipment for the printing industry.

Plan Specifics:
- Partial dividend reinvestment is not available.
- No Discount.
- OCP: not available.

- Selling fees include brokerage commissions.
- Certificate safekeeping is available.
- The company is not currently paying a dividend.

Performance Rating: **

DRIP Rating: 👍

Ball Corp. (NYSE:BLL)
345 S. High St.
PO Box 2407
Muncie, IN 47307-0407
(317) 747-6100   (800) 446-2617

Business Profile: Manufactures and markets packaging products and provides aerospace systems and professional services to the federal sector.

Plan Specifics:
- Partial dividend reinvestment is not available.
- 5 percent discount on reinvested dividends.
- OCP: $25 to $3000 per quarter.
- Stock is purchased quarterly with OCPs.
- Selling costs are brokerage commissions plus transfer fee.
- Approximately 3200 shareholders in plan.
- Dividends are paid March, June, September, and December.

Performance Rating: ***

DRIP Rating: 👍

Baltimore Gas and Electric Co. (NYSE:BGE)
PO Box 1475
Baltimore, MD 21203-1475
(800) 258-0499

Business Profile: Electric and gas utility serving central Maryland.

Plan Specifics:

- Partial dividend reinvestment is available.
- No Discount.
- OCP: $10 to $100,000 per year.
- Stock is purchased monthly with OCPs.
- Nominal purchasing fees when stock is bought on open market.
- Must go through own broker to sell shares.
- 44 percent of common shareholders are in the plan.
- Dividends are paid January, April, July, and October.

Performance Rating: ****

DRIP Rating: 👍

Banc One Corp. (NYSE:ONE)
PO Box 7700
111 Monument Circle, Ste. 1611
Indianapolis, IN 46277-0116
(317) 321-8110   (800) 573-4048

Business Profile: Major bank holding company deals in retail banking, including extensive credit card processing operations.

Plan Specifics:

- Partial dividend reinvestment is not available.
- No Discount.
- OCP: $10 to $5000 per quarter.
- Selling costs may include brokerage fees and $1 liquidation fee.
- Company purchases stock quarterly with OCPs.
- Dividends are paid March, June, September, and December.

Performance Rating: ****

DRIP Rating: 👍

Bancorp Hawaii, Inc.
(NYSE:BOH)
130 Merchant St.
Honolulu, HI 96813
(808) 537-8239

Business Profile: Holding company for the largest commercial bank in Hawaii.

Plan Specifics:

- Partial dividend reinvestment is available.
- No Discount.
- OCP: $25 to $5000 per quarter.
- Company purchases stock on the 10th business day of each month with OCPs.
- Selling costs include brokerage commissions, applicable taxes, and service charges.
- Hawaii state residents may make initial purchases of stock directly through the company (minimum $250).
- Approximately 4000 shareholders are in the plan.
- Dividends are paid March, June, September, and December.

Performance Rating: ****

DRIP Rating: 👍

BancorpSouth, Inc.
(NASDAQ:BOMS)
One Mississippi Plaza
Tupelo, MS 38801
(601) 680-2000

Business Profile: Bank holding company with operations in Mississippi and Tennessee.

Plan Specifics:

- Partial dividend reinvestment is not available.
- No Discount.
- OCP: $25 to $5000 per quarter.

- There are no fees for selling shares from the plan.
- Company purchases stock quarterly with OCPs.
- Dividends are paid January, April, July, and October.

Performance Rating: ****

DRIP Rating: 👍

Bandag, Inc. (NYSE:BDG)
c/o First National
 Bank of Boston
PO Box 1681
Boston, MA 02105-1681
(800) 730-4001

Business Profile: Leading manufacturer of precured tread rubber used in the process of retreading truck and bus tires.

Plan Specifics:

- Partial dividend reinvestment is available.
- No Discount.
- OCP: $50 to $10,000 per quarter.
- Selling costs are brokerage commissions, transfer taxes, and a 5 percent service charge (minimum $1; maximum $5).
- Company purchases stock twice quarterly with OCPs.
- Dividends are paid January, April, July, and October.

Performance Rating: ****

DRIP Rating: 👍

Bando McGlocklin Capital Corp.
 (NASDAQ:BMCC)
c/o First Wisconsin Trust Co.
777 E. Wisconsin Ave.
Milwaukee, WI 53202
(800) 637-7549

Business Profile: Diversified closed-end investment concern that makes loans to and investments in small businesses.

Plan Specifics:

- Partial dividend reinvestment is available.
- No Discount.
- OCP: $25 to $3000 per quarter.
- Selling costs are brokerage commissions.
- Company purchases stock quarterly with OCPs.
- Dividends are paid January, April, July, and October.

Performance Rating: ***

DRIP Rating: 👍

Bangor Hydro-Electric Co.
 (NYSE:BGR)
PO Box 1599
33 State St.
Bangor, ME 04401-1599
(207) 945-5621

Business Profile: Second largest electric utility in Maine, serving the eastern portion of the state.

Plan Specifics:

- Partial dividend reinvestment is available.
- No Discount.
- OCP: $25 to $25,000 per year.
- Selling costs are brokerage commissions.
- Stock is purchased quarterly with OCPs.
- Preferred dividends may be reinvested for additional common shares under the plan.
- Dividends are paid January, April, July, and October.

Performance Rating: **

DRIP Rating: 👍

Bank of Boston Corp.
 (NYSE:BKB)
c/o Bank of Boston
PO Box 1681
Boston, MA 02105
(800) 442-2001

Business Profile: Bank holding company in New England region.

Plan Specifics:

- Partial dividend reinvestment is available.
- 3 percent discount on reinvested dividends.
- OCP: $25 to $5000 per month.
- Stock is purchased monthly with OCPs.
- Selling costs are brokerage commissions and transfer taxes.
- Company will only sell up to 1000 shares and will sell within roughly 10 trading days after receiving request to sell.
- Preferred stock dividends may be reinvested for additional common shares under the plan.
- Dividends are paid February, May, August, and November.

Performance Rating: ***

DRIP Rating: 👍

Bank of Granite Corp.
 (NASDAQ:GRAN)
Investor Relations Dept.
PO Box 128
Granite Falls, NC 28630
(704) 496-2000

Business Profile: North Carolina bank holding company.

Plan Specifics:

- Partial dividend reinvestment is not available.
- No Discount.

- OCP: not available.
- Must go through own broker to sell shares.
- Approximately 960 shareholders are in the plan.
- Dividends are paid January, April, July, and October.

Performance Rating: ***

DRIP Rating: 👎

Bank of New York Co., Inc.
 (NYSE:BK)
Attn: Dividend Reinvestment
PO Box 11260, Church St. Sta.
New York, NY 10277-0760
(800) 524-4458

Business Profile: Commercial and retail banking in New York City and suburbs. Active in securities clearing and processing.

Plan Specifics:

- Partial dividend reinvestment is not available.
- No Discount.
- OCP: $25 to no maximum.
- Selling costs include brokerage fees and $2.50 service fee per transaction.
- Company purchases stock monthly with OCPs.
- Interest on debt securities is eligible for reinvestment for additional common shares under the plan.
- Dividends are paid February, May, August, and November.

Performance Rating: ***

DRIP Rating: 👍

Bank South Corp.
 (NASDAQ:BKSO)
c/o Chemical Mellon
PO Box 750
Pittsburgh, PA 15230
(800) 756-3353

Business Profile: Multibank holding company headquartered in Atlanta with offices throughout Georgia.

Plan Specifics:
- Partial dividend reinvestment is available.
- No Discount.
- OCP: $25 to $5000 per month.
- Company purchases stock monthly with OCPs.
- Selling costs are a $5 fee, any brokerage charges or applicable taxes.
- Dividends are paid January, April, July, and October.

Performance Rating: ***
DRIP Rating: 👍

BankAmerica Corp. (NYSE:BAC)
c/o Chemical Bank
Attn: Dividend Reinvestment
JAF Bldg., PO Box 3069
New York, NY 10116-3069
(800) 642-9880

Business Profile: Holding company for banks in California, Illinois, and Washington.

Plan Specifics:
- Partial dividend reinvestment is available.
- No Discount.
- OCP: $100 to $10,000 per month.
- Stock is purchased monthly with OCPs.
- No selling fees.
- Dividends are paid March, June, September, and December.

Performance Rating: ***
DRIP Rating: 👍

Bankers First Corp.
 (NASDAQ:BNKF)
Attn: Office of the Secretary
One 10th St.
Augusta, GA 30901
(706) 849-3200   (800) 446-2617

Business Profile: Georgia-based savings and loan institution.

Plan Specifics:
- Partial dividend reinvestment is not available.
- 5 percent discount on reinvested dividends.
- OCP: $50 to $5000 per quarter.
- Stock is purchased around the 15th day of the month with OCPs.
- Selling costs are brokerage commission and any transfer taxes.
- Dividends are paid February, May, August, and November.

Performance Rating: ***
DRIP Rating: 👍

Bankers Trust New York Corp.
 (NYSE:BT)
PO Box 9050, Church St. Sta.
New York, NY 10249
(800) 547-9794

Business Profile: Bank holding company. Concentrates efforts on commercial services with significant international business.

Plan Specifics:
- Partial dividend reinvestment is available.
- No Discount.
- OCP: $25 to $5000 per month.

- Stock is purchased monthly with OCPs.
- Selling costs are brokerage fees and transfer taxes.
- Dividends are paid January, April, July, and October.

Performance Rating: ***

DRIP Rating: 👍

**Banknorth Group, Inc.
 (NASDAQ:BKNG)
300 Financial Plaza
PO Box 5420
Burlington, VT 05401
(800) 526-0801   (802) 658-2492**

Business Profile: Largest bank holding company in Vermont.

Plan Specifics:

- Partial dividend reinvestment is not available.
- No Discount.
- OCP: $100 to $5000 per quarter.
- Stock is purchased quarterly with OCPs.
- Selling costs are brokerage commissions and any fees.
- Dividends are paid March, June, September, and December.

Performance Rating: ***

DRIP Rating: 👍

**BanPonce Corp.
 (NASDAQ:BPOP)
209 Munoz Rivera Ave.
Hato Rey, PR 00936
(809) 765-9800**

Business Profile: Bank holding company which operates nearly 200 branches in Puerto Rico and on the U.S. mainland.

Plan Specifics:

- Partial dividend reinvestment is available.
- 5 percent discount on reinvested dividends.
- OCP: $25 to $10,000 per month.
- There are no costs for selling shares from the plan.
- Company purchases stock monthly with OCPs.
- Puerto Rican residents may purchase initial shares directly from the company (minimum $25).
- Dividends are paid January, April, July, and October.

Performance Rating: ****

DRIP Rating: 👍

**Banta Corp. (NASDAQ:BNTA)
c/o First Wisconsin Trust Co.
PO Box 2054
Milwaukee, WI 53201
(414) 765-5000   (414) 722-7777**

Business Profile: Provides printing and graphic arts services.

Plan Specifics:

- Partial dividend reinvestment is available.
- No Discount.
- OCP: $25 to $7500 per quarter.
- Stock is purchased monthly with OCPs.
- Selling costs are brokerage commissions.
- Automatic investment services are available.
- Dividends are paid January, April, July, and October.

Performance Rating: ****

DRIP Rating: 👍

Bard (C.R.), Inc. (NYSE:BCR)
c/o First Chicago Trust Co.-NY
PO Box 2533
Jersey City, NJ 07303-2533
(800) 446-2617

Business Profile: Supplies medical, diagnostic, and surgical products and is the largest manufacturer of urological products.
Plan Specifics:
- Partial dividend reinvestment is available.
- No Discount.
- OCP: $10 to $5000 per month.
- Stock is purchased monthly with OCPs.
- Selling costs are brokerage fees and any other costs of sale.
- Dividends are paid February, May, August, and November.

Performance Rating: *****
DRIP Rating: 👍

Barnes Group, Inc. (NYSE:B)
123 Main St., PO Box 489
Bristol, CT 06011-0489
(203) 583-7070   (800) 288-9541

Business Profile: World's largest producer of precision mechanical springs; significant operations in aerospace component production and repair for jet engines and air frames.
Plan Specifics:
- Partial dividend reinvestment is not available.
- No Discount.
- OCP: $10 to $10,000 per quarter.
- Stock is purchased at least quarterly with OCPs.
- Selling costs are brokerage commissions.

- Dividends are paid March, June, September, and December.

Performance Rating: ***
DRIP Rating: 👍

Barnett Banks, Inc. (NYSE:BBI)
c/o Shareholder Services Dept.
PO Box 40789
Jacksonville, FL 32203-0789
(800) 328-5822

Business Profile: Largest bank holding company in Florida.
Plan Specifics:
- Initial purchases may be made directly from the company ($250 minimum investment).
- Partial dividend reinvestment is available.
- No Discount.
- OCP: $25 to $10,000 per month.
- Selling costs are brokerage commissions.
- Company purchases stock on the first and fifteenth of the month with OCPs.
- Automatic investment services are available.
- IRA option is available.
- Direct deposit of dividends is available.
- Preferred stock dividends may be reinvested for additional common shares.
- Approximately 25,100 shareholders are in the plan.
- Dividends are paid January, April, July, and October.

Performance Rating: ****
DRIP Rating: 👍

Bausch & Lomb, Inc.
 (NYSE:BOL)
Shareholder Relations
PO Box 54, 1 Lincoln First Sq.
Rochester, NY 14601-0054
(716) 338-6025   (800) 730-4001

Business Profile: Manufacturer of health-care products and optical devices. Leading producer of contact lenses and related accessories.

Plan Specifics:
- Partial dividend reinvestment is not available.
- No Discount.
- OCP: $25 to $60,000 per year.
- Stock is purchased monthly with OCPs.
- Selling costs are brokerage fees and transfer taxes plus a nominal service fee.
- Dividends are paid January, April, July, and October.

Performance Rating: ****
DRIP Rating: 👍

Baxter International, Inc.
 (NYSE:BAX)
Stockholder Services Dept.
One Baxter Parkway
Deerfield, IL 60015
(800) 446-2617   (708) 948-2000

Business Profile: Worldwide leading manufacturer and marketer of health-care products, systems, and services.

Plan Specifics:
- Partial dividend reinvestment is available.
- No Discount.
- OCP: $25 to $25,000 per year.
- Stock is purchased monthly with OCPs.

- Cost of selling shares includes brokerage fees.
- Dividends are paid January, April, July, and October.

Performance Rating: ****
DRIP Rating: 👍

Bay State Gas Co. (NYSE:BGC)
c/o First Nat'l Bank of Boston
PO Box 1681
Boston, MA 02105
(508) 836-7000   (800) 736-3001

Business Profile: Natural gas distributor in Massachusetts and neighboring areas.

Plan Specifics:
- Partial dividend reinvestment is available.
- No Discount.
- OCP: $10 to $2000 per month.
- Selling costs are brokerage fees.
- Company purchases stock monthly with OCPs.
- Dividends are paid March, June, September, and December.

Performance Rating: ****
DRIP Rating: 👍

Bay View Capital Corp.
 (NASDAQ:BVFS)
2121 S. El Camino Real
San Mateo, CA 94403
(415) 573-7300

Business Profile: Savings and loan holding company.

Plan Specifics:
- Partial dividend reinvestment is available.
- 5 percent discount on reinvested dividends.
- OCP: not available.

- Selling costs are brokerage commissions and a $15 fee.
- Dividends are paid January, April, July, and October.

Performance Rating: **

DRIP Rating: 👎

BayBanks, Inc. (NASDAQ:BBNK)
Shareholder Relations
175 Federal St.
Boston, MA 02110
(617) 482-1040

Business Profile: Multibank holding company headquartered in Boston.

Plan Specifics:

- Partial dividend reinvestment is not available.
- No Discount.
- OCP: $10 to $1000 per month.
- Stock is purchased monthly with OCPs.
- Purchasing fees are low brokerage commissions.
- Selling costs are brokerage commissions plus a handling fee of 5 percent on net proceeds not to exceed $2.50.
- Safekeeping services are available.
- Dividends are paid March, June, September, and December.

Performance Rating: ***

DRIP Rating: 👍

BCE, Inc. (NYSE:BCE)
1000 rue de La Gauchetiere Ouest
Bureau 3700
Montreal, Quebec H3B 4Y7
Canada
(514) 397-7310

Business Profile: Canada's largest telecommunications company.

Plan Specifics:

- Partial dividend reinvestment is not available.
- No Discount.
- OCP: no minimum to $20,000 (Canadian) per year.
- Stock is purchased monthly with OCPs.
- Selling fees are nominal brokerage commissions.
- Dividends paid on preferred shares of BCE and interest paid on Bell Canada bonds may be used to purchase additional common.
- Dividends are paid January, April, July, and October.

Performance Rating: ***

DRIP Rating: 👍

Beckman Instruments, Inc.
(NYSE:BEC)
2500 Harbor Blvd.
Box 3100
Fullerton, CA 92634-3100
(714) 871-4848   (212) 791-6422
(201) 324-0498

Business Profile: One of the world's leading manufacturers of laboratory instruments.

Plan Specifics:

- Partial dividend reinvestment is available.
- No Discount.
- OCP: $10 to $60,000 per year.
- Company purchases stock monthly with OCPs.
- Selling fees include brokerage commissions, a handling charge, and any other costs of sale.
- Safekeeping services are available.
- Shares may be sold via the telephone.

- Dividends are paid March, June, September, and December.

Performance Rating: ***

DRIP Rating: 👍

Becton, Dickinson and Company (NYSE:BDX)
c/o First Chicago Trust-NY
PO Box 13531
Newark, NJ 07188
(800) 446-2617   (201) 847-7178

Business Profile: Produces and markets medical supplies and devices and diagnostic systems.

Plan Specifics:

- Partial dividend reinvestment is not available.
- No Discount.
- OCP: $50 to $5000 per month.
- Stock is purchased monthly with OCPs.
- Selling costs are brokerage commissions and related expenses.
- Safekeeping services are available.
- Shares may be sold via the telephone.
- Dividends are paid March, June, September, and December.

Performance Rating: *****

DRIP Rating: 👍

Bedford Property Investors, Inc. (NYSE:BED)
270 Lafayette Circle
Lafayette, CA 94549
(510) 283-8910

Business Profile: Real estate investment trust.

Plan Specifics:

- Partial dividend reinvestment is not available.
- No Discount.
- OCP: $25 to $5000 per quarter.
- Stock is purchased quarterly with OCPs.
- Selling costs are brokerage commissions.
- Dividends are paid January, April, July, and November.

Performance Rating: *

DRIP Rating: 👍

Bell Atlantic Corp. (NYSE:BEL)
1717 Arch St.
Philadelphia, PA 19103
(215) 963-6000   (800) 631-2355

Business Profile: Telephone holding company supplying exchange telephone service to mid-Atlantic states.

Plan Specifics:

- 10 share minimum in order to enter plan.
- Partial dividend reinvestment is available.
- No Discount.
- OCP: $100 to $100,000 per year.
- Stock is purchased weekly with OCPs.
- Participants are charged $1 fee per quarter.
- Selling costs are brokerage fees, transaction fees, and transfer tax.
- Automatic investment services are available.
- Dividends are paid February, May, August, and November.

Performance Rating: *****

DRIP Rating: 👍

BellSouth Corp. (NYSE:BLS)
c/o Chemical Bank
PO Box 24611, Church St. Stat.
New York, NY 10249-0018
(800) 631-6001

Business Profile: Second-largest telephone holding company providing local exchange service to southeastern states.

Plan Specifics:

- Must have at least 10 shares in order to enroll in the plan.
- Partial dividend reinvestment is available.
- No Discount.
- OCP: $50 to $100,000 per year.
- Selling costs include brokerage fees, a termination fee, and any transfer taxes.
- Company purchases stock monthly with OCPs.
- Dividends are paid February, May, August, and November.

Performance Rating: *****
DRIP Rating: 👍

Bemis Co., Inc. (NYSE:BMS)
c/o Norwest Bank Minnesota
PO Box 738
South St. Paul, MN 55075-0738
(612) 450-4064   (612) 376-3000

Business Profile: Manufactures consumer and industrial flexible packaging products and pressure-sensitive materials.

Plan Specifics:

- Partial dividend reinvestment is not available.
- No Discount.
- OCP: $25 to $10,000 per quarter.
- Company purchases stock monthly with OCPs.

- Dividends are paid March, June, September, and December.

Performance Rating: ****
DRIP Rating: 👍

Beneficial Corp. (NYSE:BNL)
c/o First Chicago Trust-NY
PO Box 2500
Jersey City, NJ 07303-2500
(800) 446-2617   (302) 425-2500

Business Profile: Consumer-oriented financial institution providing loans for education, home improvement, and debt consolidation.

Plan Specifics:

- Partial dividend reinvestment is not available.
- No Discount.
- OCP: $10 to $1000 per month.
- Stock is purchased monthly with OCPs.
- Selling costs are brokerage commissions and other costs of sale.
- Preferred dividends are eligible for reinvestment for additional common shares under the plan.
- Dividends are paid March, June, September, and December.

Performance Rating: ****
DRIP Rating: 👍

Berkshire Gas Co.
** (NASDAQ:BGAS)**
Attn: Sec. of Dividend
** Reinvestment**
115 Cheshire Rd.
Pittsfield, MA 01201
(413) 442-1511

Business Profile: Massachusetts public utility produces and markets natural gas for residential, commercial, and industrial markets.

Plan Specifics:

- Need at least 10 shares to enroll.
- Partial dividend reinvestment is available.
- 3 percent discount on reinvested dividends and OCPs.
- OCP: $15 to $3000 per quarter.
- Stock is purchased on 15th of each month with OCPs.
- Selling costs are 5 percent on amount invested with a $5 maximum plus brokerage commissions.
- Dividends are paid January, April, July, and October.

Performance Rating: **

DRIP Rating: 👍

Berkshire Realty Company, Inc.
 (NYSE:BRI)
470 Atlantic Ave.
Boston, MA 02210
(617) 423-2233   (800) 343-0989

Business Profile: Real estate investment trust which owns and operates a number of apartments and shopping centers.

Plan Specifics:

- Partial dividend reinvestment is not available.
- No Discount.
- OCP: $10 minimum; no maximum.
- OCP is invested twice a month.
- Purchasing fees are $2.50 per transaction plus brokerage commissions.
- $5 service charge when selling shares.
- Dividends are paid February, May, August, and November.

Performance Rating: **

DRIP Rating: 👍

Bethlehem Steel Corp. (NYSE:BS)
c/o First Chicago Trust-NY
PO Box 2500
Jersey City, NY 07303-2500
(201) 324-0498

Business Profile: Produces steel and steel-related products.

Plan Specifics:

- Partial dividend reinvestment is not available.
- No Discount.
- OCP: $10 to $3000 per month.
- Stock is purchased around the 1st day of the month with OCPs.
- Selling costs are brokerage commissions and any other cost of sale.
- The firm does not currently pay a dividend.

Performance Rating: **

DRIP Rating: 👍

Bindley Western Industries, Inc.
 (NYSE:BDY)
4212 W. 71st St.
Indianapolis, IN 46268-2259
(317) 298-9900   (800) 753-7107

Business Profile: One of the nation's largest drug wholesalers.

Plan Specifics:

- Partial dividend reinvestment is not available.
- No Discount.
- OCP: $10 to $5000 per quarter.
- Company purchases stock quarterly with OCPs.
- Selling costs include $5 handling charge and brokerage commissions.

- Dividends are paid March, June, September, and December.

Performance Rating: ***

DRIP Rating: 👍

Birmingham Steel Corp. (NYSE:BIR)
1000 Urban Center Pkwy., Suite 300
Birmingham, AL 35242-2516
(800) 829-8432   (205) 970-1200

Business Profile: Operates mini-mills which produce steel and steel products.

Plan Specifics:

- Partial dividend reinvestment is not available.
- No Discount.
- OCP: $20 to $2000 per month.
- Stock is purchased monthly with OCPs.
- Selling costs are brokerage commissions.
- Dividends are paid February, May, August, and November.

Performance Rating: ***

DRIP Rating: 👍

Black & Decker Corp. (NYSE:BDK)
c/o First Chicago Trust Co.-NY
PO Box 2500
Jersey City, NJ 07303-2500
(800) 446-2617

Business Profile: Leading maker of power tools and household products.

Plan Specifics:

- Partial dividend reinvestment is not available.
- No Discount.
- OCP: $10 to $3000 per month.
- Stock is purchased monthly with OCPs.
- Selling costs are a $5 handling charge, brokerage commissions, and any other costs of sale.
- Shares may be sold via the telephone.
- Approximately 7850 shareholders are in the plan.
- Dividends are paid January, April, July, and October.

Performance Rating: ***

DRIP Rating: 👍

Black Hills Corp. (NYSE:BKH)
c/o Chemical Bank
PO Box 3069, JAF Bldg.
New York, NY 10116-3069
(800) 851-9677   (605) 348-1700

Business Profile: Supplies electricity to customers in South Dakota, Wyoming, and Montana.

Plan Specifics:

- Partial dividend reinvestment is not available.
- No Discount.
- OCP: $200 to $50,000 per quarter.
- Purchasing fees may include brokerage commissions and other fees.
- Company purchases stock monthly with OCPs.
- Selling costs are brokerage commissions and $15 termination fee.
- Dividends are paid March, June, September, and December.

Performance Rating: ****

DRIP Rating: 🏵

Block (H&R), Inc. (NYSE:HRB)
c/o Boatmen's Trust Co.
PO Box 14768, 510 Locust St.
St. Louis, MO 63178
(816) 753-6900   (800) 456-9852

Business Profile: Largest preparer of Federal income tax returns. Also owns CompuServe, a worldwide provider of computer services.

Plan Specifics:
- Partial dividend reinvestment is not available.
- No Discount.
- OCP: $25 to $2000 per month.
- Stock is purchased monthly with OCPs.
- Purchasing fee is very nominal broker commission.
- Selling costs are brokerage fees.
- Dividends are paid January, April, July, October.

Performance Rating: *****

DRIP Rating: 👍

Blount, Inc. (ASE:BLT.A)
c/o The Bank of Boston
PO Box 644
Boston, MA 02102-0644
(205) 244-4000   (617) 929-5445

Business Profile: Manufactures cutting chain for chain saws, tree harvesting equipment, specialty riding lawn mowers, small arms ammunition, ammunition reloading equipment, rotation bearings, and mechanical power transmission components.

Plan Specifics:
- Partial dividend reinvestment is available.
- 5 percent discount on reinvested dividends.
- OCP: $10 to $25,000 per year.

- Stock is purchased around the 1st business day of the month with OCPs.
- Selling costs may include brokerage fees.
- Dividends are paid January, April, July, and October.

Performance Rating: ***

DRIP Rating: 👍

BMJ Financial Corp.
** (NASDAQ:BMJF)**
PO Box 1001
243 Route 130
Bordentown, NJ 08505
(609) 298-5500

Business Profile: New Jersey-based bank holding company.

Plan Specifics:
- Partial dividend reinvestment is available.
- No Discount.
- OCP: $100 to $5000 per quarter.
- Company invests OCPs around the 10th day of the month.
- Must go through own broker to sell shares.
- Approximately 820 shareholders are in the plan.
- Dividends are paid January, April, July, and October.

Performance Rating: **

DRIP Rating: 👍

Boatmen's Bancshares, Inc.
** (NASDAQ:BOAT)**
c/o Boatmen's Trust Co.
510 Locust St.
St. Louis, MO 63101
(314) 466-1357

Business Profile: Multibank holding company headquartered in St.

Louis. Largest commercial banking firm in Missouri.

Plan Specifics:

- Partial dividend reinvestment is not available.
- No Discount.
- OCP: $100 to $10,000 per quarter.
- Stock is purchased quarterly with OCPs.
- Investors must sell full shares through own broker.
- Dividends are paid January, April, July, and October.

Performance Rating: ****

DRIP Rating: 👍

Bob Evans Farms, Inc. (NASDAQ:BOBE)
Stock Transfer Dept.
PO Box 07863
3776 S. High St.
Columbus, OH 43207
(614) 492-4950

Business Profile: Owns and operates over 362 Bob Evans Restaurants, Owens Family Restaurants, and Cantina del Rio Mexican restaurants. Also produces fresh and fully cooked sausage products and deli-style salads.

Plan Specifics:

- Initial purchases may be made directly from the company (minimum $50).
- Partial dividend reinvestment is available.
- No Discount.
- OCP: $10 to $10,000 per month.
- Stock is purchased bimonthly (1st and 15th) with OCPs.
- Purchasing fee is the pro rata share of brokerage commission.

- Selling cost is brokerage commission.
- Automatic investment services are available.
- Approximately 20,000 shareholders in plan.
- Dividends are paid March, June, September, and December.

Performance Rating: ****

DRIP Rating: 👍

Boddie-Noell Properties (ASE:BNP)
3710 One First Union Center
Charlotte, NC 28202
(704) 333-1367

Business Profile: Real estate investment trust which owns restaurant and apartment properties.

Plan Specifics:

- Partial dividend reinvestment is not available.
- No Discount.
- OCP: $25 to $3000 per quarter.
- Stock is purchased quarterly with OCPs.
- Purchasing costs include brokerage fees.
- Must sell through own broker.
- About 21 percent of all shareholders are enrolled in the plan.
- Dividends are paid February, May, August, and November.

Performance Rating: **

DRIP Rating: 👍

Boise Cascade Corp. (NYSE:BCC)
1111 W. Jefferson St.
Boise, ID 83702
(800) 544-6473

Business Profile: Important manufacturer of paper, wood products, and building materials.

Plan Specifics:
- Partial dividend reinvestment is not available.
- No Discount.
- OCP: $10 to no maximum per month.
- Purchasing and selling costs are less than 10 cents a share.
- Stock is purchased monthly with OCPs.
- Safekeeping is available.
- Dividends are paid January, April, July, and October.

Performance Rating: ***

DRIP Rating: 👍

Boston Bancorp (NASDAQ:SBOS)
460 W. Broadway
Boston, MA 02127
(800) 524-4458

Business Profile: Savings institution serving clients in Boston.

Plan Specifics:
- Partial dividend reinvestment is available.
- No Discount.
- OCP: $100 to $5000 per quarter.
- Minimal, if any, selling costs.
- Stock is purchased quarterly with OCPs.
- Dividends are paid March, June, September, and December.

Performance Rating: ***

DRIP Rating: 👍

Boston Edison Co. (NYSE:BSE)
800 Boylston St.
Boston, MA 02199
(617) 424-2000

Business Profile: Electric utility providing service in Boston and neighboring cities.

Plan Specifics:
- Partial dividend reinvestment is available.
- No Discount.
- OCP: $50 to $40,000 per year.
- Stock is purchased monthly with OCPs.
- Selling costs include brokerage fees and transfer tax.
- Selling will be done within 10 trading days after receipt of request.
- Customers of the utility may make initial purchases directly from the firm (minimum $500).
- Preferred stock is eligible for reinvestment for additional common shares.
- Approximately 15,000 shareholders are in the plan.
- Dividends are paid February, May, August, and November.

Performance Rating: ***

DRIP Rating: 👍

Bowater, Inc. (NYSE:BOW)
PO Box 4012
One Parklands Dr.
Darien, CT 06824
(800) 845-6002

Business Profile: Major supplier of newsprint in United States. Also manufactures coated publication paper, market pulp, and computer forms.

Plan Specifics:
- Partial dividend reinvestment is available.
- No Discount.
- OCP: $100 to $5000 per month.
- Stock is purchased monthly with OCPs.

- Selling costs include brokerage fees and transfer tax.
- Dividends are paid January, April, July, and October.

Performance Rating: ***

DRIP Rating: 👍

Bradley Real Estate, Inc.
(NYSE:BTR)
c/o First Nat'l Bank of Boston
PO Box 1681
Mail Stop 45-01-20
Boston, MA 02105-1681
(617) 575-3170

Business Profile: Trust specializing in owning and operating established income-producing commercial real estate in the Northeast and Midwest.

Plan Specifics:

- Must own at least 100 shares to participate.
- Partial dividend reinvestment is available.
- 3 percent discount on reinvested dividends.
- OCP: $100 to $2500 per quarter.
- Selling fees are brokerage commissions and a processing fee (minimum $1, maximum $10).
- Company purchases stock quarterly with OCPs.
- Dividends are paid March, June, September, and December.

Performance Rating: **

DRIP Rating: 👎

Brady (W. H.) Co.
(NASDAQ:BRCOA)
PO Box 571
Milwaukee, WI 53201-0571
(414) 332-8100

Business Profile: Manufactures a wide variety of products for adhesives, coatings, and graphics technologies industries at facilities located in the U.S. and six other countries.

Plan Specifics:

- Partial dividend reinvestment is not available.
- No Discount.
- OCP: not available.
- Selling costs are brokerage commissions and transfer taxes.
- Dividends are paid January, April, July, and October.

Performance Rating: ****

DRIP Rating: 👎

Braintree Savings Bank (The)
(NASDAQ:BTSB)
865 Washington St.
Braintree, MA 02184
(617) 843-9100

Business Profile: Massachusetts savings institution.

Plan Specifics:

- Partial dividend reinvestment is available.
- No Discount.
- OCP: $100 to $5000 per quarter.
- Company purchases stock roughly every 45 days as long as enough funds have accumulated to purchase 100 shares.
- Selling costs are brokerage fees.
- Dividends are paid February, May, August, and November.

Performance Rating: **

DRIP Rating: 👍

**Briggs & Stratton Corp.
(NYSE:BGG)
PO Box 702
Milwaukee, WI 53201-0702
(414) 259-5333**

Business Profile: Worldwide leading producer of gasoline engines for outdoor power equipment.

Plan Specifics:
- Partial dividend reinvestment is not available.
- No Discount.
- OCP: $25 to $5000 per quarter.
- Selling costs are brokerage commissions.
- Stock is purchased monthly with OCPs.
- Dividends are paid January, April, June, and October.

Performance Rating: ****

DRIP Rating: 👍

**Bristol-Myers Squibb Co.
(NYSE:BMY)
345 Park Ave.
New York, NY 10154
(800) 356-2026**

Business Profile: Leading producer of pharmaceuticals, including cardiovasculars and antibiotics. Supplier of medical devices and nonprescription health products.

Plan Specifics:
- Minimum 50 shares needed to enroll in the plan.
- Partial dividend reinvestment is not available.
- No Discount.
- OCP: $105 to $10,025 per month.
- Purchase fees include 4 percent

of reinvested dividends ($5 max.) and 4 percent of OCP ($25 max.).
- $15 plus commission per transaction for shares sold through the plan.
- Stock is purchased weekly with OCPs.
- Dividends are paid February, May, August, and November.

Performance Rating: *****

DRIP Rating: 👍

**British Airways PLC (NYSE:BAB)
c/o Morgan Guaranty Trust
PO Box 8205
Boston, MA 02266-8205
(800) 428-4237**

Business Profile: Major international airline.

Plan Specifics:
- Partial dividend reinvestment is not available.
- No Discount.
- OCP: $10 to $60,000 per year.
- Stock is purchased beginning on 6th day of the month with OCPs.
- Purchasing fees are proportionate share of brokerage commission and 5 percent of total funds invested ($2.50 maximum).
- Selling costs are $5 handling fee and brokerage commission.
- Dividends are paid January and July.

Performance Rating: ***

DRIP Rating: 👍

British Petroleum Co. PLC (NYSE:BP)
200 Public Square
Cleveland, OH 44114-2375
(216) 586-6077   (800) 428-4237

Business Profile: Major worldwide oil company.

Plan Specifics:

- Partial dividend reinvestment is not available.
- No Discount.
- OCP: $20 to $15,000 per quarter.
- Stock is purchased monthly with OCPs.
- Purchasing and selling fees are brokerage commissions.
- Dividends are paid February, May, August, and November.

Performance Rating: ****

DRIP Rating: 👍

Brooklyn Union Gas Co. (NYSE:BU)
One MetroTech Center
Brooklyn, NY 11201
(718) 403-3334   (800) 328-5090

Business Profile: Distributor of natural gas in New York City.

Plan Specifics:

- Partial dividend reinvestment is available.
- No Discount.
- OCP: $25 to $100,000 per year.
- Selling costs are brokerage commissions.
- Stock is purchased monthly with OCPs.
- Customers of the company may make initial purchases directly from the firm (minimum $250).
- Shareholders of preferred stock and registered bonds may reinvest dividends and interest payments in additional common shares.
- Approximately 12,500 shareholders are in the plan.
- Dividends are paid February, May, August, and November.

Performance Rating: *****

DRIP Rating: 👍

Brown-Forman Corp. (NYSE:BF.B)
PO Box 1080
Louisville, KY 40201
(502) 585-1100

Business Profile: Major provider and importer of wine and spirits with operations in china and crystal.

Plan Specifics:

- Partial dividend reinvestment is not available.
- No Discount.
- OCP: $50 to $3000 per quarter.
- Purchasing fees include brokerage costs.
- Stock is purchased monthly with OCPs.
- Selling fees include nominal brokerage commission and $1 service fee.
- Shares may be sold via the telephone.
- Dividends are paid January, April, July, and October.

Performance Rating: ****

DRIP Rating: 👍

Brown Group, Inc. (NYSE:BG)
PO Box 29
8300 Maryland Ave.
St. Louis, MO 63166
(314) 854-4000

Business Profile: Supplier and retailer of branded footwear.

Plan Specifics:
- Partial dividend reinvestment is not available.
- No Discount.
- OCP: $25 to $1000 per month.
- Selling costs are brokerage fees.
- Stock is purchased monthly with OCPs.
- Dividends are paid January, April, July, and October.

Performance Rating: **
DRIP Rating: 👍

Browning-Ferris Industries, Inc. (NYSE:BFI)
c/o First Chicago Trust-NY
PO Box 2500
Jersey City, NJ 07303-2500
(713) 870-7827   (800) 446-2617

Business Profile: Collects, processes, and disposes of solid and liquid waste material for commercial, industrial, and residential customers.

Plan Specifics:
- Partial dividend reinvestment is available.
- No Discount.
- OCP: $25 to $60,000 per year.
- Selling costs are brokerage commissions and any other costs of sale.
- Company purchases stock around the 10th of the month with OCPs.

- Shares may be sold via the telephone.
- Dividends are paid January, April, July, and October.

Performance Rating: *****
DRIP Rating: 👍

Brunswick Corp. (NYSE:BC)
1 N. Field Ct.
Lake Forest, IL 60045-4811
(708) 735-4293

Business Profile: Leading manufacturer of pleasure boats and marine engines. Provides recreation products.

Plan Specifics:
- Partial dividend reinvestment is not available.
- No Discount.
- OCP: $10 to $2000 per month.
- Selling costs are brokerage fees.
- Company purchases stock monthly with OCPs.
- Safekeeping services are available.
- Approximately 10,000 shareholders are in the plan.
- Dividends are paid March, June, September, and December.

Performance Rating: ***
DRIP Rating: 👍

Brush Wellman, Inc. (NYSE:BW)
17876 St. Clair Ave.
Cleveland, OH 44110-2697
(216) 486-4200

Business Profile: Major worldwide provider of beryllium, beryllium alloys, beryllic ceramic, and other specialty materials for the electronic, automotive, and telecommunications markets and aerospace applications.

Plan Specifics:

- Partial dividend reinvestment is not available.
- No Discount.
- OCP: $10 to $5000 per quarter.
- Selling costs are a $5 termination charge and brokerage fees.
- Company purchases stock with OCPs within 30 days of receipt if amount sufficient to purchase at least 100 shares, or a lesser number if the bank deems practicable, is received.
- Dividends are paid January, April, July, and October.

Performance Rating: ***

DRIP Rating: 👍

BSB Bancorp, Inc.
(NASDAQ:BSBN)
58-68 Exchange St.
Binghamton, NY 13902
(607) 779-2525

Business Profile: Multibank holding company based in New York.

Plan Specifics:

- Partial dividend reinvestment is available.
- No Discount.
- OCP: $50 to $5000 per month.
- Stock is purchased monthly with OCPs.
- Selling costs are brokerage commissions and a nominal service fee.
- Dividends are paid March, June, September, and December.

Performance Rating: ***

DRIP Rating: 👍

BT Financial Corp.
(NASDAQ:BTFC)
551 Main St.
Johnstown, PA 15907
(814) 532-3801

Business Profile: Bank holding company.

Plan Specifics:

- Partial dividend reinvestment is not available.
- No Discount.
- OCP: $20 to $2500 per quarter.
- Stock is purchased quarterly with OCPs.
- Selling costs are brokerage commissions, service charges, and any taxes.
- Dividends are paid March, June, September, and December.

Performance Rating: ***

DRIP Rating: 👍

Burnham Pacific Properties, Inc.
(NYSE:BPP)
610 W. Ash St.
San Diego, CA 92101
(800) 568-2722

Business Profile: Real estate investment trust with properties, primarily shopping centers, in southern California.

Plan Specifics:

- Partial dividend reinvestment is available.
- 5 percent discount on reinvested dividends.
- OCP: not available.
- Must go through own broker to sell.
- 15 percent of shares outstanding are enrolled in the plan.

- Dividends are paid March, June, September, and December.

Performance Rating: **

DRIP Rating: ☞

Cabot Corp. (NYSE:CBT)
75 State St.
Boston, MA 02109-1806
(617) 345-0100

Business Profile: Provides specialty chemicals, including carbon black and fumed silica, and energy.

Plan Specifics:
- Partial dividend reinvestment is available.
- No Discount.
- OCP: $10 to $10,000 per quarter.
- Stock is purchased 8 times per year with OCPs.
- Selling costs are brokerage commissions.
- Safekeeping services are available.
- Approximately 520 shareholders are in the plan.
- Dividends are paid March, June, September, and December.

Performance Rating: ***

DRIP Rating: 👍

Cadmus Communications Corp.
(NASDAQ:CDMS)
6620 W. Broad St., Suite 500
Richmond, VA 23230
(804) 287-5680

Business Profile: Holding company providing graphic arts services to the communications industry.

Plan Specifics:
- Partial dividend reinvestment is not available.
- No Discount.
- OCP: $25 to $3000 per quarter.
- There are no purchasing or selling fees.
- Company purchases stock quarterly with OCPs.
- Dividends are paid March, June, September, and December.

Performance Rating: ***

DRIP Rating: 👍

California Bancshares, Inc.
(NASDAQ:CABI)
100 Park Pl., Ste. 140
San Ramon, CA 94583
(510) 743-4204

Business Profile: Holding company for banking subsidiaries in northern California.

Plan Specifics:
- Partial dividend reinvestment is available.
- No Discount.
- OCP: $100 to $5000 per quarter.
- Purchasing costs are brokerage commissions.
- Selling costs are brokerage commissions, transfer taxes, and a $2.50 handling charge upon withdrawing/terminating from the plan.
- Company purchases stock quarterly with OCPs.
- Dividends are paid January, April, July, and October.

Performance Rating: ***

DRIP Rating: 👍

California Financial Holding Company (NASDAQ:CFHC)
501 W. Weber Ave.
Stockton, CA 95203
(209) 948-6870

Business Profile: Holding company for Stockton Savings Bank, FSB, which provides financial services in central San Joaquin Valley and Sierra foothills in California.

Plan Specifics:
- Partial dividend reinvestment is available.
- 3 percent discount on reinvested dividends.
- OCP: $100 to $50,000 per quarter.
- Company purchases stock monthly with OCPs.
- Selling costs are brokerage commissions.
- Dividends are paid February, May, August, and November.

Performance Rating: **

DRIP Rating: 👍

California Water Service Co. (NYSE:CWT)
1720 N. First St.
San Jose, CA 95112
(408) 453-8414

Business Profile: Public utility providing water service to California communities.

Plan Specifics:
- Partial dividend reinvestment is available.
- No Discount.
- OCP: not available.
- Must sell shares through own broker.
- Dividends are paid February, May, August, and November.

Performance Rating: ****

DRIP Rating: 👎

Callaway Golf Co. (NYSE:ELY)
2285 Rutherford Rd.
Carlsbad, CA 92008-8815
(619) 931-1771   (800) 647-4273

Business Profile: Designs, manufactures, and markets premium, innovative golf clubs.

Plan Specifics:
- Partial dividend reinvestment is available.
- No Discount.
- OCP: $50 to $5000 per quarter.
- Stock is purchased monthly with OCPs.
- Selling costs are brokerage commissions, transfer taxes, and a $15 service charge for termination.
- Dividends are paid March, May, August, and November.

Performance Rating: ***

DRIP Rating: 👍

Campbell Soup Co. (NYSE:CPB)
First Chicago Trust - NY
PO Box 2533
Jersey City, NJ 07303-2533
(800) 446-2617

Business Profile: Leading producer of soup, spaghetti sauce, frozen dinners, and bakery products.

Plan Specifics:
- Partial dividend reinvestment is available.
- No Discount.
- OCP: $25 to $25,000 per year.
- Stock is purchased around the last business day of the month with OCPs.

- Selling costs are brokerage commissions, a service fee, and any other costs of sale.
- Approximately 9000 shareholders are in the plan.
- Dividends are paid January, April, July, and October.

Performance Rating: *****

DRIP Rating: 👍

Canadian Pacific Ltd. (NYSE:CP)
PO Box 6042
Station Centre-Ville
Montreal, Quebec H3C 3E4
Canada
(514) 395-5151

Business Profile: Interests in transportation, energy, real estate, hotels and telecommunications.

Plan Specifics:
- Partial dividend reinvestment is not available.
- No Discount.
- OCP: up to $30,000 (Canadian) per calendar year.
- Must sell through own broker.
- Company purchases stock monthly with OCPs.
- Dividends are paid January, April, July, and October.

Performance Rating: ***

DRIP Rating: 👍

Capstead Mortgage Corp.
(NYSE:CMO)
2711 N. Haskell Ave., Ste. 900
Dallas, TX 75204
(214) 874-2323   (800) 527-7844

Business Profile: Leader in the acquisition and securitization of single-family jumbo first mortgage loans.

Plan Specifics:
- Initial purchases may be made directly from the plan ($250 minimum).
- Partial dividend reinvestment is available.
- 3 percent discount on reinvested dividends and OCPs.
- OCP: $50 to $10,000 per month.
- OCP is invested monthly.
- Selling costs are brokerage fees and a $5 service charge.
- Automatic investment services are available.
- Dividends are paid March, June, September, and December.

Performance Rating: **

DRIP Rating: 👍

Carlisle Companies, Inc.
(NYSE:CSL)
250 S. Clinton St., Ste. 201
Syracuse, NY 13202
(315) 474-2500

Business Profile: Operations in automotive and industrial products, data communications, and electronic products.

Plan Specifics:
- Partial dividend reinvestment is not available.
- No Discount.
- OCP: $10 to $3000 per quarter.
- Selling costs are brokerage fees and handling charges.
- Stock is purchased monthly with OCPs.
- Dividends are paid March, June, September, and December.

Performance Rating: ****

DRIP Rating: 👍

Carolina First Corp.
(NASDAQ: CAFC)
102 S. Main St.
Greenville, SC 29601
(803) 255-7913

Business Profile: Bank and savings and loan holding company serving communities throughout South Carolina.

Plan Specifics:
- Partial dividend reinvestment is not available.
- 5 percent discount on reinvested dividends.
- OCP: $25 to $10,000 per quarter.
- Company purchases stock quarterly with OCPs.
- Must go through own broker to sell shares.
- Certificate safekeeping is available.
- Dividends are paid February, May, August, and November.

Performance Rating: NR

DRIP Rating: 👍

Carolina Power & Light Co.
(NYSE:CPL)
PO Box 1551
Raleigh, NC 27602
(800) 662-7232   (919) 546-6111

Business Profile: Electric utility serving North and South Carolina.

Plan Specifics:
- Partial dividend reinvestment is available.
- No Discount.
- OCP: $20 to $2000 per month.
- Company purchases stock monthly with OCPs.
- Buying and selling costs are brokerage commissions.
- Preferred dividends may be reinvested for common shares under the program.
- Customers living in North and South Carolina may make initial purchase of stock directly from the company ($20 minimum).
- Automatic investment services are available.
- Dividends are paid February, May, August, and November.

Performance Rating: ****

DRIP Rating: 👍

Carpenter Technology Corp.
(NYSE:CRS)
c/o First Chicago Trust-NY
PO Box 2533
Jersey City, NJ 07303-2533
(800) 446-2617

Business Profile: Produces stainless steel, special alloys, and tool steel.

Plan Specifics:
- Partial dividend reinvestment is not available.
- No Discount.
- OCP: $10 to $60,000 per year.
- Stock is purchased monthly with OCPs.
- Selling costs may include brokerage fees, a service fee, and any other costs of sale.
- Dividends are paid March, June, September, and December.

Performance Rating: ***

DRIP Rating: 👍

Cascade Natural Gas Corp.
(NYSE:CGC)
222 Fairview Ave. N.
Seattle, WA 98109
(206) 624-3900

Business Profile: Distributes natural gas to Washington and Oregon communities.

Plan Specifics:

- Partial dividend reinvestment is available.
- No Discount.
- OCP: $50 to $20,000 per year.
- Stock is purchased monthly with OCPs.
- Residential customers of Cascade Natural Gas may make initial purchase of stock through the company ($250 minimum).
- Dividends are paid February, May, August, and November.

Performance Rating: ***

DRIP Rating: 👍

Caterpillar, Inc. (NYSE:CAT)
100 N.E. Adams St.
Peoria, IL 61629-7310
(309) 675-4619

Business Profile: Major supplier of construction machinery and equipment. Produces diesel and natural gas engines.

Plan Specifics:

- Partial dividend reinvestment is not available.
- No Discount.
- OCP: $10 to $60,000 per year.
- Company purchases stock monthly with OCPs.
- Purchasing fees include service charge of 5 percent on amounts reinvested (no more than $2.50) plus brokerage fees.

- Selling costs include brokerage fees and a service fee.
- Automatic investment services are available.
- Dividends are paid February, May, August, and November.

Performance Rating: ***

DRIP Rating: 👍

Cathay Bancorp, Inc.
(NASDAQ:CATY)
777 N. Broadway
Los Angeles, CA 90012
(213) 625-4700

Business Profile: Bank holding company with offices in the U.S., Hong Kong, and Taiwan providing banking services mainly to the Asian-American community.

Plan Specifics:

- Partial dividend reinvestment is available.
- 5 percent discount on reinvested dividends.
- OCP: $600 to $15,000 per quarter.
- Company purchases stock monthly with OCPs.
- Must go through own broker to sell shares from the plan.
- Dividends are paid January, April, July, and October.

Performance Rating: NR

DRIP Rating: 👎

CBI Industries, Inc. (NYSE:CBI)
c/o Shareholder Services
800 Jorie Blvd.
Oak Brook, IL 60521
(708) 572-7366

Business Profile: Production and delivery of industrial gases; construction of metal plate structures and other contracting services; oil blending and storage.

Plan Specifics:

- Partial dividend reinvestment is available.
- No Discount.
- OCP: $25 to $5000 per month.
- Company invests OCPs monthly.
- Purchasing and selling fees are brokerage commissions, service fees, and transfer tax.
- Fewer than 2200 shareholders are in the plan.
- Dividends are paid March, June, September, and December.

Performance Rating: **

DRIP Rating: 👍

CBT Corp. (NASDAQ:CBTC)
333 Broadway
Paducah, KY 42001
(502) 575-5100

Business Profile: Bank holding company.

Plan Specifics:

- Partial dividend reinvestment is available.
- No Discount.
- OCP: $50 to $3000 per quarter.
- Company purchases stock quarterly with OCPs.
- Purchasing costs are brokerage commissions.
- Selling costs are brokerage commissions and a handling charge of $2.
- Dividends are paid January, April, July, and October.

Performance Rating: NR

DRIP Rating: 👍

CCB Financial Corp. (NASDAQ:CCBF)
PO Box 931
Durham, NC 27702-0931
(919) 683-7631   (800) 368-5448

Business Profile: Bank holding company operating in central North Carolina.

Plan Specifics:

- Partial dividend reinvestment is available.
- No Discount.
- OCP: $25 to $3000 per month.
- Company purchases stock monthly with OCPs.
- Purchasing costs are brokerage commissions and other costs.
- Automatic investment services are available.
- Approximately 1300 shareholders are in the plan.
- Dividends are paid January, April, July, and October.

Performance Rating: ****

DRIP Rating: 👍

Cedar Fair LP (NYSE: FUN)
c/o Shareholder Services
PO Box 750
Pittsburgh, PA 15230-9625
(800) 756-3353

Business Profile: Operates amusement theme parks.

Plan Specifics:

- Must own at least 50 shares to enroll.
- Partial dividend reinvestment is not available.
- No Discount.
- OCP: $50 to $5000 per quarter.
- Selling costs are brokerage commissions and a $5 agent termination fee.

- Dividends are paid February, May, August, and November.

Performance Rating: ***
DRIP Rating: ☜

Center Financial Corp.
(NASDAQ:CFCX)
60 N. Main St.
Waterbury, CT 06702
(800) 288-9541

Business Profile: Connecticut-based savings bank.

Plan Specifics:

- Partial dividend reinvestment is not available.
- No Discount.
- OCP: $25 to $1000 per quarter.
- $10 termination fee.
- Selling costs include brokerage commissions.
- Company purchases stock monthly with OCPs.

Performance Rating: NR
DRIP Rating: ☝

Centerior Energy Corp.
(NYSE:CX)
PO Box 94661
Cleveland, OH 44101-4661
(800) 433-7794

Business Profile: Electric utility holding company serving residential, commercial, and industrial customers in northern Ohio.

Plan Specifics:

- Partial dividend reinvestment is available.
- No Discount.
- OCP: $10 to $40,000 per year.
- Minimal fees for purchasing and selling shares.

- Company purchases stock monthly with OCPs.
- Utility customers may make initial purchase of stock through the company (minimum $10).
- IRA option is available.
- May reinvest preferred dividends for common shares under the plan.
- Approximately 62,000 shareholders are in the plan.
- Dividends are paid February, May, August, and November.

Performance Rating: **
DRIP Rating: ☝

Central & South West Corp.
(NYSE:CSR)
PO Box 660164
Dallas, TX 75266-0164
(800) 527-5797

Business Profile: Utility holding company supplying electric and gas services to Texas, Oklahoma, Louisiana, and Arkansas customers.

Plan Specifics:

- Partial dividend reinvestment is available.
- No Discount.
- OCP: $25 to $100,000 per year.
- Company purchases stock semimonthly with OCPs.
- Selling fees are brokerage charges of 4 cents per share.
- Residents in Texas, Oklahoma, Louisiana, and Arkansas may purchase initial shares directly from the company (minimum $100).
- Automatic investment services are available.

- Safekeeping services are available.
- Dividends are paid February, May, August, and November.

Performance Rating: ****

DRIP Rating: 👍

Central Fidelity Banks, Inc. (NASDAQ:CFBS)
1021 E. Cary St.
Richmond, VA 23219
(804) 697-6942   (800) 293-2327

Business Profile: Virginia-based bank holding company.

Plan Specifics:

- Partial dividend reinvestment is available.
- No Discount.
- OCP: $25 to $10,000 per month.
- Company purchases stock monthly with OCPs.
- Selling fees are brokerage commissions.
- Residents in Maryland, North Carolina, and Virginia may make initial purchases directly from the firm (minimum $100).
- Automatic investment services are available.
- Direct deposit of dividends.
- Approximately 3000 shareholders are in the plan.
- Dividends are paid January, April, July, and October.

Performance Rating: ****

DRIP Rating: 👍

Central Hudson Gas & Electric Corp. (NYSE:CNH)
284 South Ave.
Poughkeepsie, NY 12601-4879
(914) 486-5204   (914) 452-2000

Business Profile: Distributes electricity and gas to residential, commercial, and industrial customers in Hudson River Valley region of New York.

Plan Specifics:

- Partial dividend reinvestment is available.
- No Discount.
- OCP: $25 to $10,000 per quarter.
- Company purchases stock quarterly with OCPs.
- Selling fees are brokerage commissions.
- Utility customers may make initial purchase of stock directly from company ($100 minimum).
- Dividends are paid February, May, August, and November.

Performance Rating: **

DRIP Rating: 👍

Central Louisiana Electric Co., Inc. (NYSE:CNL)
PO Box 5000
Pineville, LA 71361-5000
(318) 484-7400

Business Profile: Supplies electricity to residential, commercial, and industrial customers in portions of Louisiana.

Plan Specifics:

- Partial dividend reinvestment is available.
- No Discount.
- OCP: $25 to $5000 per month.
- Company purchases stock monthly with OCPs.
- Selling fees include brokerage fees, a handling charge, and other costs of sale.
- Preferred dividends may be

reinvested for additional common shares under the plan.
- Approximately 5400 shareholders are in the plan.
- Dividends are paid February, May, August, and November.

Performance Rating: ****
DRIP Rating: 👍

**Central Maine Power Co.
(NYSE:CTP)
83 Edison Dr.
Augusta, ME 04336
(800) 695-4267**

Business Profile: Distributes electric service to residential, industrial, and commercial customers in central and southern Maine.

Plan Specifics:
- Partial dividend reinvestment is available.
- No Discount.
- OCP: $10 to $40,000 per year.
- Company purchases stock monthly with OCPs.
- Selling fees are brokerage commissions.
- Customers of the utility who reside in the state of Maine may join the plan by making an initial cash investment of at least $25.
- Automatic investment services are available.
- Dividends are paid January, April, July, and October.

Performance Rating: **
DRIP Rating: 👍

**Central Vermont Public Service
  Corp. (NYSE:CV)
77 Grove St.
Rutland, VT 05701
(802) 773-2711   (802) 747-5406**

Business Profile: Provides electric power to residential, commercial, and industrial customers in Vermont and New Hampshire.

Plan Specifics:
- Nonshareholders in certain states are permitted to make initial cash investments from $50 to $2000 through the company.
- Partial dividend reinvestment is not available.
- No Discount.
- OCP: $50 to $2000 per month.
- Company purchases stock monthly with OCPs.
- Selling costs are brokerage commissions.
- Over 9000 shareholders are in the plan.
- Dividends are paid February, May, August, and November.

Performance Rating: ***
DRIP Rating: 👍

**Centura Banks, Inc. (NYSE:CBC)
134 N. Church St.
Rocky Mount, NC 27804
(919) 977-8201**

Business Profile: North Carolina's seventh largest bank holding company.

Plan Specifics:
- Partial dividend reinvestment is not available.
- No Discount.
- OCP: $25 to $5000 per month.
- Selling costs are brokerage commissions.
- Company purchases stock monthly with OCPs.
- Dividends are paid March, June, September, and December.

Performance Rating: ****
DRIP Rating: 👍

Century Telephone Enterprises, Inc. (NYSE:CTL)
PO Box 4065
Monroe, LA 71211-4065
(800) 527-7844   (318) 388-9500

Business Profile: Telephone holding company with operations in cellular telephone service and nationwide paging systems.

Plan Specifics:
- Partial dividend reinvestment is available.
- No Discount.
- OCP: $25 to $5000 per quarter.
- Selling costs are brokerage commissions.
- Company purchases stock monthly with OCPs.
- Dividends are paid March, June, September, and December.

Performance Rating: ****
DRIP Rating: 👍

Champion International Corp. (NYSE:CHA)
c/o Chemical Bank
PO Box 3069, JAF Bldg.
New York, NY 10116-3069
(800) 223-6554

Business Profile: Leading paper producer with interests in pulp and newsprint.

Plan Specifics:
- Partial dividend reinvestment is not available.
- No Discount.
- OCP: $10 to $5000 per month.
- Company purchases stock monthly with OCPs.
- No selling costs.

- Approximately 4000 shareholders are in the plan.
- Dividends are paid January, April, July, and October.

Performance Rating: ***
DRIP Rating: 👍

Charter One Financial, Inc. (NASDAQ:COFI)
1215 Superior Ave.
Cleveland, OH 44114
(216) 566-5300

Business Profile: Bank holding company serving businesses and consumers in Ohio.

Plan Specifics:
- Partial dividend reinvestment is not available.
- No Discount.
- OCP: $10 to $5000 per quarter.
- Company purchases stock quarterly with OCPs.
- Selling fees are 5 percent ($1 minimum, $5 maximum service charge) plus brokerage commissions.
- Dividends are paid February, May, August, and November.

Performance Rating: ***
DRIP Rating: 👍

Chase Manhattan Corp. (NYSE:CMB)
1 Chase Manhattan Plaza, 30th Floor
New York, NY 10081
(212) 552-4237   (800) 284-4262

Business Profile: Major banking concern based in New York.

Plan Specifics:
- Partial dividend reinvestment is available.

- 5 percent discount on reinvested dividends, 3 percent discount on OCPs.
- OCP: $100 to $2000 per month.
- Company purchases stock monthly with OCPs.
- Selling fees include brokerage fees.
- Dividends are paid February, May, August, and November.

Performance Rating: ***

DRIP Rating: 👍

Chemed Corp. (NYSE:CHE)
2600 Chemed Center
255 E. Fifth St.
Cincinnati, OH 45202-4726
(513) 762-6900   (800) 426-5754

Business Profile: Diversified corporation with positions in medical and dental supply manufacturing for the hospital and alternate-care markets. The firm also offers hospice care and home health-care services. Also involved in sanitary maintenance products and plumbing and drain-cleaning services.

Plan Specifics:

- 25 shares needed to enroll in the plan.
- Partial dividend reinvestment is not available.
- No Discount.
- OCP: $50 to $5000 per month.
- Stock is purchased monthly with OCPs.
- Selling costs include brokerage commissions and nominal fees.
- Dividends are paid March, June, September, and December.

Performance Rating: ***

DRIP Rating: 👍

Chemical Banking Corp.
 (NYSE:CHL)
277 Park Ave.
New York, NY 10172
(800) 647-4273   (212) 270-6000

Business Profile: Major New York-based banking company.

Plan Specifics:

- Partial dividend reinvestment is not available.
- No Discount.
- OCP: not available.
- Selling fees are brokerage commissions.
- Preferred dividends may be reinvested for common shares under the plan.
- Dividends are paid January, April, July, and October.

Performance Rating: ***

DRIP Rating: 👎

Chemical Financial Corp.
 (NASDAQ:CHFC)
c/o KeyCorp Shareholder Svcs.
PO Box 6477
Cleveland, OH 44101
(216) 813-5745

Business Profile: Bank holding company headquartered in Michigan.

Plan Specifics:

- Partial dividend reinvestment is not available.
- No Discount.
- OCP: $10 to $3000 per quarter.
- Termination fee is $5.
- Company purchases stock within 30 days of receipt of an amount sufficient to purchase at least 100 shares.
- Dividends are paid March, June, September, and December.

Performance Rating: NR
DRIP Rating: 👍

Chesapeake Corp. (NYSE:CSK)
PO Box 2350
1021 E. Cary St.
Richmond, VA 23218-2350
(804) 697-1166

Business Profile: Manufactures paper, pulp, tissue, and wood products and has operations in packaging.

Plan Specifics:
- Partial dividend reinvestment is not available.
- No Discount.
- OCP: $10 to $5000 per quarter.
- Stock is purchased monthly with OCPs.
- Selling costs are brokerage commissions plus a service charge.
- Dividends are paid February, May, August, and November.

Performance Rating: ***
DRIP Rating: 👍

Chesapeake Utilities Corp.
(NYSE:CPK)
PO Box 615
Dover, DE 19903-0615
(302) 734-6716   (800) 936-7275

Business Profile: Diversified utility company engaged in natural gas transmission and distribution, propane distribution, and information technology services.

Plan Specifics:
- Partial dividend reinvestment is available.
- No Discount.
- OCP: $50 to $15,000 per quarter.

- Selling costs are brokerage commissions and any transfer tax.
- Company purchases stock monthly with OCPs.
- Dividends are paid January, April, July, and October.

Performance Rating: **
DRIP Rating: 👍

Chevron Corp. (NYSE:CHV)
225 Bush St.
San Francisco, CA 94104
(415) 894-3940

Business Profile: Worldwide crude oil and natural gas company with important involvements in petrochemicals and minerals.

Plan Specifics:
- Partial dividend reinvestment is not available.
- No Discount.
- OCP: $25 to $1000 per month.
- Purchasing and selling fees include a bank service charge of 4 percent of the amount invested ($2.50 maximum) plus nominal brokerage charges.
- Company purchases stock monthly with OCPs.
- Dividends are paid March, June, September, and December.

Performance Rating: *****
DRIP Rating: 👍

Chiquita Brands International,
Inc. (NYSE:CQB)
250 E. Fifth St.
Cincinnati, OH 45202
(513) 784-8011

Business Profile: International marketer, processor, and producer of fresh and processed food products. The core of the company's operations is the marketing, distribution, and sourcing of bananas.

Plan Specifics:

- Must have at least 100 shares to enroll in the plan.
- Partial dividend reinvestment is not available.
- No Discount.
- OCP: not available.
- Selling costs are a $5 service fee, brokerage commissions, and any transfer tax.
- Dividends are paid March, June, September, and December.

Performance Rating: **

DRIP Rating: ☜

Chittenden Corp. (NASDAQ:CNDN)
Two Burlington Sq.
Burlington, VT 05401
(800) 642-3158   (617) 575-2900

Business Profile: Holding company for largest commercial bank in Vermont.

Plan Specifics:

- Partial dividend reinvestment is not available.
- No Discount.
- OCP: $25 to $10,000 per quarter.
- Selling costs are 5 percent of the value of the transaction ($1 minimum, $10 maximum).
- Company purchases stock quarterly with OCPs.
- Dividends are paid February, May, August, and November.

Performance Rating: ***

DRIP Rating: ☝

Chrysler Corp. (NYSE:C)
12000 Chrysler Dr.
Highland Park, MI 48288-1919
(313) 956-3007   (800) 446-2617

Business Profile: Third-largest United States motor vehicle manufacturer.

Plan Specifics:

- Partial dividend reinvestment is available.
- No Discount.
- OCP: $25 to $24,000 per year.
- Purchasing fees are brokerage commissions and a maximum service charge of $2.50.
- Selling costs are broker fees, a handling charge, and any other costs of sale.
- Company purchases stock on the 15th of each month with OCPs.
- Shares may be sold via the telephone.
- Dividends are paid January, April, July, and October.

Performance Rating: ***

DRIP Rating: ☝

Chubb Corp. (NYSE:CB)
PO Box 1615
15 Mountain View Rd.
Warren, NJ 07061-1615
(908) 903-3579

Business Profile: Interests in property-casualty insurance, life and health insurance, and real estate development.

Plan Specifics:

- Partial dividend reinvestment is not available.
- No Discount.
- OCP: $10 to $3000 per quarter.
- Purchasing fees are 5 percent of each investment (maximum

$2.50) and nominal brokerage fees.

- Selling fees are brokerage commission plus a $5 handling fee.
- Company purchases stock at least quarterly with OCPs.
- Dividends are paid January, April, July, and October.

Performance Rating: ****

DRIP Rating: 👍

**Church & Dwight Co., Inc.
  (NYSE:CHD)
c/o Chemical Bank
PO Box 3069, JAF Bldg.
New York, NY 10116-3069
(800) 851-9677**

Business Profile: Company sells baking soda and sodium bicarbonate-based products under the Arm & Hammer label.

Plan Specifics:

- Partial dividend reinvestment is available.
- No Discount.
- OCP: $250 to $5000 per quarter.
- Selling costs are brokerage commissions, a $5 service charge for termination, and a $15 fee for selling.
- Company purchases stock quarterly with OCPs.
- Dividends are paid March, June, September, and December.

Performance Rating: ***

DRIP Rating: 👎

**CIGNA Corp. (NYSE:CI)
First Chicago Trust-NY
PO Box 2533
Jersey City, NJ 07303-2533
(800) 446-2617**

Business Profile: Insurance organization providing property-casualty, group life/health, and annuity coverage.

Plan Specifics:

- Partial dividend reinvestment is available.
- No Discount.
- OCP: $10 to $5000 per month.
- Stock is purchased around the 10th business day of the month with OCPs.
- Selling costs are brokerage commission and any other costs of sale.
- Shares may be sold via the telephone.
- Dividends are paid January, April, July, and October.

Performance Rating: ****

DRIP Rating: 👍

**CILCORP, Inc. (NYSE:CER)
300 Hamilton Blvd., Ste. 300
Peoria, IL 61602
(800) 622-5514   (800) 322-3569**

Business Profile: Public utility holding company providing electricity and gas to customers in central Illinois. Other businesses provide environmental consulting and analytical services.

Plan Specifics:

- Partial dividend reinvestment is available.
- No Discount.
- OCP: $25 to $25,000 per quarter.
- Selling costs are brokerage fees.
- Stock is purchased monthly with OCPs.
- Preferred dividends may be reinvested for additional common shares under the plan. This

provision applies to preferred dividends on Central Illinois Light Company preferred stock.
- Dividends are paid March, June, September, and December.

Performance Rating: ***

DRIP Rating: 🖐

Cincinnati Bell, Inc. (NYSE:CSN)
PO Box 2301
201 E. 4th St.
Cincinnati, OH 45201
(513) 397-7877

Business Profile: Provides telephone service in southwestern Ohio, northern Kentucky, and southeastern Indiana. Engages in nonregulated communications-related businesses.

Plan Specifics:
- Partial dividend reinvestment is not available.
- No Discount.
- OCP: $25 to $5000 per month.
- Selling costs include brokerage commissions.
- Company purchases stock monthly with OCPs.
- Dividends are paid February, May, August, and November.

Performance Rating: ****

DRIP Rating: 🖐

Cincinnati Financial Corp.
(NASDAQ:CINF)
PO Box 145496
Cincinnati, OH 45250-5496
(513) 870-2000   (513) 579-6248

Business Profile: Insurance holding company. Sells property and casualty coverage and life insurance.

Plan Specifics:
- Partial dividend reinvestment is not available.
- No Discount.
- OCP: $25 to $5000 per month.
- Purchasing fees include brokerage commissions and service fees of $3 per transaction for optional cash investments and $1 to $3 per dividend reinvestment.
- Selling fees are brokerage commissions.
- Stock is purchased monthly with OCPs.
- Dividends are paid January, April, July, and October.

Performance Rating: ****

DRIP Rating: 🖐

Cincinnati Milacron, Inc.
(NYSE:CMZ)
4701 Marburg Ave.
Cincinnati, OH 45209
(412) 236-8000   (513) 841-8100

Business Profile: Leading manufacturer of machine tools and inspection equipment.

Plan Specifics:
- Partial dividend reinvestment is not available.
- No Discount.
- OCP: $25 to $1000 per month.
- Selling costs are brokerage commissions.
- Company purchases stock monthly with OCPs.
- Dividends are paid March, June, September, and December.

Performance Rating: ***

DRIP Rating: 🖐

CINergy Corp. (NYSE:CIN)
139 E. Fourth St.
Cincinnati, OH 45202
(513) 381-2000

Business Profile: Holding company owning shares of Cincinnati Gas & Electric Co. and PSI Energy, Inc.

Plan Specifics:

- Partial dividend reinvestment is available.
- No Discount.
- OCP: $25 to $100,000 per year.
- Company purchases stock monthly with OCPs.
- Selling costs are brokerage fees.
- Dividends are paid February, May, August, and November.

Performance Rating: ***

DRIP Rating: 👍

CIPSCO, Inc. (NYSE:CIP)
607 E. Adams St.
Springfield, IL 62739
(217) 525-5317   (800) 710-7726

Business Profile: CIPSCO's principal subsidiary provides electricity and gas to customers in central and southern Illinois.

Plan Specifics:

- Partial dividend reinvestment is available.
- No Discount.
- OCP: $10 to $50,000 per month.
- Brokerage commission for purchasing and selling.
- Company purchases stock monthly with OCPs.
- Preferred dividends may be reinvested in common shares provided the investor owns one share of common.
- Approximately 12,870 shareholders are in the plan.

- Dividends are paid March, June, September, and December.

Performance Rating: ***

DRIP Rating: 👍

Citicorp (NYSE:CCI)
Citicorp Investor Relations
153 E. 53rd St.
New York, NY 10043
(800) 342-6690   (800) 422-2066

Business Profile: Worldwide banking company.

Plan Specifics:

- Partial dividend reinvestment is available.
- No Discount.
- OCP: $100 to $5000 per month.
- Company purchases stock monthly with OCPs.
- Investors who wish to invest more than $5000 per month may do so with permission from the company.
- Selling costs are brokerage fees.
- Permits participation by shareholders who have shares registered in the name of their brokers.
- Accepts OCPs via wire transfer of funds from brokers.
- Approximately 36,000 shareholders are in the plan.
- Dividends are paid February, May, August, and November.

Performance Rating: ****

DRIP Rating: 👍

Citizens Bancorp
 (NASDAQ:CIBC)
14401 Sweitzer Lane
Laurel, MD 20707
(301) 206-6000

Business Profile: Holding institution

for banks in Maryland, Virginia
and Washington, D.C.

Plan Specifics:
- Partial dividend reinvestment is
  not available.
- No Discount.
- OCP: $100 to $7500 per quarter.
- Purchasing costs may include
  nominal brokerage fees.
- Selling costs are brokerage
  commission and a $1 handling
  charge.
- Company purchases stock
  monthly with OCPs.
- Approximately 2400 sharehold-
  ers are in the plan.
- Dividends are paid March, June,
  September, and December.

Performance Rating: NR

DRIP Rating: 👍

**Citizens Banking Corp.
  (NASDAQ:CBCF)
One Citizens Banking Center
Flint, MI 48502
(810) 766-7500**

Business Profile: Sixth largest bank
holding company in Michigan.

Plan Specifics:
- Partial dividend reinvestment is
  not available.
- No Discount.
- OCP: $25 to $5000 per quarter.
- Selling costs are brokerage
  commissions, taxes, and a
  service charge.
- Company purchases stock
  quarterly with OCPs.
- Dividends are paid February,
  May, August, and November.

*Performance Rating: ****

DRIP Rating: 👍

**Citizens Utilities Co.
  (NYSE:CZN.B)
High Ridge Park
Stamford, CT 06905-1390
(203) 329-8800   (800) 757-5755**

Business Profile: Company provides
telecommunications, electric, gas,
and water services in 18 states.

Plan Specifics:
- Partial dividend reinvestment is
  not available.
- No Discount.
- OCP: up to $25,000 per quarter.
- OCP is invested monthly.
- Selling fees include $15 service
  charge plus 5 cents per share.
- Dividends are paid March, June,
  September, and December.

*Performance Rating: ****

DRIP Rating: 👍

**Clarcor, Inc. (NYSE:CLC)
c/o First Chicago Trust-NY
PO Box 2533
Jersey City, NJ 07303-2533
(800) 446-2617**

Business Profile: Manufactures air,
fuel, and hydraulic filters; metal
and plastic lithographed containers; and plastic closures.

Plan Specifics:
- Partial dividend reinvestment is
  not available.
- No Discount.
- OCP: $25 to $3000 per month.
- Stock is purchased monthly with
  OCPs.
- Selling fees include $10 service
  charge and brokerage commis-
  sions.
- Dividends are paid January,
  April, July, and October.

Performance Rating: ****
DRIP Rating: 👍

Clayton Homes, Inc.
(NYSE:CMH)
c/o Trust Company Bank
Corporate Trust Dept.
PO Box 4625
Atlanta, GA 30302
(800) 568-3476

Business Profile: Leading producer and retailer of manufactured homes.

Plan Specifics:
- Partial dividend reinvestment is not available.
- No Discount.
- OCP: $100 to $5000 per quarter.
- OCP is invested quarterly.
- Selling costs include brokerage fees.
- Dividends are paid January, April, July, and October.

Performance Rating: ****
DRIP Rating: 👍

Cleveland-Cliffs, Inc.
(NYSE:CLF)
1100 Superior Ave., 18th Floor
Cleveland, OH 44114-2589
(216) 694-5459   (216) 694-5700

Business Profile: Produces and markets iron ore pellets.

Plan Specifics:
- Partial dividend reinvestment is not available.
- No Discount.
- OCP: $10 to $2000 per month.
- Selling costs may include brokerage fees.
- Company purchases stock monthly with OCPs.

- Dividends are paid March, June, September, and December.

Performance Rating: ***
DRIP Rating: 👍

Clorox Co. (NYSE:CLX)
c/o First Chicago Trust-NY
PO Box 2533
Jersey City, NJ 07303-2533
(201) 324-0498   (800) 446-2617

Business Profile: Manufactures household products, including bleach and cleaners.

Plan Specifics:
- Partial dividend reinvestment is available.
- No Discount.
- OCP: $10 to $60,000 per year.
- Company purchases stock monthly with OCPs.
- Selling costs include brokerage commissions and any other costs of sale.
- Automatic investment services are available.
- Dividends are paid February, May, August, and November.

Performance Rating: *****
DRIP Rating: 👍

CML Group, Inc. (NYSE:CML)
524 Main St.
Acton, MA 01720
(508) 264-4155

Business Profile: Specialty retailer which operates through various store chains and by mail order.

Plan Specifics:
- Partial dividend reinvestment is not available.
- No Discount.
- OCP: $25 to $10,000 per quarter.

- Selling costs are brokerage commissions and a handling charge of the lesser of 5 percent of the proceeds received or $5 ($1 minimum).
- Company purchases stock quarterly with OCPs.
- Dividends are paid March, June, September, and December.

Performance Rating: **

DRIP Rating: 👍

CMS Energy Corp. (NYSE:CMS)
Investor Service Dept.
212 W. Michigan Ave.
Jackson, MI 49201
(517) 788-1867   (517) 788-1868

Business Profile: Principal subsidiary is Consumers Power, Michigan's largest utility.

Plan Specifics:

- Initial purchases may be made directly through the plan (minimum $500).
- Partial dividend reinvestment is available.
- No Discount.
- OCP: $25 to $120,000 per year.
- Company purchases stock monthly with OCPs.
- Selling costs are brokerage fees.
- Automatic investment services are available.
- Preferred stock is eligible for reinvestment for CMS Energy common shares under the plan.
- Approximately 29,300 shareholders are in the plan.
- Dividends are paid February, May, August, and November.

Performance Rating: **

DRIP Rating: 👍

CNB Bancshares, Inc.
 (NASDAQ:CNBE)
PO Box 778
Evansville, IN 47705-0778
(812) 464-3416   (812) 464-3400
(800) 777-3949

Business Profile: Offers banking services in the Midwest.

Plan Specifics:

- Partial dividend reinvestment is available.
- 3 percent discount on reinvested dividends.
- OCP: $25 to $2000 per month.
- Company purchases stock monthly with OCPs.
- Must go through own broker to sell shares.
- Approximately 3400 shareholders are in the plan.
- Dividends are paid January, April, July, and October.

Performance Rating: ****

DRIP Rating: 👍

Coca-Cola Bottling Co.
 Consolidated (NASDAQ:COKE)
c/o First Union Nat'l Bank
CMG-5, Two First Union Center
Charlotte, NC 28288-1154
(704) 374-2697

Business Profile: Bottles, cans, and sells carbonated soft drinks and products of Coca-Cola Company.

Plan Specifics:

- Partial dividend reinvestment is not available.
- No Discount.
- OCP: $10 to $1000 per month.
- Purchasing fees include brokerage commissions and service charge of 4 percent of investment ($2.50 maximum).

- Selling cost is brokerage commission.
- Stock is purchased monthly with OCPs.
- Approximately 350 shareholders are in the plan.
- Dividends are paid March, June, September, and December.

Performance Rating: ***

DRIP Rating: 👍

The Coca-Cola Company (NYSE:KO)
PO Box 1734
Atlanta, GA 30301
(404) 676-2777   (800) 446-2617

Business Profile: World's largest soft drink company.

Plan Specifics:

- Partial dividend reinvestment is available.
- No Discount.
- OCP: $10 to $60,000 per year.
- Selling costs are brokerage commissions and any other costs of sale.
- Company purchases stock monthly with OCPs.
- Automatic investment services are available.
- Stock may be sold via the telephone.
- Dividends are paid April, July, October, and December.

Performance Rating: *****

DRIP Rating: 👍

Coca-Cola Enterprises, Inc. (NYSE:CCE)
PO Box 1778
Atlanta, GA 30301-1778
(404) 676-7997

Business Profile: World's largest

bottler of Coca-Cola beverages.

Plan Specifics:

- Partial dividend reinvestment is available.
- No Discount.
- OCP: $10 to $60,000 per year.
- Selling costs are brokerage fees and a liquidation fee.
- Company purchases stock monthly with OCPs.
- Safekeeping services are available.
- Dividends are paid January, April, July, and October.

Performance Rating: ***

DRIP Rating: 👍

Colgate-Palmolive Co. (NYSE:CL)
c/o First Chicago Trust-NY
PO Box 2533
Jersey City, NJ 07303-2533
(201) 324-0498   (800) 446-2617

Business Profile: Produces household goods including detergents, soap, bleaches, and personal care products.

Plan Specifics:

- Partial dividend reinvestment is available.
- No Discount.
- OCP: $20 to $60,000 per year.
- Stock is purchased around the 15th of the month with OCPs.
- Preferred stock is eligible for reinvestment for common shares under the plan.
- Selling costs are brokerage commissions, $10 handling charge, and any other costs of sale.
- Dividends are paid February, May, August, and November.

Performance Rating: *****
DRIP Rating: 👍

Colonial BancGroup, Inc. (AL)
(NYSE:CNB)
PO Box 1108
Montgomery, AL 36101
(205) 240-5000   (205) 240-5008

Business Profile: Alabama-based commercial banking company.

Plan Specifics:
- Partial dividend reinvestment is available.
- No Discount.
- OCP: $10 to $3000 per quarter.
- Selling costs may include brokerage fees.
- Company purchases stock quarterly with OCPs.
- Dividends are paid February, May, August, and November.

Performance Rating: ***
DRIP Rating: 👍

Colonial Gas Co.
(NASDAQ:CGES)
PO Box 3064
Lowell, MA 01853
(508) 458-3171   (800) 736-3001

Business Profile: Supplies natural gas to customers in Massachusetts regions.

Plan Specifics:
- Partial dividend reinvestment is available.
- 5 percent discount on reinvested dividends.
- OCP: $10 to $5000 per quarter.
- Company purchases stock monthly with OCPs.
- Selling costs are brokerage commissions and a handling charge of $5.

- Automatic investment services are available.
- Dividends are paid March, June, September, and December.

Performance Rating: ***
DRIP Rating: 👍

Columbia Gas System, Inc.
(NYSE:CG)
Stockholder Services Dept.
PO Box 2318
Columbus, OH 43216-2318
(302) 429-5331

Business Profile: Natural gas holding company serving mid-Atlantic and midwestern states.

Plan Specifics:
- Partial dividend reinvestment is not available.
- No Discount.
- OCP: $10 to $10,000 per quarter.
- Purchasing and selling fees are brokerage commissions.
- $1 termination fee.
- Company purchases stock quarterly with OCPs.
- The firm is currently not paying a dividend.

Performance Rating: **
DRIP Rating: 👍

Columbus Realty Trust
(NYSE:CLB)
15851 Dallas Parkway, Ste. 855
Dallas, TX 75248
(214) 387-1492   (800) 753-7107

Business Profile: Real estate investment trust which owns upscale multifamily residential properties.

Plan Specifics:
- Partial dividend reinvestment is available.

- 5 percent discount on reinvested dividends and OCPs.
- OCP: $100 to $10,000 per quarter.
- OCP is invested quarterly.
- Selling costs include brokerage fees.
- Dividends are paid January, April, July, and October.

Performance Rating: **

DRIP Rating: 👍

Comerica, Inc. (NYSE:CMA)
One Detroit Center, Ste. 3800
Detroit, MI 48226
(313) 222-4000   (800) 468-9716

Business Profile: Holding company owning Comerica Banks in Michigan, Illinois, Texas, California, Florida, and elsewhere.

Plan Specifics:

- Partial dividend reinvestment is not available.
- No Discount.
- OCP: $10 to $3000 per quarter.
- Selling costs are brokerage commissions, a $3 handling charge, and any other costs of sale.
- Company purchases stock quarterly with OCPs.
- Dividends are paid January, April, July, and October.

Performance Rating: ****

DRIP Rating: 👍

Commerce Bancorp, Inc.
(NASDAQ:COBA)
Commerce Atrium
1701 Route 70 E.
Cherry Hill, NJ 08034-5400
(609) 751-9000

Business Profile: Multibank holding company serving metropolitan Philadelphia and southern New Jersey.

Plan Specifics:

- Partial dividend reinvestment is available.
- 3 percent discount on reinvested dividends and OCPs.
- OCP: $100 to $5000 per quarter.
- Selling costs are brokerage commissions and taxes.
- Company purchases stock quarterly with OCPs.
- Preferred stock is eligible for reinvestment for common shares.
- Dividends are usually paid January, April, July, and October.

Performance Rating: ***

DRIP Rating: 👍

Commercial Assets, Inc.
(ASE:CAX)
3600 S. Yosemite St.
Denver, CO 80237
(303) 773-1221

Business Profile: Real estate investment trust.

Plan Specifics:

- Partial dividend reinvestment is not available.
- No Discount.
- OCP: $50 to $10,000 per quarter.
- Selling costs are brokerage commissions and a $5 termination fee.
- Stock is purchased monthly with OCPs.
- Dividends are generally paid January, April, July, and October.

Performance Rating: NR

DRIP Rating: 👍

Commercial Intertech Corp. (NYSE:TEC)
PO Box 239
Youngstown, OH 44501-0239
(216) 746-8011

Business Profile: Designs, produces, and sells hydraulic components, fluid purification products, and fabricated metal products.

Plan Specifics:
- Partial dividend reinvestment is not available.
- No Discount.
- OCP: $30 to $5000 per quarter.
- Purchasing costs may include nominal brokerage fees.
- Participants must go through own broker to sell shares.
- Company purchases stock quarterly with OCPs.
- Dividends are paid March, June, September, and December.

Performance Rating: ***
DRIP Rating: 👍

Commonwealth Energy System (NYSE:CES)
PO Box 9150
Cambridge, MA 02142-9150
(800) 447-1183

Business Profile: Electric and gas utility holding company serving portions of Massachusetts.

Plan Specifics:
- Partial dividend reinvestment is not available.
- No Discount.
- OCP: $10 to $5000 per month.
- Must go through own broker to sell shares.
- Company purchases stock monthly with OCPs.

- Dividends are paid February, May, August, and November.

Performance Rating: **
DRIP Rating: 👍

Commonwealth Savings Bank (NASDAQ:CMSB)
c/o Chemical Bank
Dividend Reinvestment Dept.
JAF Bldg., PO Box 3069
New York, NY 10116-3069
(800) 851-9677

Business Profile: Pennsylvania-based banking company.

Plan Specifics:
- Partial dividend reinvestment is available.
- No Discount.
- OCP: $100 to $2500 per quarter.
- OCP is invested monthly.
- Purchasing fees are a $5 service charge for OCPs.
- Selling costs may include brokerage fees.
- $15 fee for terminating account.
- $5 fee for withdrawing certificates.
- Firm charges $3 for safekeeping services.
- Dividends are paid January, April, July, and October.

Performance Rating: ***
DRIP Rating: 💰

Community Bank System, Inc. (NY) (NASDAQ:CBSI)
5790 Widewaters Parkway
DeWitt, NY 13214
(315) 445-2282

Business Profile: New York-based bank holding organization.

Plan Specifics:

- Partial dividend reinvestment is not available.
- No Discount.
- OCP: $25 to $2000 per quarter.
- Selling costs are brokerage fees and $5 termination fee.
- Company purchases stock quarterly with OCPs.
- Dividends are paid January, April, July, and October.

Performance Rating: ***

DRIP Rating: 👍

Compass Bancshares, Inc. (NASDAQ:CBSS)
PO Box 10566
Birmingham, AL 35296
(617) 575-3170

Business Profile: Multibank holding company based in Alabama.

Plan Specifics:

- Partial dividend reinvestment is not available.
- No Discount.
- OCP: $25 to $1000 per month.
- Purchasing fees are brokerage commissions and a service charge ($2.50 maximum, 25 cents minimum).
- Selling costs are brokerage commissions and a service charge ($2.50 maximum, 25 cents minimum).
- Company purchases stock monthly with OCPs.
- Dividends are paid January, April, July, and October.

Performance Rating: NR

DRIP Rating: 👍

Computer Associates Int'l, Inc. (NYSE:CA)
c/o Chemical Mellon Securities
PO Box 750
Pittsburgh, PA 15230
(800) 526-0801

Business Profile: Designs, develops, markets, and supports standardized computer software products.

Plan Specifics:

- Need 50 shares to enroll in the plan.
- Partial dividend reinvestment is not available.
- No Discount.
- OCP: $25 to $3000 per month.
- Stock is purchased monthly with OCPs.
- Purchasing fees are brokerage commissions and $1.50 service charge.
- Selling fees are brokerage commissions and $5 service charge.
- Dividends are paid January and July.

Performance Rating: ****

DRIP Rating: 👎

COMSAT Corp. (NYSE:CQ)
Shareholder Services
6560 Rock Spring Dr.
Bethesda, MD 20817
(301) 214-3200

Business Profile: Provides satellite communications service, consulting service, and video entertainment operations.

Plan Specifics:

- Initial purchases may be made directly from company ($250 minimum).

- Partial dividend reinvestment is not available.
- No Discount.
- OCP: $50 to $10,000 per month.
- Company purchases stock monthly with OCPs.
- Selling fees include a $5 fee plus 6 cents per share.
- Dividends are paid March, June, September, and December.

Performance Rating: ****

DRIP Rating: 👍

ConAgra, Inc. (NYSE:CAG)
One ConAgra Dr.
Omaha, NE 68102-5001
(402) 595-4000

Business Profile: Markets shelf-stable foods, frozen foods, processed meats, red meats, poultry, and seafood. Distributes pesticides and fertilizers. Trades and processes grain and other agricultural products.

Plan Specifics:

- Partial dividend reinvestment is available.
- No Discount.
- OCP: $50 to $50,000 per year.
- Selling costs are discounted brokerage fees and a $15 fee.
- Company purchases stock twice a month with OCPs.
- Approximately 13,000 shareholders are in the plan.
- Dividends are paid March, June, September, and December.

Performance Rating: ****

DRIP Rating: 👍

Connecticut Energy Corp. (NYSE:CNE)
PO Box 1540
Bridgeport, CT 06601
(203) 382-8156   (800) 736-3001

Business Profile: Gas utility holding company serving parts of Connecticut.

Plan Specifics:

- Partial dividend reinvestment is available.
- No Discount.
- OCP: $50 to $50,000 per year.
- Company purchases stock monthly with OCPs.
- Selling costs include a service charge, a small brokerage commission, and transfer taxes.
- Automatic investment services are available.
- IRA option is available.
- Customers of the utility may make initial purchases of stock directly from the firm ($250 minimum).
- More than 6600 shareholders are in the plan.
- Dividends are paid March, June, September, and December.

Performance Rating: ****

DRIP Rating: 👍

Connecticut Natural Gas Corp. (NYSE:CTG)
PO Box 1500
100 Columbus Blvd.
Hartford, CT 06144-1500
(203) 727-3469   (212) 613-7143

Business Profile: Provides gas to customers in central Connecticut communities.

Plan Specifics:
- Partial dividend reinvestment is available.
- No Discount.
- OCP: $25 to $5000 per quarter.
- Selling costs include brokerage costs.
- Company purchases stock monthly with OCPs.
- Preferred dividends may be reinvested for additional common shares under the plan.
- Dividends are paid March, June, September, and December.

Performance Rating: ****
DRIP Rating: 👍

Connecticut Water Service, Inc. (NASDAQ:CTWS)
93 W. Main St.
Clinton, CT 06413
(860) 669-8630

Business Profile: Holding company for Connecticut Water Co., a supplier of water and fire protection services in parts of Connecticut.

Plan Specifics:
- Partial dividend reinvestment is available.
- 5 percent discount on reinvested dividends.
- OCP: $100 to $3000 per quarter.
- Company purchases stock quarterly with OCPs.
- Selling costs include brokerage commissions and any other fees or charges.
- IRA option is available.
- Utility customers may purchase initial shares directly from company ($100 minimum).

- Dividends are paid March, June, September, and December.

Performance Rating: ***
DRIP Rating: 👍

Conrail, Inc. (NYSE:CRR)
c/o First Chicago Trust-NY
PO Box 2598
Jersey City, NJ 07303-2598
(800) 446-2617 (215) 209-4000

Business Profile: Operates a 12,400-mile railroad in 14 midwestern and northeastern states.

Plan Specifics:
- Partial dividend reinvestment is available.
- No Discount.
- OCP: up to $4000 per year.
- Selling costs are minimal brokerage commissions, a service fee and other costs of sale.
- Purchasing costs are brokerage commissions and a service charge ($2.50 maximum).
- Stock is purchased monthly with OCPs.
- Certificate safekeeping is available.
- Dividends are paid March, June, September, and December.

Performance Rating: ****
DRIP Rating: 👍

Consolidated Edison Co. of New York (NYSE:ED)
Attn: Investors Service
PO Box 149
New York, NY 10003
(800) 221-6664 (800) 522-5522

Business Profile: Supplies electric power and gas to residential and commercial customers throughout New York City.

Plan Specifics:
- Partial dividend reinvestment is available.
- No Discount.
- OCP: $20 to $12,000 per year.
- Selling costs are brokerage commissions.
- Company purchases stock every month with OCPs.
- Dividends are paid March, June, September, and December.

Performance Rating: ****

DRIP Rating: 👍

**Consolidated Natural Gas Co.
 (NYSE:CNG)
625 Liberty Ave.
Pittsburgh, PA 15222-3199
(412) 227-1183   (412) 227-1485**

Business Profile: Explores for, produces, stores, and distributes natural gas to parts of Ohio, Pennsylvania, New York, Virginia, and West Virginia.

Plan Specifics:
- Partial dividend reinvestment is available.
- No Discount.
- OCP: $25 to $5000 per quarter.
- Selling costs are brokerage commissions and a $5 termination fee.
- Company purchases stock quarterly with OCPs.
- Approximately 7500 shareholders are in the plan.
- Dividends are paid February, May, August, and November.

Performance Rating: ****

DRIP Rating: 👍

**Consolidated Papers, Inc.
 (NYSE:CDP)
c/o Harris Trust & Savings Bank
PO Box A3309
Chicago, IL 60690-3309
(715) 422-3111   (312) 461-5754**

Business Profile: Leading producer of coated and specialty papers for food and consumer product packaging. Also produces corrugated containers, paperboard, and pulp.

Plan Specifics:
- Partial dividend reinvestment is available.
- No Discount.
- OCP: $100 to $3000 per quarter.
- Selling costs are brokerage commissions and transfer taxes.
- Company purchases stock monthly with OCPs.
- Dividends are paid February, May, August, and November.

Performance Rating: ***

DRIP Rating: 👍

**Consumers Water Co.
 (NASDAQ:CONW)
PO Box 599
Three Canal Plaza
Portland, ME 04112
(800) 292-2925   (207) 773-6438**

Business Profile: Water utility holding company for portions of several northeastern states.

Plan Specifics:
- Partial dividend reinvestment is available.
- No Discount.
- OCP: $10 to $50,000 per year.
- Selling costs are brokerage commissions.

- Company purchases stock monthly with OCPs.
- Preferred shares may be reinvested for additional common shares under the plan.
- Approximately 3700 shareholders are in the plan.
- Dividends are paid February, May, August, and November.

Performance Rating: **

DRIP Rating: 👍

Cooper Industries, Inc.
(NYSE:CBE)
PO Box 4446
Houston, TX 77210
(713) 739-5400

Business Profile: Manufactures electrical power equipment, tools, and automotive parts.

Plan Specifics:

- Partial dividend reinvestment is available.
- No Discount.
- OCP: $25 to $24,000 per year.
- Selling costs are brokerage commissions.
- Company purchases or issues stock monthly with OCPs.
- Preferred stock is eligible for reinvestment for common shares under the plan.
- Approximately 7280 shareholders are in the plan.
- Dividends are paid January, April, July, and October.

Performance Rating: ***

DRIP Rating: 👍

Copley Properties, Inc.
(ASE:COP)
399 Boylston St.
Boston, MA 02116
(617) 578-1200

Business Profile: Real estate investment trust.

Plan Specifics:

- Partial dividend reinvestment is not available.
- No Discount.
- OCP: $100 to no maximum per quarter.
- Purchasing fees include brokerage commission.
- Company purchases stock quarterly with OCPs.
- Dividends are paid January, April, July, and October.

Performance Rating: **

DRIP Rating: 👎

CoreStates Financial Corp.
(NYSE:CFL)
c/o First Chicago Trust-NY
PO Box 2598
Jersey City, NJ 07303-2598
(800) 446-2617

Business Profile: Multibank holding company with banks in Pennsylvania and New Jersey.

Plan Specifics:

- Partial dividend reinvestment is available.
- No Discount.
- OCP: $50 to $5000 per month.
- Selling fees include a $10 service charge and brokerage commissions.
- Company purchases stock monthly with OCPs.
- Dividends are paid January, April, July, and October.

Performance Rating: ****
DRIP Rating: 👍

Corning, Inc. (NYSE:GLW)
c/o Harris Trust & Savings
PO Box 755
Chicago, IL 60690
(312) 461-6832

Business Profile: Manufactures products made from specialty glasses.

Plan Specifics:
- Partial dividend reinvestment is not available.
- No Discount.
- OCP: $10 to $5000 per month.
- Selling costs are brokerage commissions.
- Stock purchased on last business day of the month with OCPs.
- Dividends are paid March, June, September, and December.

Performance Rating: ****
DRIP Rating: 👍

Countrywide Credit Industries, Inc. (NYSE:CCR)
c/o Bank of New York
Dividend Reinvestment
PO Box 1958
Newark, NJ 07101-9774
(800) 524-4458   (818) 304-8400

Business Profile: Leading residential mortgage lender.

Plan Specifics:
- Partial dividend reinvestment is available.
- 4 percent discount on reinvested dividends.
- OCP: not available.
- Selling fees may include brokerage commissions plus $15 service charge.

- Dividends are paid January, April, July, and October.

Performance Rating: ***
DRIP Rating: 👍

Cousins Properties, Inc. (NYSE:CUZ)
c/o First Union National Bank of North Carolina
Two First Union Center
Charlotte, NC 28288-1154
(404) 955-2200

Business Profile: Real estate investment trust which concentrates on commercial buildings.

Plan Specifics:
- Partial dividend reinvestment is available.
- 5 percent discount on reinvested dividends.
- OCP: not available.
- Selling costs are brokerage commissions, taxes, and a transaction charge.
- Dividends are paid February, May, August, and December.

Performance Rating: **
DRIP Rating: 👍

CPC International, Inc. (NYSE:CPC)
PO Box 8000
International Plaza
Englewood Cliffs, NJ 07632-9976
(201) 894-2460   (800) 272-6360

Business Profile: International supplier of branded grocery products, including Hellmann's mayonnaise and Skippy peanut butter.

Plan Specifics:
- Partial dividend reinvestment is available.
- No Discount.
- OCP: $10 to $12,000 per year.
- Company purchases stock around the 25th of each month with OCPs.
- Selling fees are brokerage commissions.
- Approximately 5800 shareholders are in the plan.
- Dividends are paid January, April, July, and October.

Performance Rating: *****
DRIP Rating: 👍

CPI Corp. (NYSE:CPY)
c/o Continental Stock Transfer &
  Trust Co.
2 Broadway, 19th Floor
New York, NY 10004
(212) 509-4000

Business Profile: Operator of portrait studios through Sears, Roebuck and Co. Also owns a photo finishing chain and high-tech copy stores.

Plan Specifics:
- Partial dividend reinvestment is available.
- No Discount.
- OCP: $10 to $10,000 per quarter.
- Selling costs are brokerage commissions and a $5 service charge.
- Company purchases stock quarterly with OCPs.
- Dividends are paid February, May, August, and November.

Performance Rating: ***
DRIP Rating: 👍

Cracker Barrel Old Country Store,
  Inc. (NASDAQ:CBRL)
PO Box 787
Hartmann Dr.
Lebanon, TN 37088-0787
(615) 444-5533   (800) 568-3476

Business Profile: Operates "country store" restaurants located mostly in the southeastern and midwestern U.S.

Plan Specifics:
- Partial dividend reinvestment is available.
- No Discount.
- OCP: $100 to $5000 per quarter.
- Selling costs are brokerage commissions and any applicable transfer tax.
- Company purchases stock monthly with OCPs.
- Dividends are paid March, June, September, and December.

Performance Rating: ****
DRIP Rating: 👍

Crane Co. (NYSE:CR)
100 First Stamford Pl.
Stamford, CT 06902
(203) 363-7300

Business Profile: Provides engineered products for aerospace, fluid handling, automatic merchandising, and construction.

Plan Specifics:
- Partial dividend reinvestment is available.
- No Discount.
- OCP: $10 to $5000 per month.
- Selling costs are brokerage commissions and any other costs of sale.

- Company purchases stock around the 14th of the month with OCPs.
- Dividends are paid March, June, September, and December.

Performance Rating: ****

DRIP Rating: 👍

Crestar Financial Corp. (NYSE:CF)
919 E. Main St.
PO Box 26665
Richmond, VA 23261-6665
(804) 782-5619

Business Profile: Multibank holding company for Virginia, Maryland, and Washington, D.C. communities.

Plan Specifics:

- Partial dividend reinvestment is not available.
- 5 percent discount on reinvested dividends.
- OCP: $10 to $10,000 per quarter.
- Selling costs are a $5 service charge, brokerage commissions, and transfer tax.
- Company purchases stock monthly with OCPs.
- Dividends are paid February, May, August, and November.

Performance Rating: ***

DRIP Rating: 👍

Crompton & Knowles Corp. (NYSE:CNK)
One Station Place-Metro Center
Stamford, CT 06902
(203) 353-5400   (800) 526-0801

Business Profile: Manufactures dyes, fabrics, food ingredients, and extrusion equipment.

Plan Specifics:

- Need at least 50 shares to enroll in plan.
- Partial dividend reinvestment is not available.
- No Discount.
- OCP: $30 to $3000 per quarter.
- Company purchases stock quarterly with OCPs.
- Service charge for depositing stock certificates is $5.
- Selling costs are brokerage commissions and transfer taxes.
- Dividends are paid February, May, August, and November.

Performance Rating: ****

DRIP Rating: 👍

CSX Corp. (NYSE:CSX)
c/o Harris Trust & Savings
PO Box 755
Chicago, IL 60690
(800) 521-5571   (804) 782-1400

Business Profile: Offers rail, container-shipping, intermodal, barging, trucking, contract logistics, and related services worldwide.

Plan Specifics:

- Partial dividend reinvestment is not available.
- No Discount.
- OCP: $25 to $1500 per month.
- Selling fees are brokerage commissions and a $1 termination fee.
- Company purchases stock around the 15th of the month with OCPs.
- Dividends are paid March, June, September, and December.

Performance Rating: ****

DRIP Rating: 👍

Cummins Engine Co., Inc.
(NYSE:CUM)
c/o First Chicago Trust-NY
PO Box 2533
Jersey City, NJ 07303-2533
(800) 446-2617

Business Profile: Leading supplier of diesel engines, engine parts, and power systems for heavy-duty vehicles and equipment.

Plan Specifics:
- Partial dividend reinvestment is not available.
- No Discount.
- OCP: $10 to $6000 per quarter.
- Stock is purchased around the 15th of each month with OCPs.
- Participants may incur brokerage fees when selling shares from the plan.
- Dividends are paid March, June, September, and December.

Performance Rating: ***
DRIP Rating: 👍

Cyprus Amax Minerals Co.
(NYSE:CYM)
PO Box 3299
9100 E. Mineral Circle
Englewood, CO 80155
(303) 643-5000

Business Profile: Supplier of copper, coal, and other natural resources.

Plan Specifics:
- Partial dividend reinvestment is not available.
- No Discount.
- OCP: $50 to $3000 per month.
- Purchasing fees include service fee of $1.10 for each dividend payment invested and each voluntary cash payment plus brokerage fees.

- Selling costs are brokerage commissions and a $5 termination fee.
- Company purchases stock with OCPs within 30 days of receipt.
- Dividends are paid February, May, August, and November.

Performance Rating: **
DRIP Rating: 👍

D & N Financial Corp.
(NASDAQ:DNFC)
400 Quincy St.
Hancock, MI 49930
(906) 487-6225

Business Profile: Holding company of D & N Bank, one of the largest thrift institutions in Michigan.

Plan Specifics:
- Partial dividend reinvestment is not available.
- No Discount.
- OCP: $25 to $12,000 per year.
- Selling costs are brokerage commissions, transfer taxes, and handling charges.
- Company purchases stock monthly with OCPs.
- The company is not currently paying a dividend.

Performance Rating: **
DRIP Rating: 👍

Dana Corp. (NYSE:DCN)
Shareholder Relations
PO Box 1000
Toledo, OH 43697
(419) 535-4633

Business Profile: Manufactures automotive parts and industrial products for original equipment and aftermarket distribution.

Plan Specifics:
- Partial dividend reinvestment is not available.
- No Discount.
- OCP: $25 to $2000 per month.
- Selling costs are brokerage commission and service fees.
- Stock is purchased monthly with OCPs.
- Dividends are paid March, June, September, and December.

Performance Rating: ***

DRIP Rating: 👍

Dauphin Deposit Corp. (NASDAQ:DAPN)
PO Box 2961
Harrisburg, PA 17105
(717) 255-2121

Business Profile: Holding company with 100 branch banks throughout Pennsylvania.

Plan Specifics:
- Partial dividend reinvestment is not available.
- No Discount.
- OCP: $50 to $1000 per month.
- Selling costs are brokerage commissions and service charges.
- Company purchases stock monthly with OCPs.
- Dividends are paid January, April, July, and October.

Performance Rating: *****

DRIP Rating: 👍

Dayton Hudson Corp. (NYSE:DH)
Attn: Investor Relations Dept.
777 Nicollet Mall
Minneapolis, MN 55402
(612) 370-6732   (800) 446-2617

Business Profile: Operator of department and retail stores.

Plan Specifics:
- Partial dividend reinvestment is available.
- No Discount.
- OCP: $10 to $1000 per month.
- Selling costs are brokerage commissions and a service fee.
- Company purchases stock monthly with OCPs.
- Automatic investment services are available.
- Shares may be sold via the telephone.
- Dividends are paid March, June, September, and December.

Performance Rating: ****

DRIP Rating: 👍

Dean Foods Co. (NYSE:DF)
c/o Harris Trust & Savings Bank
PO Box A3309
111 W. Monroe St.
Chicago, IL 60690
(312) 461-3324   (312) 625-6200

Business Profile: A diversified food processor and distributor, producing a full line of dairy and other food products.

Plan Specifics:
- Must have at least 25 shares to enroll in the plan.
- Partial dividend reinvestment is not available.
- No Discount.
- OCP: $25 to $3000 per quarter.
- Selling costs are brokerage commissions and other expenses.
- Company purchases stock quarterly with OCPs.

- Safekeeping services are available.
- Dividends are paid March, June, September, and December.

Performance Rating: ****

DRIP Rating: 👎

Dean Witter, Discover & Co. (NYSE:DWD)
Exchange Pl.
PO Box 989
Jersey City, NJ 07311
(800) 228-0829

Business Profile: Company is involved in credit services and securities operations.

Plan Specifics:

- Initial purchases may be made directly from the company ($1000 minimum).
- Partial dividend reinvestment is available.
- No Discount.
- OCP: $100 to $40,000 per year.
- OCP is invested twice per month.
- Selling costs include brokerage fees and $5 service charge.
- Dividends are paid January, April, July, and October.

Performance Rating: ***

DRIP Rating: 👍

DeBartolo Realty Corp. (NYSE:EJD)
7620 Market St.
Youngstown, OH 44513-6085
(216) 758-7292   (800) 850-2880

Business Profile: Real estate investment trust which focuses on ownership of shopping malls.

Plan Specifics:

- Initial purchases may be made directly from the company ($500 minimum).
- Partial dividend reinvestment is available.
- No Discount.
- OCP: $50 to $30,000 per quarter.
- OCP is invested weekly.
- Purchasing fees for OCP are 5 percent of the amount invested ($10 maximum) plus brokerage commissions.
- Selling fees are $15 service charge plus brokerage commissions.
- Automatic investment services are available.
- Dividends are paid January, April, July, and October.

Performance Rating: **

DRIP Rating: 👍

Deere & Company (NYSE:DE)
John Deere Rd.
Moline, IL 61265
(309) 765-8000

Business Profile: Largest worldwide manufacturer of farm equipment with significant operations in construction and lawn equipment.

Plan Specifics:

- Partial dividend reinvestment is not available.
- No Discount.
- OCP: $50 to $10,000 per month.
- OCP is invested around the 1st of the month.
- Purchasing fees are 5 percent on each investment ($3 maximum) plus commissions.
- Selling costs are $15 service fee and brokerage commissions.

- Dividends are paid February, May, August, and November.

Performance Rating: ***

DRIP Rating: 👍

Delmarva Power & Light Co. (NYSE:DEW)
Attn: Shareholder Services
PO Box 231, 800 King St.
Wilmington, DE 19899
(800) 365-6495   (302) 429-3355

Business Profile: Supplies electricity and gas to residential, commercial, and industrial customers in parts of Delaware, Maryland, and Virginia.

Plan Specifics:
- Partial dividend reinvestment is available.
- No Discount.
- OCP: up to $100,000 per year.
- Company purchases stock monthly with OCPs.
- Company may charge brokerage fees for any shares purchased on open market for shareholders.
- Selling costs are brokerage commissions.
- Dividends are paid January, April, July, and October.

Performance Rating: ***

DRIP Rating: 👍

Delta Air Lines, Inc. (NYSE:DAL)
Hartsfield Atlanta Int'l Airport
Atlanta, GA 30320
(201) 324-0498

Business Profile: Major air carrier with route systems covering most of the United States as well as several foreign countries.

Plan Specifics:
- Partial dividend reinvestment is not available.
- No Discount.
- OCP: $25 to $10,000 per year.
- Selling costs are brokerage commissions.
- Company purchases stock around the 1st business day of the month with OCPs.
- Shares may be sold via the telephone.
- Approximately 9800 shareholders are in the plan.
- Dividends are paid March, June, September, and December.

Performance Rating: ***

DRIP Rating: 👍

Delta Natural Gas Co., Inc. (NASDAQ:DGAS)
3617 Lexington Rd.
Winchester, KY 40391
(606) 744-6171

Business Profile: Supplies natural gas to portions of Kentucky.

Plan Specifics:
- Partial dividend reinvestment is available.
- No Discount.
- OCP: $25 to $50,000 per year.
- Company purchases stock around the 15th day of the month with OCPs.
- Residents of Kentucky may make initial purchases directly from the firm (minimum $100).
- Must go through own broker to sell shares from the plan.
- Dividends are paid March, June, September, and December.

Performance Rating: ***

DRIP Rating: 👍

**Deposit Guaranty Corp.
(NASDAQ:DEPS)
PO Box 11275, Church St. Sta.
New York, NY 10277
(601) 354-8564   (601) 354-8114**

Business Profile: Holding company which provides banking and trust services to more than 40 communities in Mississippi through its Deposit Guaranty National Bank subsidiary.

Plan Specifics:

- Partial dividend reinvestment is not available.
- No Discount.
- OCP: $50 to $5000 per quarter.
- Selling costs are brokerage commissions and any taxes.
- Company purchases stock quarterly with OCPs.
- Dividends are paid January, April, July, and October.

Performance Rating: ****

DRIP Rating: 👍

**Detroit Edison Co. (NYSE:DTE)
PO Box 33380
Detroit, MI 48232
(313) 237-8666   (800) 551-5009**

Business Profile: Supplies electricity and steam to customers in southeastern Michigan.

Plan Specifics:

- Partial dividend reinvestment is not available.
- No Discount.
- OCP: $20 to $5000 per quarter.
- Purchasing fees are 50 cents per quarter administrative charge plus brokerage commissions.
- Must go through own broker to sell shares.

- Company purchases stock quarterly with OCPs.
- Preferred dividends may be reinvested for additional common shares under the plan.
- Dividends are paid January, April, July, and October.

Performance Rating: ***

DRIP Rating: 👍

**Dexter Corp. (NYSE:DEX)
1 Elm St.
Windsor Locks, CT 06096
(203) 282-3509   (203) 627-9051
(800) 288-9541**

Business Profile: Produces specialty coatings, plastics, and materials used in aerospace, automotive, electronics, medical, and food markets.

Plan Specifics:

- Partial dividend reinvestment is not available.
- No Discount.
- OCP: $25 to $3000 per month.
- Selling costs are brokerage commissions.
- Company purchases stock monthly with OCPs.
- Approximately 600 shareholders are in the plan.
- Dividends are paid January, April, July, and October.

Performance Rating: ***

DRIP Rating: 👍

**The Dial Corp (NYSE:DL)
Stockholder Services Dept.
Dial Tower
Phoenix, AZ 85077-1424
(800) 453-2235**

Business Profile: Produces consumer products, including soap and canned meats, and operates in-flight catering services.

Plan Specifics:

- Initial purchases of stock may be made directly from the company (minimum $100).
- Partial dividend reinvestment is available.
- No Discount.
- OCP: $10 to $5000 per month.
- Company purchases stock once a month with OCPs.
- No selling costs.
- Any holder of 49 shares or less in certificate form may sell all of their shares through the plan.
- Shares can be sold via the telephone.
- Dividends are paid January, April, July, and October.

Performance Rating: *****

DRIP Rating: 👍

Diebold, Inc. (NYSE:DBD)
PO Box 8230
Canton, OH 44711-8230
(800) 542-7792

Business Profile: Develops, manufactures, sells, and services ATMs, electronic and physical security systems, facility products, and software for global financial and commercial markets.

Plan Specifics:

- Partial dividend reinvestment is not available.
- No Discount.
- OCP: $10 to $5000 per quarter.
- Selling costs are brokerage commissions and a $5 service fee.
- Company purchases stock quarterly with OCPs.

- Dividends are paid March, June, September, and December.

Performance Rating: *****

DRIP Rating: 👍

Dominion Resources, Inc.
(NYSE:D)
PO Box 26532
Richmond, VA 23261
(800) 552-4034

Business Profile: Electric utility holding company serving Virginia and North Carolina.

Plan Specifics:

- Partial dividend reinvestment is available.
- No Discount.
- OCP: up to $50,000 per quarter.
- Selling costs are brokerage commissions.
- Company purchases stock around the 20th of each month with OCPs received by the 15th.
- Participants' shares will be sold at least once per week, except between the 4th business day prior to a dividend record date and the following dividend payment date.
- Customers of the utility may make initial purchase of stock directly from the company ($20 minimum).
- Approximately 150,000 shareholders are in the plan.
- Dividends are paid March, June, September, and December.

Performance Rating: ****

DRIP Rating: 👍

Donaldson Co., Inc. (NYSE:DCI)
PO Box 1299
Minneapolis, MN 55440
(612) 887-3131   (800) 551-6161

Business Profile: International producer of air cleaners and filters for internal combustion engines.

Plan Specifics:

- Partial dividend reinvestment is not available.
- No Discount.
- OCP: $10 to $1000 per month.
- Selling costs are brokerage commissions and other costs of sale.
- Company purchases stock monthly if enough funds accumulate to purchase at least 100 shares.
- Dividends are paid March, June, September, and December.

Performance Rating: ****
DRIP Rating: 👍

Donnelley (R.R.) & Sons Co.
(NYSE:DNY)
c/o First Chicago Trust-NY
PO Box 2533
Jersey City, NJ 07303-2533
(312) 326-8000   (800) 446-2617

Business Profile: Largest commercial printer in United States. Provides catalogs, magazines, books, and directories.

Plan Specifics:

- Partial dividend reinvestment is available.
- No Discount.
- OCP: $10 to $60,000 per year.
- Selling costs are brokerage fees and other sale costs.
- Company purchases stock monthly with OCPs.

- Dividends are paid March, June, September, and December.

Performance Rating: *****
DRIP Rating: 👍

Dow Chemical Co. (NYSE:DOW)
c/o Ameritrust Co.
PO Box 6477
Cleveland, OH 44101-1477
(517) 636-1463   (800) 542-7792

Business Profile: Major chemical manufacturer. Supplies organic and inorganic chemicals, plastics, hydrocarbons, and agricultural products.

Plan Specifics:

- Partial dividend reinvestment is not available.
- No Discount.
- OCP: $10 to $25,000 per quarter.
- Selling costs are brokerage fees and $5 service fee (may sell only a portion of your shares).
- Stock is purchased approximately every four weeks with OCPs.
- Dividends are paid January, April, July, and October.

Performance Rating: ****
DRIP Rating: 👍

Dow Jones & Co., Inc. (NYSE:DJ)
World Financial Center
200 Liberty St.
New York, NY 10281
(609) 520-5150

Business Profile: Publishes business newspapers (*The Wall Street Journal* and *Barron's*), provides information services, and circulates community newspapers.

Plan Specifics:
- Partial dividend reinvestment is available.
- No Discount.
- OCP: $25 to $1000 per month.
- Stock is purchased around the 1st business day of the month with OCPs.
- Selling costs are brokerage commissions.
- Dividends are paid March, June, September, and December.

Performance Rating: ****

DRIP Rating: 👍

DPL, Inc. (NYSE:DPL)
PO Box 1247
Dayton, OH 45401
(513) 259-7150   (800) 322-9244

Business Profile: Electric utility holding company serving portions of Ohio.

Plan Specifics:
- Partial dividend reinvestment is not available.
- No Discount.
- OCP: $25 to $1000 per quarter.
- Company purchases stock quarterly with OCPs.
- Selling costs are brokerage commissions.
- Approximately 23,000 shareholders are in the plan.
- Preferred dividends may be reinvested for additional common shares under the plan.
- Dividends are paid March, June, September, and December.

Performance Rating: ****

DRIP Rating: 👍

DQE (NYSE:DQE)
Dividend Reinvestment
PO Box 68
Pittsburgh, PA 15230-0068
(800) 247-0400   (412) 393-6167

Business Profile: The principal subsidiary, Duquesne Light Company, provides electric power to customers in southwestern Pennsylvania.

Plan Specifics:
- Initial purchases may be made directly from the company. Minimum initial investment is $100 plus a $5 one-time account setup fee.
- Partial dividend reinvestment is available.
- No Discount.
- OCP: $10 to $60,000 per year.
- Purchasing fees are nominal brokerage commissions.
- Company purchases stock monthly with OCPs.
- Selling costs are brokerage commissions and any handling fee.
- Automatic investment services are available.
- Preferred dividends may be reinvested for additional common shares under the plan.
- Dividends are paid January, April, July, and October.

Performance Rating: ****

DRIP Rating: 👍

Dresser Industries, Inc.
(NYSE:DI)
Shareholder Services
PO Box 718
Dallas, TX 75221
(214) 740-6708   (214) 740-6888

Business Profile: Significant supplier of products used in energy processing and oil field operations.

Plan Specifics:
- Partial dividend reinvestment is not available.
- No Discount.
- OCP: $25 to $1000 per month.
- Selling costs are brokerage fees.
- Company purchases stock around the 20th of the month with OCPs.
- Dividends are paid March, June, September, and December.

Performance Rating: ***
DRIP Rating: 👍

Du Pont (E.I.) de Nemours & Co.
(NYSE:DD)
Attn: Shareholder Relations
PO Box 470
Washington Bridge Sta.
New York, NY 10033
(302) 774-0195   (800) 526-0801

Business Profile: Nation's largest chemical producer with major operations in petroleum via its Conoco unit.

Plan Specifics:
- Partial dividend reinvestment is not available.
- No Discount.
- OCP: $20 to $5000 per quarter.
- Purchasing fees may include maximum service charge of $3 and brokerage commissions,

usually about 1 percent of investment.
- Stock is purchased approximately 8 times a year with OCPs.
- Selling costs are brokerage commissions and $5 service charge.
- Service charge for depositing certificates is $3.50.
- Preferred dividends may be reinvested for additional common shares under the plan.
- Dividends are paid March, June, September, and December.

Performance Rating: *****
DRIP Rating: 👍

Duke Power Co. (NYSE:DUK)
Attn: Investor Relations Dept.
PO Box 1005
Charlotte, NC 28201-1005
(800) 488-3853

Business Profile: Provides electricity to Piedmont regions of North and South Carolina.

Plan Specifics:
- Partial dividend reinvestment is available.
- No Discount.
- OCP: $25 to $20,000 per quarter.
- Company purchases stock monthly with OCPs.
- Selling costs are nominal brokerage fees.
- Automatic investment services are available.
- Residents of North and South Carolina may make initial purchase of stock directly through the company (minimum $25). Company is contemplating opening initial purchase option to all investors.

- Preferred dividends are eligible for reinvestment in additional common shares.
- Dividends are paid March, June, September, and December.

Performance Rating: *****

DRIP Rating: 👍

Duke Realty Investments, Inc.
(NYSE:DRE)
8888 Keystone Crossing,
Suite 1200
Indianapolis, IN 46240
(800) 278-4353   (317) 574-3531

Business Profile: Real estate investment trust which focuses on warehouses and office buildings.

Plan Specifics:

- Initial purchases may be made directly from the company (minimum $250).
- Partial dividend reinvestment is not available.
- 5 percent discount on reinvested dividends.
- OCP: $100 to $5000 per month.
- OCP is invested monthly.
- Selling fees include brokerage commissions.
- Automatic investment services are available.
- Dividends are paid February, May, August, and November.

Performance Rating: **

DRIP Rating: 👍

Duracell International, Inc.
(NYSE:DUR)
Berkshire Industrial Park
Bethel, CT 06801
(203) 796-4000   (800) 446-2617

Business Profile: Manufactures Duracell alkaline batteries and other battery types.

Plan Specifics:

- Partial dividend reinvestment is available.
- No Discount.
- OCP: $25 to $60,000 per year.
- Selling costs are brokerage commissions and any other costs of sale.
- Company purchases stock monthly with OCPs.
- Dividends are paid March, June, September, and December.

Performance Rating: ****

DRIP Rating: 👍

Duriron Co., Inc.
(NASDAQ:DURI)
c/o Bank One, Indianapolis, NA
Corporate Trust Department
Bank One Center/Tower
111 Monument Circle, Ste. 1611
Indianapolis, IN 46277-0116
(317) 321-8110

Business Profile: Manufactures equipment for chemical process markets.

Plan Specifics:

- Partial dividend reinvestment is not available.
- No Discount.
- OCP: $25 to $3000 per quarter.
- Selling costs are service charge of $3 and brokerage commissions.
- Service charge for depositing certificates is $5 for each deposit.
- Company purchases stock at least quarterly with OCPs.
- Approximately 750 shareholders are in the plan.

- Dividends are paid March, June, September, and December.

Performance Rating: ***

DRIP Rating: 👍

E'Town Corp. (NYSE:ETW)
c/o Bank of New York
1010 Barclay St.
New York, NY 10286
(908) 654-1234

Business Profile: Holding company for New Jersey water utility.

Plan Specifics:

- Partial dividend reinvestment is available.
- 5 percent discount on both OCPs and reinvested dividends.
- OCP: $100 to $2000 per month.
- Selling costs may include brokerage commissions.
- Company purchases stock once a month with OCPs.
- Dividends are paid March, June, September, and December.

Performance Rating: **

DRIP Rating: 👍

Eastern Co. (ASE:EML)
112 Bridge St.
Naugatuck, CT 06770
(203) 729-2255

Business Profile: Manufactures security locks and industrial products.

Plan Specifics:

- Partial dividend reinvestment is available.
- No Discount.
- OCP: $25 to $3000 per quarter.
- Selling costs are brokerage commissions and maximum $5 service fee.

- Company purchases stock quarterly with OCPs.
- Approximately 150 shareholders are in the plan.
- Dividends are paid March, June, September, and December.

Performance Rating: **

DRIP Rating: 👍

Eastern Enterprises (NYSE:EFU)
9 Riverside Rd.
Weston, MA 02193
(617) 647-2300

Business Profile: Has operations in natural gas utility services, barge lines, and water products and purification systems.

Plan Specifics:

- Partial dividend reinvestment is available.
- No Discount.
- OCP: $10 to $3000 per quarter.
- Selling costs are brokerage commissions and a maximum service fee of $10.
- Company purchases stock quarterly with OCPs.
- Dividends are paid January, April, July, and October.

Performance Rating: ***

DRIP Rating: 👍

Eastern Utilities Associates
 (NYSE:EUA)
PO Box 2333
Boston, MA 02107
(617) 357-9590

Business Profile: Diversified energy-services company. Distributes electric power to residential, commercial, and industrial customers in Massachusetts and Rhode Island.

Plan Specifics:
- Partial dividend reinvestment is available.
- No Discount.
- OCP: up to $5000 per quarter.
- Selling costs are brokerage commissions.
- Company purchases stock monthly with OCPs.
- Dividends are paid February, May, August, and November.

Performance Rating: **

DRIP Rating: 👍

Eastman Chemical Company (NYSE:EMN)
PO Box 511
Kingsport, TN 37662-5075
(615) 229-4647   (800) 323-1404

Business Profile: A leading international chemical company that produces a wide range of chemicals, fibers, and plastics.

Plan Specifics:
- Partial dividend reinvestment is available.
- No Discount.
- OCP: maximum $60,000 per year.
- Stock is purchased weekly with OCPs.
- Selling costs are brokerage commissions, a service fee, and any other costs of sale.
- Shares may be sold via the telephone.
- Safekeeping services are available.
- Dividends are paid January, April, July, and October.

Performance Rating: ***

DRIP Rating: 👍

Eastman Kodak Co. (NYSE:EK)
c/o First Chicago Trust-NY
PO Box 2598
Jersey City, NJ 07303-2598
(800) 253-6057

Business Profile: Largest worldwide manufacturer of photographic products.

Plan Specifics:
- Partial dividend reinvestment is available.
- No Discount.
- OCP: up to $60,000 per year.
- Selling costs are brokerage commission, a service charge, and any other costs of sale.
- Company purchases stock weekly with OCPs.
- Shares may be sold via the telephone.
- Dividends are paid January, April, July, and October.

Performance Rating: ****

DRIP Rating: 👍

Eaton Corp. (NYSE:ETN)
c/o KeyCorp Shareholder Svcs.
PO Box 6477
Cleveland, OH 44101-1477
(216) 523-4350   (800) 542-7792

Business Profile: Important producer of vehicle components and electrical controls for automotive, commercial, defense, and industrial industries.

Plan Specifics:
- Partial dividend reinvestment is available.
- No Discount.
- OCP: $10 to $60,000 per year.
- No selling costs.

- Initial OCP of $100 is required if participant is just in the OCP program.
- The company purchases stock monthly with OCPs.
- Dividends are paid February, May, August, and November.

Performance Rating: ****

DRIP Rating: 👍

Ecolab, Inc. (NYSE:ECL)
Ecolab Center
St. Paul, MN 55102
(612) 293-2233

Business Profile: Leading global developer of premium cleaning, sanitizing, and maintenance products and services for the hospitality, institutional, and industrial markets.

Plan Specifics:

- Partial dividend reinvestment is available.
- No Discount.
- OCP: $10 to $60,000 per year.
- Selling costs are brokerage fees.
- Company purchases stock monthly with OCPs.
- Approximately 1700 shareholders are in the plan.
- Dividends are paid January, April, July, and October.

Performance Rating: ***

DRIP Rating: 👍

EG&G, Inc. (NYSE:EGG)
45 William St.
Wellesley, MA 02181-4078
(617) 237-5100

Business Profile: International supplier of scientific and technological products and services for

aerospace, industrial, and defense markets.

Plan Specifics:

- Partial dividend reinvestment is not available.
- No Discount.
- OCP: $10 to $1000 per month.
- Selling costs are brokerage commissions and a service charge of 5 percent of sale price net of commission (maximum $2.50).
- Company purchases stock monthly with OCPs if enough funds accumulate to purchase at least a 100-share lot.
- Dividends are paid February, May, August, and November.

Performance Rating: ***

DRIP Rating: 👍

Elco Industries, Inc.
(NASDAQ:ELCN)
PO Box 7009
Rockford, IL 61125
(815) 397-5151

Business Profile: Leading producer of metal and plastic components for industrial and constructional use.

Plan Specifics:

- Partial dividend reinvestment is not available.
- No Discount.
- OCP: $25 to $1000 per month.
- Selling costs are brokerage fees.
- Company purchases stock monthly with OCPs.
- Dividends are paid March, June, September, and December.

Performance Rating: **

DRIP Rating: 👍

EMC Insurance Group, Inc.
(NASDAQ:EMCI)
717 Mulberry St.
Des Moines, IA 50309
(515) 280-2511

Business Profile: Holding company with interests in multiple-line property and casualty insurance, nonstandard risk automobile insurance and reinsurance.

Plan Specifics:
- Partial dividend reinvestment is available.
- No Discount.
- OCP: $100 to $9000 per quarter.
- Must go through a broker to sell shares from the plan.
- Company purchases stock quarterly with OCPs.
- Dividends are paid March, June, September, and December.

Performance Rating: **
DRIP Rating: ⚐

Emerson Electric Co.
(NYSE:EMR)
c/o Boatmen's Trust Co.
510 Locust
St. Louis, MO 63101
(314) 553-2197   (314) 982-1700

Business Profile: Manufactures electrical and electronic products for commercial, consumer, and industrial markets.

Plan Specifics:
- Partial dividend reinvestment is not available.
- No Discount.
- OCP: $25 to $2500 per quarter.
- Purchasing fees are very nominal brokerage fees.
- Selling costs are nominal.

- Company purchases stock quarterly with OCPs.
- Dividends are paid March, June, September, and December.

Performance Rating: *****
DRIP Rating: ☝

Empire District Electric Co.
(NYSE:EDE)
Attn: Shareholder Relations
PO Box 127
Joplin, MO 64802
(417) 623-4700

Business Profile: Provides electricity to residential, commercial, and industrial customers in Ozark region of Missouri and portions of neighboring states.

Plan Specifics:
- Partial dividend reinvestment is not available.
- 5 percent discount on reinvested dividends (doesn't apply to shares purchased on open market).
- OCP: $50 to $3000 per quarter.
- Selling costs are $15.
- Company purchases stock quarterly with OCPs.
- Preferred dividends may be reinvested for additional common shares under the plan.
- Approximately 35 percent of all shareholders are enrolled in the plan.
- Dividends are paid March, June, September, and December.

Performance Rating: **
DRIP Rating: ☝

Energen Corp. (NYSE: EGN)
2101 Sixth Ave., N.
Birmingham, AL 35203
(205) 326-8421   (800) 654-3206

Business Profile: Parent company for Alabama gas utility and oil and gas exploration company.

Plan Specifics:

- Partial dividend reinvestment is available.
- No Discount.
- OCP: $25 to $5000 per quarter.
- Selling costs are brokerage commissions and transfer taxes.
- Company purchases stock monthly with OCPs.
- Approximately 1100 shareholders are in the plan.
- Dividends are paid March, June, September, and December.

Performance Rating: *****
DRIP Rating: 👍

EnergyNorth, Inc. (NYSE: EI)
PO Box 329
1260 Elm St.
Manchester, NH 03105
(603) 625-4000

Business Profile: Public utility holding company supplying natural and propane gas to customers in southern and central New Hampshire.

Plan Specifics:

- Partial dividend reinvestment is available.
- 5 percent discount on reinvested dividends.
- OCP: $50 to $2500 per quarter.
- Must sell shares through own broker.
- Company purchases stock monthly with OCPs.

- Approximately 1500 shareholders are in the plan.
- Dividends are paid March, June, September, and December.

Performance Rating: ***
DRIP Rating: 👍

Engelhard Corp. (NYSE:EC)
101 Wood Ave., S.
Iselin, NJ 08830-0770
(908) 205-6000

Business Profile: Manufactures pigments and additives used in the paper, paint, and plastics industries.

Plan Specifics:

- Partial dividend reinvestment is not available.
- No Discount.
- OCP: $10 to $3000 per month.
- Stock is purchased monthly with OCPs.
- Selling costs are a $5 handling charge, brokerage commission, and any related expenses of sale.
- Dividends are paid March, June, September, and December.

Performance Rating: ***
DRIP Rating: 👍

Enron Corp. (NYSE:ENE)
1400 Smith St.
Houston, TX 77002
(713) 853-6161   (800) 446-2617

Business Profile: Operates large natural gas pipeline facility and is involved in oil and gas production.

Plan Specifics:

- Partial dividend reinvestment is not available.
- No Discount.
- OCP: $10 to $2000 per month.

- Selling costs are brokerage fees and transfer taxes.
- Company purchases stock around the 20th of the month with OCPs.
- Stock may be sold via the telephone.
- Approximately 7700 shareholders are in the plan.
- Dividends are paid March, June, September, and December.

Performance Rating: ***

DRIP Rating: 👍

Enserch Corp. (NYSE:ENS)
c/o First Chicago Trust-NY
PO Box 2533
Jersey City, NJ 07303-2533
(214) 670-2649

Business Profile: Distributes natural gas to portions of Texas and Oklahoma.

Plan Specifics:

- Partial dividend reinvestment is not available.
- No Discount.
- OCP: $10 to $15,000 per quarter.
- Selling costs are brokerage commissions and $5 fee.
- Company purchases stock at least quarterly with OCPs.
- Approximately 6000 shareholders are in the plan.
- Dividends are paid March, June, September, and December.

Performance Rating: **

DRIP Rating: 👍

Entergy Corp. (NYSE:ETR)
c/o Mellon Securities Trust Co.
PO Box 750
Pittsburgh, PA 15230
(504) 529-5262   (800) 333-4368

Business Profile: Utility holding company serving portions of Arkansas, Louisiana, Mississippi, Missouri, and Texas.

Plan Specifics:

- Partial dividend reinvestment is available.
- No Discount.
- OCP: $25 to $3000 per month.
- Purchasing costs are brokerage commissions.
- Selling costs are brokerage commissions and a transaction fee of $5.
- Company purchases stock monthly with OCPs.
- Dividends are paid March, June, September, and December.

Performance Rating: **

DRIP Rating: 👍

Equifax, Inc. (NYSE:EFX)
PO Box 4081
1600 Peachtree St. NW
Atlanta, GA 30302
(404) 885-8000

Business Profile: Provides information services to businesses for insurance claims and credit evaluation purposes.

Plan Specifics:

- Partial dividend reinvestment is not available.
- No Discount.
- OCP: $10 to $5000 per quarter.
- Selling costs are brokerage commissions.
- Company purchases stock around 15th of the month with OCPs.
- Approximately 3900 shareholders are in the plan.

- Dividends are paid March, June, September, and December.

Performance Rating: *****

DRIP Rating: 👍

Equitable Companies, Inc.
(NYSE:EQ)
787 Seventh Ave.
New York, NY 10019
(800) 437-8736

Business Profile: Financial services organization involved in the sale of individual life insurance and annuities and in asset management and investment banking.

Plan Specifics:

- Partial dividend reinvestment is not available.
- No Discount.
- OCP: $25 to $60,000 per year.
- Stock is purchased once a month with OCPs.
- Selling costs are brokerage commissions, a service fee, and any other costs of sale.
- Dividends are paid March, June, September, and December.

Performance Rating: ***

DRIP Rating: 👍

Equitable of Iowa Companies
(NYSE:EIC)
c\o Boatmen's Trust Co.
PO Box 14768
St. Louis, MO 63178
(800) 456-9852   (515) 245-6911

Business Profile: Company offers life insurance, annuities, and other financial products.

Plan Specifics:

- Partial dividend reinvestment is available.

- No Discount.
- OCP: $25 to $5000 per month.
- OCP is invested monthly.
- Selling costs are brokerage commissions.
- Dividends are paid March, June, September, and December.

Performance Rating: ***

DRIP Rating: 👍

Equitable Resources, Inc.
(NYSE:EQT)
420 Boulevard of the Allies
Pittsburgh, PA 15219
(412) 553-5877

Business Profile: Provides natural gas and transmission services. Operations in production and marketing of natural gas and oil.

Plan Specifics:

- Partial dividend reinvestment is not available.
- No Discount.
- OCP: $25 to $5000 per month.
- Selling costs are approximately 10 cents per share plus a $5 handling fee.
- Company purchases stock monthly with OCPs.
- Approximately 2900 shareholders are in the plan.
- Dividends are paid March, June, September, and December.

Performance Rating: ****

DRIP Rating: 👍

Essex County Gas Company
(NASDAQ:ECGC)
7 N. Hunt Rd.
Amesbury, MA 01913
(508) 388-4000

Business Profile: Purchases, distributes, and sells natural gas to customers in northeastern Massachusetts.

Plan Specifics:

- Partial dividend reinvestment is available.
- 5 percent discount on reinvested dividends.
- OCP: up to $5000 per quarter.
- Selling costs include brokerage commissions.
- Company purchases stock quarterly with OCPs.
- Certificate safekeeping is available.
- Dividends are paid January, April, July, and October.

Performance Rating: ***

DRIP Rating: 👍

Ethyl Corp. (NYSE:EY)
c/o Harris Trust and Savings
311 W. Monroe, 11th Floor
PO Box 755
Chicago, IL 60690-9971
(312) 461-6879

Business Profile: Manufactures fuel and lubricant additives for worldwide industrial markets.

Plan Specifics:

- Partial dividend reinvestment is not available.
- No Discount.
- OCP: $25 to $1000 per month.
- Selling costs are brokerage fees.
- Company purchases stock monthly with OCPs.
- Dividends are paid January, April, July, and October.

Performance Rating: ***

DRIP Rating: 👍

Evergreen Bancorp, Inc.
(NASDAQ:EVGN)
237 Glen St.
PO Box 311
Glens Falls, NY 12801-0311
(518) 792-1151

Business Profile: Bank holding company.

Plan Specifics:

- Partial dividend reinvestment is available (25 share minimum).
- No Discount.
- OCP: $25 to $3000 per quarter.
- Selling costs are brokerage commissions and a $5 termination fee.
- Company purchases stock quarterly with OCPs.
- Dividends are paid February, May, August, and November.

Performance Rating: **

DRIP Rating: 👍

Exxon Corp. (NYSE:XON)
PO Box 160369
Irving, TX 75016
(800) 252-1800

Business Profile: Major factor in worldwide petroleum markets.

Plan Specifics:

- Initial purchases may be made directly through the plan (minimum $250).
- Partial dividend reinvestment is available.
- No Discount.
- OCP: $50 to $100,000 per year.
- OCP is invested weekly.
- Selling costs include brokerage fees.
- Automatic investment services are available.

- IRA option is available ($20 annual administrative fee).
- Direct deposit of dividends is available.
- Dividends are paid March, June, September, and December.

Performance Rating: *****

DRIP Rating: 👍

F & M Bancorp
(NASDAQ:FMBN)
110 Thomas Johnson Dr.
PO Box 518
Frederick, MD 21701
(301) 694-4000

Business Profile: Bank holding company serving businesses and individuals in and around Frederick County, Maryland.

Plan Specifics:

- Partial dividend reinvestment is available.
- 5 percent discount on reinvested dividends.
- OCP: $25 to $3000 per quarter.
- Company purchases stock quarterly with OCPs.
- Dividends are paid February, May, August, and November.

Performance Rating: NR

DRIP Rating: 👍

F & M National Corp. (VA)
(NYSE:FMN)
PO Box 2800
Winchester, VA 22604
(703) 665-4200

Business Profile: Virginia-based commercial banking firm.

Plan Specifics:

- Partial dividend reinvestment is available.

- 5 percent discount on reinvested dividends.
- OCP: $25 to $5000 per quarter.
- Selling costs are brokerage commissions.
- Company purchases stock monthly with OCPs.
- Dividends are paid January, April, July, and October.

Performance Rating: ***

DRIP Rating: 👍

Fay's, Inc. (NYSE:FAY)
7245 Henry Clay Blvd.
Liverpool, NY 13088
(315) 451-8000

Business Profile: Operates retail stores in New York, Pennsylvania, Vermont, and New Hampshire.

Plan Specifics:

- Partial dividend reinvestment is available.
- No Discount.
- OCP: $25 to $5000 per month.
- Selling costs are brokerage commissions.
- Company purchases stock each month with OCPs.
- Dividends are paid January, April, July, and October.

Performance Rating: **

DRIP Rating: 👍

Federal-Mogul Corp.
(NYSE:FMO)
PO Box 1966
Detroit, MI 48235
(800) 521-8607   (800) 524-4458

Business Profile: Global distributor and manufacturer of precision parts for vehicles and machinery, serving the aftermarket and original equipment market.

Plan Specifics:

- Partial dividend reinvestment is available.
- No Discount.
- OCP: $10 to $25,000 per year.
- Purchasing fees are brokerage commissions and a service charge of 5 percent of the total funds invested ($3 maximum).
- Selling costs are brokerage commissions and a handling charge of $5.
- Company purchases stock monthly with OCPs.
- Dividends are paid March, June, September, and December.

Performance Rating: ***
DRIP Rating: 👍

Federal National Mortgage Association (Fannie Mae) (NYSE:FNM)
c/o Chemical Bank
Dividend Reinvestment Dept.
PO Box 24850, Church St. Sta.
New York, NY 10249
(800) 910-8277

Business Profile: Nation's largest mortgage lender.

Plan Specifics:

- Partial dividend reinvestment is available.
- No Discount.
- OCP: $10 to $5000 per month.
- Stock is purchased monthly with OCPs.
- Purchasing fees are a $5 service charge for each OCP investment plus brokerage commissions.
- Selling costs include brokerage fees and $15 handling charge.
- $5 termination fee.

- Dividends are paid February, May, August, and November.

Performance Rating: ****
DRIP Rating: 👍

Federal Paper Board Co., Inc. (NYSE:FBO)
75 Chestnut Ridge Rd.
Montvale, NJ 07645
(201) 391-1776

Business Profile: Manufactures paper, paperboard, pulp, and wood products.

Plan Specifics:

- Partial dividend reinvestment is not available.
- No Discount.
- OCP: $10 to $3000 per quarter.
- Purchasing fees are brokerage commissions and a service charge (maximum $2.50).
- Selling costs are brokerage commissions and any other costs of sale.
- Company purchases stock quarterly with OCPs.
- Dividends are paid January, April, July, and October.

Performance Rating: ***
DRIP Rating: 👍

Federal Realty Investment Trust (NYSE:FRT)
4800 Hampden Lane, Ste. 500
Bethesda, MD 20814
(301) 652-3360

Business Profile: Real estate investment trust.

Plan Specifics:

- Partial dividend reinvestment is available.
- No Discount.

- OCP: $50 to $15,000 per quarter.
- Selling costs may include brokerage fees.
- Company purchases stock monthly with OCPs.
- Dividends are paid January, April, July, and October.

Performance Rating: ***

DRIP Rating: 👍

Federal Signal Corp. (NYSE:FSS)
c/o Harris Trust & Savings
PO Box A3309
Chicago, IL 60690
(312) 461-3932   (708) 954-2000

Business Profile: Manufactures fire trucks, street cleaning trucks, signaling equipment, signs, and electronic message displays. Operations in industrial tools.

Plan Specifics:

- Must own 50 shares in order to enroll in the plan.
- Partial dividend reinvestment is available.
- No Discount.
- OCP: $100 to $5000 per quarter.
- Stock is purchased at least quarterly with OCPs.
- Selling costs are approximately 6 cents per share.
- Dividends are paid March, June, September, and December.

Performance Rating: ****

DRIP Rating: 👍

Ferro Corp. (NYSE:FOE)
1000 Lakeside Ave.
Cleveland, OH 44114-1183
(216) 641-8580   (216) 575-2658

Business Profile: Manufacturer of specialty materials such as colors, plastics, coatings, chemicals, and ceramics for the construction, appliance, furnishings, industrial, and transportation markets.

Plan Specifics:

- Partial dividend reinvestment is available.
- No Discount.
- OCP: $10 to $3000 per month.
- Selling costs are brokerage commissions.
- Company purchases stock monthly with OCPs.
- Dividends are paid March, June, September, and December.

Performance Rating: ***

DRIP Rating: 👍

Fifth Third Bancorp
(NASDAQ:FITB)
c/o Fifth Third Bank
38 Fountain Square Plaza
Dept. 00855
Cincinnati, OH 45263
(513) 579-5300   (513) 744-8677

Business Profile: Multibank holding company with operations in Ohio, Kentucky, and Indiana.

Plan Specifics:

- Partial dividend reinvestment is not available.
- No Discount.
- OCP: $25 to $2500 per month.
- Selling costs include brokerage commissions.
- Company purchases stock monthly with OCPs.
- Dividends are paid January, April, July, and October.

Performance Rating: *****

DRIP Rating: 👍

Figgie International, Inc.
 (NASDAQ:FIGI)
4420 Sherwin Rd.
Willoughby, OH 44094
(216) 953-2700

Business Profile: Manufactures fire extinguishers, security systems, maintenance equipment, and other industrial and technical equipment.

Plan Specifics:
- Partial dividend reinvestment is not available.
- No Discount.
- OCP: $10 to $5000 per quarter.
- Selling costs are brokerage commissions and a service charge (maximum $5, minimum $1).
- Company purchases stock monthly with OCPs.
- The company is not currently paying a dividend.

Performance Rating: *
DRIP Rating: 👍

FINA, Inc. (ASE:FI)
c/o First Chicago Trust-NY
PO Box 2533
Jersey City, NJ 07303-2533
(800) 446-2617

Business Profile: Integrated oil and petrochemical firm active in refining and marketing petroleum products and producing petrochemicals, crude oil, and natural gas.

Plan Specifics:
- Partial dividend reinvestment is not available.
- No Discount.

- OCP: $10 to $1000 per month.
- Fees for purchasing stock are nominal brokerage commissions plus a service charge of 5 percent of the amount of each investment not to exceed $2.50.
- Stock is purchased on the 15th of each month with OCPs.
- Dividends are paid March, June, September, and December.

Performance Rating: ***
DRIP Rating: 👍

Financial Trust Corp.
 (NASDAQ:FITC)
PO Box 220
Carlisle, PA 17013
(717) 243-3212

Business Profile: Multibank holding company.

Plan Specifics:
- Partial dividend reinvestment is not available.
- No Discount.
- OCP: $100 to $1000 per quarter.
- Purchasing fees will be incurred if shares are purchased in the market.
- Must go through a broker to sell shares from the plan. There is a $3 service fee for withdrawing from the plan.
- Company purchases stock quarterly with OCPs.
- Dividends are paid February, May, August, and November.

Performance Rating: ***
DRIP Rating: 👎

First American Corp. (TN) (NASDAQ:FATN)
First American Center
Shareholder Services
Nashville, TN 37237-0721
(615) 748-2100   (615) 748-2441

Business Profile: Tennessee-based multibank holding company.

Plan Specifics:

- Partial dividend reinvestment is available.
- 5 percent discount on reinvested dividends.
- OCP: $25 to $15,000 per quarter.
- Must go through own broker to sell shares.
- Company purchases stock once a month with OCPs.
- Approximately 3700 shareholders are in the plan.
- Dividends are paid February, May, August, and November.

Performance Rating: ***
DRIP Rating: 👍

First Bank System, Inc. (NYSE:FBS)
PO Box 522
601 Second Ave., S.
Minneapolis, MN 55480
(800) 446-2617

Business Profile: Multistate bank holding company based in Minnesota.

Plan Specifics:

- Partial dividend reinvestment is available.
- No Discount.
- OCP: $25 to $5000 per quarter.
- Company purchases stock once a month with OCPs.
- Selling costs are $5 service fee and brokerage fees.

- Approximately 9000 shareholders are in the plan.
- Dividends are paid March, June, September, and December.

Performance Rating: ***
DRIP Rating: 👍

First Chicago Corp. (NYSE:FNB)
Office of the Treasurer
PO Box 2533
Jersey City, NJ 07303-2533
(312) 732-4812

Business Profile: Chicago-based multibank holding company.

Plan Specifics:

- Partial dividend reinvestment is available.
- No Discount.
- OCP: $25 to $5000 per month.
- Stock is purchased around the 1st of the month with OCPs.
- Selling costs are brokerage commission of 12 cents per share and a $10 service charge.
- Dividends are paid January, April, July, and October.

Performance Rating: ***
DRIP Rating: 👍

First Citizens BancShares, Inc. (NASDAQ:FCNCA)
3128 Smoketree Court
PO Box 27131
Raleigh, NC 27611
(919) 755-7000

Business Profile: Bank holding company.

Plan Specifics:

- Partial dividend reinvestment is available.
- 5 percent discount on reinvested dividends.

- OCP: $25 to $25,000 per year.
- Company purchases stock monthly with OCPs.
- Dividends are paid January, April, July, and October.

Performance Rating: ***

DRIP Rating: 👍

First Colony Corporation (NYSE:FCL)
700 Main St.
Lynchburg, VA 24505
(804) 948-5223

Business Profile: Insurance holding company that sells individual life insurance and annuity products.

Plan Specifics:
- Partial dividend reinvestment is not available.
- No Discount.
- OCP: $25 to $1000 per month.
- Stock is purchased monthly with OCPs.
- Selling costs are brokerage commissions.
- Dividends are paid January, April, July, and October.

Performance Rating: **

DRIP Rating: 👍

First Commerce Corp. (NASDAQ:FCOM)
c/o First Chicago Trust-NY
PO Box 2533
Jersey City, NJ 07303-2533
(800) 446-2617   (504) 582-2900

Business Profile: Multibank holding company serving mainly Louisiana and Mississippi.

Plan Specifics:
- Partial dividend reinvestment is available.

- 5 percent discount on reinvested dividends.
- OCP: $50 to $3000 per quarter.
- Stock is purchased quarterly with OCPs.
- Selling costs are brokerage commission, service charges, and other expenses related to sale.
- Preferred dividends are eligible for reinvestment for additional common shares under the plan.
- Dividends are paid January, April, July, and October.

Performance Rating: ***

DRIP Rating: 👍

First Commercial Corp. (NASDAQ:FCLR)
400 W. Capitol
Little Rock, AR 72201
(501) 371-7000

Business Profile: Multibank holding company which owns banks in Arkansas; Memphis, Tennessee; and Texas.

Plan Specifics:
- Partial dividend reinvestment is available.
- 5 percent discount on reinvested dividends.
- OCP: $25 to $2000 per quarter.
- Company purchases stock monthly with OCPs.
- Dividends are paid January, April, July, and October.

Performance Rating: ****

DRIP Rating: 👍

First Commonwealth Financial Corp. (NYSE:FCF)
22 N. Sixth St.
Indiana, PA 15701
(412) 349-7220

Business Profile: Bank holding company serving central and western Pennsylvania.

Plan Specifics:
- Partial dividend reinvestment is available.
- 5 percent discount on reinvested dividends and OCPs.
- OCP: $25 to $10,000 per quarter.
- Stock is purchased monthly with OCPs.
- Selling costs are brokerage commission and bank service fees.
- Dividends are paid January, April, July, and October.

Performance Rating: NR

DRIP Rating: 👍

First Empire State Corp. (ASE:FES)
c/o First Nat'l Bank of Boston
PO Box 644
Boston, MA 02102
(716) 842-5445

Business Profile: Bank holding company based in Buffalo, New York.

Plan Specifics:
- Partial dividend reinvestment is not available.
- No Discount.
- OCP: $10 to $1000 per quarter.
- Purchasing fees are brokerage commissions and a service charge (5 percent of total funds invested with a $2.50 maximum).

- Selling costs are brokerage commissions and transfer taxes.
- Company purchases stock quarterly with OCPs.
- Dividends are paid March, June, September, and December.

Performance Rating: ****

DRIP Rating: 👍

First Federal Capital Corp. (NASDAQ:FTFC)
605 State St.
La Crosse, WI 54602-1868
(608) 784-8000   (800) 657-4636

Business Profile: Bank holding company with facilities in western and southcentral Wisconsin.

Plan Specifics:
- Partial dividend reinvestment is available.
- No Discount.
- OCP: $50 to $5000 per quarter.
- OCP is invested quarterly.
- Selling costs are brokerage commissions.
- Dividends are paid March, June, September, and December.

Performance Rating: **

DRIP Rating: 👍

First Fidelity Bancorp. (NYSE:FFB)
550 Broad St.
Newark, NJ 07102
(609) 895-6800   (800) 524-4458

Business Profile: Bank holding company in New Jersey.

Plan Specifics:
- Partial dividend reinvestment is not available.
- 3 percent discount on reinvested dividends.

- OCP: $50 to $60,000 per year.
- Company purchases stock monthly with OCPs.
- Selling costs are a $3 fee.
- Preferred stock is eligible for reinvestment for common shares under the plan.
- Dividends are paid February, May, August, and November.

Performance Rating: ***

DRIP Rating: 👍

First Financial Holdings, Inc. (NASDAQ:FFCH)
34 Broad St.
Charleston, SC 29401
(803) 529-5931

Business Profile: Savings and loan holding company in Charleston, South Carolina.

Plan Specifics:

- Partial dividend reinvestment is not available.
- No Discount.
- OCP: $25 to $2000 per month.
- Selling costs may include brokerage fees.
- Company purchases stock once a month with OCPs.
- Dividends are paid February, May, August, and November.

Performance Rating: **

DRIP Rating: 👍

First Harrisburg Bancor, Inc. (NASDAQ:FFHP)
PO Box 1111
234 N. 2nd St.
Harrisburg, PA 17108
(717) 232-6661

Business Profile: Holding company for savings and loan institution in Pennsylvania.

Plan Specifics:

- Partial dividend reinvestment is available.
- No Discount.
- OCP: not available.
- Selling costs may include brokerage fees.
- 60 to 70 percent of total shareholders are in the plan.
- Dividends are paid February, May, August, and November.

Performance Rating: NR

DRIP Rating: 👎

First Interstate Bancorp (NYSE:I)
c/o First Interstate Bank, Ltd.
PO Box 4207
Woodland Hills, CA 91365-9784
(800) 522-6645

Business Profile: Multibank holding company serving western states.

Plan Specifics:

- Partial dividend reinvestment is available.
- No Discount.
- OCP: not available.
- Selling costs include brokerage commission.
- Dividends are paid February, May, August, and November.

Performance Rating: ***

DRIP Rating: 👎

First Michigan Bank Corp. (NASDAQ:FMBC)
Shareholder Services Dept.
One Financial Plaza
Holland, MI 49423
(616) 396-9000

Business Profile: Multibank holding company serving western Michigan.

Plan Specifics:

- Partial dividend reinvestment is available.
- 5 percent discount on reinvested dividends.
- OCP: $100 to $1000 per quarter.
- Selling costs are a 4 cents per share fee, brokerage commissions and service charges.
- Company purchases stock quarterly with OCPs.
- Dividends are paid January, April, July, and October.

Performance Rating: ****

DRIP Rating: 👍

First Midwest Bancorp, Inc.
 (NASDAQ:FMBI)
c/o American Stock Transfer
 & Trust Co.
40 Wall St.
New York, NY 10005
(800) 937-5449   (708) 778-8700

Business Profile: Multibank holding company based in Illinois.

Plan Specifics:

- Partial dividend reinvestment is available.
- No Discount.
- OCP: $100 to $5000 per quarter.
- Company purchases stock monthly with OCPs.
- May have to go through own broker to sell whole shares.
- Dividends are paid January, April, July, and October.

Performance Rating: ***

DRIP Rating: 👍

First Mississippi Corp.
 (NYSE:FRM)
PO Box 1249
700 North St.
Jackson, MS 39215-1249
(601) 948-7550   (216) 737-4127

Business Profile: Operations in fertilizer, industrial chemicals, gold, and environmental technology.

Plan Specifics:

- Partial dividend reinvestment is not available.
- No Discount.
- OCP: $25 to $3000 per month.
- Stock is purchased monthly with OCPs.
- Selling costs are $5 termination charge and brokerage fees.
- Service charge of $5 for depositing certificates.
- Dividends are paid January, April, July, and October.

Performance Rating: ***

DRIP Rating: 👍

First National Bancorp (GA)
 (NASDAQ:FBAC)
303 Jesse Jewell Parkway,
 Suite 700
PO Drawer 937
Gainesville, GA 30501
(404) 503-2000

Business Profile: Bank holding company.

Plan Specifics:

- Partial dividend reinvestment is available.
- No Discount.
- OCP: not available.
- Selling costs are brokerage commissions and any applicable taxes.

- Dividends are paid January, April, July, and October.

Performance Rating: NR

DRIP Rating: 👎

**First Northern Savings Bank
  (NASDAQ:FNGB)
201 N. Monroe Ave.
PO Box 23100
Green Bay, WI 54305-3100
(414) 437-7101   (800) 999-3675**

Business Profile: Bank operating in northeastern Wisconsin.

Plan Specifics:

- Need at least 50 shares to enroll in the plan.
- Partial dividend reinvestment is available.
- No Discount.
- OCP: $25 to $3000 per quarter
- Must go through a broker to sell shares from the plan.
- Company purchases stock quarterly with OCPs.
- Dividends are paid February, May, August, and November.

Performance Rating: ***

DRIP Rating: 👎

**First of America Bank Corp.
  (NYSE:FOA)
225 N. Rose St.
Kalamazoo, MI 49007
(616) 376-7320   (800) 782-4040**

Business Profile: Multibank holding company serving parts of Michigan, Indiana, Illinois, and Florida.

Plan Specifics:

- Partial dividend reinvestment is not available.
- 5 percent discount on reinvested dividends.

- OCP: $25 to $25,000 per quarter.
- Selling costs are brokerage commissions and service charges.
- Company purchases stock monthly with OCPs.
- Dividends are paid January, April, July, and October.

Performance Rating: ***

DRIP Rating: 👍

**First Security Corp.
  (NASDAQ:FSCO)
Stock Transfer Svcs., 5th Floor
PO Box 30007
Salt Lake City, UT 84130
(801) 246-5289**

Business Profile: Multibank holding company serving customers in Utah, Idaho, Oregon, Wyoming, Nevada, and New Mexico.

Plan Specifics:

- Partial dividend reinvestment is available.
- No Discount.
- OCP: $50 to $5000 per month.
- Must go through own broker to sell shares.
- Company purchases stock monthly with OCPs.
- Approximately 1900 shareholders are in the plan.
- Dividends are paid March, June, September, and December.

Performance Rating: ****

DRIP Rating: 👍

First Tennessee National Corp. (NASDAQ:FTEN)
Attn: Treasury
PO Box 84
Memphis, TN 38101
(901) 523-5630   (800) 468-9716

Business Profile: Holding company for banks in Tennessee.

Plan Specifics:

- Partial dividend reinvestment is available.
- No Discount.
- OCP: $25 to $5000 per quarter.
- Must go through own broker to sell shares.
- Company purchases stock monthly with OCPs.
- Dividends are paid January, April, July, and October.

Performance Rating: ****

DRIP Rating: 👍

First Union Corp. (NYSE:FTU)
First Union Center
Charlotte, NC 28288-0206
(704) 374-6782

Business Profile: Interstate bank holding company headquartered in North Carolina.

Plan Specifics:

- Partial dividend reinvestment is not available.
- 1 percent discount on reinvested dividends and OCPs.
- OCP: $25 to $2000 per month.
- If shares are purchased in the open market, participants will pay brokerage fees and any other expenses.
- Participants with less than 100 shares may sell shares through the plan, and the company will pay commission costs; over 100

shares must go through own broker.

- Stock is purchased monthly with OCPs.
- Dividends are paid March, June, September, and December.

Performance Rating: ****

DRIP Rating: 👍

First Union Real Estate Investments (NYSE:FUR)
55 Public Square, Ste. 1900
Cleveland, OH 44113
(216) 781-4030   (216) 575-2532

Business Profile: Real estate investment trust.

Plan Specifics:

- Partial dividend reinvestment is available.
- No Discount.
- OCP: $20 to $5000 per month.
- Purchasing fees include brokerage commissions and a bank fee of 5 percent of the dividend and OCP invested (maximum $3).
- Selling costs are brokerage commissions.
- Company purchases stock monthly with OCPs.
- Dividends are paid January, April, July, and October.

Performance Rating: *

DRIP Rating: 👍

First Virginia Banks, Inc. (NYSE:FVB)
6400 Arlington Blvd.
Falls Church, VA 22042-2336
(703) 241-3669   (703) 241-4000

Business Profile: Multibank holding company with a major presence in Virginia and member banks in Maryland and Tennessee.

Plan Specifics:
- Partial dividend reinvestment is not available.
- No Discount.
- OCP: $25 to $5000 per quarter.
- Company purchases stock monthly with OCPs.
- Selling costs are brokerage commissions and a service charge of $1.
- Dividends are paid January, April, July, and October.

Performance Rating: ****

DRIP Rating: 👍

**First Western Bancorp, Inc.
  (NASDAQ:FWBI)
101 E. Washington St.
PO Box 1488
New Castle, PA 16103-1488
(412) 652-8550**

Business Profile: Bank holding company providing a wide range of commercial banking, residential mortgage, and trust services.

Plan Specifics:
- Partial dividend reinvestment is available.
- No Discount.
- OCP: $25 to $10,000 per quarter.
- Company purchases stock monthly with OCPs.
- Selling costs are brokerage fees.
- Dividends are paid February, May, August, and November.

Performance Rating: NR

DRIP Rating: 👍

**Firstar Corp. (NYSE:FSR)
777 E. Wisconsin Ave.
Milwaukee, WI 53202
(414) 765-4321**

Business Profile: Multibank holding company controlling banks in Wisconsin, Illinois, Iowa, Minnesota, Arizona, and Florida.

Plan Specifics:
- Partial dividend reinvestment is available.
- No Discount.
- OCP: $50 to $10,000 per month.
- Stock is purchased monthly with OCPs.
- Selling costs are brokerage and administrative fees.
- Automatic investment services are available.
- Dividends are paid February, May, August, and November.

Performance Rating: ***

DRIP Rating: 👍

**Firstbank of Illinois Co.
  (NASDAQ:FBIC)
205 S. Fifth St.
PO Box 19264
Springfield, IL 62794-9264
(217) 753-7543   (217) 753-7358**

Business Profile: Bank holding company.

Plan Specifics:
- Partial dividend reinvestment is not available.
- No Discount.
- OCP: $25 to $3000 per quarter.
- Company purchases stock quarterly with OCPs.
- Dividends are paid January, April, July, and October.

Performance Rating: ****

DRIP Rating: 👍

FirstMerit Corp.
(NASDAQ:FMER)
121 S. Main St., Ste. 200
Akron, OH 44308-1440
(216) 384-7347

Business Profile: Ohio-based multibank holding company.

Plan Specifics:
- Partial dividend reinvestment is not available.
- No Discount.
- OCP: $25 to $5000 per quarter.
- Selling costs include service fees of $2.50 for partial sales and $5 for full liquidation, plus brokerage commissions.
- Company purchases stock quarterly with OCPs.
- Approximately 2500 shareholders are in the plan.
- Dividends are paid March, June, September, and December.

Performance Rating: ***
DRIP Rating: ⚬

Fleet Financial Group, Inc.
(NYSE:FLT)
50 Kennedy Plaza
Providence, RI 02903
(401) 278-5800   (401) 278-3900

Business Profile: New England multibank holding company.

Plan Specifics:
- Partial dividend reinvestment is not available.
- 3 percent discount on reinvested dividends.
- OCP: $10 to $2500 per month.
- May have to sell shares through own broker.
- Company purchases stock monthly with OCPs.

- Dividends are paid January, April, July, and October.

Performance Rating: ***
DRIP Rating: ⚬

Fleming Companies, Inc.
(NYSE:FLM)
PO Box 26647
6301 Waterford Blvd.
Oklahoma City, OK 73126-0647
(405) 840-7200

Business Profile: Important distributor of wholesale food and related products.

Plan Specifics:
- Partial dividend reinvestment is available.
- 5 percent discount on reinvested dividends.
- OCP: $25 to $5000 per quarter.
- Stock is purchased around the 10th of each month with OCPs.
- Selling costs include brokerage fees.
- Dividends are paid March, June, September, and December.

Performance Rating: ***
DRIP Rating: ⚬

Florida Progress Corp.
(NYSE:FPC)
PO Box 33042
St. Petersburg, FL 33733
(800) 352-1121   (813) 824-6416

Business Profile: Holding company for Florida electric utility. Operations in coal mining, real estate, and technology development.

Plan Specifics:
- Partial dividend reinvestment is available.
- No Discount.

- OCP: $10 to $100,000 per year.
- Purchasing fees are brokerage commissions and other fees.
- Selling costs are brokerage commissions and any other fees.
- Company purchases stock monthly with OCPs.
- Florida residents may make initial purchase of stock directly from the company ($100 minimum).
- Dividends are paid March, June, September, and December.

Performance Rating: ****

DRIP Rating: 👍

Florida Public Utilities Co. (ASE:FPU)
PO Box 3395
W. Palm Beach, FL 33402-3395
(407) 832-2461

Business Profile: Supplies electricity, water, and gas services to communities in Florida.

Plan Specifics:

- Partial dividend reinvestment is available.
- No Discount.
- OCP: $25 to $2000 per quarter.
- Selling costs are brokerage fees.
- Stock is purchased quarterly with OCPs.
- Approximately 312 shareholders are in the plan.
- Dividends are paid January, April, July, and October.

Performance Rating: ***

DRIP Rating: 👍

Flowers Industries, Inc. (NYSE:FLO)
U.S. Highway 19
PO Box 1338
Thomasville, GA 31799
(912) 226-9110   (800) 633-4236

Business Profile: Produces bread and baked goods for grocery and food service industries.

Plan Specifics:

- Partial dividend reinvestment is available.
- No Discount.
- OCP: $25 to $3000 per month.
- Selling costs are brokerage fees.
- Company purchases stock once a month with OCPs.
- Approximately 2000 shareholders are in the plan.
- Dividends are paid February, May, August, and November.

Performance Rating: ***

DRIP Rating: 👍

Fluor Corporation (NYSE:FLR)
c/o Chemical Bank
PO Box 3069, JAF Bldg.
New York, NY 10116-3069
(800) 356-2017   (714) 975-2000

Business Profile: One of the world's largest international engineering, construction, and related services companies.

Plan Specifics:

- Participants must enroll with and maintain a balance of not less than 50 shares.
- Partial dividend reinvestment is not available.
- No Discount.
- OCP: $100 to $10,000 per quarter.
- Company purchases stock monthly with OCPs.

- There is a charge of $1.50 for each check or money order processed by the bank. Purchasing fees are brokerage commissions.
- Selling costs are brokerage commissions and a $15 service fee.
- Dividends are paid January, April, July, and October.

Performance Rating: ****

DRIP Rating: ☜

FNB Corp. (NASDAQ:FNBN)
PO Box 1328
Asheboro, NC 27204
(910) 626-8300

Business Profile: Bank holding company.

Plan Specifics:

- Partial dividend reinvestment is available.
- No Discount.
- OCP: $25 to $1000 per quarter.
- OCP is invested quarterly.
- Must go through broker to sell.
- Dividends are paid January, April, July, and October.

Performance Rating: NR

DRIP Rating: 👍

Food Lion, Inc.
(NASDAQ:FDLN.A)
c/o Wachovia Bank of North
Carolina, N.A.
PO Box 3001
Winston-Salem, NC 27102
(800) 633-4236

Business Profile: Operates a chain of retail supermarkets in the southeastern United States.

Plan Specifics:

- Partial dividend reinvestment is not available.
- No Discount.
- OCP: $10 to $2500 per month.
- Company purchases stock monthly with OCPs.
- Selling costs are brokerage commissions and any other costs of sale.
- Dividends are paid March, May, July, and October.

Performance Rating: **

DRIP Rating: 👍

Ford Motor Co. (NYSE:F)
c/o Chemical Bank
JAF Bldg., PO Box 3069
New York, NY 10116-3069
(800) 279-1237   (313) 322-3000

Business Profile: Second largest motor vehicle manufacturer.

Plan Specifics:

- Partial dividend reinvestment is available.
- No Discount.
- OCP: $50 to $12,000 per quarter.
- Purchasing costs are nominal brokerage fees plus service charge of 5 percent of funds invested (maximum of $3).
- Selling costs are $15 handling fee and brokerage fees.
- Company purchases stock monthly with OCPs.
- Dividends are paid March, June, September, and December.

Performance Rating: ***

DRIP Rating: 👍

**Fort Wayne National Corp.
 (NASDAQ:FWNC)
c/o Fort Wayne National Bank
PO Box 110
Fort Wayne, IN 46801
(219) 426-0555**

Business Profile: Bank holding company with 43 offices in Indiana.

Plan Specifics:
- Partial dividend reinvestment is not available.
- No Discount.
- OCP: not available.
- Selling costs are brokerage commissions.
- Dividends are paid January, April, July, and October.

Performance Rating: NR
DRIP Rating: ☜

**Foster Wheeler Corp.
 (NYSE:FWC)
c/o Mellon Securities
PO Box 750
Pittsburgh, PA 15230
(800) 526-0801   (908) 730-4090**

Business Profile: Provides engineering services and products to petroleum, gas, petrochemical, and power-generation industries.

Plan Specifics:
- Partial dividend reinvestment is not available.
- No Discount.
- OCP: $10 to no maximum per month.
- Selling fees include a $3.50 service charge and any applicable brokerage charges.
- Company purchases stock around the 1st business day of the month with OCPs.

- Dividends are paid March, June, September, and December.

Performance Rating: ***
DRIP Rating: 👍

**FPL Group, Inc. (NYSE:FPL)
c/o The Bank of Boston
PO Box 1681
Boston, MA 02105
(407) 694-6304   (617) 929-5445
(800) 736-3001**

Business Profile: Florida-based electric utility holding company.

Plan Specifics:
- Partial dividend reinvestment is available.
- No Discount.
- OCP: $100 to $100,000 per year.
- Selling costs are brokerage commissions.
- Company purchases stock quarterly with OCPs.
- Preferred dividends are eligible for dividend reinvestment under the plan.
- Dividends are paid March, June, September, and December.

Performance Rating: ****
DRIP Rating: 👍

**Franklin Resources, Inc.
 (NYSE:BEN)
777 Mariners Island Blvd.
San Mateo, CA 94404
(800) 524-4458**

Business Profile: Provides investment management, share distribution, transfer agent, and administrative services to open-end investment companies.

Plan Specifics:
- Partial dividend reinvestment is not available.
- No Discount.
- OCP: $50 to $10,000 per quarter.
- Selling costs are brokerage commissions, transfer taxes, and a bank fee of $3.
- Company purchases stock monthly with OCPs.
- Dividends are paid January, April, July, and October.

Performance Rating: ★★★★

DRIP Rating: 👍

Frontier Corp. (NYSE:FRO)
c/o Bank of Boston
PO Box 1681
Mail Stop 45-01-01
Boston, MA 02105-1681
(800) 836-7370

Business Profile: Provides integrated telecommunications services to more than two million customers.

Plan Specifics:
- Partial dividend reinvestment is available.
- No Discount.
- OCP: $25 to $50,000 per month.
- Stock is purchased monthly with OCPs.
- Selling costs are brokerage fees and a nominal service fee (no charge if staying in the program).
- Approximately 12,900 shareholders in plan.
- Dividends are paid February, May, August, and November.

Performance Rating: ★★★★

DRIP Rating: 👍

Fuller (H.B.) Co.
(NASDAQ:FULL)
2400 Energy Park Dr.
St. Paul, MN 55108-1591
(612) 645-3401   (800) 468-9716

Business Profile: Worldwide producer of adhesives, sealants, coatings, paints, and waxes.

Plan Specifics:
- Partial dividend reinvestment is available.
- 3 percent discount on reinvested dividends.
- OCP: $10 to $6000 per month.
- Selling costs include $3 sale fee and brokerage commission of 20 cents per share.
- Company purchases stock around the 10th of each month provided there are enough funds to purchase at least 100 shares.
- Electronic deposit of dividends is available.
- Dividends are paid February, May, August, and November.

Performance Rating: ★★★

DRIP Rating: 👍

Fulton Financial Corp.
(NASDAQ:FULT)
#1 Penn Square
Lancaster, PA 17602
(717) 291-2546

Business Profile: Pennsylvania-based bank holding company.

Plan Specifics:
- Partial dividend reinvestment is available.
- No Discount.
- OCP: $25 to $1000 per month.
- Stock is purchased monthly with OCPs.

- Selling costs are $35 fee and brokerage fees.
- Approximately 3200 shareholders in plan.
- Dividends are paid January, April, July, October.

Performance Rating: NR
DRIP Rating: 👎

Gannett Co., Inc. (NYSE:GCI)
c/o Norwest Bank
PO Box 738
161 N. Concord Exchange
South St. Paul, MN 55075-0738
(800) 778-3299

Business Profile: Operations in newspaper publishing, broadcasting, and outdoor advertising.
Plan Specifics:
- Partial dividend reinvestment is available.
- No Discount.
- OCP: $10 to $5000 per month.
- Selling costs are brokerage fees and any service charge.
- Company purchases stock monthly with OCPs.
- Dividends are paid January, April, July, and October.

Performance Rating: *******
DRIP Rating: 👍

GATX Corp. (NYSE:GMT)
c/o Chemical Bank
PO Box 3069, JAF Bldg.
New York, NY 10116-3069
(800) 851-9677

Business Profile: Interests in railcar leasing, tank terminal operations, and shipping services.
Plan Specifics:
- Partial dividend reinvestment is not available.

- No Discount.
- OCP: $25 to $3000 per month.
- Stock is purchased quarterly, and most likely more frequently, with OCPs.
- Selling costs may include brokerage fees.
- Dividends are paid March, June, September, and December.

Performance Rating: *****
DRIP Rating: 👍

GenCorp, Inc. (NYSE:GY)
175 Ghent Rd.
Fairlawn, OH 44333-3300
(216) 869-4453   (216) 869-4200

Business Profile: Technology-based company with strong positions in the defense/automotive and polymer products markets.
Plan Specifics:
- Partial dividend reinvestment is not available.
- No Discount.
- OCP: $10 to $3000 per quarter.
- Selling costs are brokerage commissions.
- Company purchases stock every 45 days with OCPs.
- Dividends are paid February, May, August, and November.

Performance Rating: ****
DRIP Rating: 👍

General Electric Co. (NYSE:GE)
Reinvestment Plan Services
PO Box 120068
Stamford, CT 06912
(203) 373-2816   (800) 786-2543

Business Profile: Operations in aerospace, aircraft engines, major appliances, power systems, broadcasting, and financial services.

Plan Specifics:
- Partial dividend reinvestment is available.
- No Discount.
- OCP: $10 to $10,000 per month.
- Stock is purchased monthly with OCPs.
- Selling cost is approximately 15 cents per share.
- Dividends are paid January, April, July, and October.

Performance Rating: *****
DRIP Rating: 👍

General Housewares Corp. (NYSE:GHW)
1536 Beech St.
PO Box 4066
Terre Haute, IN 47804
(800) 446-2617

Business Profile: Produces a variety of household products, including cookware and cutlery.

Plan Specifics:
- Partial dividend reinvestment is not available.
- No Discount.
- OCP: $10 to $1000 per month.
- Company purchases stock monthly with OCPs.
- Selling costs are brokerage commissions, a handling charge of $5, and any other costs of sale.
- Dividends are paid March, June, September, and December.

Performance Rating: **
DRIP Rating: 👍

General Mills, Inc. (NYSE:GIS)
c/o Norwest Bank Minnesota
PO Box 738
161 N. Concord Exchange St.
South St. Paul, MN 55075
(612) 540-3888   (800) 670-4763

Business Profile: Produces consumer foods.

Plan Specifics:
- Partial dividend reinvestment is available.
- No Discount.
- OCP: $10 to $3000 per quarter.
- Selling costs are brokerage commissions and any service fees.
- Company purchases stock monthly with OCPs.
- Approximately 40 percent of all shareholders are in the plan.
- Dividends are paid February, May, August, and November.

Performance Rating: ****
DRIP Rating: 👍

General Motors Corp. (NYSE:GM)
3044 W. Grand Blvd.
Detroit, MI 48202
(313) 556-2044   (800) 331-9922

Business Profile: World's largest automobile manufacturer.

Plan Specifics:
- Partial dividend reinvestment is available.
- No Discount.
- OCP: $25 to $4000 per month.
- Participants will pay nominal brokerage costs if stock is purchased on the open market.
- Selling costs are $5 liquidation fee and approximately 10 cents per share.

- Company purchases stock monthly with OCPs.
- Approximately 158,300 shareholders are in the plan.
- Dividends are paid March, June, September, and December.

Performance Rating: ***

DRIP Rating: 👍

General Public Utilities Corp. (NYSE:GPU)
c/o Chemical Bank
PO Box 3069, JAF Bldg.
New York, NY 10116-3069
(800) 263-1310

Business Profile: Electric utility holding company serving New Jersey and Pennsylvania regions.

Plan Specifics:

- Partial dividend reinvestment is not available.
- No Discount.
- OCP: $50 to $6000 per quarter.
- Company purchases stock monthly with OCPs.
- Selling costs are brokerage commissions and $15 transaction fee.
- $5 fee for issuance of certificates.
- $3 service fee for safekeeping feature.
- Approximately 9800 shareholders are in the plan.
- Dividends are paid February, May, August, and November.

Performance Rating: ***

DRIP Rating: 👍

General Re Corp. (NYSE:GRN)
PO Box 10351
Financial Center
Stamford, CT 06904-2351
(203) 328-5000   (800) 524-4458

Business Profile: Holding company for largest property-casualty reinsurance firm in country.

Plan Specifics:

- Partial dividend reinvestment is not available.
- No Discount.
- OCP: $10 to $10,000 per quarter.
- Selling costs are brokerage fees.
- Company purchases stock monthly with OCPs.
- Dividends are paid March, June, September, and December.

Performance Rating: *****

DRIP Rating: 👍

General Signal Corp. (NYSE:GSX)
PO Box 10010
High Ridge Park
Stamford, CT 06904
(203) 329-4100   (203) 329-4344

Business Profile: Produces equipment and systems for process controls, electrical equipment, semiconductor, and telecommunications industries.

Plan Specifics:

- Partial dividend reinvestment is not available.
- No Discount.
- OCP: $25 to $10,000 per quarter.
- Must go through own broker to sell shares.
- Company purchases stock around 15th of the month with OCPs.
- Dividends are paid January, April, July, and October.

Performance Rating: ***

DRIP Rating: 👍

Genuine Parts Co. (NYSE:GPC)
2999 Circle 75 Parkway
Atlanta, GA 30339
(404) 588-7822   (404) 953-1700

Business Profile: Supplies automotive and industrial replacement parts and office products.

Plan Specifics:

- Partial dividend reinvestment is not available.
- No Discount.
- OCP: $10 to $3000 per quarter.
- Purchasing and selling fees are brokerage commissions.
- OCP is invested within roughly 30 days provided at least a 100-share lot can be purchased.
- Dividends are paid January, April, July, and October.

Performance Rating: *****
DRIP Rating: 👍

Georgia-Pacific Corp. (NYSE:GP)
c/o First Chicago Trust-NY
PO Box 2533
Jersey City, NJ 07303-2533
(800) 446-2617   (201) 324-0498

Business Profile: Leading provider of plywood, lumber, paper, and pulp.

Plan Specifics:

- Partial dividend reinvestment is available.
- No Discount.
- OCP: $25 to $5000 per month.
- Stock is purchased around the 10th of the month with OCPs.
- Purchase fees include 5 percent of total amount invested with a $2.50 maximum charge per investment.
- Selling costs are brokerage

commissions and any other costs of sale.

- Stock may be sold via the telephone.
- Dividends are paid March, June, September, and December.

Performance Rating: ***
DRIP Rating: 👍

Giant Food, Inc. (ASE:GFS.A)
Office of the Sec. (Dept. 559)
PO Box 1804
Washington, DC 20013
(301) 341-8480

Business Profile: Operates chain of food and drug supermarkets in metropolitan Washington, Baltimore, and nearby areas.

Plan Specifics:

- Partial dividend reinvestment is not available.
- No Discount.
- OCP: $10 to $1000 per quarter.
- Selling costs are $3 service charge and brokerage commissions.
- Company purchases stock once a month with OCPs.
- Dividends are paid March, June, September, and December.

Performance Rating: ****
DRIP Rating: 👍

Giddings & Lewis, Inc.
 (NASDAQ:GIDL)
c/o First Wisconsin Trust
PO Box 2077
Milwaukee, WI 53201
(800) 637-7549

Business Profile: Largest industrial automation supplier in North America and the fourth largest in the world.

Plan Specifics:
- Partial dividend reinvestment is not available.
- No Discount.
- OCP: not available.
- Selling costs are brokerage commissions and transfer taxes.
- Dividends are paid March, June, September, and December.

Performance Rating: **

DRIP Rating: 👎

Gillette Co. (NYSE:G)
c/o Bank of Boston
Shareholder Services
PO Box 644
Boston, MA 02102
(617) 575-3170   (800) 730-4001
(800) 291-7675

Business Profile: Manufactures razor blades, toiletries, cosmetics, and electric shavers.

Plan Specifics:
- Partial dividend reinvestment is not available.
- No Discount.
- OCP: $10 to $5000 per month.
- Selling costs are brokerage commissions.
- Company purchases stock monthly with OCP.
- Approximately 13,500 shareholders are in the plan.
- Dividends are paid March, June, September, and December.

Performance Rating: *****

DRIP Rating: 👍

GoodMark Foods, Inc.
(NASDAQ:GDMK)
6131 Falls of Neuse Rd.
Raleigh, NC 27609
(919) 790-9940

Business Profile: Leading producer of meat snacks in the United States. Also manufactures and distributes nonmeat snack foods and is a regional supplier of packaged meat products.

Plan Specifics:
- Partial dividend reinvestment is not available.
- 2 percent discount on reinvested dividends and OCPs.
- OCP: $25 to $500 per month.
- Stock is purchased monthly with OCPs.
- Selling costs are brokerage fees.
- Dividends are paid February, May, August, and November.

Performance Rating: ****

DRIP Rating: 👍

Goodrich (B.F.) Co. (NYSE:GR)
3925 Embassy Parkway
Akron, OH 44313
(216) 374-2613

Business Profile: Produces specialty chemicals and aerospace products.

Plan Specifics:
- Partial dividend reinvestment is not available.
- No Discount.
- OCP: $25 to $1000 per month.
- Selling costs are brokerage commissions.
- Company purchases stock around last day of month with OCPs.
- Dividends are paid March, June, September, and December.

Performance Rating: ***

DRIP Rating: 👍

Goodyear Tire & Rubber Co. (NYSE:GT)
1144 E. Market St.
Akron, OH 44316
(216) 796-3751   (216) 796-2121

Business Profile: Supplies tires and rubber-related products to original equipment and replacement markets.

Plan Specifics:
- Partial dividend reinvestment is available.
- No Discount.
- OCP: $10 to $15,000 per quarter.
- Company purchases stock every month with OCPs.
- Selling costs are $10 transaction fee, brokerage fees, service charges, and a $5 termination fee.
- Approximately 11,000 shareholders are in the plan.
- Dividends are paid March, June, September, and December.

Performance Rating: ***

DRIP Rating: 👍

Gorman-Rupp Co. (ASE:GRC)
PO Box 1217
Mansfield, OH 44901-1217
(419) 755-1011

Business Profile: Develops pumps, sewage pumping stations, and powered pumps for liquid handling applications.

Plan Specifics:
- Partial dividend reinvestment is available.
- No Discount.
- OCP: $20 to $1000 per month.
- Company purchases stock once a month with OCPs.
- Selling costs may include brokerage fees.
- Dividends are paid March, June, September, and December.

Performance Rating: ***

DRIP Rating: 👍

Goulds Pumps, Inc. (NASDAQ:GULD)
240 Fall St.
Seneca Falls, NY 13148
(315) 568-2811   (800) 937-5449

Business Profile: Produces service pumps, motors, and accessories for industrial and agricultural use.

Plan Specifics:
- Partial dividend reinvestment is not available.
- No Discount.
- OCP: $10 to $5000 per month.
- Stock is purchased monthly with OCPs.
- Selling costs are brokerage commissions.
- Dividends are paid January, April, July, and October.

Performance Rating: ***

DRIP Rating: 👍

Grace (W.R.) & Co. (NYSE:GRA)
One Town Center Rd.
Boca Raton, FL 33486-1010
(800) 648-8392   (407) 362-2000

Business Profile: Produces wide range of specialty chemicals. Also involved in specialty businesses.

Plan Specifics:
- Need at least 50 shares to enroll in plan.
- Partial dividend reinvestment is not available.
- No Discount.
- OCP: $100 to $100,000 per year.

- Selling costs are brokerage commissions, a $5 handling fee for each sale transaction, and a $15 service charge.
- Company purchases stock once a month with OCPs.
- Approximately 4500 shareholders are in the plan.
- Dividends are paid March, June, September and December.

Performance Rating: ***

DRIP Rating: ☜

Graco, Inc. (NYSE:GGG)
c/o Norwest Bank MN
161 N. Concord Exchange
PO Box 738
South St. Paul, MN 55075-0738
(612) 450-4064

Business Profile: Supplies specialized fluid-handling pumps and equipment.

Plan Specifics:

- Partial dividend reinvestment is not available.
- No Discount.
- OCP: $25 to $1000 per quarter.
- Stock is purchased monthly with OCPs.
- Selling costs are brokerage commissions and service charges.
- Approximately 600 shareholders in plan.
- Dividends are paid February, May, August, and November.

Performance Rating: ***

DRIP Rating: 👍

Grand Metropolitan PLC
(NYSE:GRM)
c/o Morgan Guaranty Trust Co. of New York
410 Park Ave.
New York, NY 10022
(800) 428-4237

Business Profile: British-based international producer of consumer products with interests in food for humans and pets, wine and spirits, eyewear, restaurants, and property management.

Plan Specifics:

- Partial dividend reinvestment is available.
- No Discount.
- OCP: $25 to $25,000 per year.
- Purchasing fees are brokerage commissions.
- Selling costs are brokerage commissions, a $5 handling charge, and any other costs of sale.
- Company purchases stock in April and October with OCPs.
- Dividends are paid April and October.

Performance Rating: ****

DRIP Rating: 👍

Great Southern Bancorp, Inc.
(NASDAQ:GSBC)
c/o Registrar and Transfer Co.
10 Commerce Dr.
Cranford, NJ 07016
(800) 749-7113

Business Profile: Company provides savings and trust services in southwestern and central Missouri.

Plan Specifics:
- Partial dividend reinvestment is not available.
- No Discount.
- OCP: $25 to $2500 per quarter.
- Selling costs are brokerage commissions and any transfer tax.
- Company purchases stock quarterly with OCPs.
- Dividends are paid January, April, July, and October.

Performance Rating: NR

DRIP Rating: 👍

Great Western Financial Corp. (NYSE:GWF)
9200 Oakdale Ave., N 11 75
Chatsworth, CA 91311
(818) 775-3411   (800) 522-6645

Business Profile: Holding company for thrift bank with operations primarily in Florida and California.

Plan Specifics:
- Partial dividend reinvestment is available.
- 3 percent discount on reinvested dividends.
- OCP: $100 to $10,000 per quarter.
- Selling costs include brokerage fees and transfer taxes.
- Company purchases stock quarterly with OCPs.
- Dividends are paid February, May, August, and November.

Performance Rating: **

DRIP Rating: 👍

Green Mountain Power Corp. (NYSE:GMP)
PO Box 850
25 Green Mountain Dr.
South Burlington, VT 05402
(802) 864-5731

Business Profile: Vermont-based electric utility serving residential, commercial, and industrial customers.

Plan Specifics:
- Partial dividend reinvestment is available.
- 5 percent discount on reinvested dividends.
- OCP: $50 to $40,000 per year.
- Company purchases stock monthly with OCPs.
- Selling costs are brokerage fees.
- Residents of Vermont may make initial purchases directly from the firm (minimum $50).
- Approximately 4000 shareholders are in the plan.
- Dividends are paid March, June, September, and December.

Performance Rating: **

DRIP Rating: 👍

GTE Corp. (NYSE:GTE)
c/o Bank of Boston
PO Box 9092
Boston, MA 02205-9092
(800) 225-5160

Business Profile: Operates large telephone system and engages in manufacture of telecommunication and electrical products.

Plan Specifics:
- Partial dividend reinvestment is available.
- No Discount.
- OCP: $25 to $100,000 per year.

- A quarterly fee equal to the lesser of $1 or 5 percent of the quarterly dividend and cash investment amount will be charged.
- Selling costs are brokerage commissions.
- Company purchases stock once a quarter with OCPs.
- IRA option is available.
- Preferred dividends are eligible for reinvestment for additional common shares under the plan.
- Dividends are paid January, April, July, and October.

Performance Rating: ****

DRIP Rating: 👍

Guardsman Products, Inc. (NYSE:GPI)
PO Box 1521
3033 Orchard Vista Dr., SE
Grand Rapids, MI 49501-1521
(616) 957-2600   (212) 613-7147

Business Profile: Manufactures industrial coatings and home-care products.

Plan Specifics:

- Partial dividend reinvestment is not available.
- No Discount.
- OCP: $200 to $3000 per quarter.
- Selling costs are $15 service charge and any brokerage commission.
- Company purchases stock quarterly with OCPs.
- Dividends are paid March, June, September, and December.

Performance Rating: ***

DRIP Rating: 👎

Hancock Holding Company (NASDAQ:HBHC)
One Hancock Plaza
Gulfport, MS 39501
(601) 868-4414

Business Profile: Bank holding company.

Plan Specifics:

- Partial dividend reinvestment is available.
- No Discount.
- OCP: $50 to $5000 per quarter.
- Purchasing fees include brokerage commissions.
- Selling costs are brokerage commissions and any transfer tax.
- Company purchases stock quarterly with OCPs.
- Dividends are paid March, June, September, and December.

Performance Rating: NR

DRIP Rating: 👍

Handleman Co. (NYSE:HDL)
500 Kirts Blvd.
Troy, MI 48084-5299
(800) 257-1770   (810) 362-4400

Business Profile: Supplier of prerecorded music and videocassettes, books, and computer software.

Plan Specifics:

- Partial dividend reinvestment is not available.
- No Discount.
- OCP: $10 to $3000 per month.
- Selling costs are $1 handling fee and brokerage commission.
- Stock is purchased monthly with OCPs.
- Dividends are paid January, April, July, and October.

Performance Rating: **

DRIP Rating: 👍

Handy & Harman (NYSE:HNH)
850 Third Ave.
New York, NY 10022
(212) 661-2400

Business Profile: Produces and refines precious metals. Manufactures automotive components for original equipment and replacement industries.

Plan Specifics:
- Partial dividend reinvestment is not available.
- No Discount.
- OCP: $10 to $60,000 per year.
- Selling costs include brokerage commissions.
- Company purchases stock each month with OCPs.
- Dividends are paid March, June, September, and December.

Performance Rating: **

DRIP Rating: 👍

Hanna (M. A.) Co. (NYSE:MAH)
200 Public Square, Ste. 36-5000
Cleveland, OH 44114-2304
(216) 589-4000   (800) 321-1954

Business Profile: Produces formulated polymers, plastics, and rubber compounds.

Plan Specifics:
- Partial dividend reinvestment is available.
- No Discount.
- OCP: $25 to $3000 per month.
- Selling costs are brokerage fees.
- Company purchases stock every month with OCPs.
- Dividends are paid March, June, September, and December.

Performance Rating: ***

DRIP Rating: 👍

Hannaford Brothers Co.
(NYSE:HRD)
145 Pleasant Hill Rd.
Scarborough, ME 04074
(207) 883-2911

Business Profile: Major food retailer.

Plan Specifics:
- Partial dividend reinvestment is available.
- No Discount.
- OCP: $25 to $2000 per month.
- Selling costs are brokerage commissions and a handling charge of 5 percent of the amount invested (maximum of $2.50).
- Company purchases stock monthly with OCPs.
- Dividends are paid March, June, September, and December.

Performance Rating: ****

DRIP Rating: 👍

Hanson PLC (NYSE:HAN)
c/o Citibank
Sort 3196
111 Wall St., 5th Floor
New York, NY 10043
(800) 422-2066   (212) 826-0098

Business Profile: British-based holding company.

Plan Specifics:
- Partial dividend reinvestment is available.
- No Discount.
- OCP: $50 to $60,000 per year.
- Company purchases stock once a month with OCPs.
- Purchasing costs include brokerage commissions and a $2.50 service charge for each OCP.
- Selling costs include a $3 administrative charge plus brokerage

commissions.
- Dividends are paid January, April, July, and October.

Performance Rating: ****

DRIP Rating: 👍

Harcourt General, Inc. (NYSE:H)
PO Box 1000
27 Boylston St.
Chestnut Hill, MA 02167
(617) 232-8200   (800) 442-2001

Business Profile: Major trade publisher with equity interest in Neiman Marcus Group.

Plan Specifics:
- Partial dividend reinvestment is not available.
- No Discount.
- OCP: $25 to $2500 per quarter.
- Selling costs are brokerage commissions and bank charges of $10 per transaction.
- Stock is purchased approximately 8 times a year with OCPs.
- Dividends are paid January, April, July, and October.

Performance Rating: ****

DRIP Rating: 👍

Harland (John H.) Company
(NYSE:JH)
c/o Trust Company Bank
PO Box 4625
Atlanta, GA 30302
(800) 568-3476

Business Profile: Provides products and services to the financial industry.

Plan Specifics:
- Partial dividend reinvestment is not available.

- No Discount.
- OCP: $25 to $3000 per quarter.
- OCP is invested monthly.
- Selling costs are brokerage charges.
- Company purchases stock monthly with OCPs if enough is received to purchase a minimum of 100 shares.
- Dividends are paid March, June, September, and December.

Performance Rating: ****

DRIP Rating: 👍

Harley-Davidson, Inc.
(NYSE:HDI)
3700 W. Juneau Ave.
PO Box 653
Milwaukee, WI 53201
(800) 637-7549   (414) 342-4680

Business Profile: Only U.S. motorcycle maker. The company also produces recreational and commercial vehicles.

Plan Specifics:
- Partial dividend reinvestment is not available.
- No Discount.
- OCP: $30 to $5000 per quarter.
- Stock is purchased monthly with OCPs.
- Selling costs are brokerage fees.
- Dividends are paid March, June, September, and December.

Performance Rating: ****

DRIP Rating: 👍

Harleysville Group, Inc.
(NASDAQ:HGIC)
355 Maple Ave.
Harleysville, PA 19438
(215) 256-5000   (800) 288-9541

Business Profile: Regional holding

company engaged in the property and casualty insurance business.

Plan Specifics:
- Partial dividend reinvestment is available.
- No Discount.
- OCP: $100 to $25,000 per year.
- Selling costs are brokerage commissions.
- Company purchases stock quarterly with OCPs.
- Dividends are paid March, June, September, and December.

Performance Rating: ***

DRIP Rating: 👍

Harris Corp. (NYSE:HRS)
1025 W. NASA Blvd.
Melbourne, FL 32919
(407) 727-9100

Business Profile: Manufactures electronic systems, semiconductors, and communication equipment.

Plan Specifics:
- Partial dividend reinvestment is not available.
- No Discount.
- OCP: $10 to $5000 per quarter.
- Stock is purchased monthly with OCPs.
- Selling costs may include brokerage commissions.
- Dividends are paid March, June, September, and December.

Performance Rating: ***

DRIP Rating: 👍

Harsco Corp. (NYSE:HSC)
PO Box 8888
Camp Hill, PA 17001-8888
(717) 763-7064   (800) 526-0801

Business Profile: A diversified industrial manufacturing and service company.

Plan Specifics:
- Partial dividend reinvestment is not available.
- No Discount.
- OCP: $10 to no maximum per month.
- Company purchases stock monthly with OCPs.
- Selling costs are $5 service charge and brokerage commissions.
- Service charge of $5 for deposit of certificates.
- Approximately 2600 shareholders are in the plan.
- Dividends are paid February, May, August, and November.

Performance Rating: ****

DRIP Rating: 👍

Hartford Steam Boiler Inspection
** & Insurance Co. (NYSE:HSB)**
One State St.
Hartford, CT 06102
(203) 722-1866   (800) 730-4001

Business Profile: Underwriter of property insurance for boilers and machinery.

Plan Specifics:
- Partial dividend reinvestment is not available.
- No Discount.
- OCP: $10 to $1000 per month.
- Stock is purchased monthly with OCPs.
- Selling costs are brokerage fees and a maximum handling charge of $3.
- Dividends are paid January, April, July, and October.

Performance Rating: ***
DRIP Rating: 👍

**Haverfield Corp.
  (NASDAQ:HVFD)
Terminal Tower
50 Public Square, Ste. 444
Cleveland, OH 44113-2203
(216) 348-2800**

Business Profile: Savings and loan holding company based in Ohio.

Plan Specifics:

- Partial dividend reinvestment is not available.
- No Discount.
- OCP: $20 to $1000 per month.
- Company purchases stock monthly with OCPs.
- Administrative fees include a fee of 5 percent of the dividend and OCP reinvested (maximum $3) and brokerage fees.
- There is a service charge of $2 for termination.
- Dividends are paid March, June, September, and December.

Performance Rating: **
DRIP Rating: 👍

**Hawaiian Electric Industries, Inc.
  (NYSE:HE)
PO Box 730
Honolulu, HI 96808-0730
(808) 532-5868   (808) 543-5662**

Business Profile: Hawaii-based electric utility holding company.

Plan Specifics:

- Partial dividend reinvestment is available.
- No Discount.
- OCP: $25 to $100,000 per year.
- Company purchases stock once a month with OCPs.

- Selling costs are brokerage fees and a $10 service charge.
- Residents of the state of Hawaii may make initial purchases of stock directly through the company (minimum $100).
- Automatic investment services are available.
- Preferred stock is eligible for reinvestment for common shares under the plan.
- Approximately 28,500 shareholders are in the plan.
- Dividends are paid March, June, September, and December.

Performance Rating: ***
DRIP Rating: 👍

**Health & Retirement Properties
  Trust (NYSE:HRP)
400 Centre St.
Newton, MA 02158-2076
(617) 332-3990**

Business Profile: Real estate investment trust investing in income-producing health-care real estate.

Plan Specifics:

- Partial dividend reinvestment is not available.
- No Discount.
- OCP: up to $10,000 per quarter.
- Company purchases stock quarterly with OCPs.
- Selling costs include brokerage fees and $2.50 service fee.
- Dividends are paid February, May, August, and November.

Performance Rating: **
DRIP Rating: 👍

Health Care REIT, Inc. (NYSE:HCN)
PO Box 1475
Toledo, OH 43603-1475
(419) 247-2800

Business Profile: Real estate investment trust investing in nursing homes, retirement homes, and psychiatric hospitals.

Plan Specifics:
- Partial dividend reinvestment is available.
- 4 percent discount on both reinvested dividends and OCPs.
- OCP: $10 to $5000 per quarter.
- Selling costs include brokerage fees and a handling charge of $15.
- Company purchases stock each quarter with OCPs.
- Dividends are paid February, May, August, and November.

Performance Rating: **

DRIP Rating: 👍

Heilig-Meyers Company (NYSE:HMY)
2235 Staples Mill Rd.
Richmond, VA 23230
(804) 359-9171   (800) 633-4236

Business Profile: Primarily engaged in the retail sale of home furnishings.

Plan Specifics:
- Partial dividend reinvestment is available.
- No Discount.
- OCP: $10 to $2500 per month.
- Stock is purchased once a month with OCPs.
- Selling costs are brokerage commissions.
- Dividends are paid February, May, August, and November.

Performance Rating: ***

DRIP Rating: 👍

Heinz (H.J.) Co. (NYSE:HNZ)
c/o Mellon Bank
PO Box 444
Pittsburgh, PA 15230-0444
(412) 236-8000   (800) 253-3399

Business Profile: Produces ketchup, tuna fish, frozen potatoes, and other consumer items, as well as weight loss services.

Plan Specifics:
- Partial dividend reinvestment is not available.
- No Discount.
- OCP: $25 to $5000 per month.
- Stock is purchased around the 10th of each month with OCPs.
- Selling costs are brokerage commissions and a $2.50 service charge.
- Dividends are paid January, April, July, and October.

Performance Rating: *****

DRIP Rating: 👍

Hercules, Inc. (NYSE:HPC)
c/o Chemical Mellon
Shareholder Services
PO Box 750
Pittsburgh, PA 15230
(800) 237-9980

Business Profile: Operations in specialty chemicals, aerospace, and fiber products.

Plan Specifics:
- Partial dividend reinvestment is available.
- No Discount.

- OCP: $50 to $2000 per month.
- Purchasing costs are brokerage commissions. There is a $5 service charge for each OCP.
- Selling costs are brokerage fees and $15 handling charge.
- Stock is purchased monthly with OCPs.
- Safekeeping services are available.
- Dividends are paid March, June, September, and December.

Performance Rating: ***

DRIP Rating: 👍

Hershey Foods Corp. (NYSE:HSY)
PO Box 810
100 Crystal A Dr.
Hershey, PA 17033-0810
(717) 534-7527   (800) 851-4216

Business Profile: Leading producer of chocolate, confectionery, and pasta products.

Plan Specifics:

- Partial dividend reinvestment is available.
- No Discount.
- OCP: $50 to $20,000 per year.
- Purchasing fees are brokerage fee (approximately 8 to 12 cents per share) for OCP plus service fee of 5 percent of total contribution (maximum $5).
- Selling costs are sales fee of $15 per transaction plus brokerage commissions.
- $5 charge for withdrawal of certificates.
- Stock is purchased monthly with OCPs.
- Approximately 15,000 shareholders are in the plan.

- Dividends are paid March, June, September, and December.

Performance Rating: *****

DRIP Rating: 👍

Hibernia Corp. (NYSE:HIB)
PO Box 61540
313 Carondelet St.
New Orleans, LA 70161
(800) 647-4273   (504) 533-3333

Business Profile: Holding company for banks in Louisiana.

Plan Specifics:

- Partial dividend reinvestment is available.
- 5 percent discount on reinvested dividends.
- OCP: $100 to $3000 per month.
- Selling costs are brokerage commissions.
- Company purchases stock once a month with OCPs.
- Approximately 2453 shareholders are in the plan.
- Dividends are paid February, May, August, and November.

Performance Rating: **

DRIP Rating: 👍

Home Depot, Inc. (NYSE:HD)
2727 Paces Ferry Rd.
Atlanta, GA 30339
(800) 442-2001

Business Profile: Operates a chain of retail warehouse-style stores which sell a wide variety of building materials and home improvement products.

Plan Specifics:

- Partial dividend reinvestment is not available.
- No Discount.

- OCP: $10 to $4000 per month.
- Purchasing fees include a service charge of 5 percent of the amount invested up to a maximum of $2.50.
- Selling costs are brokerage commissions and any other costs of sale.
- Company purchases stock monthly with OCPs.
- Dividends are paid March, June, September, and December.

Performance Rating: ****

DRIP Rating: 👍

**Homestake Mining Co.
(NYSE:HM)
c/o First National Bank of Boston
PO Box 1681
Boston, MA 02105-1681
(800) 442-2001**

Business Profile: Major gold producer in United States.

Plan Specifics:

- Partial dividend reinvestment is not available.
- No Discount.
- OCP: $25 to $5000 per month.
- There are no costs for selling shares from the plan.
- Company purchases stock monthly with OCPs.
- Dividends are paid February, May, August, and November.

Performance Rating: **

DRIP Rating: 👍

**Honeywell, Inc. (NYSE:HON)
PO Box 524
Honeywell Plaza
Minneapolis, MN 55440
(612) 951-1000   (800) 647-7147**

Business Profile: Manufactures and supplies automation and control systems for homes, industrial, and space and aviation markets.

Plan Specifics:

- Partial dividend reinvestment is not available.
- No Discount.
- OCP: $25 to $3000 per month.
- Selling costs are brokerage commissions and related expenses of sale.
- Company purchases stock beginning on the 20th day of the month with OCPs.
- Dividends are paid March, June, September, and December.

Performance Rating: ****

DRIP Rating: 👍

**Hormel Foods Corp. (NYSE:HRL)
c/o Norwest Bank
161 N. Concord Exchange
South St. Paul, MN 55075-0738
(612) 450-4064**

Business Profile: Processes pork, poultry, and fish food items.

Plan Specifics:

- Partial dividend reinvestment is not available.
- No Discount.
- OCP: $25 to $20,000 per quarter.
- Stock is purchased around the 15th of each month with OCPs, provided there are enough funds to purchase at least 100 shares.
- Selling costs are a $3 sales fee and 20 cents per share brokerage fee.
- Dividends are paid February, May, August, and November.

Performance Rating: ****

DRIP Rating: 👍

Houghton Mifflin Company (NYSE:HTN)

222 Berkeley St.
Boston, MA 02116-3764
(617) 351-5114

Business Profile: Publisher deriving most of its revenues from the sale of textbooks and educational services. Company also produces reference publications and fiction and nonfiction for adults and young readers.

Plan Specifics:

- Partial dividend reinvestment is not available.
- No Discount.
- OCP: $25 to $3000 per quarter.
- Selling costs are brokerage commissions and a service charge (maximum $5).
- Company purchases stock quarterly with OCPs.
- Dividends are paid February, May, August, and November.

Performance Rating: ***
DRIP Rating: 👍

Household International, Inc. (NYSE:HI)

2700 Sanders Rd.
Prospect Heights, IL 60070
(708) 564-5000

Business Profile: Major provider of finance and banking services and consumer insurance and investment products.

Plan Specifics:

- Partial dividend reinvestment is not available.
- 2½ percent discount on reinvested dividends.
- OCP: $50 to $5000 per quarter.
- Selling costs are brokerage commissions, handling charges, and any transfer taxes.
- Stock is purchased on the 15th of each month with OCPs.
- Preferred dividends are eligible for reinvestment for additional common shares under the plan.
- Dividends are paid January, April, July, and October.

Performance Rating: ****
DRIP Rating: 👍

Houston Industries, Inc. (NYSE:HOU)

Investor Services Dept.
PO Box 4505
Houston, TX 77210
(713) 629-3000   (800) 231-6406

Business Profile: Electric utility holding company provides electricity to regions of the Texas Gulf Coast.

Plan Specifics:

- Initial purchases may be made directly from company ($250 minimum).
- Partial dividend reinvestment is available.
- No Discount.
- OCP: $50 to $120,000 per year.
- Company purchases stock twice per month with OCPs.
- Selling costs are brokerage fees.
- Houston Industries debentures, first mortgage bonds, and preferred stock are eligible for reinvestment.
- Dividends are paid March, June, September, and December.

Performance Rating: ***
DRIP Rating: 👍

HRE Properties (NYSE:HRE)
c/o Bank of New York
101 Barclay St., 11th Floor E.
New York, NY 10007
(212) 642-4800

Business Profile: Real estate investment trust.

Plan Specifics:
- Partial dividend reinvestment is available.
- No Discount.
- OCP: not available.
- Selling costs are brokerage commissions.
- Approximately 400 shareholders are in the plan.
- Dividends are paid January, April, July, and October.

Performance Rating: **

DRIP Rating: ᧐

Hubbell, Inc. (NYSE:HUB.B)
c/o Chemical Bank
PO Box 3069, JAF Bldg.
New York, NY 10116-3069
(203) 799-4100

Business Profile: Manufactures a variety of electrical equipment and supplies.

Plan Specifics:
- Partial dividend reinvestment is available.
- No Discount.
- OCP: $100 to $1000 per quarter.
- Stock is purchased monthly with OCPs.
- Selling costs include brokerage commissions and service charges.
- $5 fee for issuance of certificates.
- Safekeeping services are available.

- Dividends are paid January, April, July, and October.

Performance Rating: *****

DRIP Rating: ᧐

HUBCO, Inc. (NASDAQ:HUBC)
3100 Bergenline Ave.
Union City, NJ 07087
(201) 348-2300

Business Profile: Bank holding company with 31 branches throughout New Jersey.

Plan Specifics:
- Partial dividend reinvestment is not available.
- No Discount.
- OCP: $10 to $2000 per quarter.
- Company purchases stock quarterly with OCPs.
- Dividends are paid March, June, September, and December.

Performance Rating: ****

DRIP Rating: ᧐

Huffy Corp. (NYSE:HUF)
PO Box 1204
Dayton, OH 45401
(513) 866-6251

Business Profile: Largest United States manufacturer of bicycles.

Plan Specifics:
- Need 25 shares to enroll.
- Partial dividend reinvestment is not available.
- No Discount.
- OCP: $10 to $1000 per month.
- Company purchases stock monthly with OCPs.
- Selling costs are brokerage commissions and a $1 service charge.

- Dividends are paid February, May, August, and November.

Performance Rating: **

DRIP Rating: 👍

Huntington Bancshares, Inc. (NASDAQ:HBAN)
c/o Huntington National Bank
41 S. High St.
Columbus, OH 43287
(614) 480-8300

Business Profile: Multibank holding company headquartered in Ohio.

Plan Specifics:

- Partial dividend reinvestment is available.
- 5 percent discount on reinvested dividends.
- OCP: $25 to $10,000 per quarter.
- Selling costs are minimal.
- Company purchases stock monthly with OCPs.
- Automatic investment services are available.
- Approximately 15,000 shareholders are in the plan.
- Dividends are paid January, April, July, and October.

Performance Rating: ***

DRIP Rating: 👍

Idaho Power Co. (NYSE:IDA)
PO Box 70
Boise, ID 83707
(800) 635-5406

Business Profile: Electric utility serving Idaho and sections of Oregon and Nevada.

Plan Specifics:

- Partial dividend reinvestment is available.

- No Discount.
- OCP: $10 to $15,000 per quarter.
- Purchasing fees are approximately 4 cents per share.
- Must go through own broker to sell shares.
- Company purchases stock quarterly with OCPs.
- Residential customers may make initial purchase of stock directly from the firm ($10 minimum).
- Approximately 14,000 shareholders are in the plan.
- Dividends are paid February, May, August, November.

Performance Rating: ***

DRIP Rating: 👍

IES Industries, Inc. (NYSE:IES)
200 First St. SE
Cedar Rapids, IA 52401
(800) 247-9785

Business Profile: Holding company for electric utility in Iowa.

Plan Specifics:

- Partial dividend reinvestment is available.
- No Discount.
- OCP: $25 to $120,000 per year.
- Selling costs include brokerage fees.
- Company purchases stock once a month with OCPs.
- Utility customers may purchase initial shares directly from the company (minimum $50).
- Dividends are paid January, April, July, and October.

Performance Rating: **

DRIP Rating: 👍

Illinois Tool Works, Inc.
(NYSE:ITW)
3600 W. Lake Ave.
Glenview, IL 60025-5811
(708) 724-7500

Business Profile: Producer of industrial components and other specialty products and equipment for high-volume manufacturing.

Plan Specifics:

- Partial dividend reinvestment is available.
- No Discount.
- OCP: $25 to $5000 per quarter.
- There are no costs for selling shares from the plan.
- Company purchases stock quarterly with OCPs.
- Dividends are paid January, April, July, and October.

Performance Rating: ****

DRIP Rating: 🖐

Illinova Corp. (NYSE:ILN)
Attn: Shareholder Services
500 S. 27th St.
Decatur, IL 62525-1805
(800) 800-8220

Business Profile: Provides electric and gas services to residential, industrial, and commercial customers in Illinois.

Plan Specifics:

- Partial dividend reinvestment is available.
- No Discount.
- OCP: $25 to $5000 per quarter.
- Stock is purchased monthly with OCPs.
- Selling costs are brokerage commissions and other fees.

- Preferred dividends are eligible for reinvestment for common shares under the plan.
- Dividends are paid February, May, August, and November.

Performance Rating: **

DRIP Rating: 🖐

Imo Industries, Inc.
(NYSE:IMD)
3450 Princeton Pike
PO Box 6550
Lawrenceville, NJ 08648
(609) 896-7600

Business Profile: Producer of analytical and optical instruments, electronic and mechanical controls, and engineered power products.

Plan Specifics:

- Partial dividend reinvestment is not available.
- No Discount.
- OCP: $100 to $5000 per quarter.
- Selling costs are brokerage commissions and a handling charge of $2.50 when terminating.
- Company purchases stock quarterly with OCPs.
- The company does not pay a dividend.

Performance Rating: **

DRIP Rating: 🖐

Imperial Holly Corp. (ASE:IHK)
c/o The Bank of New York
PO Box 11258, Church St. Sta.
New York, NY 10286-1258
(800) 524-4458

Business Profile: One of the largest U.S. producers and marketers of refined sugar.

Plan Specifics:
- Partial dividend reinvestment is not available.
- No Discount.
- OCP: $100 to $5000 per quarter.
- Company purchases stock monthly with OCPs.
- Selling fees include a $5 service charge and brokerage commissions.

Performance Rating: **

DRIP Rating: 👍

Imperial Oil Ltd. (ASE:IMO)
111 St. Clair Ave., W.
Toronto, Ont. M5W 1K3 Canada
(416) 968-5076

Business Profile: Produces crude oil, natural gas, and petroleum in Canada; 70 percent owned by Exxon.

Plan Specifics:
- Partial dividend reinvestment is available.
- No Discount.
- OCP: $50 to $5000 (Canadian) per quarter.
- Must go through own broker to sell shares.
- Company purchases stock four times a year with OCPs.
- Dividends are paid January, April, July, and October.

Performance Rating: ****

DRIP Rating: 👍

Inco Ltd. (NYSE:N)
One New York Plaza
New York, NY 10004
(800) 457-1464

Business Profile: Leading producer of nickel with operations in copper and other metals.

Plan Specifics:
- Partial dividend reinvestment is available.
- No Discount.
- OCP: $30 to $10,000 per quarter.
- Selling costs are brokerage fees and any service charges.
- Company purchases stock quarterly with OCPs.
- Approximately 16,500 shareholders are in the plan.
- Dividends are paid March, June, September, and December.

Performance Rating: **

DRIP Rating: 👍

Independence Bancorp, Inc. (NASDAQ:IBNJ)
1100 Lake St.
Ramsey, NJ 07446
(201) 825-1000

Business Profile: Bank holding company.

Plan Specifics:
- Partial dividend reinvestment is available.
- No Discount.
- OCP: $500 to $2000 per quarter.
- Selling costs are service charges and taxes.
- Company purchases stock quarterly with OCPs.
- Dividends are paid January, April, July, and October.

Performance Rating: NR

DRIP Rating: 👎

Independent Bank Corp. (MI)
(NASDAQ:IBCP)
c/o Security Transfer Services
PO Box 8204
Boston, MA 02266-8204
(800) 257-1770   (616) 527-9450

Business Profile: Michigan-based bank holding company.

Plan Specifics:

- Partial dividend reinvestment is available.
- 5 percent discount on reinvested dividends.
- OCP: $25 to $2500 per quarter.
- Selling cost includes brokerage fees and $5 termination fee.
- Stock is purchased quarterly with OCPs.
- Dividends are paid January, April, July, and October.

Performance Rating: ****
DRIP Rating: 👍

Indiana Energy, Inc. (NYSE:IEI)
1630 N. Meridian St.
Indianapolis, IN 46202-1496
(317) 926-3351   (800) 446-2617

Business Profile: Holding company for Indiana-based natural gas distributor.

Plan Specifics:

- Partial dividend reinvestment is available.
- No Discount.
- OCP: $25 to $50,000 per calendar year.
- Selling costs are brokerage fees and a $5 handling charge.
- Company purchases stock each month with OCPs.
- Stock may be sold via the telephone.

- Dividends are paid March, June, September, and December.

Performance Rating: *****
DRIP Rating: 👍

Ingersoll-Rand Co. (NYSE:IR)
c/o Bank of New York
PO Box 11258, Church St. Sta.
New York, NY 10286
(201) 573-0123   (800) 524-4458

Business Profile: Designs and produces compressed air systems for mining, construction, and automotive markets.

Plan Specifics:

- Partial dividend reinvestment is not available.
- No Discount.
- OCP: $10 to $3000 per quarter.
- Selling cost is pro rata share of brokerage fees.
- Stock is purchased around the 1st of each month with OCPs.
- Dividends are paid March, June, September, and December.

Performance Rating: ***
DRIP Rating: 👍

Inland Steel Industries, Inc.
(NYSE:IAD)
30 W. Monroe St.
Chicago, IL 60603
(312) 346-0300   (312) 461-3932

Business Profile: Major integrated steel producer.

Plan Specifics:

- Partial dividend reinvestment is not available.
- No Discount.
- OCP: $25 to $10,000 per month.
- Company purchases stock once a month with OCPs.

- Dividends are paid February, May, August, and November.

Performance Rating: ***

DRIP Rating: 👍

Insteel Industries, Inc. (NYSE:III)
c/o First Union Nat'l Bank of N.C.
Dividend Reinvestment
  Service—CMG-5
Charlotte, NC 28288-1154
(800) 829-8432

Business Profile: One of the largest wire manufacturers in the United States.

Plan Specifics:
- Partial dividend reinvestment is not available.
- No Discount.
- OCP: $10 per month minimum (no maximum).
- Selling costs are general costs of sale.
- Company purchases stock monthly with OCPs.
- Dividends are paid January, April, July, and October.

Performance Rating: **

DRIP Rating: 👍

Intel Corp. (NASDAQ:INTC)
2200 Mission College Blvd.
Santa Clara, CA 95052
(800) 298-0146

Business Profile: World's leading semiconductor manufacturer. Company also produces micro-computer components, modules, and systems.

Plan Specifics:
- Partial dividend reinvestment is not available.
- No Discount.

- OCP: $25 to $15,000 per quarter.
- Selling costs are brokerage commissions.
- Company purchases stock quarterly with OCPs.
- Dividends are paid March, June, September, and December.

Performance Rating: ****

DRIP Rating: 👍

Interchange Financial Services
  Corp. (ASE:ISB)
Park 80 West/Plaza Two
Saddle Brook, NJ 07662
(201) 703-2265

Business Profile: Holding company operating commercial banking offices in Bergen and Passaic counties, New Jersey.

Plan Specifics:
- Initial purchases may be made directly from the company ($100 minimum investment).
- Partial dividend reinvestment is not available.
- No Discount.
- OCP: $25 per month to no maximum (in multiples of $10).
- Company purchases stock monthly with OCPs.
- Purchasing fees are brokerage commissions.
- Selling costs are commissions and fees.
- Dividends are paid January, April, July, and October.

Performance Rating: ***

DRIP Rating: 👍

**International Business Machines
Corp. (NYSE:IBM)**
c/o First Chicago Trust-NY
PO Box 2530, Ste. 4688
Jersey City, NJ 07303
(201) 324-0405   (800) 446-2617

Business Profile: Largest producer
of mainframe, small business, and
personal computers.

Plan Specifics:
- Partial dividend reinvestment is
  available.
- No Discount.
- OCP: $10 to $25,000 per quarter.
- Stock is purchased around the
  10th of the month with OCPs.
- Purchasing fees are 2 percent of
  amount invested (maximum $3).
- Selling costs are approximately
  10 cents per share and a $7.50
  fee.
- Dividends are paid March, June,
  September, and December.

Performance Rating: ****
DRIP Rating: 👍

**International Flavors &
Fragrances, Inc. (NYSE: IFF)**
521 W. 57th St.
New York, NY 10019
(212) 765-5500

Business Profile: Leading maker of
products used by other manufacturers to improve flavor or fra-
grance in a variety of consumer
goods.

Plan Specifics:
- Partial dividend reinvestment is
  not available.
- No Discount.
- OCP: $25 to $5000 per month.
- Must go through own broker to
  sell shares.

- Company purchases stock
  monthly with OCPs.
- Dividends are paid January,
  April, July, and October.

Performance Rating: *****
DRIP Rating: 👍

**International Multifoods Corp.
(NYSE:IMC)**
PO Box 2942
Multifoods Tower
Minneapolis, MN 55402-0942
(612) 340-3300   (800) 446-2617

Business Profile: International food
company with operations in frozen
foods and bakery items.

Plan Specifics:
- Partial dividend reinvestment is
  available.
- No Discount.
- OCP: $10 to $60,000 per year.
- Selling costs are brokerage fees
  and service charges.
- Company purchases stock
  beginning on the 15th day of
  each month with OCPs.
- Dividends are paid January,
  April, July, and October.

Performance Rating: ***
DRIP Rating: 👍

International Paper Co. (NYSE:IP)
2 Manhattanville Rd.
Purchase, NY 10577
(914) 397-1500   (800) 678-8715

Business Profile: Leading manufacturer of paper and related items.

Plan Specifics:
- Partial dividend reinvestment is
  available.
- No Discount.
- OCP: $25 to $20,000 per year.

- Stock is purchased monthly with OCPs.
- Selling costs include brokerage commissions.
- Dividends are paid March, June, September, and December.

Performance Rating: ****

DRIP Rating: 👍

Interpublic Group of Companies, Inc. (NYSE:IPG)
1271 Ave. of the Americas
New York, NY 10020
(212) 399-8000

Business Profile: Leading advertising agency system.

Plan Specifics:
- Partial dividend reinvestment is not available.
- No Discount.
- OCP: $10 to $3000 per quarter.
- Stock is purchased quarterly with OCPs.
- Purchasing fees are 5 percent of total funds invested with a $2.50 maximum and brokerage commission of about 1 percent.
- Selling costs are brokerage commission and other costs of sale.
- Safekeeping services are available.
- Dividends are paid March, June, September, and December.

Performance Rating: ****

DRIP Rating: 👍

Interstate Power Co. (NYSE:IPW)
PO Box 769
1000 Main St.
Dubuque, IA 52004-0769
(319) 582-5421

Business Profile: Provides electric power and natural gas to Iowa, Minnesota, and Illinois.

Plan Specifics:
- Partial dividend reinvestment is available.
- No Discount.
- OCP: $25 to $2000 per month.
- Purchasing and selling costs are brokerage commissions.
- Company purchases stock once a month with OCPs.
- Customers of the company may make initial purchase of stock directly from the company ($50 minimum).
- Dividends are paid March, June, September, and December.

Performance Rating: **

DRIP Rating: 👍

IPALCO Enterprises, Inc. (NYSE:IPL)
25 Monument Circle
PO Box 1595
Indianapolis, IN 46206-1595
(317) 261-8394   (800) 877-0153

Business Profile: Holding company for electric utility serving Indianapolis.

Plan Specifics:
- Partial dividend reinvestment is available.
- No Discount.
- OCP: $25 to $5000 per month.
- Purchasing and selling fees are brokerage commissions.
- Company purchases stock once a month with OCPs.
- Dividends are paid January, April, July, and October.

Performance Rating: ****

DRIP Rating: 👍

IRT Property Co. (NYSE:IRT)
200 Galleria Pkwy., Ste. 1400
Atlanta, GA 30339
(404) 955-4406

Business Profile: Real estate investment trust.

Plan Specifics:
- Partial dividend reinvestment is available.
- 5 percent discount on reinvested dividends.
- OCP: not available.
- Selling costs may include brokerage fees.
- Approximately 1000 shareholders are in the plan.
- Dividends are paid March, June, September, and December.

Performance Rating: **

DRIP Rating: ☞

ITT Corp. (NYSE:ITT)
PO Box 1507
Secaucus, NJ 07096-1507
(201) 601-4202   (800) 342-5488

Business Profile: Operations in gaming, entertainment, and information services.

Plan Specifics:
- Partial dividend reinvestment is not available.
- No Discount.
- OCP: $50 to $60,000 per year.
- Selling costs are brokerage commissions.
- Company purchases stock every month with OCPs.
- Dividends are paid January, April, July, October.

Performance Rating: ***

DRIP Rating: 👍

IWC Resources Corp.
(NASDAQ:IWCR)
PO Box 1220
1220 Waterway Blvd.
Indianapolis, IN 46206
(317) 263-6358   (317) 639-1501

Business Profile: Holding company for public water utility serving Indianapolis-area communities.

Plan Specifics:
- Partial dividend reinvestment is available.
- 3 percent discount on reinvested dividends and OCPs.
- OCP: $100 to $100,000 per year.
- Selling costs are brokerage commissions and other charges.
- Company purchases stock twice per month with OCPs.
- Utility customers may make initial purchase of stock directly from company (minimum $100).
- Dividends are paid March, June, September, and December.

Performance Rating: ***

DRIP Rating: 👍

Jacobson Stores, Inc.
(NASDAQ:JCBS)
3333 Sargent Rd.
Jackson, MI 49201
(517) 764-6400

Business Profile: Operates specialty department stores in the Midwest and Florida, showcasing fashion apparel, home furnishings, and accessories.

Plan Specifics:
- Partial dividend reinvestment is available.
- No Discount.
- OCP: $10 to $1000 per month.

- Selling costs include transfer taxes.
- Company purchases stock monthly with OCPs.
- Dividends are paid January, April, July, and October.

Performance Rating: **

DRIP Rating: 👍

James River Corp. (NYSE: JR)
120 Tredegar St.
Richmond, VA 23219
(804) 644-5411   (800) 633-4236

Business Profile: Leading manufacturer of consumer and commercial tissue products.

Plan Specifics:

- Partial dividend reinvestment is available.
- No Discount.
- OCP: $100 to $5000 per month.
- OCP is invested monthly.
- Purchasing and selling fees are approximately 9 cents per share.
- Dividends are paid March, June, September, and December.

Performance Rating: ***

DRIP Rating: 👍

Jefferson Bankshares, Inc.
 (NASDAQ:JBNK)
123 E. Main St.
Charlottesville, VA 22901
(804) 972-1115   (804) 972-1100

Business Profile: Virginia-based bank holding company.

Plan Specifics:

- Partial dividend reinvestment is available.
- No Discount.
- OCP: $25 to $5000 per quarter.
- Company purchases stock monthly with OCP.

- Selling costs are brokerage commissions, an administrative fee of $2.50, and applicable taxes.
- Approximately 2500 shareholders are in the plan.
- Dividends are paid January, April, July, and October.

Performance Rating: ***

DRIP Rating: 👍

Jefferson-Pilot Corp. (NYSE:JP)
c/o First Union Nat'l Bank
Dividend Reinvestment Service
230 S. Tryon St.
Charlotte, NC 28288-1154
(800) 829-8432   (910) 691-3000

Business Profile: Insurance holding company with operations in life insurance, television, and radio communications.

Plan Specifics:

- Partial dividend reinvestment is not available.
- No Discount.
- OCP: $20 to $2000 per month.
- Shares will be purchased at least monthly if funds are available for round-lot purchase.
- Selling costs may include brokerage fees.
- Dividends are paid March, June, September, and December.

Performance Rating: ****

DRIP Rating: 👍

Johnson & Johnson (NYSE:JNJ)
One Johnson & Johnson Plaza
New Brunswick, NJ 08933
(800) 328-9033

Business Profile: Leading supplier of health-care products and consumer products.

Plan Specifics:
- Partial dividend reinvestment is available.
- No Discount.
- OCP: $25 to $50,000 per year.
- Selling costs are brokerage commissions and other costs of sale.
- Company purchases stock beginning on the 7th of the month with OCPs.
- Shares may be sold via the telephone.
- Dividends are paid March, June, September, and December.

Performance Rating: *****
DRIP Rating: 👍

Johnson Controls, Inc. (NYSE:JCI)
Shareholder Services
PO Box 591
Milwaukee, WI 53201-0591
(414) 276-3737   (414) 228-2363
(414) 228-2135

Business Profile: Major producer of automated building controls, batteries, automotive seating, and plastics.

Plan Specifics:
- Initial purchases of stock may be made through the company ($50 minimum).
- Partial dividend reinvestment is available.
- No Discount.
- OCP: $50 to $15,000 per quarter.
- Company purchases stock once a month with OCPs.
- Selling costs are minimal brokerage fees and $5 termination fee.
- Approximately 28,000 shareholders are in the plan.

- Dividends are paid January, March, June, and September.

Performance Rating: ****
DRIP Rating: 👍

Jostens, Inc. (NYSE:JOS)
c/o Norwest Bank Minnesota
PO Box 738
South St. Paul, MN 55075
(612) 450-4064   (612) 830-3287

Business Profile: Leading provider of class rings, yearbooks, and diplomas for schools and universities.

Plan Specifics:
- Partial dividend reinvestment is not available.
- No Discount.
- OCP: $25 to $1000 per month.
- Selling costs are brokerage commissions and service fees.
- Company purchases stock monthly with OCPs.
- Dividends are paid March, June, September, and December.

Performance Rating: ***
DRIP Rating: 👍

Justin Industries, Inc.
** (NASDAQ:JSTN)**
PO Box 425
2821 W. Seventh St.
Fort Worth, TX 76101
(817) 390-2415   (800) 527-7844

Business Profile: Manufactures western-style footwear, building materials, and industrial equipment.

Plan Specifics:
- Partial dividend reinvestment is not available.
- No Discount.

- OCP: $25 to $1000 per month.
- Company purchases stock monthly with OCPs.
- Purchasing fees are service charge of $2 per investment plus brokerage costs.
- Company suggests having a quarterly dividend of at least $20 to enroll.
- Selling costs are brokerage fees.
- Dividends are paid January, April, July, and October.

Performance Rating: ***

DRIP Rating: ☜

K N Energy, Inc. (NYSE:KNE)
PO Box 15265
Lakewood, CO 80215-0265
(303) 989-1740

Business Profile: Natural gas company serving customers in Colorado, Kansas, Nebraska, and Wyoming.

Plan Specifics:
- Partial dividend reinvestment is available.
- No Discount.
- OCP: $25 to $8000 per quarter.
- Company purchases stock once a week with OCPs.
- Purchasing fees are brokerage commissions.
- Must go through own broker to sell stock.
- Automatic investment services are available.
- Preferred dividends are eligible for reinvestment for additional common shares under the plan.
- Approximately 3500 shareholders are in the plan.
- Dividends are paid March, June, September, and December.

Performance Rating: ***

DRIP Rating: 👍

Kaman Corp.
(NASDAQ:KAMNA)
c/o Chemical Bank
PO Box 3068, JAF Bldg.
New York, NY 10116-3068
(800) 851-9677

Business Profile: Manufactures helicopters and aircraft components. Provides scientific systems and services for government. Distributes industrial parts. Manufactures and distributes musical instruments.

Plan Specifics:
- Partial dividend reinvestment is not available.
- No Discount.
- OCP: $25 to $5000 per quarter.
- Selling costs are brokerage fees.
- Company purchases stock at least once a month with OCPs.
- Dividends are paid January, April, July, and October.

Performance Rating: ***

DRIP Rating: 👍

Kansas City Power & Light Co.
(NYSE:KLT)
1201 Walnut
Kansas City, MO 64106
(800) 245-5275

Business Profile: Supplies electricity to over 419,000 customers in western Missouri and eastern Kansas, primarily in metropolitan Kansas City.

Plan Specifics:
- Partial dividend reinvestment is available.
- No Discount.

- OCP: $100 to $5000 per month.
- Stock is purchased monthly with OCPs.
- Fees are roughly 5 cents per share when buying and 10 cents per share when selling.
- Dividends are paid March, June, September, and December.

Performance Rating: ***

DRIP Rating: 👍

Keithley Instruments, Inc.
(ASE:KEI)
28775 Aurora Rd.
Solon, OH 44139
(216) 248-0400   (800) 542-7792

Business Profile: One of the world's leading designers, developers, and manufacturers of precision electrical measuring instruments.

Plan Specifics:
- Partial dividend reinvestment is available.
- No Discount.
- OCP: $10 to $4000 per month.
- Stock is purchased monthly with OCPs.
- Selling costs are brokerage commissions and a $5 termination fee.
- Dividends are paid March, June, September, and December.

Performance Rating: ***

DRIP Rating: 👍

Kellogg Co. (NYSE:K)
One Kellogg Square
PO Box 3599
Battle Creek, MI 49016-3599
(616) 961-2380   (800) 323-6138

Business Profile: Leading supplier of cereals and other breakfast items.

Plan Specifics:
- Partial dividend reinvestment is available.
- No Discount.
- OCP: $25 to $25,000 per year.
- Company purchases stock around the 15th of the month with OCPs.
- Selling costs are brokerage commission and other expenses.
- Dividends are paid March, June, September, and December.

Performance Rating: *****

DRIP Rating: 👍

Kellwood Company
(NYSE:KWD)
600 Kellwood Parkway
Chesterfield, MO 63017
(314) 576-3100

Business Profile: Manufacturer and marketer of value-oriented apparel and recreational camping products.

Plan Specifics:
- Initial stock purchases may be made directly from the company ($100 minimum).
- Partial dividend reinvestment is available.
- No Discount.
- OCP: $25 to $3000 per month.
- Stock is purchased monthly with OCPs.
- Selling costs include a $5 termination fee and brokerage fees.
- Dividends are paid March, June, September, and December.

Performance Rating: ***

DRIP Rating: 👍

Kennametal, Inc. (NYSE:KMT)
PO Box 231
Latrobe, PA 15650
(412) 539-5204   (412) 539-5000

Business Profile: Manufactures cemented carbide tools, ceramics, and metalworking supplies.

Plan Specifics:

- Partial dividend reinvestment is not available.
- 5 percent discount on reinvested dividends.
- OCP: $25 to $4000 per quarter.
- Selling costs include brokerage fees and service charges.
- Company purchases stock quarterly with OCPs.
- Approximately 1000 shareholders are in the plan.
- Dividends are paid February, May, August, and November.

Performance Rating: ****
DRIP Rating: 👍

Kerr-McGee Corp. (NYSE:KMG)
c/o Liberty National Bank
PO Box 25848
Oklahoma City, OK 73125
(405) 231-6711   (405) 270-1313
(800) 786-2556

Business Profile: Produces oil and natural gas, industrial chemicals and coal.

Plan Specifics:

- Initial purchases may be made directly from the company ($750 minimum).
- Partial dividend reinvestment is available.
- No Discount.
- OCP: $10 to $3000 per quarter.
- Stock is purchased monthly with OCPs.

- No buying or selling costs.
- Dividends are paid January, April, July, and October.

Performance Rating: ****
DRIP Rating: 👍

KeyCorp (NYSE:KEY)
127 Public Square
Cleveland, OH 44114-1306
(216) 689-6300

Business Profile: Interstate bank holding company.

Plan Specifics:

- Partial dividend reinvestment is available.
- No Discount.
- OCP: $10 to $10,000 per month.
- Company purchases stock monthly with OCPs.
- Selling costs include brokerage fees.
- Dividends are paid March, June, September, and December.

Performance Rating: ****
DRIP Rating: 👍

Keystone Financial, Inc.
(NASDAQ:KSTN)
One Keystone Plaza
Front & Market Streets
PO Box 3660
Harrisburg, PA 17105-3660
(717) 233-1555

Business Profile: Pennsylvania multibank holding company.

Plan Specifics:

- Partial dividend reinvestment is not available.
- No Discount.
- OCP: $100 to $5000 per quarter.
- Stock is purchased quarterly with OCPs.

- Selling costs are brokerage fees.
- Approximately 2700 shareholders are in the plan.
- Dividends are paid January, April, July, and October.

Performance Rating: ***

DRIP Rating: ☞

Keystone Heritage Group, Inc. (ASE:KHG)
PO Box 1285
Lebanon, PA 17042-1285
(717) 274-6800

Business Profile: Bank holding company based in Pennsylvania.

Plan Specifics:
- Partial dividend reinvestment is not available.
- No Discount.
- OCP: $10 to $2000 per quarter.
- Participants may have to pay brokerage costs if shares are purchased on the open market.
- $3 termination fee.
- Participants may have to go through own broker to sell stock.
- Company purchases stock quarterly with OCPs.
- Dividends are paid February, May, August, November.

Performance Rating: ***

DRIP Rating: ☞

Keystone International, Inc. (NYSE:KII)
9600 W. Gulf Bank Dr.
PO Box 40010
Houston, TX 77240
(713) 937-5301

Business Profile: Produces flow control equipment and systems.

Plan Specifics:
- Partial dividend reinvestment is available.
- No Discount.
- OCP: $25 to $4000 per month.
- Selling costs are brokerage commissions.
- Company purchases stock monthly with OCPs.
- Safekeeping services are available.
- Dividends are paid February, May, August, and November.

Performance Rating: ***

DRIP Rating: 👍

Kimberly-Clark Corp. (NYSE:KMB)
PO Box 619100
Dallas, TX 75261-9100
(214) 830-1200   (800) 442-2001

Business Profile: Produces facial tissues, feminine napkins, disposable diapers, and paper towels.

Plan Specifics:
- Partial dividend reinvestment is available.
- No Discount.
- OCP: $25 to $3000 per quarter.
- Stock is purchased approximately 8 times a year with OCPs.
- Selling costs include brokerage fees plus service charge (minimum $1; maximum, $10).
- Direct deposit of dividends is available.
- Dividends are paid January, April, July, October.

Performance Rating: *****

DRIP Rating: 👍

Kmart Corp. (NYSE:KM)
3100 W. Big Beaver Rd.
Troy, MI 48084
(800) 336-6981

Business Profile: One of the world's largest mass merchandise retailers.

Plan Specifics:

- Holders of record of 10 or more shares are eligible to participate.
- Partial dividend reinvestment is available.
- No Discount.
- OCP: $25 to $100,000 per year.
- Company purchases stock monthly with OCPs.
- Selling costs are brokerage commissions, a $10 service charge, and any applicable taxes.
- Dividends are paid March, June, September, and December.

Performance Rating: ***

DRIP Rating: 👍

Knape & Vogt Manufacturing Company (NASDAQ:KNAP)
c/o Harris Trust
PO Box A3309
Chicago, IL 60690
(616) 459-3311   (800) 323-1849

Business Profile: Leading manufacturer of shelving and storage products for the do-it-yourself home improvement market.

Plan Specifics:

- Partial dividend reinvestment is not available.
- No Discount.
- OCP: $25 to $1000 per month.
- Company purchases stock monthly with OCPs.
- Selling costs are brokerage commissions and transfer taxes.

- Dividends are paid March, June, September, and December.

Performance Rating: ***

DRIP Rating: 👍

Knight-Ridder, Inc. (NYSE:KRI)
One Herald Plaza
Miami, FL 33132
(305) 376-3938   (800) 851-9677

Business Profile: Leading newspaper publisher with operations in electronic information distribution.

Plan Specifics:

- Partial dividend reinvestment is not available.
- No Discount.
- OCP: $25 to $1000 per month.
- Selling costs include brokerage fees.
- Company purchases stock monthly with OCPs.
- Dividends are paid January, April, July, and October.

Performance Rating: ****

DRIP Rating: 👍

Kollmorgen Corp. (NYSE:KOL)
c/o First Nat'l Bank of Boston
PO Box 1681
Boston, MA 02105-1681
(617) 890-5655

Business Profile: Producer of motors, controls, and electro-optical instruments for industrial and military use.

Plan Specifics:

- Partial dividend reinvestment is not available.
- No Discount.
- OCP: $25 to $1000 per month.
- Selling costs are brokerage commissions, transfer tax, and

bank charges of 5 percent of the gross proceeds up to a maximum of $5.

- Company purchases stock monthly with OCPs.
- Dividends are paid March, June, September, and December.

Performance Rating: **

DRIP Rating: 👍

**Kranzco Realty Trust (NYSE:KRT)
c/o First Fidelity Bank, N.A., New Jersey
PO Box 11031, Church St. Sta.
New York, NY 10286
(800) 524-4458**

Business Profile: Real estate investment trust which owns and operates community shopping centers in Connecticut, Maryland, New Jersey, New York, Pennsylvania, Rhode Island, and Virginia.

Plan Specifics:

- Partial dividend reinvestment is available.
- No Discount.
- OCP: $100 to $5000 per quarter.
- Selling costs are brokerage fees and any other costs of sale.
- Company purchases stock monthly with OCPs.
- Dividends are paid January, April, July, and October.

Performance Rating: **

DRIP Rating: 👍

**KU Energy Corp. (NYSE:KU)
One Quality St.
Lexington, KY 40507
(606) 288-1188**

Business Profile: Owner of Kentucky Utilities Co., a coal-based

utility company that provides electric service to customers in Kentucky and Virginia.

Plan Specifics:

- Partial dividend reinvestment is available.
- No Discount.
- OCP: $20 to $10,000 per quarter.
- Purchasing fees include brokerage commissions.
- Selling costs are brokerage commissions and any other fees or transfer taxes.
- Company purchases stock quarterly with OCPs.
- Dividends are paid March, June, September, and December.

Performance Rating: ****

DRIP Rating: 👍

**Kuhlman Corp. (NYSE:KUH)
1 Skidaway Village Walk, Suite 201
Savannah, GA 31411
(912) 598-7809**

Business Profile: Holding company involved in the manufacturing of distribution, power and instrument transformers; electrical and electronic wire and cable products; and spring products.

Plan Specifics:

- Partial dividend reinvestment is available.
- No Discount.
- OCP: $10 to $3000 per quarter.
- Company purchases stock once a month with OCPs.
- Selling costs are brokerage commissions and a handling charge.
- Dividends are paid January, April, July, and October.

Performance Rating: **

DRIP Rating: 👍

**Kysor Industrial Corp.
(NYSE:KZ)
One Madison Ave.
Cadillac, MI 49601-9785
(800) 426-5523**

Business Profile: Manufactures a variety of refrigerated display cases and original equipment components for heavy-duty trucks, commercial, military, and off-road vehicles; and marine equipment.

Plan Specifics:

- Partial dividend reinvestment is not available.
- No Discount.
- OCP: $10 to $12,000 per year.
- Selling costs are brokerage commissions, applicable taxes, and a handling charge of $3.
- Company purchases stock monthly with OCPs.
- Dividends are paid January, April, July, and October.

Performance Rating: ***

DRIP Rating: 👍

**La-Z-Boy Chair Co. (NYSE:LZB)
1284 N. Telegraph Rd.
Monroe, MI 48162-3390
(212) 936-5100**

Business Profile: Manufactures reclining chairs and upholstered furniture.

Plan Specifics:

- Partial dividend reinvestment is not available.
- No Discount.
- OCP: $25 to $1000 per month.
- Selling costs are brokerage commissions and charge of $5.

- Company purchases stock each month with OCPs.
- Dividends are paid March, June, September, and December.

Performance Rating: ***

DRIP Rating: 👍

**Laclede Gas Co. (NYSE:LG)
720 Olive St.
St Louis, MO 63101
(314) 466-1754   (800) 456-9852**

Business Profile: Retail supplier of natural gas in St. Louis communities.

Plan Specifics:

- Partial dividend reinvestment is not available.
- No Discount.
- OCP: $100 to $30,000 per year.
- Selling costs are brokerage commissions.
- Company purchases stock quarterly with OCPs.
- Dividends are paid January, April, July, and October.

Performance Rating: *****

DRIP Rating: 👍

**Lafarge Corp. (NYSE:LAF)
c/o Wachovia Bank of North
 Carolina, N.A.
PO Box 3001
Winston-Salem, NC 27102-3001
(800) 633-4236**

Business Profile: Produces cement and other construction materials.

Plan Specifics:

- Partial dividend reinvestment is not available.
- 5 percent discount on reinvested dividends.
- OCP: not available.

- Must go through own broker to sell shares.
- Dividends are paid March, June, September, and December.

Performance Rating: **

DRIP Rating: ℗

Lancaster Colony Corp. (NASDAQ:LANC)
37 W. Broad St.
Columbus, OH 43215
(614) 224-7141

Business Profile: Maker of automotive products, specialty food products, glassware, and candles.

Plan Specifics:
- Partial dividend reinvestment is available.
- No Discount.
- OCP: not available.
- Dividends are paid March, June, September, and December.

Performance Rating: ****

DRIP Rating: ℗

Lance, Inc. (NASDAQ:LNCE)
PO Box 32368
Charlotte, NC 28232
(704) 554-1421   (800) 438-1880

Business Profile: Produces snack foods and bakery items.

Plan Specifics:
- Partial dividend reinvestment is not available.
- No Discount.
- OCP: $10 to $1000 per month.
- Service charge of 4 percent of amount invested with OCPs up to maximum of $2.50.
- Selling costs are brokerage fees.
- Company purchases stock monthly with OCPs.

- Dividends are paid February, May, August, and November.

Performance Rating: ***

DRIP Rating: ♦

LG&E Energy Corp. (NYSE:LGE)
PO Box 32030
Louisville, KY 40232
(502) 627-3445   (800) 235-9705

Business Profile: An energy services company that provides electric and natural-gas services to industrial, commercial, governmental, and residential customers and other utilities.

Plan Specifics:
- Partial dividend reinvestment is available.
- No Discount.
- OCP: $25 to $40,000 per year.
- Selling costs are brokerage commissions.
- Company purchases stock around the 15th of the month with OCPs.
- Preferred dividends are eligible for reinvestment for additional common shares under the plan.
- Dividends are paid January, April, July, and October.

Performance Rating: ****

DRIP Rating: ♦

Lilly (Eli) & Co. (NYSE:LLY)
Shareholder Services
Lilly Corporate Center
Indianapolis, IN 46285
(317) 276-3219

Business Profile: Leading supplier of prescription drugs including antibiotics.

Plan Specifics:

- Need 5 shares to enroll in plan.
- Partial dividend reinvestment is not available.
- No Discount.
- OCP: $25 to $50,000 per year.
- Company purchases stock monthly with OCPs.
- Fees include a $5 transaction fee on each OCP investment and $1.50 on each dividend reinvestment.
- Approximately 22,500 shareholders are in the plan.
- Dividends are paid March, June, September, and December.

Performance Rating: *****

DRIP Rating: 👍

Lilly Industries, Inc. (NASDAQ:LICIA)
PO Box 946
Indianapolis, IN 46206-0946
(317) 634-8512

Business Profile: Leading producer of industrial paints and coatings for manufacturers of furniture and a wide variety of metal products.

Plan Specifics:

- Partial dividend reinvestment is available.
- No Discount.
- OCP: $25 to $5000 per quarter.
- Selling costs are brokerage commissions, a $1 service charge, and other costs of sale.
- Company purchases stock quarterly with OCPs.
- Dividends are paid January, April, July, and October.

Performance Rating: ***

DRIP Rating: 👍

Limited, (The) Inc. (NYSE:LTD)
c/o First Chicago Trust-NY
PO Box 2533
Jersey City, NJ 07303-2533
(800) 446-2617   (614) 479-7000

Business Profile: Leading retailer of women's apparel.

Plan Specifics:

- Partial dividend reinvestment is not available.
- No Discount.
- OCP: $30 to $6000 per quarter.
- Selling costs are brokerage commissions, a service fee, and related expenses.
- Company purchases stock quarterly with OCPs.
- Dividends are paid March, June, September, and December.

Performance Rating: ****

DRIP Rating: 👍

Lincoln National Corp. (NYSE:LNC)
c/o First Nat'l Bank of Boston
PO Box 644
Boston, MA 02102
(800) 442-2001   (219) 455-2000

Business Profile: Owns and operates financial services businesses with emphasis on annuities, life insurance, property-casualty insurance and life-health reinsurance.

Plan Specifics:

- Partial dividend reinvestment is available.
- No Discount.
- OCP: $25 to $5000 per month.
- Stock is purchased monthly with OCPs.
- Selling costs are $1 fee plus brokerage fees.

- Preferred dividends are eligible for reinvestment for additional common shares under the plan.
- Dividends are paid February, May, August, and November.

Performance Rating: ****

DRIP Rating: 👍

Lincoln Telecommunications Co. (NASDAQ:LTEC)
PO Box 81309
Lincoln, NE 68501
(402) 436-5277

Business Profile: Provides telecommunication products and services in Nebraska.

Plan Specifics:
- Partial dividend reinvestment is not available.
- No Discount.
- OCP: $100 to $3000 per quarter.
- Company purchases stock quarterly with OCPs.
- Selling costs are brokerage commissions and applicable service fees.
- Approximately 1500 shareholders are in the plan.
- Dividends are paid January, April, July, and October.

Performance Rating: ****

DRIP Rating: 👎

Liz Claiborne, Inc. (NYSE:LIZ)
c/o First Chicago Trust-NY
PO Box 2533
Jersey City, NJ 07303-2533
(800) 446-2617   (201) 324-0498

Business Profile: Markets men's and women's apparel, cosmetics, and accessories.

Plan Specifics:
- Partial dividend reinvestment is not available.
- No Discount.
- OCP: $25 to $1000 per month.
- Selling costs are a $5 service charge and brokerage commissions.
- Company purchases stock each month with OCPs.
- Stock may be sold via the telephone.
- Dividends are paid March, June, September, and December.

Performance Rating: ***

DRIP Rating: 👍

Lockheed Martin Corp. (NYSE:LMT)
6801 Rockledge Dr.
Bethesda, MD 20817
(301) 897-6000   (800) 446-2617

Business Profile: The company, formed via the merger of Lockheed and Martin Marietta, is a major defense and space contractor.

Plan Specifics:
- Partial dividend reinvestment is available.
- No Discount.
- OCP: $50 to $100,000 per year.
- OCP is invested monthly.
- Selling costs are brokerage fees.
- Dividends are paid March, June, September, and December.

Performance Rating: ****

DRIP Rating: 👍

Loctite Corp. (NYSE:LOC)
c/o First Nat'l Bank of Boston
PO Box 1681
Boston, MA 02105
(800) 730-4001   (203) 520-5000

Business Profile: Manufactures chemical adhesives and sealants.

Plan Specifics:
- Partial dividend reinvestment is available.
- No Discount.
- OCP: $25 to $1000 per month.
- There are no costs for selling shares from the plan.
- Company purchases stock each month with OCPs if there are enough funds to purchase at least a 100-share lot.
- Dividends are paid January, April, July, and October.

Performance Rating: ****
DRIP Rating: 👍

Long Island Lighting Company (NYSE:LIL)
175 E. Old Country Rd.
Hicksville, NY 11801
(516) 755-6000   (800) 524-4458

Business Profile: Supplier of electricity and gas to customers in Long Island, New York and in sections of Queens, New York City. Company services some 2,700,000 people.

Plan Specifics:
- Partial dividend reinvestment is not available.
- No Discount.
- OCP: $25 to $5000 per quarter.
- Selling costs are brokerage commissions and other fees.
- Company purchases stock quarterly with OCPs.

- Dividends are paid January, April, July, and October.

Performance Rating: **
DRIP Rating: 👍

Louisiana Land & Exploration Company (NYSE:LLX)
c/o First Chicago Trust-NY
PO Box 2533
Jersey City, NJ 07303-2533
(800) 446-2617

Business Profile: Explores for, develops, and sells oil, gas, and natural gas.

Plan Specifics:
- Partial dividend reinvestment is not available.
- No Discount.
- OCP: $10 to $3000 per month.
- Selling costs are brokerage commissions, $5 handling charge, and any other costs of sale.
- Company purchases stock monthly with OCPs.
- Dividends are paid March, June, September, and December.

Performance Rating: **
DRIP Rating: 👍

Louisiana-Pacific Corp. (NYSE:LPX)
111 SW 5th Ave.
Portland, OR 97204
(503) 221-0800

Business Profile: Leading manufacturer of lumber, particleboard, plywood, and pulp.

Plan Specifics:
- Partial dividend reinvestment is not available.
- No Discount.

- OCP: $25 to $12,000 per year.
- Selling costs are brokerage commissions and a $10 service fee.
- Stock is purchased monthly with OCPs.
- Dividends are paid March, June, September, and December.

Performance Rating: ***

DRIP Rating: 👍

**Lowe's Companies, Inc.
(NYSE:LOW)
PO Box 1111
N. Wilkesboro, NC 28656-0001
(910) 651-4000**

Business Profile: Sells lumber, building materials, home decorations, and hardware through retail outlets.

Plan Specifics:

- Partial dividend reinvestment is not available.
- No Discount.
- OCP: $10 to $1000 per month.
- Selling costs are brokerage fees.
- Stock is purchased monthly with OCPs.
- Dividends are paid January, April, July, and October.

Performance Rating: ****

DRIP Rating: 👍

**LTC Properties, Inc. (NYSE:LTC)
300 Esplanade Dr., Ste. 1860
Oxnard, CA 93030
(805) 981-8655**

Business Profile: Real estate investment trust which invests in healthcare facilities.

Plan Specifics:

- Partial dividend reinvestment is available.

- No Discount.
- OCP: $25 to $1000 per month.
- Company purchases stock monthly with OCPs.
- Selling costs are brokerage commissions and a nominal bank charge.
- Dividends are paid January, April, July, and October.

Performance Rating: **

DRIP Rating: 👍

**Lubrizol Corp. (NYSE:LZ)
29400 Lakeland Blvd.
Wickliffe, OH 44092-2298
(216) 943-1200   (800) 542-7792**

Business Profile: Large supplier of chemical additives used in automotive and industrial lubricants. Also produces specialty vegetable oils.

Plan Specifics:

- Partial dividend reinvestment is not available.
- No Discount.
- OCP: $25 to $5000 per quarter.
- Selling costs include a $5 service fee and brokerage costs.
- Company purchases stock quarterly with OCPs.
- Safekeeping services are available.
- Dividends are paid March, June, September, and December.

Performance Rating: ****

DRIP Rating: 👍

**Luby's Cafeterias, Inc.
(NYSE:LUB)
PO Box 33069
San Antonio, TX 78265-3069
(210) 654-9000**

Business Profile: Operates a cafeteria-style chain of restaurants primarily in the southern United States.

Plan Specifics:

- Partial dividend reinvestment is available.
- No Discount.
- OCP: $20 to $5000 per quarter.
- Selling costs are brokerage commissions and charges.
- Company purchases stock once a month with OCPs.
- Dividends are paid March, June, September, and December.

Performance Rating: ****

DRIP Rating: 👍

Lukens, Inc. (NYSE:LUC)
c/o American Stock Transfer &
** Trust Co.**
40 Wall St.
New York, NY 10005
(718) 921-8200   (610) 383-2000

Business Profile: Supplies carbon, alloy, and clad plate steels; stainless steel sheet, strip and plate products; and industrial products and services.

Plan Specifics:

- Partial dividend reinvestment is not available.
- No Discount.
- OCP: $50 to $6000 per month.
- Stock is purchased around the 15th of the month with OCPs.
- Selling costs are brokerage commissions and other expenses.
- Dividends are paid February, May, August, and November.

Performance Rating: ***

DRIP Rating: 👍

Lyondell Petrochemical Co.
** (NYSE:LYO)**
c/o Bank of New York
PO Box 11260, Church St. Sta.
New York, NY 10277-0760
(713) 652-7367   (713) 652-7200

Business Profile: Produces petrochemicals and refines petroleum products.

Plan Specifics:

- Partial dividend reinvestment is not available.
- No Discount.
- OCP: $25 to $10,000 per quarter.
- Selling costs are brokerage commissions and $5 handling fee.
- Company purchases stock quarterly with OCPs.
- Dividends are paid March, June, September, and December.

Performance Rating: **

DRIP Rating: 👍

MacDermid, Inc.
** (NASDAQ:MACD)**
PO Box 671
Waterbury, CT 06720
(203) 575-5813   (203) 575-5700

Business Profile: Manufactures specialty chemicals, equipment, and supplies for electronic and metal markets.

Plan Specifics:

- Partial dividend reinvestment is available with at least 25 shares.
- No Discount.
- OCP: minimum of $50 and no maximum.
- Selling costs may include brokerage fees and $1 service charge.
- Stock is purchased at least

quarterly, and between dividend-payment dates if demand is sufficient, with OCPs.
- Dividends are paid January, April, July, and October.

Performance Rating: ****
DRIP Rating: 👍

Madison Gas & Electric Co.
(NASDAQ:MDSN)
PO Box 1231
133 S. Blair St.
Madison, WI 53701-1231
(800) 356-6423

Business Profile: Wisconsin-based electric and gas utility.

Plan Specifics:
- Partial dividend reinvestment is available.
- No Discount.
- OCP: $10 to $4000 per quarter.
- Company purchases stock around the 15th of month with OCPs.
- Participants pay brokerage fees when shares are purchased.
- Minimal, if any, selling costs.
- Approximately 8500 shareholders are in the plan.
- Dividends are paid March, June, September, and December.

Performance Rating: ****
DRIP Rating: 👍

Magna Group, Inc.
(NASDAQ:MAGI)
PO Box 523
222 E. Main St.
Belleville, IL 62222
(618) 233-2120

Business Profile: Illinois multibank holding company.

Plan Specifics:
- Partial dividend reinvestment is available.
- No Discount.
- OCP: $25 to $5000 per month.
- Selling costs are brokerage commission.
- Company purchases stock twice a month with OCPs.
- Approximately 3000 shareholders are in the plan.
- Dividends are paid March, June, September, and December.

Performance Rating: **
DRIP Rating: 👍

Mallinckrodt Group, Inc.
(NYSE:MKG)
7733 Forsyth Blvd.
St. Louis, MO 63105-1820
(314) 854-5200

Business Profile: Manufactures medical products, specialty chemicals, and animal health products.

Plan Specifics:
- Partial dividend reinvestment is not available.
- No Discount.
- OCP: $10 to $1000 per month.
- Selling costs are brokerage commissions, a handling charge, and any other costs of sale.
- Company purchases stock once a month with OCPs.
- Approximately 2600 shareholders are in the plan.
- Dividends are paid March, June, September, and December.

Performance Rating: ***
DRIP Rating: 👍

Manitowoc Company, Inc.
 (NYSE:MTW)
PO Box 66
Manitowoc, WI 54221-0066
(414) 684-4410   (800) 446-2617

Business Profile: Manufacturer of
heavy-lift cranes for the utility,
petroleum, mining, and construction industries. Also makes ice-
making machines and operates a
shipyard.

Plan Specifics:
- Partial dividend reinvestment is
  not available.
- No Discount.
- OCP: $10 to $60,000 per year.
- Selling costs are brokerage
  commissions, a $5 handling
  charge, and other costs of sale.
- Company purchases stock once a
  month with OCPs.
- Dividends are paid March, June,
  September, and December.

Performance Rating: **
DRIP Rating: 👍

Manpower, Inc. (NYSE:MAN)
PO Box 2053
5301 N. Ironwood Rd.
Milwaukee, WI 53201
(414) 961-1000   (800) 446-2617

Business Profile: World's largest
nongovernmental temporary
employment services organization.

Plan Specifics:
- Partial dividend reinvestment is
  available.
- No Discount.
- OCP: $25 to $10,000 per year.
- Stock is purchased monthly with
  OCPs.

- Selling costs are brokerage
  commissions, a service fee, and
  any other costs of sale.
- Dividends are paid June and
  December.

Performance Rating: ****
DRIP Rating: 👍

MAPCO, Inc. (NYSE:MDA)
PO Box 645
Tulsa, OK 74101-0645
(918) 599-6045   (212) 701-7607

Business Profile: Operations in retail
gas transportation, refining, gas
transmission, and coal production.

Plan Specifics:
- Partial dividend reinvestment is
  not available.
- No Discount.
- OCP: $10 to $3000 per quarter.
- Company purchases stock
  monthly with OCPs.
- Must sell shares through broker.
- Dividends are paid March, June,
  September, and December.

Performance Rating: ***
DRIP Rating: 👍

Mark Twain Bancshares, Inc.
 (NASDAQ:MTWN)
8820 Ladue Rd.
St. Louis, MO 63124
(314) 727-1000   (216) 737-5000

Business Profile: Multibank holding
company serving the St. Louis and
Kansas City metropolitan areas
with banks in Missouri, Illinois,
and Kansas. Operations in brokerage and trust services.

Plan Specifics:
- Partial dividend reinvestment is
  available.

- No Discount.
- OCP: $10 to $2000 per month.
- Stock is purchased twice per month with OCPs.
- Selling costs are a service charge of $5 and brokerage commissions.
- $5 termination fee.
- Dividends are paid February, May, August, and November.

Performance Rating: ****

DRIP Rating: 👍

Marriott International, Inc. (NYSE:MAR)
Marriott Dr.
Washington, DC 20058
(301) 380-3000   (800) 446-2617

Business Profile: Major lodging and food-service company.

Plan Specifics:

- Partial dividend reinvestment is available.
- No Discount.
- OCP: $25 to $60,000 per year.
- OCP is invested monthly.
- Selling fees are a $10 service charge and approximately 12 cents per share.
- Dividends are paid January, April, July, and October.

Performance Rating: *****

DRIP Rating: 👍

Marsh & McLennan Companies, Inc. (NYSE:MMC)
1166 Ave. of the Americas
New York, NY 10036
(212) 345-5000

Business Profile: Insurance and reinsurance brokerage company with operations in investment services and consulting.

Plan Specifics:

- Partial dividend reinvestment is not available.
- No Discount.
- OCP: $10 to $3000 per quarter.
- Stock is purchased quarterly with OCPs.
- Purchasing fees are 5 percent of amount invested ($2.50 maximum) and proportionate share of brokerage commission.
- Selling costs are brokerage commissions and other costs of sale.
- Dividends are paid February, May, August, and November.

Performance Rating: *****

DRIP Rating: 👍

Marsh Supermarkets, Inc. (NASDAQ:MARSA)
9800 Crosspoint Blvd.
Indianapolis, IN 46256
(317) 594-2100

Business Profile: Manages midwestern supermarkets and convenience stores.

Plan Specifics:

- Partial dividend reinvestment is available.
- No Discount.
- OCP: $100 to $5000 per month.
- Company purchases stock monthly with OCPs.
- Selling costs include brokerage fees and a $2.50 administrator's fee.
- Dividends are paid February, May, August, and November.

Performance Rating: ***

DRIP Rating: 👍

**Marshall & Ilsley Corp.
(NASDAQ:MRIS)**
770 N. Water St.
PO Box 2035
Milwaukee, WI 53201
(414) 765-7801

Business Profile: Holding company for Wisconsin-based banks.

Plan Specifics:

- Partial dividend reinvestment is not available.
- No Discount.
- OCP: $25 to $3000 per quarter.
- Selling costs are service fee of $5 and brokerage fees.
- Company purchases stock around the first of the month with OCPs.
- Dividends are paid March, June, September, and December.

Performance Rating: ****
DRIP Rating: 👍

**MASSBANK Corp.
(NASDAQ:MASB)**
159 Haven St.
Reading, MA 01867
(617) 662-0100

Business Profile: Massachusetts-based bank holding company.

Plan Specifics:

- Partial dividend reinvestment is available.
- No Discount.
- OCP: $50 to $1500 per quarter.
- Selling costs are brokerage commissions.
- Company purchases stock quarterly with OCPs.
- Approximately 400 shareholders are in the plan.
- Dividends are paid February, May, August, and November.

Performance Rating: ***
DRIP Rating: 👍

Mattel, Inc. (NYSE:MAT)
c/o Bank of Boston
Mail Stop 45-01-06
PO Box 1681
Boston, MA 02105-1681
(310) 524-2000

Business Profile: World's largest toy company.

Plan Specifics:

- Partial dividend reinvestment is available.
- No Discount.
- OCP: $25 to $1000 per month.
- Stock is purchased monthly with OCPs.
- Selling costs are brokerage commissions plus a $5 bank charge.
- Safekeeping services are available.
- Dividends are paid January, April, July, and October.

Performance Rating: ****
DRIP Rating: 👍

**May Department Stores
Company (NYSE:MA)**
c/o Bank of New York
PO Box 11258, Church St. Sta.
New York, NY 10286-1258
(800) 524-4458

Business Profile: One of the nation's largest retail companies whose merchandise is targeted toward medium and upscale buyers.

Plan Specifics:

- Partial dividend reinvestment is not available.
- No Discount.

- OCP: $25 minimum (no maximum).
- Purchasing fees include 5 percent of amount (maximum $2) per dividend reinvestment; $2 fee per OCP.
- Selling costs are commissions and service charges.
- Company purchases stock every Friday with OCPs.
- Dividends are paid March, June, September, and December.

Performance Rating: ****

DRIP Rating: 👍

Maytag Corp. (NYSE:MYG)
403 W. 4th St., N.
Newton, IA 50208
(515) 792-7000   (515) 792-8000

Business Profile: Supplier of laundry equipment and kitchen appliances.

Plan Specifics:

- Partial dividend reinvestment is not available.
- No Discount.
- OCP: $25 to $5000 per month.
- Selling costs are brokerage commissions.
- Company purchases stock around the 15th of the month with OCPs.
- Dividends are paid March, June, September, and December.

Performance Rating: **

DRIP Rating: 👍

McCormick & Co., Inc.
(NASDAQ:MCCRK)
18 Loveton Circle
Sparks, MD 21152-6000
(410) 771-7301

Business Profile: Manufactures

spices, flavorings, seasonings, and specialty foods.

Plan Specifics:

- Partial dividend reinvestment is available.
- No Discount.
- OCP: $100 to $3000 per quarter.
- Selling costs include brokerage commissions.
- Company purchases stock quarterly with OCPs.
- Dividends are paid January, April, July, and October.

Performance Rating: ****

DRIP Rating: 👍

McDermott International, Inc.
(NYSE:MDR)
PO Box 61961
1450 Poydras St.
New Orleans, LA 70161-1961
(504) 587-5682   (212) 679-3960

Business Profile: Constructs power generation systems and fabricates and installs drilling and production platforms and oil and gas pipelines.

Plan Specifics:

- Partial dividend reinvestment is available.
- No Discount.
- OCP: $25 to $15,000 per quarter.
- Selling costs include brokerage fees.
- Company purchases stock every quarter with OCPs.
- Preferred dividends and interest on 10 percent subordinated debentures are eligible for reinvestment in common shares under the plan.
- Approximately 2300 shareholders are in the plan.

- Dividends are paid January, April, July, and October.

Performance Rating: **

DRIP Rating: 👍

McDonald's Corp. (NYSE:MCD)
c/o First Chicago Trust-NY
PO Box 2591
Jersey City, NJ 07303-2591
(800) 621-7825

Business Profile: Worldwide leader in the fast-food industry.

Plan Specifics (Proposed plan at press time):

- Initial purchase may be made directly from the company. Investors may enroll either by investing $1000 or by authorizing automatic monthly withdrawals of at least $100.
- Partial dividend reinvestment is not available.
- No Discount.
- OCP: $100 to $250,000 per year.
- Company purchases stock weekly with OCPs.
- Participants will incur various fees when buying and selling shares in the plan.
- Automatic investment services are available.
- IRA option is available.
- Dividends are paid March, June, September, and December.

Performance Rating: *****

DRIP Rating: 👍

McGraw-Hill Cos., Inc.
(NYSE:MHP)
1221 Ave. of the Americas
New York, NY 10020
(212) 512-4150   (212) 512-2000

Business Profile: Publishes educa-tional and professional books and magazines and offers financial informational services.

Plan Specifics:

- Partial dividend reinvestment is not available.
- No Discount.
- OCP: $10 to $1000 per quarter.
- Stock is purchased quarterly with OCPs.
- Selling costs are brokerage commission and $1 termination fee.
- $5 service fee for withdrawal of certificates.
- Dividends are paid March, June, September, and December.

Performance Rating: ****

DRIP Rating: 👍

McKesson Corp. (NYSE:MCK)
One Post St.
San Francisco, CA 94104
(415) 983-8367

Business Profile: Manages health-care costs through pharmaceutical distribution.

Plan Specifics:

- Partial dividend reinvestment is available.
- No Discount.
- OCP: $10 to $60,000 per year.
- Selling costs include brokerage fees and any service fee.
- Company purchases stock monthly with OCPs.
- Dividends are paid January, April, July, and October.

Performance Rating: ***

DRIP Rating: 👍

MCN Corp. (NYSE:MCN)
500 Griswold St.
Detroit, MI 48226
(800) 548-4655   (313) 256-5500

Business Profile: Natural gas holding company serving portions of Michigan.

Plan Specifics:

- Partial dividend reinvestment is available.
- No Discount.
- OCP: $25 to $50,000 per year.
- Company purchases stock monthly with OCPs.
- Selling costs include brokerage commissions (currently 12 cents per share) and a service fee (maximum $10).
- Automatic investment services are available.
- Approximately 12,100 shareholders are in the plan.
- Dividends are paid February, May, August, and November.

Performance Rating: *****
DRIP Rating: ⚡

MDU Resources Group, Inc. (NYSE:MDU)
400 N. 4th St.
Bismarck, ND 58501
(701) 222-7621

Business Profile: A natural resources company with business lines in natural gas distribution and transmission, electricity, lignite coal, and oil and gas production.

Plan Specifics:

- Partial dividend reinvestment is available.
- No Discount.
- OCP: $50 to $5000 per quarter.
- Selling costs include brokerage fees and any other costs of sale.
- Company purchases stock quarterly with OCPs.
- Approximately 5600 shareholders are in the plan.
- Dividends are paid January, April, July, and October.

Performance Rating: ****
DRIP Rating: ⚡

Mead Corp. (NYSE:MEA)
Courthouse Plaza NE
Dayton, OH 45463
(513) 495-3710

Business Profile: Manufactures paper, paperboard, and packaging systems.

Plan Specifics:

- Partial dividend reinvestment is not available.
- No Discount.
- OCP: $25 to $2000 per month.
- Selling costs include brokerage fees.
- Company purchases stock every month with OCPs.
- Approximately 5200 shareholders are in the plan.
- Dividends are paid March, June, September, and December.

Performance Rating: ***
DRIP Rating: ⚡

Medford Savings Bank (NASDAQ:MDBK)
29 High St.
Medford, MA 02155
(617) 395-7700   (800) 426-5523

Business Profile: Savings bank providing a wide variety of banking services throughout Massachusetts.

Plan Specifics:
- Partial dividend reinvestment is available.
- No Discount.
- OCP: $100 to $1000 per quarter.
- Company purchases stock quarterly with OCPs.
- Selling fees include brokerage commissions, service charges, and any transfer taxes.
- Certificate safekeeping is available.
- Dividends are paid January, April, July, and October.

Performance Rating: NR

DRIP Rating: 👍

Media General, Inc.
(ASE: MEG.A)
PO Box C-32333
Richmond, VA 23293-0001
(804) 649-6000

Business Profile: Operations in newspaper publishing, newsprint, and broadcasting.

Plan Specifics:
- Partial dividend reinvestment is available.
- 5 percent discount on reinvested dividends.
- OCP: $25 to $5000 per month.
- Selling costs include brokerage fees.
- Company purchases stock monthly with OCPs.
- Dividends are paid March, June, September, and December.

*Performance Rating: ***

DRIP Rating: 👍

Meditrust (NYSE:MT)
c/o Fleet Bank-RI
Stock Transfer Dept.
RI/OP/0317
PO Box 366
Providence, RI 02901-0366
(800) 538-1516   (617) 433-6000

Business Profile: Real estate investment trust which invests in healthcare facilities.

Plan Specifics:
- Partial dividend reinvestment is available.
- No Discount.
- OCP: $100 to $5000 per quarter.
- OCP is invested quarterly.
- Must go through broker to sell shares.
- Dividends are paid February, May, August, and November.

*Performance Rating: ***

DRIP Rating: 👍

Medtronic, Inc. (NYSE:MDT)
c/o Norwest Bank MN
161 N. Concord Exchange
PO Box 738
South St. Paul, MN 55075-0738
(612) 450-4064

Business Profile: Designs, makes, and sells implantable cardiac pacemakers and other cardiac devices.

Plan Specifics:
- Partial dividend reinvestment is not available.
- No Discount.
- OCP: $25 to $4000 per month.
- Selling costs are brokerage commissions and service charges.
- Company purchases stock monthly with OCPs.

- Dividends are paid January, April, July, and October.

Performance Rating: *****

DRIP Rating: 👍

Medusa Corp. (NYSE:MSA)
3008 Monticello Blvd.
Cleveland Heights, OH 44118
(216) 371-4000   (216) 575-2532

Business Profile: Makes gray portland cements, masonry cements, and several specialty cements. The company also mines and processes industrial limestone products used in concrete and blacktop surfaces.

Plan Specifics:

- Partial dividend reinvestment is available.
- No Discount.
- OCP: $10 to $5000 per month.
- Selling costs are brokerage commissions.
- Company purchases stock monthly with OCPs.
- Dividends are paid March, June, September, and December.

Performance Rating: ***

DRIP Rating: 👍

Mellon Bank Corp. (NYSE:MEL)
PO Box 444
Pittsburgh, PA 15230
(412) 236-8000

Business Profile: Pittsburgh-based holding company for banks in Pennsylvania, Maryland, and Delaware.

Plan Specifics:

- Partial dividend reinvestment is not available.
- No Discount.

- OCP: $100 to $50,000 per month. For shareholders holding less than 100 shares of common stock, the maximum per month purchase limit is $100.
- Selling costs are brokerage commissions.
- Company purchases stock each month with OCPs.
- Dividends are paid February, May, August, and November.

Performance Rating: ***

DRIP Rating: 👎

Mercantile Bancorp., Inc.
(NYSE:MTL)
c/o Society National Bank
PO Box 6477
Cleveland, OH 44101-9990
(314) 241-4002   (314) 425-2525

Business Profile: Holding company for Missouri and Illinois banks.

Plan Specifics:

- Partial dividend reinvestment is not available.
- No Discount.
- OCP: $10 to $3000 per month.
- No selling costs.
- Company purchases stock at least quarterly and most likely monthly if enough funds accumulate to purchase at least 100 shares.
- Dividends are paid January, April, July, and October.

Performance Rating: ***

DRIP Rating: 👍

Mercantile Bankshares Corp.
 (NASDAQ:MRBK)
PO Box 2438
Baltimore, MD 21203
(410) 237-5900

Business Profile: Maryland-based bank holding company.

Plan Specifics:

- Partial dividend reinvestment is not available.
- 5 percent discount on reinvested dividends.
- OCP: $25 to $5000 per quarter.
- Must go through own broker to sell shares.
- Company purchases stock quarterly with OCPs.
- Dividends are paid March, June, September, and December.

Performance Rating: *****

DRIP Rating: 🖐

Merck & Co., Inc. (NYSE:MRK)
PO Box 100
Whitehouse Sta., NJ 08889-0100
(908) 423-6627   (800) 613-2104

Business Profile: Leading producer of human and animal pharmaceuticals and specialty chemicals.

Plan Specifics:

- Partial dividend reinvestment is available.
- No Discount.
- OCP: $25 to $50,000 per year.
- Purchasing fees are brokerage commissions, 4 percent of dividends reinvested (maximum $2), and a $5 fee for OCP.
- Selling costs are brokerage commissions plus $5.
- Company purchases stock monthly with OCPs.

- Approximately 130,000 shareholders are in the plan.
- Dividends are paid January, April, July, and October.

Performance Rating: *****

DRIP Rating: 🖐

Mercury Finance Company
 (NYSE:MFN)
c/o Harris Trust
PO Box A-3309
Chicago, IL 60690-9939
(312) 461-7369

Business Profile: Consumer finance company which concentrates on financing used cars for new and used car dealers.

Plan Specifics:

- Partial dividend reinvestment is not available.
- No Discount.
- OCP: not available.
- Selling costs are brokerage commissions and other fees.
- Dividends are paid March, June, September, and December.

Performance Rating: ****

DRIP Rating: ☜

Meridian Bancorp, Inc.
 (NASDAQ:MRDN)
PO Box 1102
35 N. 6th St.
Reading, PA 19603
(610) 655-2000

Business Profile: A bank and financial services holding company in Pennsylvania, Delaware, and New Jersey.

Plan Specifics:

- Must have at least 50 shares to enroll in the plan.

- Partial dividend reinvestment is available.
- 5 percent discount on reinvested dividends.
- OCP: $10 to $4000 per quarter.
- Selling costs are brokerage commissions.
- Company purchases stock quarterly with OCPs.
- Preferred dividends are eligible for reinvestment for additional common shares under the plan.
- Dividends are paid March, June, September, and December.

Performance Rating: ***

DRIP Rating: 👎

Meridian Diagnostics, Inc. (NASDAQ: KITS)
3471 River Hills Dr.
Cincinnati, OH 45244
(800) 837-2755   (513) 579-6016
(800) 543-1980

Business Profile: Manufactures and markets immunodiagnostic test kits and related products.

Plan Specifics:

- Partial dividend reinvestment is not available.
- No Discount.
- OCP: $25 to $1000 monthly.
- OCP is invested monthly.
- Purchasing fees are $3 per OCP investment and 5 percent of dividends reinvested (minimum $1, maximum $3).
- Selling costs may include brokerage fees.
- Dividends are paid February, May, August, and December.

Performance Rating: ***

DRIP Rating: 👍

Merrill Lynch & Co., Inc. (NYSE:MER)
World Financial Center
New York, NY 10281-1332
(201) 557-2118   (212) 449-1000

Business Profile: Major financial services holding organization.

Plan Specifics:

- Partial dividend reinvestment is not available.
- No Discount.
- OCP: not available.
- Selling costs are brokerage fees and transfer taxes.
- Dividends are paid February, May, August, and November.

Performance Rating: ****

DRIP Rating: 👎

Merry Land & Investment Co., Inc. (NYSE:MRY)
624 Ellis St.
Augusta, GA 30901
(800) 829-8432

Business Profile: Acquires, develops, and manages real estate properties primarily in Georgia and South Carolina.

Plan Specifics:

- Partial dividend reinvestment is available.
- 5 percent discount on reinvested dividends and OCPs.
- OCP: $25 to $5000 per quarter.
- Company purchases stock quarterly with OCPs.
- Must go through own broker to sell shares.
- Preferred dividends are eligible for reinvestment for additional common shares under the plan.
- Dividends are paid March, June, September, and December.

Performance Rating: ***
DRIP Rating: 👍

Mid Am, Inc. (NASDAQ:MIAM)
222 S. Main St.
PO Box 428
Bowling Green, OH 43402
(419) 352-5271   (800) 426-5523

Business Profile: Multibank holding company with offices in northwestern, west-central, and southwestern Ohio, and southern Michigan.

Plan Specifics:
- Partial dividend reinvestment is available.
- No Discount.
- OCP: $20 to $3000 per quarter.
- Company purchases stock quarterly with OCPs.
- Selling costs are brokerage commissions and transfer taxes.
- Preferred dividends are eligible for reinvestment for additional common shares under the plan.
- Dividends are paid March, June, September, and December.

Performance Rating: ***
DRIP Rating: 👍

Mid-America Realty Investments (NYSE:MDI)
11506 Nicholas St., Ste. 100
Omaha, NE 68154
(402) 496-3300

Business Profile: Equity real estate investment trust which invests in income-producing properties, mainly enclosed malls and neighborhood shopping centers.

Plan Specifics:
- Partial dividend reinvestment is not available.

- No Discount.
- OCP: $25 to $7500 per quarter.
- Company purchases stock quarterly with OCPs.
- There are no costs for selling shares from the plan.
- Dividends are paid February, May, August, and November.

Performance Rating: *
DRIP Rating: 👍

MidAmerican Energy Co.
(NYSE: MEC)
666 Grand Ave.
PO Box 9244
Des Moines, IA 50306-9244
(800) 247-5211

Business Profile: Electric utility holding company.

Plan Specifics:
- Partial dividend reinvestment is available.
- No Discount.
- OCP: $25 to $10,000 per month.
- OCP is invested monthly.
- Purchasing and selling fees are 5 cents per share.
- Automatic investment services are available.
- Dividends are paid March, June, September, and December.

Performance Rating: ***
DRIP Rating: 👍

Middlesex Water Co.
(NASDAQ:MSEX)
PO Box 1500
Iselin, NJ 08830-0452
(908) 634-1500

Business Profile: Supplies water service to customers throughout New Jersey communities.

Plan Specifics:
- Partial dividend reinvestment is available.
- 5 percent discount on reinvested dividends and OCPs.
- OCP: $25 to $25,000 per quarter.
- Selling costs are brokerage commissions.
- Company purchases stock each month with OCPs.
- Preferred dividends are eligible for reinvestment for additional common shares under the plan.
- Dividends are paid March, June, September, and December.

Performance Rating: ***

DRIP Rating: 👍

Midlantic Corp.
(NASDAQ:MIDL)
c/o First Chicago Trust-NY
PO Box 2533
Jersey City, NJ 07303-2533
(800) 446-2617   (908) 321-8000

Business Profile: Multibank holding firm serving areas in New Jersey, Pennsylvania, and New York.

Plan Specifics:
- Partial dividend reinvestment is not available.
- 3 percent discount on reinvested dividends.
- OCP: $50 to $3000 per month.
- Stock is purchased monthly with OCPs.
- Selling cost is a brokerage fee.
- Dividends are paid February, May, August, and November.

Performance Rating: ***

DRIP Rating: 👍

Millipore Corp. (NYSE:MIL)
80 Ashby Rd.
Bedford, MA 01730
(617) 275-9200   (617) 575-2900

Business Profile: Manufactures products used in analysis and purification of liquids.

Plan Specifics:
- Partial dividend reinvestment is not available.
- No Discount.
- OCP: $25 to $3000 per quarter.
- Selling costs are brokerage commissions and a termination fee of 5 percent (maximum of $3).
- Company purchases stock quarterly with OCPs.
- Dividends are paid January, April, July, and October.

Performance Rating: ****

DRIP Rating: 👍

Minnesota Mining & Mfg. Co.
(NYSE:MMM)
3M Center
St. Paul, MN 55144-1000
(800) 468-9716   (612) 450-4064
(612) 733-1110

Business Profile: Manufactures industrial, electronic, medical, and consumer products.

Plan Specifics:
- Partial dividend reinvestment is not available.
- No Discount.
- OCP: $10 to $10,000 per quarter.
- Selling costs are brokerage commissions and service charges.
- Company purchases stock once a month with OCPs.

- Approximately 30,000 share-holders are in the plan.
- Dividends are paid March, June, September, and December.

Performance Rating: *****
DRIP Rating: 👍

Minnesota Power & Light Co. (NYSE:MPL)
30 W. Superior St.
Duluth, MN 55802-2093
(218) 723-3974   (800) 535-3056

Business Profile: Provides electric services in a 26,000-square mile area of upper Minnesota and northwestern Wisconsin. Provides water services in Wisconsin, Florida, North Carolina, and South Carolina.

Plan Specifics:

- Partial dividend reinvestment is available.
- No Discount.
- OCP: $10 to $10,000 per quarter.
- Company will sell up to 25 shares; otherwise must go through own broker to sell shares.
- Company purchases stock monthly with OCPs.
- Preferred dividends are eligible for reinvestment for additional common shares under the plan.
- Customers in Wisconsin and Minnesota may make initial purchases directly through the plan (minimum $10).
- Dividends are paid March, June, September, and December.

Performance Rating: ***
DRIP Rating: 👍

Mobil Corp. (NYSE:MOB)
3225 Gallows Rd.
Fairfax, VA 22037-0001
(800) 648-9291   (703) 849-3000

Business Profile: Leading world-wide integrated oil company.

Plan Specifics:

- Initial shares may be purchased directly from the company (minimum $250).
- Partial dividend reinvestment is not available.
- No Discount.
- OCP: $10 to $7500 per month.
- Company purchases stock twice a month with OCPs.
- Selling costs are brokerage commission plus $5 service charge.
- IRA option is available.
- Safekeeping services are available.
- Approximately 52,000 share-holders are in the plan.
- Dividends are paid March, June, September, and December.

Performance Rating: ****
DRIP Rating: 👍

Mobile Gas Service Corp. (NASDAQ:MBLE)
PO Box 2248
Mobile, AL 36652
(205) 476-2720

Business Profile: Distributes natural gas to residential, commercial, and industrial customers in southwest Alabama, principally within the greater metropolitan area of Mobile.

Plan Specifics:

- Partial dividend reinvestment is available.

- No Discount.
- OCP: not available.
- Selling costs are brokerage commissions.
- Dividends are paid January, April, July, and October.

Performance Rating: ***

DRIP Rating: 👍

**Modine Manufacturing Co.
(NASDAQ:MODI)
1500 DeKoven Ave.
Racine, WI 53403
(414) 636-1200   (800) 937-5449**

Business Profile: Produces heat-transfer equipment for heating and cooling engines, transmissions, vehicles, industrial equipment, and buildings.

Plan Specifics:

- Partial dividend reinvestment is not available.
- No Discount.
- OCP: $10 to $5000 per month.
- Selling costs may include brokerage fees.
- Company purchases stock each month with OCPs.
- Dividends are paid March, June, September, and December.

Performance Rating: ***

DRIP Rating: 👍

**Monmouth Real Estate
Investment Corp.
(NASDAQ:MNRTA)
125 Wyckoff Rd.
PO Box 335
Eatontown, NJ 07724
(908) 542-4927**

Business Profile: Real estate investment company whose equity portfolio consists mostly of warehouses and distribution centers in several states, including New York and New Jersey.

Plan Specifics:

- Partial dividend reinvestment is available.
- 5 percent discount on reinvested dividends and OCPs.
- OCP: $500 to $40,000 per month.
- Company purchases stock monthly with OCPs.
- There are no selling fees.
- Dividends are paid March, June, September, and December.

Performance Rating: **

DRIP Rating: 👍

**Monsanto Co. (NYSE:MTC)
800 N. Lindbergh Blvd.
St. Louis, MO 63167
(314) 694-5392   (314) 694-1000**

Business Profile: Manufactures herbicides, industrial chemicals, plastics, pharmaceuticals, and low calorie sweeteners.

Plan Specifics:

- Partial dividend reinvestment is not available.
- No Discount.
- OCP: $10 to $3000 per quarter.
- The company purchases stock monthly with OCPs.
- Selling costs include brokerage fees.
- Purchasing costs are 3 percent service charge (maximum $2 per dividend or OCP) plus brokerage fees.
- Dividends are paid March, June, September, and December.

Performance Rating: ****

DRIP Rating: 👍

Montana Power Co. (NYSE:MTP)
40 E. Broadway
Butte, MT 59701-9394
(800) 245-6767   (406) 723-5421

Business Profile: Supplies electric power and natural gas to Montana customers. Operations in coal mining, oil production, and telecommunications.

Plan Specifics:
- Partial dividend reinvestment is available.
- No Discount.
- OCP: $10 to $60,000 per year.
- Company purchases stock monthly with OCPs.
- Selling costs are brokerage commissions and any applicable taxes.
- Automatic investment services are available.
- Investors in 17 states may make initial purchase of stock directly from the firm ($100 minimum).
- Preferred dividends are eligible for reinvestment for additional common shares under the plan.
- Over 23,320 shareholders are in the plan.
- Dividends are paid February, May, August, and November.

Performance Rating: ***
DRIP Rating: 👍

Moore Corp. (NYSE:MCL)
1 First Canadian Pl.
PO Box 78
Toronto, Ontario M5X 1G5
Canada
(416) 364-2600

Business Profile: Leading supplier of business forms and related products.

Plan Specifics:
- Partial dividend reinvestment is not available.
- No Discount.
- OCP: $50 to $5000 (Canadian) per quarter.
- OCP is invested quarterly.
- Must sell shares through own broker.
- Dividends are paid January, April, July, and October.

Performance Rating: ****
DRIP Rating: 👍

Morgan (J.P.) & Co., Inc.
(NYSE:JPM)
c/o First Chicago Trust-NY
PO Box 2550, Ste. 4666
Jersey City, NJ 07303
(800) 446-2617   (212) 483-2323

Business Profile: Leading bank holding company emphasizing services for corporations.

Plan Specifics:
- Partial dividend reinvestment is available.
- No Discount.
- OCP: $50 to $5000 per month.
- Stock is purchased around the 15th of the month with OCPs.
- Selling costs are $10 service charge and a commission of 12 cents per share.
- Shares may be sold via the telephone.
- Dividends are paid January, April, July, and October.

Performance Rating: *****
DRIP Rating: 👍

Morrison Knudsen Corp. (NYSE:MRN)
PO Box 73
Boise, ID 83707
(208) 386-5000

Business Profile: Operations in construction, engineering, and rail systems.

Plan Specifics:
- Partial dividend reinvestment is not available.
- No Discount.
- OCP: $50 to $2000 per month.
- Company purchases stock monthly with OCPs.
- Selling fees are brokerage commissions and service charges.
- Dividends are paid March, June, September, and December.

Performance Rating: *

DRIP Rating: 👍

Morton International, Inc. (NYSE:MII)
100 N. Riverside Plaza
Chicago, IL 60606-1596
(800) 990-1010

Business Profile: Diversified company with interests in automotive airbags, specialty chemicals, and salt.

Plan Specifics:
- Initial purchases may be made directly from the company's transfer agent ($1000 minimum).
- Partial dividend reinvestment is available.
- No Discount.
- OCP: $50 to $60,000 per year.
- Stock is purchased at least monthly with OCPs.
- Minimum dividend reinvest-

ment fee of 3 percent of the amount to be reinvested or $2.50, whichever is smaller.
- Purchasing fees for OCPs are 5 percent of the amount invested (maximum $10) and 12 cents per share.
- Selling fees are a transaction fee ($15 plus 12 cents per share sold).
- Shares may be sold via the telephone.
- Automatic investment services are available ($25 minimum).
- IRA option is available.
- Dividends are paid March, June, September, and December.

Performance Rating: *****

DRIP Rating: 👍

Motorola, Inc. (NYSE:MOT)
c/o Harris Trust
PO Box A3309
Chicago, IL 60690
(312) 461-5535   (708) 576-5000

Business Profile: Provides radio communication systems, semiconductors, and cellular telephone systems.

Plan Specifics:
- Partial dividend reinvestment is available.
- No Discount.
- OCP: $25 to $5000 per quarter.
- Selling costs are brokerage commissions and other expenses.
- Company purchases stock monthly if there is enough money to buy at least a 100-share lot.
- Dividends are paid January, April, July, and October.

Performance Rating: *****
DRIP Rating: 👍

Nalco Chemical Co. (NYSE:NLC)
One Nalco Center
Naperville, IL 60563-1198
(708) 305-1000   (800) 446-2617

Business Profile: Manufactures specialty chemicals, including water and waste treatment, process chemicals, and petroleum chemicals.

Plan Specifics:
- Partial dividend reinvestment is available.
- No Discount.
- OCP: $50 to $15,000 per quarter.
- Selling costs include brokerage fees.
- Stock is purchased quarterly with OCPs.
- Shares may be sold via the telephone.
- Dividends are paid March, June, September, and December.

Performance Rating: ****
DRIP Rating: 👍

Nash-Finch Co.
(NASDAQ:NAFC)
PO Box 355
Minneapolis, MN 55440-0355
(612) 832-0534

Business Profile: Wholesale and retail food distribution.

Plan Specifics:
- Partial dividend reinvestment is available.
- No Discount.
- OCP: $10 to $1000 per month.
- Selling costs are brokerage commissions.

- Company purchases stock monthly if enough funds accumulate to purchase at least a 100-share lot.
- Dividends are paid March, June, September, and December.

Performance Rating: ***
DRIP Rating: 👍

Nashua Corp. (NYSE:NSH)
44 Franklin St.
Nashua, NH 03060
(603) 880-2323

Business Profile: Manufactures toners, developers, tapes, facsimile paper, carbonless paper, thermosensitive label paper, pressure sensitive labels, and OPC drums; remanufactures laser printer cartridges; provides mail-order photo finishing services.

Plan Specifics:
- Partial dividend reinvestment is not available.
- No Discount.
- OCP: $100 to $5000 per quarter.
- Company purchases stock approximately 8 times a year.
- Minimal, if any, brokerage fees when selling.
- Approximately 320 shareholders are in the plan.
- Dividends are paid January, April, July, and October.

Performance Rating: **
DRIP Rating: 👍

**National City Bancshares, Inc.
(NASDAQ:NCBE)**
227 Main St.
PO Box 868
Evansville, IN 47705-0868
(812) 464-9800
Business Profile: Bank holding
company.
Plan Specifics:
- Partial dividend reinvestment is
  available.
- No Discount.
- OCP: $100 to $10,000 per quarter.
- Company purchases stock
  quarterly with OCPs.
- Dividends are paid January,
  April, July, and October.
Performance Rating: NR
DRIP Rating: 👍

National City Corp. (NYSE:NCC)
PO Box 92301
Cleveland, OH 44193-0900
(216) 575-2640   (800) 622-8100
Business Profile: Multibank holding
company serving Ohio, Kentucky,
and Indiana.
Plan Specifics:
- Partial dividend reinvestment is
  available.
- 3 percent discount on reinvested
  dividends and OCPs.
- OCP: $20 to $500 per month.
- Selling costs are brokerage fees.
- Company purchases stock
  monthly with OCPs.
- Dividends are paid February,
  May, August, and November.
*Performance Rating: ****
DRIP Rating: 👍

**National Commerce Bancorp.
(TN) (NASDAQ:NCBC)**
One Commerce Square
Memphis, TN 38150
(800) 524-4458
Business Profile: Tennessee-based
banking institution.
Plan Specifics:
- Partial dividend reinvestment is
  available.
- No Discount.
- OCP: $100 to $10,000 per quarter.
- Selling costs include brokerage
  fees and service charges.
- Company purchases stock at
  least quarterly with OCPs.
- Dividends are paid January,
  April, July, and October.
Performance Rating: NR
DRIP Rating: 👍

National Data Corp. (NYSE:NDC)
c/o Wachovia Bk. of North
  Carolina, NA
PO Box 3001
Winston-Salem, NC 27102
(800) 633-4236
Business Profile: Provides data
processing services, including
credit card processing, bank
deposit reporting, money transfer
functions, and health-care data
services.
Plan Specifics:
- Partial dividend reinvestment is
  not available.
- No Discount.
- OCP: $25 to $1000 per quarter.
- Stock is purchased quarterly
  with OCPs.
- Purchasing costs include brokerage fees.

- Selling costs include brokerage fees.
- Dividends are paid February, May, August, and November.

Performance Rating: ****

DRIP Rating: 👍

National Fuel Gas Co.
 (NYSE:NFG)
10 Lafayette Square
Buffalo, NY 14203
(716) 857-7548

Business Profile: An integrated natural gas operation with utility operations, pipeline and storage, and exploration and production.

Plan Specifics:

- Partial dividend reinvestment is not available.
- No Discount.
- OCP: $25 to $5000 per month.
- Stock is purchased monthly with OCPs.
- Selling costs include brokerage commissions, transfer taxes, and $15 bank service charge.
- Residential customers of the company may make initial purchase of stock directly from the company ($200 minimum).
- Dividends are paid January, April, July, and October.

Performance Rating: ****

DRIP Rating: 👍

National Health Investors, Inc.
 (NYSE:NHI)
100 Vine St.
Murfreesboro, TN 37130
(615) 890-9100

Business Profile: Real estate investment trust which invests in income-producing health-care facilities.

Plan Specifics:

- Partial dividend reinvestment is not available.
- No Discount.
- OCP: $100 to $3000 per quarter.
- OCP is invested at least quarterly.
- Purchasing fees may include nominal brokerage commissions.
- Selling costs are brokerage fees.
- Dividends are paid February, May, August, and November.

Performance Rating: ***

DRIP Rating: 👎

National Penn Bancshares, Inc.
 (NASDAQ:NPBC)
Philadelphia & Reading Aves.
Boyertown, PA 19512
(610) 367-6001   (800) 526-0801

Business Profile: Bank holding company.

Plan Specifics:

- Partial dividend reinvestment is not available.
- No Discount.
- OCP: not available.
- Participants are charged the actual cost (including brokerage commissions) of common shares purchased in the open market.
- Must go through a broker to sell shares from the plan.
- Dividends are paid February, May, August, and November.

Performance Rating: NR

DRIP Rating: 👎

National Service Industries, Inc. (NYSE:NSI)
c/o Wachovia Bk. of North Carolina, N.A.
PO Box 3001
Winston-Salem, NC 27102
(800) 633-4236   (404) 853-1000

Business Profile: Produces lighting equipment and has operations in textiles and chemicals.

Plan Specifics:

- Partial dividend reinvestment is not available.
- No Discount.
- OCP: $10 to $4000 per month.
- Purchasing fees are service charge of 5 percent of the amount invested (maximum of $2.50) plus brokerage commissions.
- Selling costs are brokerage commissions and other costs of sale.
- Dividends are paid January, April, July, and October.

Performance Rating: ****
DRIP Rating: 👍

National-Standard Co. (NYSE:NSD)
1618 Terminal Rd.
Niles, MI 49120
(616) 683-8100   (800) 777-1618

Business Profile: Manufactures carbon and steel wires and related products for reinforcement of rubber products.

Plan Specifics:

- Partial dividend reinvestment is not available.
- No Discount.
- OCP: $10 to $3000 per month.

- Stock is purchased monthly with OCPs.
- There are no selling fees.
- The company is not currently paying a dividend.

Performance Rating: *
DRIP Rating: 👍

NationsBank Corp. (NYSE:NB)
100 N. Tryon St.
Charlotte, NC 28255
(704) 386-5000

Business Profile: Multibank holding company.

Plan Specifics:

- Partial dividend reinvestment is available.
- No Discount.
- OCP: $50 to $3000 per quarter.
- Company purchases stock monthly with OCPs.
- Selling costs are brokerage commissions and any transfer tax.
- Direct deposit of dividends is available.
- Dividends are paid March, June, September, and December.

Performance Rating: ****
DRIP Rating: 👍

Nationwide Health Properties, Inc. (NYSE:NHP)
4675 MacArthur Ct., Ste. 1170
Newport Beach, CA 92660
(714) 251-1211

Business Profile: Real estate investment trust specializing in the ownership of long-term health-care facilities.

Plan Specifics:

- Partial dividend reinvestment is available.

- No Discount.
- OCP: not available.
- Dividends are paid March, June, September, and December.

Performance Rating: ***
DRIP Rating: ☜

NBD Bancorp, Inc. (NYSE:NBD)
611 Woodward Ave.
Detroit, MI 48226
(313) 225-1000   (800) 336-6982

Business Profile: Holding company for banks in Michigan, Illinois, Indiana, Ohio, and Florida.

Plan Specifics:
- Partial dividend reinvestment is not available.
- No Discount.
- OCP: $10 to $10,000 per quarter.
- Selling costs include brokerage fees and $3 service charge.
- Company purchases stock at least quarterly with OCPs.
- Dividends are paid February, May, August, and November.

Performance Rating: ****
DRIP Rating: 👍

Neiman-Marcus Group, Inc.
(NYSE:NMG)
27 Boylston St.
Chestnut Hill, MA 02167
(617) 232-0760   (617) 575-2900

Business Profile: Owns and operates fashion apparel stores.

Plan Specifics:
- Partial dividend reinvestment is not available.
- No Discount.
- OCP: $25 to $2500 per quarter.
- Stock is purchased monthly with OCPs.

- Selling costs are brokerage fees and any transfer taxes.
- Dividends are paid January, April, July, and October.

Performance Rating: ***
DRIP Rating: 👍

Nestle S.A. (NASDAQ:NSRGY)
c/o Morgan Guaranty Trust
PO Box 8205
Boston, MA 02266-8205
(617) 774-4237   (800) 428-4237

Business Profile: International consumer-products company.

Plan Specifics:
- Partial dividend reinvestment is available.
- No Discount.
- OCP: $20 to $60,000 per year.
- Company purchases stock monthly with OCPs.
- Purchasing costs are brokerage fees and any other costs.
- Selling costs are brokerage commissions and any other costs of sale.
- Dividends are paid June and December.

Performance Rating: ****
DRIP Rating: 👍

Nevada Power Co. (NYSE:NVP)
PO Box 98669
Las Vegas, NV 89193-8669
(702) 367-5609   (800) 344-9239

Business Profile: Provides electric service to Las Vegas area.

Plan Specifics:
- Partial dividend reinvestment is available only on stock certificates.
- No Discount.

- OCP: $25 to $25,000 per quarter.
- Company purchases stock twice a month with OCPs.
- Selling costs include brokerage fees.
- Customers may make initial investments directly through the plan (minimum $25).
- Automatic investment services are available.
- Preferred dividends are eligible for reinvestment for additional common stock under the plan.
- Approximately 35,000 shareholders are in the plan.
- Dividends are paid February, May, August, and November.

Performance Rating: ***

DRIP Rating: 👍

New England Electric System (NYSE:NES)
PO Box 770
Westborough, MA 01581-0770
(508) 366-9011

Business Profile: Supplies electric power to communities in Massachusetts, Rhode Island, and New Hampshire.

Plan Specifics:

- Partial dividend reinvestment is available.
- No Discount.
- OCP: $25 to $5000 per month.
- Company purchases stock monthly with OCPs.
- Selling costs are brokerage commissions.
- Automatic investment services are available.
- Approximately 20,000 shareholders are in the plan.
- Dividends are paid January, April, July, and October.

Performance Rating: ***

DRIP Rating: 👍

New Jersey Resources Corp. (NYSE:NJR)
PO Box 1468
1415 Wyckoff Rd.
Wall, NJ 07719
(908) 938-1480   (908) 938-1230

Business Profile: Holding company with the principal subsidiary a natural gas utility serving New Jersey communities.

Plan Specifics:

- Partial dividend reinvestment is not available.
- No Discount.
- OCP: $25 to $60,000 per year.
- Selling costs are brokerage commissions.
- Company purchases stock twice a month with OCPs.
- Customers of the utility may make initial purchase of stock directly from the company ($25 minimum).
- Approximately 15,000 shareholders are in the plan.
- Dividends are paid January, April, July, and October.

Performance Rating: ****

DRIP Rating: 👍

New Plan Realty Trust (NYSE:NPR)
1120 Ave. of the Americas
New York, NY 10036
(212) 869-3000

Business Profile: Real estate investment trust.

Plan Specifics:

- Partial dividend reinvestment is available.

- 5 percent discount on reinvested dividends.
- OCP: $100 to $20,000 per quarter.
- Selling costs are brokerage fees.
- Company purchases stock at least quarterly with OCPs.
- Dividends are paid January, April, July, and October.

Performance Rating: ***

DRIP Rating: 👍

New York State Electric & Gas Corp. (NYSE:NGE)
PO Box 3200
Ithaca, NY 14852-3200
(800) 225-5643   (607) 729-2551

Business Profile: Supplies electricity and gas in New York State.

Plan Specifics:

- Partial dividend reinvestment is not available.
- No Discount.
- OCP: $25 to $100,000 per year.
- Selling costs are brokerage commissions.
- Company purchases stock around the 1st of each month with OCPs.
- Dividends are paid February, May, August, and November.

Performance Rating: **

DRIP Rating: 👍

New York Times Co.
(ASE:NYT.A)
c/o First Chicago Trust-NY
PO Box 2533
Jersey City, NJ 07303-2533
(800) 446-2617   (212) 556-1234

Business Profile: Publishes newspapers and magazines, operates radio and television stations, and provides broadcasting and information services.

Plan Specifics:

- Partial dividend reinvestment is not available.
- No Discount.
- OCP: $10 to $3000 per quarter.
- Stock is purchased quarterly with OCPs.
- Selling costs are brokerage commission and costs of sale.
- Dividends are paid March, June, September, and December.

Performance Rating: ****

DRIP Rating: 👍

Newell Co. (NYSE:NWL)
c/o First Chicago Trust Co.-NY
PO Box 2533
Jersey City, NJ 07303-2533
(800) 424-1941   (815) 235-4171

Business Profile: Manufactures consumer hardware, housewares, and certain industrial products for volume purchasers.

Plan Specifics:

- Partial dividend reinvestment is available.
- No Discount.
- OCP: $10 to $30,000 per year.
- Selling costs are brokerage commissions and costs of sale.
- Company purchases stock monthly with OCPs.
- Dividends are paid March, June, September, and December.

Performance Rating: ****

DRIP Rating: 👍

**Niagara Mohawk Power Corp.
(NYSE:NMK)
PO Box 7058
Syracuse, NY 13202
(800) 448-5450**

Business Profile: Electric and gas utility serving portions of New York.

Plan Specifics:

- Partial dividend reinvestment is not available.
- No Discount.
- OCP: $25 to $50,000 per year.
- Selling costs are brokerage commissions.
- There is a 50 cent quarterly service charge.
- Company purchases stock monthly with OCPs.
- Preferred dividends are eligible for reinvestment for additional common shares under the plan.
- Dividends are paid February, May, August, and November.

Performance Rating: **

DRIP Rating: 👍

**NICOR, Inc. (NYSE:GAS)
PO Box 3014
1844 Ferry Rd.
Naperville, IL 60566-7014
(708) 305-9500**

Business Profile: Operations in gas distribution and containerized shipping.

Plan Specifics:

- Partial dividend reinvestment is not available.
- No Discount.
- OCP: $50 to $5000 per month.
- Must go through own broker to sell shares.

- Company purchases stock around the 1st of month with OCPs.
- Preferred dividends are eligible for reinvestment for additional common shares under the plan.
- Approximately 14,200 shareholders are in the plan.
- Dividends are paid February, May, August, and November.

Performance Rating: ****

DRIP Rating: 👍

**NIPSCO Industries, Inc.
(NYSE:NI)
5265 Hohman Ave.
Hammond, IN 46320
(219) 853-5200**

Business Profile: Indiana-based electric and gas utility holding company.

Plan Specifics:

- Partial dividend reinvestment is not available.
- No Discount.
- OCP: $25 to $5000 per quarter.
- Selling costs are brokerage commissions and a $5 service charge.
- Company purchases stock monthly with OCPs.
- Approximately 16,400 shareholders are in the plan.
- Dividends are paid February, May, August, and November.

Performance Rating: ****

DRIP Rating: 👍

Nooney Realty Trust, Inc.
 (NASDAQ:NRTI)
7701 Forsyth Blvd.
St. Louis, MO 63105-1877
(314) 863-7700

Business Profile: Real estate investment trust.

Plan Specifics:

- Partial dividend reinvestment is not available.
- No Discount.
- OCP: minimum of $50 per payment.
- Stock is purchased at least quarterly with OCPs.
- Purchasing fees are 5 percent of amount invested ($2.50 maximum) and brokerage commissions.
- Selling costs are brokerage commissions and $1 termination fee.
- Dividends are paid March, June, September, and December.

Performance Rating: NR

DRIP Rating: 👍

NorAm Energy Corp.
 (NYSE:NAE)
PO Box 2628
1600 Smith St.
Houston, TX 77002
(800) 526-0801   (713) 654-7502

Business Profile: Explores for, produces, transports, and distributes natural gas in south central United States.

Plan Specifics:

- Initial purchase of stock may be made directly from the company ($200 minimum).
- Partial dividend reinvestment is available.

- 3 percent discount on reinvested dividends.
- OCP: $25 to $60,000 per year.
- Stock is purchased twice a month with OCPs.
- Selling costs include brokerage commissions.
- Automatic investment services are available.
- Safekeeping services are available.
- Direct deposit of dividends is available.
- Dividends are paid March, June, September, and December.

*Performance Rating: ***

DRIP Rating: 👍

Nordson Corp.
 (NASDAQ:NDSN)
28601 Clemens Rd.
Westlake, OH 44145-1148
(216) 892-1580

Business Profile: Engineers, manufactures, and markets equipment and systems used to apply advanced technology adhesives, sealants, and coatings during manufacturing processes.

Plan Specifics:

- Partial dividend reinvestment is not available.
- No Discount.
- OCP: $10 to $4000 per quarter.
- Selling costs include brokerage fees and $5 termination fee.
- Company purchases stock at least quarterly with OCPs.
- Dividends are paid March, June, September, and December.

*Performance Rating: *****

DRIP Rating: 👍

Norfolk Southern Corp.
(NYSE:NSC)
c/o First Chicago Trust-NY
PO Box 2533
Jersey City, NJ 07303-2533
(800) 446-2617   (804) 533-4811

Business Profile: Major railroad concern with operations in coal.

Plan Specifics:
- Partial dividend reinvestment is not available.
- No Discount.
- OCP: $10 to $3000 per quarter.
- Stock is purchased quarterly with OCPs.
- Purchasing fees are pro rata portion of brokerage commission and 5 percent on each investment ($2.50 maximum).
- Selling costs are pro rata portion of brokerage commission and termination fee of $5.
- Approximately 5000 shareholders are in the plan.
- Dividends are paid March, June, September, and December.

Performance Rating: *****

DRIP Rating: 👍

North Carolina Natural Gas Corp.
(NYSE:NCG)
PO Box 909
Fayetteville, NC 28302-0909
(910) 483-0315

Business Profile: Provides natural gas to customers in south central and eastern North Carolina.

Plan Specifics:
- Partial dividend reinvestment is available.
- 5 percent discount on reinvested dividends.
- OCP: $25 to $3000 per quarter.

- Company purchases stock quarterly with OCPs.
- Selling fees are brokerage commissions.
- Approximately 1860 shareholders are in the plan.
- Dividends are paid March, June, September, and December.

Performance Rating: ***

DRIP Rating: 👍

North Fork Bancorporation, Inc.
(NYSE:NFB)
9025 Main Rd.
Mattituck, NY 11952-9339
(516) 298-5000

Business Profile: Bank holding company for parts of New York.

Plan Specifics:
- Partial dividend reinvestment is available.
- No Discount.
- OCP: $200 to $15,000 per month.
- Selling costs include brokerage fee and a handling charge of $10 per transaction.
- Company purchases stock monthly with OCPs.
- Dividends are paid February, May, August, and November.

Performance Rating: **

DRIP Rating: 👎

Northeast Utilities Service Co.
(NYSE:NU)
PO Box 5006
Berlin, CT 06102-5006
(203) 665-4801   (800) 999-7269

Business Profile: Electric utility serving parts of Connecticut, Massachusetts, and New Hampshire.

Plan Specifics:
- Partial dividend reinvestment is available.
- No Discount.
- OCP: $100 to $25,000 per month.
- Purchasing and selling costs are brokerage fees and an administrative fee.
- Company purchases stock once a month with OCPs.
- Approximately 59,000 shareholders are in the plan.
- Dividends are paid March, June, September, and December.

Performance Rating: **

DRIP Rating: 👍

Northern States Power Co. (NYSE:NSP)
414 Nicollet Mall
Minneapolis, MN 55401
(800) 527-4677

Business Profile: Distributes electric power and gas to upper Midwest customers.

Plan Specifics:
- Partial dividend reinvestment is available.
- No Discount.
- OCP: $10 to $10,000 per quarter.
- May sell up to 25 shares through the plan.
- Company purchases stock once a month with OCPs.
- Residents of Minnesota, North Dakota, South Dakota, Wisconsin, and Michigan may make initial purchase of stock directly through the plan ($10 minimum).
- Preferred dividends are eligible for reinvestment for additional

shares of common stock under the plan.
- Approximately 39,000 shareholders are in the plan.
- Dividends are paid January, April, July, and October.

Performance Rating: *****

DRIP Rating: 👍

Northern Telecom Ltd. (NYSE:NT)
c/o Montreal Trust Company
151 Front St. W, 8th Floor
Toronto, Ont. M5J 2N1 Canada
(416) 981-9633

Business Profile: Leading global manufacturer of telecommunications equipment.

Plan Specifics:
- Partial dividend reinvestment is not available.
- No Discount.
- OCP: $40 to $5000 (United States) per quarter.
- Selling costs include brokerage fees.
- Company purchases stock quarterly with OCPs.
- Dividends are paid March, June, September, and December.

Performance Rating: ***

DRIP Rating: 👍

Northrop Grumman Corp. (NYSE:NOC)
c/o Chemical Bank
PO Box 3069, JAF Bldg.
New York, NY 10116-3069
(800) 851-9677   (310) 553-6262

Business Profile: Manufacturer of military aircraft and other defense products.

Plan Specifics:
- Partial dividend reinvestment is not available.
- No Discount.
- OCP: $100 to $1000 per month.
- Stock is purchased around the 15th of the month with OCPs.
- Dividends are paid March, June, September, and December.

Performance Rating: ***

DRIP Rating: 👍

Northwest Natural Gas Co. (NASDAQ:NWNG)
Shareholder Services
220 NW 2nd Ave.
Portland, OR 97209
(503) 220-2591

Business Profile: Distributes natural gas to customers in Oregon and Washington.

Plan Specifics:
- Partial dividend reinvestment is available.
- No Discount.
- OCP: up to $50,000 per year.
- Selling costs include a service fee and brokerage commissions.
- Firm will sell shares from a participant's account within 5 business days after receiving notice to sell, except between ex-dividend and dividend payment dates.
- Company purchases stock once a month with OCPs.
- Approximately 7000 shareholders are in the plan.
- Dividends are paid February, May, August, and November.

Performance Rating: ****

DRIP Rating: 👍

Northwestern Public Service Co. (NYSE:NPS)
33 Third St., SE
PO Box 1318
Huron, SD 57350
(605) 352-8411

Business Profile: Provides electric service to communities in South Dakota. Supplies natural gas in Nebraska and South Dakota.

Plan Specifics:
- Partial dividend reinvestment is available.
- No Discount.
- OCP: $10 to $2000 per month.
- Selling costs are brokerage commissions and other fees.
- Company purchases stock once a month with OCPs.
- Customers of the utility may make initial purchases directly from the company (minimum $10).
- Approximately 4600 shareholders are in the plan.
- Dividends are paid March, June, September, and December.

Performance Rating: ****

DRIP Rating: 👍

Norwest Corp. (NYSE:NOB)
6th & Marquette
Minneapolis, MN 55479
(612) 450-4180

Business Profile: Bank holding institution with outlets in the upper Midwest and Arizona.

Plan Specifics:
- Partial dividend reinvestment is available.
- No Discount.
- OCP: $25 to $30,000 per quarter.

- Selling costs are brokerage commissions and service charges.
- Company purchases stock monthly with OCPs.
- Dividends are paid March, June, September, and December.

Performance Rating: ★★★★

DRIP Rating: 👍

NOVA Corporation (NYSE:NVA)
PO Box 2535
Station "M"
Calgary, Alberta T2P 2N6 Canada
(800) 661-8686   (403) 290-6000

Business Profile: Operations in petrochemicals, petroleum, gas transmission, and pipeline development.

Plan Specifics:

- Partial dividend reinvestment is not available.
- No Discount.
- OCP: $50 to $5000 (Canadian) per quarter.
- Must go through own broker to sell stock.
- Preferred dividends are eligible for reinvestment for additional common shares under the plan.
- Company purchases stock quarterly with OCPs.
- Dividends are paid February, May, August, and November.

Performance Rating: ★★

DRIP Rating: 👍

Novo-Nordisk A/S (NYSE:NVO)
c/o First Chicago Trust-NY
PO Box 2533
Jersey City, NJ 07303-2533
(800) 446-2617   (212) 867-0131
(617) 774-4237

Business Profile: Denmark-based company that manufactures insulin and industrial enzymes.

Plan Specifics:

- Partial dividend reinvestment is not available.
- No Discount.
- OCP: not available.
- Purchasing fees are proportionate share of brokerage commission and 5 percent of total funds invested ($2.50 maximum).
- Selling costs are $5 handling charge, brokerage commissions, and any other costs of sale.
- Dividends are paid in May.

Performance Rating: ★★★★

DRIP Rating: 👍

Nucor Corp. (NYSE:NUE)
2100 Rexford Rd.
Charlotte, NC 28211
(704) 366-7000   (800) 829-8432

Business Profile: Leading manufacturer of steel joists and steel products.

Plan Specifics:

- Partial dividend reinvestment is not available.
- No Discount.
- OCP: $10 to $3000 per quarter.
- Selling costs include brokerage fees and a handling charge.
- Company purchases stock approximately 8 times a year with OCPs.
- Dividends are paid February, May, August, and November.

Performance Rating: ★★★★

DRIP Rating: 👍

NUI Corp. (NYSE:NUI)
PO Box 760
550 Route 202-206
Bedminster, NJ 07921-0760
(908) 781-0500

Business Profile: Transports, distributes, and markets natural gas in parts of New Jersey, Florida, Pennsylvania, North Carolina, Maryland, and New York.

Plan Specifics:

- Partial dividend reinvestment is available.
- No Discount.
- OCP: $25 to $60,000 per year.
- Selling costs are brokerage commissions, service charges, and an administrative fee.
- Company purchases stock once a month with OCPs.
- Automatic investment services are available.
- Direct deposit of dividends is available.
- Customers and residents of the states in which the company conducts its operations (NJ, FL, NC, NY, PA, MD) can purchase initial shares directly from the company ($125 minimum).
- Dividends are paid March, June, September, and December.

Performance Rating: **

DRIP Rating: 👍

NYNEX Corp. (NYSE:NYN)
c/o Bank of Boston
PO Box 9176
Boston, MA 02205-9176
(800) 358-1133   (914) 644-6400

Business Profile: Major telephone holding company in New York and New England. Firm is in-

volved in telecommunications, cable television, directory publishing, video entertainment, and information network and delivery services.

Plan Specifics:

- Need at least 5 shares to enroll in plan.
- Partial dividend reinvestment is available.
- No Discount.
- OCP: $25 to $100,000 per year.
- Selling costs are brokerage commissions.
- Company purchases stock each month with OCPs.
- Dividends are paid February, May, August, and November.

Performance Rating: *****

DRIP Rating: 👍

Occidental Petroleum Corp. (NYSE:OXY)
10889 Wilshire Blvd.
Los Angeles, CA 90024
(213) 879-1700   (800) 622-9231

Business Profile: Refines, produces, and markets natural gas and oil. Also has operations in chemicals.

Plan Specifics:

- Need at least 25 shares to enroll in plan.
- Partial dividend reinvestment is available (must have 25 shares reinvested at all times).
- No Discount.
- OCP: $50 to $1000 per month.
- $5 fee for withdrawal of full-share certificates.
- Stock is purchased monthly with OCPs.

- Selling costs are $15 plus any brokerage fees.
- Preferred dividends are eligible for reinvestment for additional common shares under the plan.
- Approximately 33,500 shareholders are in the plan.
- Dividends are paid January, April, July, and October.

Performance Rating: **

DRIP Rating: 👎

**Ohio Casualty Corp.
(NASDAQ:OCAS)
136 N. Third St.
Hamilton, OH 45025-0001
(513) 867-3903   (800) 446-2617**

Business Profile: Insurance holding company with emphasis in property-casualty insurance.

Plan Specifics:

- Partial dividend reinvestment is available.
- No Discount.
- OCP: $10 to $5000 per month.
- OCP is invested monthly.
- Purchasing fees are 5 percent of the amount received up to a maximum charge of $3 plus nominal brokerage fees.
- Selling costs are brokerage fees plus $1 service charge.
- Dividends are paid March, June, September, and December.

Performance Rating: ***

DRIP Rating: 👍

**Ohio Edison Co. (NYSE:OEC)
76 S. Main St.
Akron, OH 44308-1890
(216) 384-5151**

Business Profile: Electric utility serving Ohio and Pennsylvania.

Plan Specifics:

- Partial dividend reinvestment is available.
- No Discount.
- OCP: $10 to $50,000 per year.
- Company purchases stock every month with OCPs.
- Selling costs are brokerage commissions and a service charge.
- Preferred dividends are eligible for reinvestment for additional common shares under the plan.
- Dividends are paid March, June, September, and December.

Performance Rating: **

DRIP Rating: 👍

**Oklahoma Gas & Electric Co.
(NYSE:OGE)
PO Box 321
Oklahoma City, OK 73101-0321
(800) 395-2662**

Business Profile: Provides electricity to customers in Oklahoma and portions of Arkansas.

Plan Specifics:

- Partial dividend reinvestment is available.
- No Discount.
- OCP: $10 to $5000 per quarter.
- Selling costs are brokerage commissions.
- Company purchases stock each month with OCPs.
- Preferred dividends are eligible for reinvestment in additional common shares under the plan.
- Customers of the company may make initial purchase of stock directly from the company ($25 minimum).

- Dividends are paid January, April, July, and October.

Performance Rating: ***

DRIP Rating: 🖐️

**Old Kent Financial Corp.
(NASDAQ:OKEN)
One Vandenberg Center
Grand Rapids, MI 49503
(800) 652-2657   (616) 771-5482**

Business Profile: Bank holding company engaged in commercial banking and related services.

Plan Specifics:

- Partial dividend reinvestment is not available.
- No Discount.
- OCP: $100 to $5000 per quarter.
- Selling costs are brokerage commissions, transfer taxes, and a $20 service charge.
- Company purchases stock quarterly with OCPs.
- Dividends are paid March, June, September, and December.

Performance Rating: ****

DRIP Rating: 👍

**Old National Bancorp (IN)
(NASDAQ:OLDB)
PO Box 718
Evansville, IN 47705
(812) 464-1296   (812) 464-1442**

Business Profile: Indiana-based holding company for banks in Indiana, Kentucky, and Illinois.

Plan Specifics:

- Partial dividend reinvestment is available.
- 3 percent discount on reinvested dividends, 2½ percent discount on OCPs.

- OCP: $100 to $3500 per quarter.
- Must go through own broker to sell shares.
- Company purchases stock once each quarter with OCPs.
- Approximately 7000 shareholders are in the plan.
- Dividends are paid March, June, September, and December.

Performance Rating: ***

DRIP Rating: 🖐️

**Old Republic International Corp.
(NYSE:ORI)
c/o First Chicago Trust-NY
PO Box 2533
Jersey City, NJ 07303-2533
(800) 446-2617   (312) 346-8100**

Business Profile: Chicago-based insurance holding firm. Writes and sells property and liability, life and disability, and mortgage guaranty insurance.

Plan Specifics:

- Partial dividend reinvestment is available.
- No Discount.
- OCP: $100 to $5000 per quarter.
- Stock is purchased quarterly with OCPs.
- Selling costs are brokerage commissions and transfer taxes.
- Dividends are paid March, June, September, and December.

Performance Rating: ***

DRIP Rating: 🖐️

Olin Corp. (NYSE:OLN)
c/o Chemical Bank
PO Box 3069, JAF Bldg.
New York, NY 10116-3069
(800) 851-9677   (203) 356-2000

Business Profile: Producer of industrial and specialty chemicals, metals, and defense products.

Plan Specifics:
- Partial dividend reinvestment is not available.
- No Discount.
- OCP: $50 to $5000 per month.
- Stock is purchased monthly with OCPs.
- Purchasing fees are brokerage commissions and 5 percent service charge (maximum $2.50) plus $5 fee for each investment of OCPs.
- Selling costs are brokerage commissions and $15 handling charge.
- $5 fee for issuance of certificates.
- Dividends are paid March, June, September, and December.

Performance Rating: ***

DRIP Rating: 🏴

OM Group, Inc.
 (NASDAQ:OMGI)
3800 Terminal Tower
Cleveland, OH 44113
(800) 321-9696   (216) 781-0083

Business Profile: A leading producer and international marketer of value added metal-based specialty chemicals.

Plan Specifics:
- Partial dividend reinvestment is available.
- No Discount.
- OCP: $10 to $5000 per month.

- Stock is purchased monthly with OCPs.
- Selling costs are brokerage commissions.
- Dividends are paid February, May, August, and November.

Performance Rating: ***

DRIP Rating: 👍

Omnicare, Inc. (NYSE:OCR)
2800 Chemed Center
255 E. Fifth St.
Cincinnati, OH 45202
(513) 762-6666

Business Profile: Provides pharmacy management services.

Plan Specifics:
- Partial dividend reinvestment is not available.
- No Discount.
- OCP: $10 to $1000 per month.
- Selling costs are brokerage commissions.
- Stock is purchased monthly with OCPs.
- Dividends are paid March, June, September, and December.

Performance Rating: ****

DRIP Rating: 👍

One Valley Bancorp of West
 Virginia, Inc.
 (NASDAQ:OVWV)
PO Box 1793
Charleston, WV 25326
(304) 348-7023

Business Profile: Multibank holding company.

Plan Specifics:
- Partial dividend reinvestment is available.
- No Discount.

- OCP: $25 to $3000 per quarter.
- There are no costs for selling shares from the plan.
- Company purchases stock quarterly with OCPs.
- Dividends are paid March, June, September, and December.

Performance Rating: NR

DRIP Rating: 👍

Oneida Ltd. (NYSE:OCQ)
Executive Offices
Oneida, NY 13421
(315) 361-3636   (312) 461-7369

Business Profile: Produces stainless steel and silver-plated flatware. Operations in industrial wire products.

Plan Specifics:

- Partial dividend reinvestment is available.
- No Discount.
- OCP: not available.
- Selling costs are brokerage fees and service charges.
- Dividends are paid March, June, September, and December.

Performance Rating: **

DRIP Rating: 👍

Oneok, Inc. (NYSE:OKE)
PO Box 871
Tulsa, OK 74102-0871
(800) 395-2662   (918) 588-7158

Business Profile: Natural gas utility in Oklahoma with interests in gas and oil exploration and production.

Plan Specifics:

- Initial purchases may be made directly from the company (minimum $100).

- Partial dividend reinvestment is available.
- 3 percent discount on reinvested dividends.
- OCP: $25 to $100,000 per year.
- Company purchases stock twice a month with OCPs.
- Selling costs are brokerage commissions.
- Automatic investment services are available.
- IRA option is available.
- Preferred dividends are eligible for reinvestment for additional common shares under the plan.
- Dividends are paid February, May, August, and November.

Performance Rating: ***

DRIP Rating: 👍

Orange & Rockland Utilities, Inc.
(NYSE:ORU)
c/o Chemical Bank
PO Box 3069, JAF Bldg.
New York, NY 10116-3069
(800) 851-9677   (914) 352-6000

Business Profile: Provides electric and gas services to portions of New York, New Jersey, and Pennsylvania.

Plan Specifics:

- Partial dividend reinvestment is available.
- No Discount.
- OCP: $25 to $5000 per quarter.
- Stock is purchased monthly with OCPs.
- Selling costs are brokerage commission.
- Preferred dividends are eligible for reinvestment for additional common shares under the plan.

- Dividends are paid February, May, August, and November.

Performance Rating: ***

DRIP Rating: 👍

Otter Tail Power Co.
 (NASDAQ:OTTR)
215 S. Cascade St.
Fergus Falls, MN 56537
(218) 739-8479

Business Profile: Supplies electric power to customers in Minnesota and the Dakotas.

Plan Specifics:

- Partial dividend reinvestment is not available.
- No Discount.
- OCP: $10 to $2000 per month.
- Company purchases stock monthly with OCPs.
- Preferred dividends are eligible for reinvestment for additional common shares under the plan.
- Certificate safekeeping is available.
- 7000 shareholders are in the plan.
- Dividends are paid March, June, September, and December.

Performance Rating: ****

DRIP Rating: 👍

Outboard Marine Corp.
 (NYSE:OM)
100 Sea-Horse Dr.
Waukegan, IL 60085
(708) 689-6200   (312) 407-4589

Business Profile: Designs, makes, and distributes marine products.

Plan Specifics:

- Partial dividend reinvestment is not available.

- No Discount.
- OCP: $10 to $3000 per quarter.
- Company purchases stock monthly with OCPs.
- Purchasing fees are brokerage commissions and 5 percent service charge (min. $1; max. $3).
- Selling fees are brokerage commissions and a service fee.
- Automatic investment services are available.
- Dividends are paid February, May, August, and November.

Performance Rating: ***

DRIP Rating: 👍

Owens & Minor, Inc.
 (NYSE:OMI)
4800 Cox Rd.
PO Box 27626
Richmond, VA 23261-7626
(804) 747-9794   (800) 633-4236

Business Profile: Distributes medical and surgical supplies, pharmaceuticals, and related products.

Plan Specifics:

- Partial dividend reinvestment is available.
- No Discount.
- OCP: $25 to $25,000 per year.
- Selling costs are brokerage commissions and a $5 handling charge.
- Company purchases stock monthly with OCPs.
- Dividends are paid March, June, September, and December.

Performance Rating: ***

DRIP Rating: 👍

Pacific Enterprises (NYSE:PET)
633 W. Fifth St., Ste. 5400
Los Angeles, CA 90071-2006
(800) 722-5483

Business Profile: California-based natural gas holding company.

Plan Specifics:
- Partial dividend reinvestment is available.
- No Discount.
- OCP: $25 to $25,000 per quarter.
- Company purchases stock monthly with OCPs.
- Must go through own broker to sell shares.
- Preferred dividends are eligible for reinvestment for additional common shares under the plan.
- Safekeeping services are available.
- Dividends are paid February, May, August, and November.

Performance Rating: ***

DRIP Rating: 👍

Pacific Gas & Electric Co. (NYSE:PCG)
Shareholder Services, B26B
77 Beale St., Room 2600
PO Box 770000
San Francisco, CA 94177
(800) 367-7731

Business Profile: Natural gas and electric utility serving regions of California.

Plan Specifics:
- Partial dividend reinvestment is not available.
- No Discount.
- OCP: not available.
- Company will sell less than 100 shares for participants for no

charge; otherwise must go through own broker to sell shares.
- Preferred dividends are eligible for reinvestment for additional common shares under the plan.
- Dividends are paid January, April, July, and October.

Performance Rating: **

DRIP Rating: 👎

Pacific Telesis Group (NYSE:PAC)
c/o Bank of Boston
PO Box 9154
Boston, MA 02209-9154
(800) 637-6373   (415) 394-3000

Business Profile: Telephone holding company serving portions of California and Nevada.

Plan Specifics:
- Need a minimum of 2 shares to enroll in the plan.
- Partial dividend reinvestment is available.
- No Discount.
- OCP: $50 to $20,000 per month.
- Fees are $1 per quarter.
- Selling costs are $6 plus 25 cents per share.
- Company purchases stock monthly with OCPs.
- Automatic investment services are available.
- Dividends are paid February, May, August, and November.

Performance Rating: ****

DRIP Rating: 👍

PacifiCorp (NYSE:PPW)
700 N.E. Multnomah St.,
 Suite 1600
Portland, OR 97232-4107
(800) 233-5453   (503) 731-2000

Business Profile: Electric and telephone holding company with operations in resource development.

Plan Specifics:

- Partial dividend reinvestment is available.
- No Discount.
- OCP: $25 to $25,000 per quarter.
- Purchasing and selling fees are approximately 5 to 10 cents per share, with no fee charged on original issue investments.
- Company purchases stock every month with OCPs.
- Preferred dividends are eligible for reinvestment for additional common shares under the plan.
- Dividends are paid February, May, August, and November.

Performance Rating: ****

DRIP Rating: 👍

PaineWebber Group, Inc.
 (NYSE:PWJ)
1285 Ave. of the Americas,
 14th Floor
New York, NY 10019
(212) 713-2000

Business Profile: Holding company for investment services firm.

Plan Specifics:

- Partial dividend reinvestment is not available.
- No Discount.
- OCP: $10 to $3000 per quarter.
- Stock is purchased at least quarterly with OCPs.

- Selling costs are brokerage commission and any taxes.
- Dividends are paid January, April, July, and October.

Performance Rating: **

DRIP Rating: 👍

Pall Corp. (NYSE:PLL)
2200 Northern Blvd.
East Hills, NY 11548
(516) 484-5400   (800) 633-4236

Business Profile: Manufacturer of filtration products used in the health care, aeropower, and fluid processing markets.

Plan Specifics:

- Need at least 50 shares to enroll in plan.
- Partial dividend reinvestment is available.
- No Discount.
- OCP: $100 to $5000 per month.
- Stock is purchased once a month with OCPs.
- Selling costs include brokerage fees and any other costs of sale.
- Dividends are paid February, May, August, and November.

Performance Rating: ****

DRIP Rating: 👍

Panhandle Eastern Corp.
 (NYSE:PEL)
Shareholder Services
PO Box 1642
Houston, TX 77251-1642
(713) 627-5400   (800) 225-5838

Business Profile: Transports and markets natural gas in midwestern and eastern states.

Plan Specifics:

- Partial dividend reinvestment is available.

- No Discount.
- OCP: $25 to $60,000 per year.
- Must sell shares through own broker, although the company will buy back holdings of less than 50 shares.
- Company purchases stock monthly with OCPs.
- Safekeeping services are available.
- Approximately 11,500 shareholders are in the plan.
- Dividends are paid March, June, September, and December.

Performance Rating: ***

DRIP Rating: 👍

Parker Hannifin Corp. (NYSE:PH)
17325 Euclid Ave.
Cleveland, OH 44112-1290
(216) 531-3000

Business Profile: Creates devices for fluid power systems used in industrial, aerospace, and automotive markets.

Plan Specifics:
- Partial dividend reinvestment is not available.
- No Discount.
- OCP: $10 to $1000 per month.
- Stock is purchased with OCPs within 30 days of receipt of any amount sufficient to purchase at least 100 shares.
- Selling costs are brokerage commissions and a termination fee.
- Dividends are paid March, June, September, and December.

Performance Rating: ***

DRIP Rating: 👍

Paychex, Inc. (NASDAQ:PAYX)
911 Panorama Trail S.
Rochester, NY 14625
(716) 385-6666   (800) 937-5449

Business Profile: Largest payroll accounting services concern in the United States which provides services to small and medium-sized firms across the country.

Plan Specifics:
- Partial dividend reinvestment is not available.
- No Discount.
- OCP: $100 to $10,000 per quarter.
- Stock is purchased once a month with OCPs.
- Selling costs are brokerage commissions.
- Dividends are paid February, May, August, and November.

Performance Rating: *****

DRIP Rating: 👍

PECO Energy Co. (NYSE:PE)
Shareholder Relations
PO Box 8699
Philadelphia, PA 19101
(800) 626-8729

Business Profile: Supplies electricity and natural gas to customers in southeastern Pennsylvania.

Plan Specifics:
- Partial dividend reinvestment is available.
- No Discount.
- OCP: $25 to $50,000 per year.
- Selling costs are brokerage fees and service charge.
- Stock is purchased monthly with OCPs.
- Preferred dividends are eligible

for reinvestment for additional
common shares under the plan.
- Dividends are paid March, June,
September, and December.

Performance Rating: **

DRIP Rating: 👍

Penney (J.C.) Co., Inc. (NYSE:JCP)
PO Box 10001
Dallas, TX 75301
(214) 431-1000   (800) 842-9470

Business Profile: Major retailer with
outlets in all 50 states.

Plan Specifics:
- Partial dividend reinvestment is
available.
- No Discount.
- OCP: $20 to $10,000 per month.
- Selling costs are a $15 service
charge for each sale of shares.
- Company purchases stock twice
a month with OCPs.
- Dividends are paid February,
May, August, and November.

Performance Rating: ****

DRIP Rating: 👍

Pennsylvania Enterprises, Inc.
(NYSE:PNT)
Wilkes-Barre Center
39 Public Square
Wilkes-Barre, PA 18711-0601
(717) 829-8843

Business Profile: Distributor of
natural gas and water, with gas
utility operations as well.

Plan Specifics:
- Partial dividend reinvestment is
available.
- No Discount.
- OCP: not available.

- Selling costs are brokerage
commissions, any service charge,
and applicable transfer taxes.
- Dividends are paid March, June,
September, and December.

Performance Rating: **

DRIP Rating: 👎

Pennzoil Co. (NYSE:PZL)
PO Box 2967
Houston, TX 77252-2967
(713) 546-4000

Business Profile: Explores for,
produces, and refines natural gas
and crude oil. Operations in sulfur,
motor oil, and auto parts.

Plan Specifics:
- Partial dividend reinvestment is
available.
- No Discount.
- OCP: $50 to $60,000 per year.
- Company purchases stock
monthly with OCPs.
- Selling costs are a $15 adminis-
trative charge and brokerage
fees.
- Automatic investment services
are available.
- Direct deposit of dividends is
available.
- Safekeeping services are avail-
able.
- Approximately 5300 sharehold-
ers are in the plan.
- Dividends are paid March, June,
September, and December.

Performance Rating: ***

DRIP Rating: 👍

Pentair, Inc. (NASDAQ:PNTA)
c/o Norwest Bank MN
PO Box 738
161 N. Concord Exchange
South St. Paul, MN 55075-0738
(612) 450-4064   (612) 636-7920

Business Profile: Manufactures industrial equipment.

Plan Specifics:

- Partial dividend reinvestment is not available.
- No Discount.
- OCP: $10 to $3000 per quarter.
- Selling costs are brokerage commissions and service charges.
- Company purchases stock monthly with OCPs.
- Dividends are paid February, May, August, and November.

Performance Rating: ****
DRIP Rating: 👍

Peoples Energy Corp.
(NYSE:PGL)
130 E. Randolph Dr.
PO Box 2000
Chicago, IL 60690-2000
(312) 240-4292   (800) 228-6888

Business Profile: A holding company for two natural gas utilities which serve nearly one million customers in Chicago and communities in northeastern Illinois.

Plan Specifics:

- Partial dividend reinvestment is not available.
- No Discount.
- OCP: $25 to $3000 per month.
- Selling costs include brokerage fees.
- Company purchases stock every month with OCPs.

- Dividends are paid January, April, July, and October.

Performance Rating: ***
DRIP Rating: 👍

Pep Boys - Manny, Moe & Jack
(NYSE:PBY)
3111 W. Allegheny Ave.
Philadelphia, PA 19132
(215) 229-9000

Business Profile: Retailer of automotive parts and accessories and a provider of automotive maintenance, parts installation, and other related services.

Plan Specifics:

- Partial dividend reinvestment is available.
- No Discount.
- OCP: $100 to $10,000 per quarter.
- Selling costs are brokerage commissions, service charges, and taxes.
- Company purchases stock quarterly with OCPs.
- Dividends are paid January, April, July, and October.

Performance Rating: ****
DRIP Rating: 👍

PepsiCo, Inc. (NYSE:PEP)
700 Anderson Hill Rd.
Purchase, NY 10577
(914) 253-3055   (800) 226-0083

Business Profile: Produces soft drinks and snack foods (Frito-Lay) and owns several fast-food restaurants (Pizza Hut, KFC, and Taco Bell).

Plan Specifics:

- Need at least 5 shares to enroll in plan.

- Partial dividend reinvestment is available.
- No Discount.
- OCP: $25 to $5000 per month.
- Selling costs are brokerage commissions and a $5 charge.
- Stock is purchased monthly with OCPs.
- Safekeeping services are available.
- Dividends are paid January, March, June, and September.

Performance Rating: *****

DRIP Rating: 👍

Perkin-Elmer Corp. (NYSE:PKN)
761 Main Ave.
Norwalk, CT 06859-0001
(203) 762-1000   (617) 575-2900

Business Profile: Manufactures scientific analytical instruments and combustion, electric arc, and plasma thermal spray equipment.

Plan Specifics:

- Partial dividend reinvestment is available.
- No Discount.
- OCP: not available.
- Selling costs include brokerage commissions and a handling charge of $2.50.
- Dividends are paid January, April, July, and October.

Performance Rating: ***

DRIP Rating: 👍

Petroleum Heat and Power Co., Inc. (NASDAQ: HEAT)
c/o Chemical Bank
PO Box 3069, JAF Bldg.
New York, NY 10116-3069
(800) 851-9677

Business Profile: The company is the largest retail distributor of home heating oil in the U.S. The firm also distributes propane.

Plan Specifics:

- Partial dividend reinvestment is available.
- 5 percent discount on reinvested dividends and 3 percent discount on OCPs.
- OCP: $500 to $5000 per quarter.
- OCP is invested quarterly.
- Selling costs include brokerage fees.
- $5 fee for issuing certificates.
- Dividends are paid January, April, July, and October.

Performance Rating: ***

DRIP Rating: 👍

Pfizer, Inc. (NYSE:PFE)
Shareholder Services
235 E. 42nd St.
New York, NY 10017-5755
(212) 573-3704

Business Profile: Produces health-care products, consumer products, pharmaceuticals, and animal health-care items.

Plan Specifics:

- Partial dividend reinvestment is available.
- No Discount.
- OCP: $25 to $10,000 per month.

- Company purchases stock monthly with OCPs.
- There are no selling fees.
- Dividends are paid March, June, September, and December.

Performance Rating: *****

DRIP Rating: 👍

Phelps Dodge Corp. (NYSE:PD)
2600 N. Central Ave.
Phoenix, AZ 85004-3014
(602) 234-8199   (602) 234-8100

Business Profile: Leading United States copper provider with interests in carbon black and truck wheels and rims.

Plan Specifics:

- Partial dividend reinvestment is not available.
- No Discount.
- OCP: $10 to $2000 per quarter.
- Selling costs are $5 termination fee.
- Company purchases stock quarterly with OCPs.
- Dividends are paid March, June, September, and December.

Performance Rating: ****

DRIP Rating: 👍

Philadelphia Suburban Corp. (NYSE:PSC)
762 Lancaster Ave.
Bryn Mawr, PA 19010-3489
(610) 527-8000

Business Profile: Philadelphia-based water utility holding company.

Plan Specifics:

- Partial dividend reinvestment is available.
- 5 percent discount on reinvested dividends.

- OCP: $25 to $10,000 per year.
- Company purchases stock three times a year with OCPs.
- Selling costs are brokerage commission and taxes.
- Customers may periodically make initial purchases of stock directly from the company ($250 minimum).
- Must be a shareholder of record 15 days prior to record date to participate in the plan.
- Dividends are paid March, June, September, and December.

Performance Rating: ***

DRIP Rating: 👍

Philip Morris Companies, Inc. (NYSE:MO)
c/o First Chicago Trust-NY
PO Box 2533
Jersey City, NJ 07303-2533
(800) 446-2617   (800) 442-0077

Business Profile: Major supplier of cigarettes (Marlboro), beer (Miller), and consumer foods (Oscar Mayer, Maxwell House, Jell-O).

Plan Specifics:

- Partial dividend reinvestment is available.
- No Discount.
- OCP: $10 to $60,000 per year.
- Stock is purchased around the 10th day of the month with OCPs.
- Selling costs are brokerage commission, a handling charge, and other costs of sale.
- Automatic investment services are available.
- Dividends are paid January, April, July, and October.

Performance Rating: *****
DRIP Rating: 👍

Phillips Petroleum Co. (NYSE:P)
Stockholder Records
4 A4 PB
Bartlesville, OK 74004
(800) 356-0066

Business Profile: Major integrated crude oil and natural gas concern with operations in chemicals.

Plan Specifics:
- Partial dividend reinvestment is not available.
- No Discount.
- OCP: $10 to $10,000 per month.
- Selling costs are brokerage commissions and a handling charge.
- Stock is purchased weekly with OCPs.
- Dividends are paid March, June, September, and December.

Performance Rating: **
DRIP Rating: 👍

Piccadilly Cafeterias, Inc.
(NYSE:PIC)
PO Box 2467
Baton Rouge, LA 70821-2467
(504) 293-9440

Business Profile: Manages chain of cafeterias in southern and southwestern states.

Plan Specifics:
- Partial dividend reinvestment is available.
- 5 percent discount on reinvested dividends.
- OCP: $100 to $5000 per quarter.
- Selling costs are brokerage commissions, termination fee, and transfer taxes.
- Company purchases stock quarterly with OCPs.
- Dividends are paid January, April, July, and October.

Performance Rating: **
DRIP Rating: 👍

Piedmont Natural Gas Co.
(NYSE:PNY)
PO Box 33068
Charlotte, NC 28233
(800) 438-8410

Business Profile: Provides natural gas to Piedmont region of North and South Carolina and metropolitan Nashville, Tennessee.

Plan Specifics:
- Partial dividend reinvestment is available.
- 5 percent discount on reinvested dividends.
- OCP: $25 to $3000 per month.
- Selling costs are brokerage commissions and any transfer tax.
- Stock is purchased monthly with OCPs.
- Dividends are paid January, April, July, and October.

Performance Rating: ****
DRIP Rating: 👍

Pinnacle West Capital Corp.
(NYSE:PNW)
PO Box 52133
Phoenix, AZ 85072-2133
(800) 457-2983   (602) 379-2500

Business Profile: Electric utility holding company providing services to portions of Arizona.

Plan Specifics:
- Initial purchases may be made directly from the company ($50 minimum).
- Partial dividend reinvestment is available.
- No Discount.
- OCP: up to $60,000 per year.
- Purchasing and selling fees are brokerage commissions and related service charges.
- Company purchases stock monthly with OCPs.
- Preferred dividends may be reinvested in common stock.
- Dividends are paid March, June, September, and December.

Performance Rating: **
DRIP Rating: 👍

Pioneer Hi-Bred International, Inc. (NASDAQ:PHYB)
c/o First Nat'l Bank of Boston
PO Box 1681
Boston, MA 02105-1681
(800) 730-4001

Business Profile: Leading supplier of hybrid seed corn in North America. Also produces other seeds and makes inoculants for livestock and crop production.

Plan Specifics:
- Partial dividend reinvestment is not available.
- No Discount.
- OCP: $50 to $1500 per month.
- Selling costs are brokerage commissions, transfer taxes, and bank charges of 5 percent (maximum $3).
- Company purchases stock monthly with OCPs.

- Dividends are paid January, April, July, and October.

Performance Rating: ***
DRIP Rating: 👍

Pioneer-Standard Electronics, Inc. (NASDAQ:PIOS)
4800 E. 131st St.
Cleveland, OH 44105
(216) 587-3600   (800) 542-7792

Business Profile: Third largest distributor of industrial electronic components in the United States.

Plan Specifics:
- Partial dividend reinvestment is available.
- No Discount.
- OCP: $25 to $5000 per month.
- Stock is purchased monthly with OCPs.
- Selling costs are brokerage commissions and a $5 service fee.
- Dividends are paid February, May, August, and November.

Performance Rating: ****
DRIP Rating: 👍

Pitney Bowes, Inc. (NYSE:PBI)
World Headquarters
Stamford, CT 06926-0700
(203) 351-6659   (800) 648-8170

Business Profile: Leading provider of products and services which manage the movement of messages and packages through relevant networks.

Plan Specifics:
- Partial dividend reinvestment is available.
- No Discount.
- OCP: $100 to $3000 per quarter.

- Selling costs are brokerage commissions, taxes, and a service fee of $15.
- Company purchases stock monthly with OCPs.
- Dividends are paid March, June, September, and December.

Performance Rating: ****
DRIP Rating: 👍

**Ply Gem Industries, Inc.
(NYSE:PGI)
777 Third Ave.
New York, NY 10017
(212) 832-1550   (800) 492-9877**

Business Profile: National manufacturer and distributor of specialty home improvement products.
Plan Specifics:
- Partial dividend reinvestment is not available.
- No Discount.
- OCP: $10 to $2000 per month.
- Selling costs include a handling charge of $1.50, brokerage commissions, and any other costs of sale.
- Safekeeping services are available.
- Company purchases stock monthly with OCPs.
- Dividends are paid March, June, September, and December.

Performance Rating: ***
DRIP Rating: 👍

**PMC Capital, Inc. (ASE:PMC)
Presidential Circle
4000 Hollywood Blvd.,
  Suite 435-5
Hollywood, FL 33021
(305) 966-8868   (800) 937-5449**

Business Profile: Registered closed-end investment company.
Plan Specifics:
- Partial dividend reinvestment is available.
- 2 percent discount on reinvested dividends and OCPs.
- OCP: $50 to $10,000 per month.
- Selling costs are brokerage commissions and any transfer tax.
- Company purchases stock monthly with OCPs.
- Dividends are paid January, April, July, and October.

Performance Rating: ***
DRIP Rating: 👍

**PMC Commercial Trust
  (ASE:PCC)
17290 Preston Rd., 3rd Fl.
Dallas, TX 75252
(214) 380-0044   (800) 937-5449**

Business Profile: Company originates small business loans secured by first liens on real estate.
Plan Specifics:
- Partial dividend reinvestment is available.
- 2 percent discount on reinvested dividends and OCPs.
- OCP: $50 to $10,000 per month.
- Selling costs are brokerage commissions and any transfer tax.
- Company purchases stock monthly with OCPs.
- Dividends are paid January, April, July, and October.

Performance Rating: **
DRIP Rating: 👍

PNC Bank Corp. (NYSE:PNC)
One PNC Plaza
Fifth Ave. and Wood St.
Pittsburgh, PA 15265
(800) 843-2206

Business Profile: Multibank holding company serving Pennsylvania, Indiana, Kentucky, Ohio, New Jersey, and Delaware.

Plan Specifics:

- Partial dividend reinvestment is available.
- No Discount.
- OCP: $50 to $5000 per month.
- Selling costs are brokerage commissions and $15 handling fee.
- Company purchases stock monthly with OCPs.
- Automatic investment services are available.
- Preferred dividends are eligible for reinvestment for additional common shares under the plan.
- Dividends are paid January, April, July, and October.

Performance Rating: ***

DRIP Rating: 👍

Polaroid Corp. (NYSE:PRD)
549 Technology Square
Cambridge, MA 02139
(617) 386-2000   (800) 730-4001

Business Profile: Leading manufacturer of instant cameras, photographic equipment, and film.

Plan Specifics:

- Partial dividend reinvestment is not available.
- No Discount.
- OCP: $10 to $3000 per quarter.
- Stock is purchased every quarter with OCPs.

- Purchasing fees include 5 percent of reinvested dividends and optional cash payments ($2.50 maximum).
- Selling costs are brokerage commissions and a service charge ($5 maximum).
- Dividends are paid March, June, September, and December.

Performance Rating: ***

DRIP Rating: 👍

Portland General Corp.
(NYSE:PGN)
c/o First Chicago Trust-NY
PO Box 2533
Jersey City, NJ 07303-2533
(800) 446-2617   (503) 464-8599

Business Profile: Electric utility holding company serving residential, commercial, and industrial customers in Oregon.

Plan Specifics:

- Initial purchases may be made directly from the company ($250 minimum).
- Partial dividend reinvestment is available.
- No Discount.
- OCP: $25 to $75,000 per year.
- Selling and buying costs are brokerage commissions.
- Company purchases stock weekly with OCPs.
- IRA option is available.
- Automatic investment services are available.
- Dividends are paid January, April, July, and October.

Performance Rating: ***

DRIP Rating: 👍

Portsmouth Bank Shares, Inc.
  (NASDAQ:POBS)
333 State St.
Portsmouth, NH 03801
(603) 436-6630

Business Profile: New Hampshire-based bank holding company.

Plan Specifics:

- Partial dividend reinvestment is not available.
- No Discount.
- OCP: not available.
- Purchasing costs are low brokerage fees.
- Selling costs are brokerage commission and handling fee of 5 percent of amount invested (maximum of $5).
- Dividends are paid March, June, September, and December.

Performance Rating: NR
DRIP Rating: 👎

Potlatch Corp. (NYSE:PCH)
PO Box 193591
San Francisco, CA 94119-3591
(415) 576-8803   (415) 576-8800

Business Profile: Manufactures lumber, plywood, paper, paperboard, and pulp products.

Plan Specifics:

- Partial dividend reinvestment is not available.
- No Discount.
- OCP: $25 to $1000 per month.
- Selling costs are brokerage commissions.
- Company purchases stock monthly with OCPs.
- Dividends are paid March, June, September, and December.

Performance Rating: ***
DRIP Rating: 👍

Potomac Electric Power Co.
  (NYSE:POM)
Shareholder Service Dept.
PO Box 1936
Washington, DC 20013
(800) 527-3726

Business Profile: Provides electric service in Washington, D.C. and Maryland.

Plan Specifics:

- Partial dividend reinvestment is available.
- No Discount.
- OCP: $25 to $5000 per month.
- Stock is purchased monthly with OCPs.
- Selling costs are $5 service fee and brokerage fees.
- Dividends are paid March, June, September, and December.

Performance Rating: ***
DRIP Rating: 👍

PP&L Resources, Inc. (NYSE:PPL)
Two N. Ninth St.
Allentown, PA 18101-1179
(800) 345-3085

Business Profile: Provides customers in east-central Pennsylvania with electric power.

Plan Specifics:

- Partial dividend reinvestment is available.
- No Discount.
- OCP: up to $80,000 per year.
- Selling costs are 10 cents per share brokerage fees.
- Company purchases stock once a month with OCPs.
- Preferred dividends are eligible for reinvestment for additional common shares under the plan.

- Approximately 60,000 share-holders are in the plan.
- Dividends are paid January, April, July, and October.

Performance Rating: **

DRIP Rating: 👍

PPG Industries, Inc. (NYSE:PPG)
One PPG Pl.
Pittsburgh, PA 15272
(412) 434-2120   (412) 434-3131

Business Profile: Produces glass, protective and decorative coatings for automotive and industrial markets, and specialty chemicals.

Plan Specifics:

- Partial dividend reinvestment is not available.
- No Discount.
- OCP: $10 to $3000 per quarter.
- Selling costs are brokerage commissions, any other costs, and administrative charge of $1.
- Company purchases stock monthly with OCPs.
- Dividends are paid March, June, September, and December.

Performance Rating: ****

DRIP Rating: 👍

Praxair, Inc. (NYSE:PX)
39 Old Ridgebury Rd.
Danbury, CT 06810-5113
(203) 837-2000   (800) 524-4458

Business Profile: Largest supplier of industrial gases in North and South America and one of the three largest in the world. The company also is a leading world-wide supplier of metallic and ceramic coatings and powders.

Plan Specifics:

- Partial dividend reinvestment is available.
- No Discount.
- OCP: $50 to $24,000 per year.
- Company purchases stock monthly with OCPs.
- Selling costs are brokerage commissions, $5 handling fee, and any transfer tax.
- Automatic investment services are available.
- Dividends are paid March, June, September, and December.

Performance Rating: ***

DRIP Rating: 👍

Premier Industrial Corp.
** (NYSE:PRE)**
4500 Euclid Ave.
Cleveland, OH 44103-3780
(216) 391-8300

Business Profile: Distributes electronic and electrical products used in the production and maintenance of equipment.

Plan Specifics:

- Partial dividend reinvestment is not available.
- No Discount.
- OCP: $10 to $5000 per quarter.
- Bank charges an administration fee ($3 maximum per transaction).
- Buying and selling costs include brokerage fees.
- Stock is purchased monthly with OCPs.
- Dividends are paid January, April, July, and October.

Performance Rating: ****

DRIP Rating: 👍

Presidential Realty Corp.
(ASE:PDL.B)
c/o American Stock Transfer
99 Wall St.
New York, NY 10005
(212) 936-5100   (914) 948-1300

Business Profile: Real estate investment trust.

Plan Specifics:

- Partial dividend reinvestment is available.
- 5 percent discount on reinvested dividends.
- OCP: $100 to $10,000 per quarter.
- Stock is purchased monthly with OCPs.
- Selling costs are brokerage commission and any transfer taxes.
- Dividends are paid March, June, September, and December.

Performance Rating: **

DRIP Rating: 👍

Prime Bancorp, Inc.
(NASDAQ:PSAB)
6425 Rising Sun Ave.
Philadelphia, PA 19111
(215) 742-5300

Business Profile: Company owns Prime Savings Bank, which has operations in the Philadelphia metropolitan area.

Plan Specifics:

- Partial dividend reinvestment is available.
- No Discount.
- OCP: $50 to $5000 per quarter.
- Selling costs are brokerage commissions.
- Company purchases stock quarterly with OCPs.

- Dividends are paid February, May, August, and November.

Performance Rating: NR

DRIP Rating: 👍

Procter & Gamble Co. (NYSE:PG)
PO Box 5572
Cincinnati, OH 45201-5572
(800) 742-6253

Business Profile: Markets household items, personal-care products, and consumer foods.

Plan Specifics:

- Initial purchases may be made directly from company (minimum $100).
- Partial dividend reinvestment is available.
- No Discount.
- OCP: $100 to $120,000 per year.
- OCP is invested twice a month.
- Purchasing and selling fees are $1 plus nominal brokerage fees. The firm also charges up to $1 per reinvested dividend.
- Automatic investment services are available.
- Dividends are paid February, May, August, and November.

Performance Rating: *****

DRIP Rating: 👍

Providence Energy Corp.
(ASE:PVY)
100 Weybosset St.
Providence, RI 02903
(401) 272-9191   (800) 426-5523

Business Profile: Rhode Island natural gas holding company.

Plan Specifics:

- Partial dividend reinvestment is available.

- No Discount.
- OCP: $25 to $5000 per quarter.
- Selling costs are brokerage commissions and a $3 termination fee.
- Company purchases stock around the 15th of the month with OCPs.
- Dividends are paid February, May, August, and November.

Performance Rating: **

DRIP Rating: 👍

Provident Bankshares Corp. (NASDAQ:PBKS)
114 E. Lexington St.
Baltimore, MD 21202
(410) 281-7000

Business Profile: Bank holding company.

Plan Specifics:
- Partial dividend reinvestment is not available.
- No Discount.
- OCP: $100 to $10,000 per quarter.
- Stock is purchased monthly with OCPs.
- Must go through own broker to sell shares from the plan.
- Dividends are paid February, May, August, and November.

Performance Rating: NR

DRIP Rating: 👍

Providian Corp. (NYSE:PVN)
PO Box 32830
Louisville, KY 40232
(502) 560-2000

Business Profile: Life insurance holding company. Writes accident, health, annuity, life, and property-casualty insurance.

Plan Specifics:
- Partial dividend reinvestment is available.
- No Discount.
- OCP: $10 to $60,000 per year.
- Company purchases stock monthly with OCPs.
- Selling costs are brokerage fees plus a service fee.
- Automatic investment services are available.
- Dividends are paid March, June, September, and December.

Performance Rating: ***

DRIP Rating: 👍

Public Service Co. of Colorado (NYSE:PSR)
Ste. 600, PO Box 840
Denver, CO 80201-0840
(303) 294-2566   (201) 324-0498

Business Profile: Provides electricity and natural gas service to Colorado regions.

Plan Specifics:
- Partial dividend reinvestment is available.
- No Discount.
- OCP: $25 to $100,000 per year.
- Participants may incur small brokerage fees if company purchases stock in open market.
- Selling costs are a $10 processing fee plus 12 cents per share brokerage commissions.
- Company purchases stock monthly with OCPs.
- Approximately 33,000 shareholders are in the plan.
- Dividends are paid February, May, August, and November.

Performance Rating: **

DRIP Rating: 👍

Public Service Co. of North Carolina (NYSE:PGS)
Shareholder Service
PO Box 1398
Gastonia, NC 28053-1398
(704) 834-6448   (800) 784-6443

Business Profile: Provides natural gas to clients in 26 counties in North Carolina.

Plan Specifics:

- Partial dividend reinvestment is available.
- 5 percent discount on reinvested dividends.
- OCP: $25 to $6000 per quarter.
- Company purchases stock around 1st of the month with OCPs.
- Selling fees are nominal.
- Automatic investment services are available.
- Dividends are paid January, April, July, and October.

Performance Rating: ***

DRIP Rating: 👍

Public Service Enterprise Group, Inc. (NYSE:PEG)
PO Box 1171
Newark, NJ 07101-1171
(800) 242-0813

Business Profile: New Jersey-based public utility holding company.

Plan Specifics:

- Partial dividend reinvestment is available.
- No Discount.
- OCP: $25 to $100,000 per year.
- Selling costs are brokerage fees.
- Company purchases stock monthly with OCPs.
- Dividends are paid March, June, September, and December.

Performance Rating: **

DRIP Rating: 👍

Puget Sound Power & Light Co. (NYSE:PSD)
PO Box 96010
Bellevue, WA 98009-9610
(206) 462-3719   (800) 997-8438

Business Profile: Provides electric service to nearly 1.8 million people in the state of Washington.

Plan Specifics:

- Partial dividend reinvestment is not available.
- No Discount.
- OCP: $25 to $100,000 per year.
- Purchasing and selling fees are brokerage commission of 5 cents per share.
- Company purchases stock twice a month with OCPs.
- Preferred dividends may be reinvested for additional common shares.
- Residents of the state of Washington may make initial purchase of stock directly through the company ($25 minimum).
- Dividends are paid February, May, August, and November.

Performance Rating: **

DRIP Rating: 👍

Quaker Oats Co. (NYSE:OAT)
c/o Harris Trust & Savings
PO Box 95894
Chicago, IL 60690-9938
(800) 344-1198

Business Profile: Important producer of cereals, beverages, flavored rice and pasta products, pancake mixes, and frozen breakfast items.

Plan Specifics:

- Partial dividend reinvestment is available.
- No Discount.
- OCP: $10 to $30,000 per year.
- Selling costs are brokerage commissions and service charges.
- Company purchases stock every month with OCPs.
- Approximately 25,000 shareholders are in the plan.
- Dividends are paid January, April, July, and October.

Performance Rating: ****

DRIP Rating: 👍

Quaker State Corp. (NYSE:KSF)
PO Box 989
255 Elm St.
Oil City, PA 16301
(814) 676-7676   (800) 526-0801

Business Profile: Produces and markets motor oil and provides vehicle maintenance services.

Plan Specifics:

- Partial dividend reinvestment is not available.
- No Discount.
- OCP: $10 to $3000 per quarter.
- Selling costs are brokerage commissions.
- Company purchases stock at least quarterly with OCPs.
- Dividends are paid March, June, September, and December.

Performance Rating: ***

DRIP Rating: 👍

Quanex Corp. (NYSE:NX)
1900 W. Loop S., Ste. 1500
Houston, TX 77027
(800) 231-8176

Business Profile: Manufactures carbon and alloy steel bars, steel tubing, and aluminum building materials.

Plan Specifics:

- Partial dividend reinvestment is available.
- No Discount.
- OCP: $50 to $10,000 per quarter.
- Selling costs are a $15 service fee and brokerage commissions.
- Company purchases stock the 1st business day of the month with OCPs.
- Approximately 3000 shareholders are in the plan.
- Dividends are paid March, June, September, and December.

Performance Rating: **

DRIP Rating: 👍

Questar Corp. (NYSE:STR)
PO Box 45433
Salt Lake City, UT 84145-0433
(801) 534-5885   (801) 534-5804

Business Profile: Energy-based holding company engaged in retail distribution, interstate transmission, exploration, and storage of natural gas. The firm is also involved in microwave communications and commercial real estate.

Plan Specifics:

- Partial dividend reinvestment is available.
- No Discount.
- OCP: $50 to $15,000 per quarter.
- Participants may incur brokerage fees if company purchases stock in the open market.
- Company purchases stock each month with OCPs.

- Approximately 5100 shareholders are in the plan.
- Dividends are paid March, June, September, and December.

Performance Rating: ****

DRIP Rating: 👍

Ralston-Ralston Purina Group (NYSE:RAL)
Attn: Investors Relations
Checkerboard Square
St. Louis, MO 63164
(314) 982-3002

Business Profile: Produces pet food and batteries.

Plan Specifics:
- Partial dividend reinvestment is available.
- No Discount.
- OCP: $10 to $25,000 per year.
- Stock is purchased monthly with OCPs.
- Selling costs include brokerage fees.
- Dividends are paid March, June, September, and December.

Performance Rating: ****

DRIP Rating: 👍

Raymond Corp.
(NASDAQ:RAYM)
Corporate Headquarters
Greene, NY 13778
(607) 656-2311

Business Profile: Manufactures materials for the handling of equipment for the transportation and storage of materials.

Plan Specifics:
- Partial dividend reinvestment is not available.
- No Discount.
- OCP: $10 to $3000 per month.

- Company purchases stock monthly with OCPs.
- Selling costs are brokerage commissions.
- The company currently does not pay a cash dividend.

Performance Rating: ***

DRIP Rating: 👍

Raytheon Co. (NYSE:RTN)
141 Spring St.
Lexington, MA 02173
(617) 862-6600   (617) 575-2900
(800) 360-4519

Business Profile: Has operations in defense electronics, commercial aircraft, appliances, and engineering.

Plan Specifics:
- Partial dividend reinvestment is not available.
- No Discount.
- OCP: $10 to $5000 per quarter.
- Purchasing and selling fees are service charge of 5 percent (maximum of $2.50) plus brokerage commissions.
- Stock is purchased approximately 8 times a year with OCPs.
- Dividends are paid January, April, July, and October.

Performance Rating: *****

DRIP Rating: 👍

Real Estate Investment Trust of CA (NYSE:RCT)
12011 San Vicente Blvd., Suite 700
Los Angeles, CA 90049
(310) 476-7793

Business Profile: Real estate investment trust.

Plan Specifics:
- Partial dividend reinvestment is available.
- No Discount.
- OCP: $500 to $25,000 per quarter.
- OCP is invested quarterly.
- Must go through own broker to sell shares.
- Dividends are paid January, April, July, and October.

Performance Rating: **

DRIP Rating: ℘

Regions Financial Corp.
(NASDAQ:RGBK)
PO Box 5260
Montgomery, AL 36102-1448
(334) 832-8450   (800) 638-6431
(800) 251-7589

Business Profile: Multibank holding company serving primarily Alabama and northwestern Florida.

Plan Specifics:
- Initial investments in the company may be made directly through the plan (minimum $500).
- Partial dividend reinvestment is not available.
- No Discount.
- OCP: $100 to $10,000 per month.
- Company purchases stock monthly with OCPs.
- Selling costs include brokerage commissions. In addition, a $50 charge will be assessed if account is closed within six months of its opening.
- Automatic investment services are available.

- Approximately 10,000 shareholders are in the plan.
- Dividends are paid January, April, July, and October.

Performance Rating: *****

DRIP Rating: ♨

ReliaStar Financial Corp.
(NYSE: RLR)
20 Washington Ave., S.
Minneapolis, MN 55401
(612) 450-4064   (800) 468-9716

Business Profile: Holding company whose subsidiaries specialize in life insurance and related financial services.

Plan Specifics:
- Need 50 shares to enroll.
- Partial dividend reinvestment is not available.
- 4 percent discount on reinvested dividends; 1 percent discount on OCPs.
- OCP: $50 to $5000 per month.
- Selling costs are brokerage commissions, service charges, and transfer taxes.
- Company purchases stock monthly with OCPs.
- Dividends are paid February, May, August, and November.

Performance Rating: ***

DRIP Rating: ℘

Reynolds & Reynolds Co.
(NYSE:REY)
PO Box 2608
Dayton, OH 45401
(513) 443-2000

Business Profile: Supplies automotive, business, and medical markets with business forms and computer systems.

Plan Specifics:
- Partial dividend reinvestment is not available.
- No Discount.
- OCP: $100 to $1000 per quarter.
- Selling costs are $1 bank service charge and brokerage fees.
- Company purchases stock quarterly with OCPs.
- Approximately 510 shareholders are in the plan.
- Dividends are paid January, April, June, and September.

Performance Rating: ***

DRIP Rating: ☞

Reynolds Metals Co.
(NYSE:RLM)
PO Box 27003
Richmond, VA 23261-7003
(804) 281-2812   (804) 281-2000

Business Profile: Supplies aluminum cans, aluminum foil, and other food wraps, building materials, and metal for automotive use.

Plan Specifics:
- Partial dividend reinvestment is not available.
- No Discount.
- OCP: $25 to $3000 per quarter.
- Selling costs are brokerage commission and a $5 service charge.
- Company purchases stock monthly with OCPs.
- Approximately 2500 shareholders are in the plan.
- Dividends are paid January, April, July, and October.

Performance Rating: ***

DRIP Rating: ☜

Rhone-Poulenc Rorer, Inc.
(NYSE:RPR)
500 Arcola Rd.
Collegeville, PA 19426-0107
(800) 524-4458

Business Profile: Develops, manufactures, and sells pharmaceuticals.

Plan Specifics:
- Partial dividend reinvestment is available.
- No Discount.
- OCP: $25 to $3000 per quarter.
- Selling costs are brokerage commissions.
- Company purchases stock quarterly with OCPs.
- Dividends are paid February, May, August, and November.

Performance Rating: ****

DRIP Rating: ☜

Rite Aid Corp. (NYSE:RAD)
c/o Harris Trust
PO Box A3309
Chicago, IL 60690
(312) 461-7369   (717) 761-2633

Business Profile: Operates chain of retail drugstores.

Plan Specifics:
- Partial dividend reinvestment is available.
- No Discount.
- OCP: $25 to $25,000 per year.
- Selling costs are brokerage commissions and other related expenses of sale.
- Company purchases stock monthly with OCPs.
- Dividends are paid February, May, July, and October.

Performance Rating: ****

DRIP Rating: ☜

RLI Corp. (NYSE:RLI)
9025 N. Lindbergh Dr.
Peoria, IL 61615
(309) 692-1000   (800) 468-9716

Business Profile: Holding company providing specialty property and casualty insurance and contact lens insurance. Also offers extended service programs, a computerized office automation system for eye care practitioners, and distributes contact lenses.

Plan Specifics:

- Partial dividend reinvestment is not available.
- No Discount.
- OCP: $25 to $2000 per month.
- Company purchases stock monthly with OCPs.
- Selling costs include brokerage commissions and service charges.
- Safekeeping services are available.
- Dividends are paid January, April, July, and October.

Performance Rating: ***

DRIP Rating: 👍

Roadway Services, Inc.
(NASDAQ:ROAD)
1077 Gorge Blvd.
PO Box 88
Akron, OH 44309
(216) 384-8184

Business Profile: Transportation holding company offering long-haul, regional, small package, and express services.

Plan Specifics:

- Partial dividend reinvestment is not available.
- No Discount.

- OCP: $10 to $3000 per month.
- Purchasing fees are brokerage commissions.
- Selling costs include $5 service charge and brokerage commissions.
- Company purchases stock monthly with OCPs.
- Dividends are paid February, May, August, and November.

Performance Rating: ****

DRIP Rating: 👍

Roanoke Electric Steel Corp.
(NASDAQ:RESC)
c/o Wachovia Bank of North
Carolina, N.A.
PO Box 3001
Winston-Salem, NC 27102
(800) 633-4236

Business Profile: Producer of merchant steel products.

Plan Specifics:

- Partial dividend reinvestment is not available.
- No Discount.
- OCP: not available.
- There are no costs for selling shares from the plan.
- Dividends are paid February, May, August, and November.

Performance Rating: ***

DRIP Rating: 👎

Roanoke Gas Company
(NASDAQ:RGCO)
519 Kimball Ave., NE
Roanoke, VA 24016
(703) 983-3800   (800) 829-8432

Business Profile: Sells and distributes natural gas in Virginia and West Virginia.

Plan Specifics:
- Partial dividend reinvestment is not available.
- No Discount.
- OCP: $25 to $20,000 per year.
- Must go through a broker to sell shares from the plan.
- Company purchases stock monthly with OCPs.
- Dividends are paid February, May, August, and November.

Performance Rating: NR

DRIP Rating: 👍

Rochester Gas & Electric Corp. (NYSE:RGS)
c/o Bank of Boston
Shareholder Services Division
Mail Stop 45-02-09
PO Box 644
Boston, MA 02102-0644
(800) 736-3001

Business Profile: Supplies electric and gas service to the city of Rochester, New York and an adjacent nine-county area.

Plan Specifics:
- 10 shares needed to enroll in plan.
- Partial dividend reinvestment is available.
- No Discount.
- OCP: $50 to $5000 per month.
- Selling costs are approximately 7 cents per share brokerage fee and a maximum $5 service charge.
- Company purchases stock monthly with OCPs.
- Approximately 16,000 shareholders are in the plan.
- Dividends are paid January, April, July, and October.

Performance Rating: **

DRIP Rating: 👍

Rockwell International Corp. (NYSE:ROK)
625 Liberty Ave.
Pittsburgh, PA 15222-3123
(412) 565-7120   (412) 236-8000

Business Profile: Operations in space systems, defense systems, military equipment, and automotive components.

Plan Specifics:
- Partial dividend reinvestment is not available.
- No Discount.
- OCP: $10 to $1000 per month.
- Stock is purchased 8 times per year with OCPs.
- Dividends are paid March, June, September, and December.

Performance Rating: ****

DRIP Rating: 👍

Rollins Environmental Services, Inc. (NYSE:REN)
c/o Registrar & Transfer Co.
10 Commerce Dr.
PO Box 1010
Cranford, NJ 07016
(800) 368-5948

Business Profile: Hazardous waste management company.

Plan Specifics:
- Partial dividend reinvestment is not available.
- No Discount.
- OCP: $25 to $2500 per month.
- 5 percent service fee (maximum $5) for OCPs.
- Selling costs are a 5 percent service fee (maximum $5) and a termination fee of $2.50.

- Company purchases stock monthly with OCPs.
- The company is not currently paying a dividend.

Performance Rating: **

DRIP Rating: 👍

Rollins, Inc. (NYSE:ROL)
2170 Piedmont Rd. NE
Atlanta, GA 30324
(404) 888-2000

Business Profile: Operations in pest control, protective services, and lawn care.

Plan Specifics:
- Must have a minimum of 50 shares to enroll in the plan.
- Partial dividend reinvestment is not available.
- No Discount.
- OCP: not available.
- Selling costs are brokerage commission.
- Dividends are paid March, June, September, and December.

Performance Rating: *****

DRIP Rating: 👍

Rollins Truck Leasing Corp.
(NYSE:RLC)
c/o Registrar and Transfer
Company
10 Commerce Dr.
PO Box 1010
Cranford, NJ 07016
(800) 525-7686   (302) 426-2700

Business Profile: A major provider of truck leasing and rental services.

Plan Specifics:
- Partial dividend reinvestment is not available.

- No Discount.
- OCP: $25 to $2500 per month.
- 5 percent service fee (maximum $5) for OCP.
- Selling costs are a 5 percent service fee (maximum $5) and a $2.50 fee for termination.
- Company purchases stock monthly with OCPs.
- Dividends are paid March, June, September, and December.

Performance Rating: ****

DRIP Rating: 👍

Roosevelt Financial Group, Inc.
(NASDAQ:RFED)
900 Roosevelt Parkway
Chesterfield, MO 63017
(800) 323-1849

Business Profile: Bank holding company operating in the St. Louis metropolitan area.

Plan Specifics:
- Partial dividend reinvestment is not available.
- No Discount.
- OCP: $25 to $1000 per quarter.
- Selling costs are brokerage commissions and other expenses.
- Company purchases stock quarterly with OCPs.
- Dividends are paid February, May, August, and November.

Performance Rating: NR

DRIP Rating: 👍

Rouse Co. (NASDAQ:ROUS)
10275 Little Patuxent Parkway
Columbia, MD 21044-3456
(410) 992-6000

Business Profile: Engages in possession, development, and management of income-producing real estate.

Plan Specifics:

- Partial dividend reinvestment is not available.
- No Discount.
- OCP: minimum of $50 per quarter.
- Purchasing fees are any applicable brokerage commissions.
- May have to go through own broker to sell shares.
- Company purchases stock quarterly with OCPs.
- Approximately 587 shareholders are in the plan.
- Dividends are paid March, June, September, and December.

Performance Rating: ***

DRIP Rating: 👍

RPM, Inc. (NASDAQ:RPOW)
PO Box 777
Medina, OH 44258
(216) 273-5090   (800) 542-7792

Business Profile: Manufactures protective coatings for waterproofing and rustproofing, wallcoverings, and fabrics for industrial and hobby markets.

Plan Specifics:

- Partial dividend reinvestment is not available.
- No Discount.
- OCP: $25 to $5000 per month.
- Company purchases stock around the 10th and last business days of each month with OCPs.
- There are no selling fees.
- Approximately 27,000 shareholders are in the plan.

- Dividends are paid January, April, July, and October.

Performance Rating: *****

DRIP Rating: 👍

Rubbermaid, Inc. (NYSE:RBD)
1147 Akron Rd.
Wooster, OH 44691-0800
(216) 264-6464   (800) 736-3001

Business Profile: Manufactures rubber and plastic houseware products, children's toys, and institutional products.

Plan Specifics:

- Need 10 shares to enroll.
- Partial dividend reinvestment is not available.
- No Discount.
- OCP: $50 to $5000 per month.
- Service fee of $2 for each OCP.
- Selling costs include brokerage fees, 5 percent termination fee ($1 minimum, $10 maximum).
- Stock is purchased monthly with OCPs.
- Safekeeping services are available.
- Dividends are paid March, June, September, and December.

Performance Rating: *****

DRIP Rating: 👍

Russell Corp. (NYSE:RML)
PO Box 272
Alexander City, AL 35010
(205) 329-4832

Business Profile: Manufactures and sells leisure apparel, athletic uniforms, knit shirts, and woven fabrics.

Plan Specifics:

- Partial dividend reinvestment is not available.

- No Discount.
- OCP: $10 to $2000 per month.
- Selling costs include brokerage commissions and any applicable taxes.
- Company purchases stock monthly with OCPs.
- Dividends are paid February, May, August, and November.

Performance Rating: ****

DRIP Rating: 👍

Ryder System, Inc. (NYSE:R)
3600 NW 82nd Ave.
Miami, FL 33166
(305) 593-3726

Business Profile: Provides truck leasing, truck rental, automobile hauling, and school bus transportation services.

Plan Specifics:

- Partial dividend reinvestment is available.
- No Discount.
- OCP: $25 to $60,000 per year.
- Selling costs are minimal brokerage commissions and a service charge.
- Company purchases stock monthly with OCPs.
- Dividends are paid March, June, September, and December.

Performance Rating: ***

DRIP Rating: 👍

Rykoff-Sexton, Inc. (NYSE:RYK)
761 Terminal St.
Los Angeles, CA 90021
(213) 622-4131

Business Profile: Manufacturer and distributor of foods and related nonfood products and services for the food service industry.

Plan Specifics:

- Partial dividend reinvestment is not available.
- No Discount.
- OCP: $50 to $500 per quarter.
- Selling costs are brokerage commissions and a $1 service charge for termination.
- Company purchases stock monthly with OCPs.
- Dividends are paid in February and July.

Performance Rating: ***

DRIP Rating: 👍

RYMAC Mortgage Investment Corp. (ASE:RM)
c/o Amer. Stock Transfer & Trust
40 Wall St.
New York, NY 10005
(800) 666-6960   (800) 937-5449

Business Profile: Real estate investment trust which maintains a portfolio of residential mortgage-backed securities.

Plan Specifics:

- Partial dividend reinvestment is available.
- No Discount.
- OCP: $50 to $1000 per quarter.
- Purchasing fees are service charges, brokerage commissions, and other charges.
- Selling costs are brokerage commissions, service charges, and other related expenses.
- Company purchases stock quarterly with OCPs.
- The company is not currently paying a dividend.

Performance Rating: *

DRIP Rating: 👍

Safety-Kleen Corp. (NYSE:SK)
c/o First Chicago Trust-NY
PO Box 2533
Jersey City, NJ 07303-2533
(800) 446-2617

Business Profile: World's largest
recycler of automotive and industrial hazardous and nonhazardous
fluids.

Plan Specifics:
- Partial dividend reinvestment is
  not available.
- No Discount.
- OCP: $25 to $5000 per month.
- Selling costs are brokerage
  commissions and other costs of
  sale.
- Company purchases stock
  monthly with OCPs.
- Stock can be sold via the tele-
  phone.
- Dividends are paid March, June,
  September, and December.

Performance Rating: ****
DRIP Rating: 👍

St. Joseph Light & Power Co.
(NYSE:SAJ)
520 Francis St.
St. Joseph, MO 64502
(816) 233-8888

Business Profile: Provides electric
power and natural gas to regions
of northwestern Missouri.

Plan Specifics:
- Partial dividend reinvestment is
  not available.
- No Discount.
- OCP: $100 to $7500 per quarter.
- Selling costs are brokerage
  commissions and any other
  expenses.

- Company purchases stock
  quarterly with OCPs.
- Dividends are paid February,
  May, August, and November.

Performance Rating: ****
DRIP Rating: 👍

St. Paul Bancorp, Inc.
 (NASDAQ:SPBC)
c/o Bank of Boston
PO Box 1681
Boston, MA 02105
(617) 575-2900   (312) 622-5000

Business Profile: Chicago savings
bank holding company.

Plan Specifics:
- Partial dividend reinvestment is
  not available.
- No Discount.
- OCP: $50 to $1500 per quarter.
- Selling costs are brokerage
  commissions, transfer tax, and 5
  percent administrative charges
  (max. $3).
- Company purchases stock
  quarterly, and more frequently if
  enough funds accumulate, with
  OCPs.
- Dividends are paid February,
  May, August, and November.

Performance Rating: ***
DRIP Rating: 👍

St. Paul Companies, Inc.
 (NYSE:SPC)
385 Washington St.
St. Paul, MN 55102
(612) 221-7911

Business Profile: Provider of property-liability insurance.

Plan Specifics:
- **Partial dividend reinvestment is**
  available.

- No Discount.
- OCP: $10 to $60,000 per year.
- Selling costs are brokerage fees.
- Company purchases stock monthly with OCPs.
- Approximately 2500 shareholders are in the plan.
- Dividends are paid January, April, July, and October.

Performance Rating: ****

DRIP Rating: 👍

Salomon, Inc. (NYSE:SB)
1 New York Plaza
New York, NY 10004
(800) 772-7865   (800) 446-2617

Business Profile: Investment banking and market making holding firm.

Plan Specifics:

- Partial dividend reinvestment is not available.
- No Discount.
- OCP: $10 to $3000 per quarter.
- Selling costs are brokerage commissions.
- Company purchases stock quarterly with OCPs.
- Dividends are paid January, April, July, and October.

Performance Rating: ***

DRIP Rating: 👍

San Diego Gas & Electric
Company (NYSE:SDO)
101 Ash St.
San Diego, CA 92101
(619) 696-2020   (800) 243-5454

Business Profile: Provides electric and gas services to customers in southern California.

Plan Specifics:

- Partial dividend reinvestment is available.
- No Discount.
- OCP: $25 to $25,000 per quarter.
- Selling costs are brokerage commissions, service charges, and a $2.50 handling fee.
- Company purchases stock monthly with OCPs.
- Customers may join the plan by making an initial investment directly ($25 minimum).
- Dividends are paid January, April, July, and October.

Performance Rating: ***

DRIP Rating: 👍

Santa Fe Pacific Pipeline
Partners, LP (NYSE:SFL)
888 S. Figueroa St.
Los Angeles, CA 90017
(213) 486-7766

Business Profile: Owns and operates petroleum pipelines serving six western states.

Plan Specifics:

- Partial dividend reinvestment is not available.
- No Discount.
- OCP: $100 to $1000 per month.
- OCP is invested monthly.
- Selling costs are brokerage fees and a $3 service charge.
- Dividends are paid February, May, August, and November.

Performance Rating: ***

DRIP Rating: 👍

Sara Lee Corp. (NYSE:SLE)
3 First National Plaza
Chicago, IL 60602-4260
(312) 558-8450

Business Profile: Produces packaged meats, bakery, and coffee products and has operations in food service and personal items.

Plan Specifics:

- Partial dividend reinvestment is not available.
- No Discount.
- OCP: $10 to $5000 per quarter.
- Selling costs are brokerage commissions, transfer taxes, and 5 percent service charge ($10 maximum).
- Stock is purchased approximately 8 times a year with OCPs.
- Dividends are paid January, April, July, and October.

Performance Rating: *****
DRIP Rating: 👍

Savannah Foods & Industries, Inc. (NYSE:SFI)
PO Box 339
Savannah, GA 31402-0339
(912) 234-1261

Business Profile: Refines and markets beet and cane sugar.

Plan Specifics:

- Partial dividend reinvestment is not available.
- No Discount.
- OCP: $10 to $3000 per month.
- Selling costs are brokerage commissions.
- Company purchases stock monthly with OCPs.
- Dividends are paid April, July, October, and December.

Performance Rating: **
DRIP Rating: 👍

SBC Communications, Inc. (NYSE:SBC)
c/o The Bank of New York
PO Box 11272, Church St. Stat.
New York, NY 10277-0123
(800) 351-7221

Business Profile: Telecommunications holding company providing local exchange service in Arkansas, Kansas, Missouri, Oklahoma, and Texas, and other domestic and international communication services.

Plan Specifics:

- Partial dividend reinvestment is available.
- No Discount.
- OCP: $50 to $100,000 per year.
- Company purchases stock weekly with OCPs.
- Selling costs are approximately 8 cents per share and any transfer tax.
- $5 termination fee.
- IRA option is available.
- Automatic investment services are available.
- Dividends are paid February, May, August, and November.

Performance Rating: *****
DRIP Rating: 👍

SCANA Corp. (NYSE:SCG)
Shareholder Services 054
Columbia, SC 29218
(803) 733-6817   (800) 763-5891

Business Profile: Public utility holding company supplying electric power and gas service to South Carolina residents.

Plan Specifics:
- Initial purchases may be made directly ($250 minimum).
- Partial dividend reinvestment is available.
- No Discount.
- OCP: $25 to $100,000 per year.
- Company purchases stock twice monthly with OCPs.
- Selling costs are brokerage commissions and any transfer tax.
- Approximately 24,800 shareholders are in the plan.
- Dividends are paid January, April, July, and October.

Performance Rating: ****

DRIP Rating: 👍

SCEcorp (NYSE:SCE)
PO Box 400-Secretary's Dept.
Rosemead, CA 91770
(800) 347-8625

Business Profile: Electric utility holding company.

Plan Specifics:
- Partial dividend reinvestment is available.
- No Discount.
- OCP: up to $10,000 per month.
- Must go through own broker to sell shares.
- Company purchases stock monthly with OCPs.
- Dividends are paid January, April, July, and October.

Performance Rating: ****

DRIP Rating: 👍

Schering-Plough Corp.
(NYSE:SGP)
1 Giralda Farms
Madison, NJ 07940-1000
(201) 822-7000

Business Profile: Major supplier of pharmaceuticals and consumer products.

Plan Specifics:
- Partial dividend reinvestment is available.
- No Discount.
- OCP: $25 to $36,000 per year.
- Selling costs are a fee of $2.50 for termination and brokerage fees.
- Company purchases stock around the 10th and the 25th of each month with OCPs.
- Dividends are paid February, May, August, and November.

Performance Rating: *****

DRIP Rating: 👍

Schwab (Charles) Corp.
(NYSE:SCH)
c/o Harris Trust Company
PO Box A3309
Chicago, IL 60690-3309
(312) 461-2288

Business Profile: Nation's largest discount brokerage firm serving over two million active customer accounts.

Plan Specifics:
- Partial dividend reinvestment is available.
- No Discount.
- OCP: $25 to $5000 per month.
- Company purchases stock monthly with OCPs.
- Dividends are paid February, May, August, and November.

Performance Rating: ****
DRIP Rating: 👍

Scientific-Atlanta, Inc.
 (NYSE:SFA)
One Technology Parkway, S.
Atlanta, GA 30092-2967
(404) 903-4821   (800) 524-4458

Business Profile: Makes electronic communications products, including transmitting and receiving equipment, antennae and cable TV equipment.
Plan Specifics:
- Partial dividend reinvestment is not available.
- No Discount.
- OCP: $25 to $40,000 per year.
- Selling costs include brokerage fees.
- Company purchases stock monthly with OCPs.
- Dividends are paid March, June, September, and December.

Performance Rating: *****
DRIP Rating: 👍

Seafield Capital Corp.
 (NASDAQ:SFLD)
c/o First Chicago Trust-NY
PO Box 2533
Jersey City, NJ 07303-2533
(800) 446-2617

Business Profile: Insurance-based holding company.
Plan Specifics:
- Partial dividend reinvestment is available.
- No Discount.
- OCP: $25 to $5000 per quarter.
- Stock is purchased quarterly with OCPs.

- Purchasing fees are brokerage commissions.
- Selling costs are brokerage commissions and any other costs of sale.
- Dividends are paid March, June, September, and December.

Performance Rating: ***
DRIP Rating: 👍

Sears, Roebuck & Co. (NYSE:S)
c/o First Chicago Trust-NY
PO Box 2533
Jersey City, NJ 07303-2533
(312) 875-3000   (800) 732-7780

Business Profile: Manages general merchandise stores nationwide and engages in insurance and financial services operations.
Plan Specifics:
- Partial dividend reinvestment is not available.
- No Discount.
- OCP: $25 to $3000 per month.
- Stock is purchased monthly with OCPs.
- Purchasing fees are brokerage commissions and 5 percent of total amount invested ($2.50 maximum).
- Selling costs are a $5 charge and brokerage commissions.
- Dividends are paid January, April, July, and October.

Performance Rating: ***
DRIP Rating: 👍

Second Bancorp, Inc.
(NASDAQ:SECD)
108 Main St.
Warren, OH 44482
(216) 841-0123   (412) 236-8128

Business Profile: Ohio bank holding company.

Plan Specifics:
- Partial dividend reinvestment is not available.
- No Discount.
- OCP: $50 to $5000 per quarter.
- Selling costs are brokerage commissions.
- Company purchases stock monthly with OCPs.
- Dividends are paid January, April, July, and October.

Performance Rating: ****

DRIP Rating: 👍

Selective Insurance Group, Inc.
(NASDAQ:SIGI)
40 Wantage Ave.
Branchville, NJ 07890
(201) 948-3000

Business Profile: Insurance holding company offering property-casualty coverage.

Plan Specifics:
- Partial dividend reinvestment is available.
- No Discount.
- OCP: $100 to $1000 per quarter.
- Selling costs are brokerage commissions and other costs of sale.
- Company purchases stock quarterly with OCPs.
- Dividends are paid March, June, September, and December.

Performance Rating: ***

DRIP Rating: 👍

ServiceMaster Limited
Partnership (NYSE:SVM)
One ServiceMaster Way
Downers Grove, IL 60515-1700
(708) 964-1300   (800) 858-0840

Business Profile: Provider of housekeeping, maintenance, and management services to health-care facilities as well as to residential, commercial, educational, and industrial customers.

Plan Specifics:
- Partial dividend reinvestment is available.
- No Discount.
- OCP: $25 to $25,000 per year.
- Selling costs are brokerage commissions and other costs of sale.
- Company purchases stock monthly with OCPs.
- Dividends are paid January, April, July, and October.

Performance Rating: ****

DRIP Rating: 👍

Sherwin-Williams (The)
Company (NYSE:SHW)
101 Prospect Ave., NW
Cleveland, OH 44115-1075
(216) 566-2000   (800) 542-7792

Business Profile: Manufacturer and retailer of paints, varnishes, and associated products.

Plan Specifics:
- Partial dividend reinvestment is not available.
- No Discount.
- OCP: $10 to $2000 per month.
- No selling costs.
- Stock is purchased monthly with OCPs.

- Dividends are paid March, June, September, and December.

Performance Rating: *****

DRIP Rating: 👍

Shoreline Financial Corp. (NASDAQ: SLFC)
823 Riverview Dr.
Benton Harbor, MI 49022
(616) 927-2251

Business Profile: Bank holding company.

Plan Specifics:

- Partial dividend reinvestment is available.
- 5 percent discount on reinvested dividends.
- OCP: not available.
- Selling costs are brokerage commissions, service charges, and transfer taxes.
- Dividends are paid March, June, September, and December.

Performance Rating: NR

DRIP Rating: 👎

Sierra Pacific Resources (NYSE:SRP)
PO Box 30150
6100 Neil Rd.
Reno, NV 89520-3150
(800) 662-7575   (702) 689-3610

Business Profile: Public utility holding company supplying electric, gas, and water service to customers in portions of Nevada and California.

Plan Specifics:

- Partial dividend reinvestment is not available.
- No Discount.
- OCP: $25 to $5000 per quarter.

- Selling costs are brokerage commissions and any transfer tax.
- Company purchases stock quarterly with OCPs.
- 47 percent of the shareholders are in the plan.
- Dividends are paid February, May, August, and November.

Performance Rating: ***

DRIP Rating: 👍

SIFCO Industries, Inc. (ASE:SIF)
970 E. 64th St.
Cleveland, OH 44103-1694
(216) 881-8600   (216) 575-2532

Business Profile: Provides metal-working products and services to aerospace, shipbuilding, and defense industries.

Plan Specifics:

- Partial dividend reinvestment is not available.
- No Discount.
- OCP: $20 to $3000 per quarter.
- Selling costs are brokerage charges.
- Company purchases stock monthly with OCPs.
- The company is not currently paying a dividend.

Performance Rating: **

DRIP Rating: 👍

Signet Banking Corp. (NYSE:SBK)
c/o Mellon Bank, N.A.
PO Box 750
Pittsburgh, PA 15230
(800) 451-7392   (804) 747-2000

Business Profile: Multibank holding company serving Virginia, Maryland, and Washington, D.C. areas.

Plan Specifics:
- Partial dividend reinvestment is not available.
- 5 percent discount on reinvested dividends.
- OCP: $10 to $10,000 per month.
- Selling costs are brokerage commissions.
- Company purchases stock on the 1st and 15th of every month with OCPs.
- Dividends are paid February, May, August, and November.

Performance Rating: ***

DRIP Rating: 👍

Simpson Industries, Inc.
 (NASDAQ:SMPS)
32100 Telegraph Rd.
Birmingham, MI 48010
(810) 540-6200

Business Profile: Manufactures machined components and assemblies for vehicle original equipment makers.

Plan Specifics:
- Partial dividend reinvestment is not available.
- No Discount.
- OCP: $10 to $1000 per month.
- Selling costs include brokerage fees and a handling charge of $3.
- Stock is purchased monthly with OCPs.
- Dividends are paid March, June, September, and December.

Performance Rating: ***

DRIP Rating: 👍

Sizeler Property Investors, Inc.
 (NYSE:SIZ)
2542 Williams Blvd.
Kenner, LA 70062
(504) 466-5363

Business Profile: Self-administered equity real estate investment trust.

Plan Specifics:
- Partial dividend reinvestment is available.
- No Discount.
- OCP: $10 to $20,000 per quarter (in increments of $10).
- Purchasing fees are the lesser of $3 or 5 percent of the amount invested.
- Selling costs are a $5 termination fee.
- Company purchases stock monthly with OCPs.
- Dividends are paid March, June, September, and December.

Performance Rating: **

DRIP Rating: 👍

Smith (A.O.) Corp. (ASE:SMC)
11270 W. Park Pl.
Milwaukee, WI 53223-0972
(414) 359-4000   (414) 359-4060

Business Profile: Manufactures truck frames and components, electric motors, and fiberglass piping systems.

Plan Specifics:
- Partial dividend reinvestment is not available.
- No Discount.
- OCP: up to $5000 per quarter.
- Selling costs are handling charges and brokerage fees.
- Company purchases stock at least quarterly with OCPs.

- Dividends are paid February, May, August, and November.

Performance Rating: **

DRIP Rating: 👍

Smucker (J.M.) Co. (NYSE:SJM)
Strawberry Lane
Orrville, OH 44667-0280
(216) 682-3000

Business Profile: Producer of jellies, preserves, syrups, peanut butter, and fruit-related items.

Plan Specifics:

- Partial dividend reinvestment is available.
- No Discount.
- OCP: $20 to $1500 per month.
- Selling costs are brokerage charges.
- Company purchases stock around the first business day of the month with OCPs.
- Dividends are paid March, June, September, and December.

Performance Rating: ****

DRIP Rating: 👍

Snap-on, Inc. (NYSE:SNA)
2801 80th St.
Kenosha, WI 53141-1410
(414) 656-5200   (800) 524-0687

Business Profile: Largest manufacturer and distributor of hand tools, storage units, and diagnostic equipment for professional mechanics and industry.

Plan Specifics:

- Partial dividend reinvestment is available.
- No Discount.
- OCP: $100 to $5000 per quarter.
- Company purchases stock monthly with OCPs.

- Selling costs are brokerage commissions.
- Dividends are paid March, June, September, and December.

Performance Rating: ***

DRIP Rating: 👍

Sonat, Inc. (NYSE:SNT)
c/o Chemical Bank
PO Box 3069, JAF Bldg.
New York, NY 10116-3069
(800) 851-9677

Business Profile: Natural gas pipeline concern with operations in oil-field services.

Plan Specifics:

- Partial dividend reinvestment is not available.
- No Discount.
- OCP: $25 to $6000 per quarter.
- Selling costs include $15 handling charge and brokerage commissions.
- Stock is purchased monthly with OCPs.
- Dividends are paid March, June, September, and December.

Performance Rating: **

DRIP Rating: 👍

Sonoco Products Co. (NYSE:SON)
N. Second St.
Hartsville, SC 29550-0160
(803) 383-7277   (803) 383-7000

Business Profile: International supplier of industrial and consumer packaging items.

Plan Specifics:

- Partial dividend reinvestment is not available.
- No Discount.
- OCP: $10 to $500 per month.

- Selling and purchasing costs include brokerage fees of approximately 8 cents a share.
- Company purchases stock monthly with OCPs.
- Dividends are paid March, June, September, and December.

Performance Rating: ****

DRIP Rating: 👍

Sotheby's Holdings, Inc.
(NYSE:BID)
c/o Mellon Securities Trust
PO Box 750
Pittsburgh, PA 15230-0750
(800) 526-0801   (212) 606-7040

Business Profile: World's largest auctioneer of fine art, specializing in paintings, jewelry, decorative art, and other property.

Plan Specifics:

- Partial dividend reinvestment is available.
- No Discount.
- OCP: $100 to $5000 per month.
- Company purchases stock monthly with OCPs.
- Selling costs are brokerage commissions and a handling charge.
- Dividends are paid March, June, September, and December.

Performance Rating: **

DRIP Rating: 👍

South Jersey Industries, Inc.
(NYSE:SJI)
One S. Jersey Plaza, Route 54
Folsom, NJ 08037
(609) 561-9000

Business Profile: New Jersey gas utility holding company with operations in sand mining.

Plan Specifics:

- Partial dividend reinvestment is available.
- No Discount.
- OCP: $25 to $100,000 per year.
- Selling costs are approximately 7 cents per share brokerage commissions and a handling charge.
- Company purchases stock quarterly with OCPs.
- Dividends are paid March, June, September, and December/early January.

Performance Rating: ****

DRIP Rating: 👍

South West Property Trust, Inc.
(NYSE:SWP)
5949 Sherry Lane, Ste. 1400
Dallas, TX 75225
(214) 369-1995   (800) 527-7844

Business Profile: Real estate investment trust which manages real estate in the southwestern U.S.

Plan Specifics:

- Partial dividend reinvestment is available.
- 5 percent discount on reinvested dividends and OCPs.
- OCP: $500 to $5000 per quarter.
- OCP is invested quarterly.
- Selling fees are brokerage commissions.
- Dividends are paid January, April, July, and October.

Performance Rating: **

DRIP Rating: 👎

Southeastern Michigan Gas Enterprises (NASDAQ:SMGS)
405 Water St.
PO Box 5026
Port Huron, MI 48061-5026
(810) 987-2200   (800) 255-7647

Business Profile: Supplier of natural gas to parts of Michigan.

Plan Specifics:
- Partial dividend reinvestment is available.
- No Discount.
- OCP: $25 to $5000 per month.
- Company purchases stock monthly with OCPs.
- Must go through own broker to sell if 100 shares or more.
- Purchasing fees are 10 cents per share.
- Approximately 78 percent of the shareholders are in the plan.
- Dividends are paid February, May, August, and November.

Performance Rating: ***

DRIP Rating: 👍

Southern California Water Co. (NYSE:SCW)
630 E. Foothill Blvd.
San Dimas, CA 91773
(909) 394-3600

Business Profile: Provides water and, to a lesser extent, electric services in regions of northern and southern California.

Plan Specifics:
- Partial dividend reinvestment is available.
- No Discount.
- OCP: $50 to $12,000 per year.
- Company purchases stock quarterly with OCPs.
- Brokerage commissions and other fees are included in the weighted average purchase price.
- Must sell shares through own broker.
- Dividends are paid March, June, September, and December.

Performance Rating: ***

DRIP Rating: 👍

Southern Co. (NYSE:SO)
PO Box 88300
Atlanta, GA 30356
(800) 554-7626   (404) 668-2774

Business Profile: Electric utility holding company serving much of the Southeast.

Plan Specifics:
- Partial dividend reinvestment is available.
- No Discount.
- OCP: $25 to $6000 per quarter.
- Selling costs are approximately 6 cents per share.
- Company purchases stock quarterly with OCPs.
- Approximately 143,800 shareholders are in the plan.
- Dividends are paid March, June, September, and December.

Performance Rating: *****

DRIP Rating: 👍

Southern Indiana Gas & Electric Co. (NYSE:SIG)
20 NW 4th St.
Evansville, IN 47741-0001
(812) 464-4553   (812) 424-6411

Business Profile: Distributes electricity and natural gas in southwestern Indiana.

Plan Specifics:

- Partial dividend reinvestment is available.
- No Discount.
- OCP: $25 to $5000 per month.
- Selling costs are brokerage fees and any commissions.
- Company purchases stock monthly with OCPs.
- Approximately 4300 shareholders are in the plan.
- Dividends are paid March, June, September, and December.

Performance Rating: *****

DRIP Rating: 👍

Southern National Corp.
(NYSE:SNB)
PO Box 1489
Lumberton, NC 28359
(910) 671-2000

Business Profile: Multibank holding company with over 150 branch offices in North and South Carolina.

Plan Specifics:

- Partial dividend reinvestment is not available.
- No Discount.
- OCP: $25 to $5000 per month.
- Purchasing fees are nominal.
- Must go through a broker to sell shares from the plan.
- Company purchases stock monthly with OCPs.
- Dividends are paid February, May, August, and November.

Performance Rating: ****

DRIP Rating: 👍

Southern New England
Telecommunications Corp.
(NYSE:SNG)
PO Box 1101
New Haven, CT 06504
(800) 243-1110

Business Profile: Telecommunications holding company providing service throughout Connecticut.

Plan Specifics:

- Partial dividend reinvestment is not available.
- No Discount.
- OCP: up to $10,000 per quarter.
- Selling costs are brokerage fees.
- Company purchases stock quarterly with OCPs.
- Approximately 20,000 shareholders are in the plan.
- Dividends are paid January, April, July, and October.

Performance Rating: ***

DRIP Rating: 👍

SouthTrust Corp.
(NASDAQ:SOTR)
PO Box 2554
Birmingham, AL 35290
(205) 254-5509

Business Profile: Alabama-based multibank holding company serving clients in Alabama, Florida, Georgia, North Carolina, South Carolina, Mississippi, and Tennessee.

Plan Specifics:

- Partial dividend reinvestment is available.
- No Discount.
- OCP: $25 to $10,000 per month.
- May have to pay brokerage fees on any shares purchased in the open market.

- Selling costs are brokerage commissions.
- Stock is purchased monthly with OCPs.
- Dividends are paid January, April, July, and October.

Performance Rating: ****

DRIP Rating: 👍

**Southwest Gas Corp.
(NYSE:SWX)
Attn: Shareholder Relations
PO Box 98510
Las Vegas, NV 89193-8510
(702) 876-7280**

Business Profile: Supplies natural gas to areas of Arizona, Nevada, and California. Activities in savings and loan.

Plan Specifics:

- Partial dividend reinvestment is available at 50 percent if account has 250 shares.
- No Discount.
- OCP: $25 to $50,000 per year.
- Selling costs are approximately 5 cents a share.
- Company purchases stock twice a month with OCPs.
- Customers of the company may make initial investments directly through the firm ($100 minimum).
- Dividends are paid March, June, September, and December.

Performance Rating: **

DRIP Rating: 👍

**Southwest Water Co.
(NASDAQ:SWWC)
225 N. Barranca Ave.,
Suite 200
West Covina, CA 91791-1605
(818) 915-1551**

Business Profile: Parent company of Suburban Water Systems (water service in Los Angeles and Orange counties, CA); New Mexico Utilities, Inc. (water supply and sewage collection services northwest of Albuquerque); and ECO Resources, Inc. (services for water supply and wastewater treatment facilities in western, southwestern, and southeastern United States).

Plan Specifics:

- Partial dividend reinvestment is available.
- 5 percent discount on reinvested dividends.
- OCP: $25 to $3000 per quarter.
- Must go through own broker to sell shares.
- Company purchases stock quarterly with OCPs.
- Approximately 1100 shareholders are in the plan.
- Dividends are paid January, April, July, and October.

Performance Rating: **

DRIP Rating: 👍

**Southwestern Energy Co.
(NYSE:SWN)
c/o First Chicago Trust-NY
PO Box 2533
Jersey City, NJ 07303-2533
(800) 446-2617   (501) 521-1141**

Business Profile: Natural gas holding company. Utility operation serves parts of Arkansas and Missouri.

Plan Specifics:

- Partial dividend reinvestment is not available.
- No Discount.
- OCP: $25 to $1000 per month.

- Selling costs are brokerage commissions and any applicable taxes.
- Purchasing fees are proportionate share of broker commissions, service charge of 5 percent per dividend investment (maximum $3), and $3 charge per OCP.
- Company purchases stock monthly with OCPs.
- Dividends are paid February, May, August, and November.

Performance Rating: **

DRIP Rating: 👍

Southwestern Public Service Co. (NYSE:SPS)
PO Box 1261
Amarillo, TX 79170
(806) 378-2841

Business Profile: Electric utility serving portions of Kansas, New Mexico, Oklahoma, and Texas.

Plan Specifics:

- Partial dividend reinvestment is available.
- No Discount.
- OCP: $25 to $3000 per quarter.
- Purchasing and selling fees are brokerage commissions.
- Company purchases stock monthly with OCPs.
- Approximately 13,300 shareholders are in the plan.
- Dividends are paid March, June, September, and December.

Performance Rating: ***

DRIP Rating: 👍

Sprint Corp. (NYSE:FON)
PO Box 11315
Kansas City, MO 64112
(913) 624-3000   (816) 860-7745

Business Profile: Operates telephone system and is the third largest long distance carrier.

Plan Specifics:

- Partial dividend reinvestment is available.
- No Discount.
- OCP: $25 to $5000 per quarter.
- Selling costs are brokerage commissions and a $2 administrative charge.
- Company purchases stock monthly with OCPs.
- Dividends are paid March, June, September, and December.

Performance Rating: ****

DRIP Rating: 👍

SPX Corp. (NYSE:SPW)
700 Terrace Point Dr.
Muskegon, MI 49443
(616) 724-5000   (800) 524-4458

Business Profile: Manufactures specialty service tools and original equipment components for the motor vehicle industry.

Plan Specifics:

- Partial dividend reinvestment is not available.
- No Discount.
- OCP: $25 to $10,000 per quarter.
- Selling costs are brokerage commissions, transfer taxes, and bank's fee of $2.50.
- Company purchases stock around the 1st of each month with OCPs.
- Dividends are paid March, June, September, and December.

Performance Rating: **

DRIP Rating: 👍

Standard Commercial Corp.
(NYSE:STW)
PO Box 450
Wilson, NC 27894-0450
(919) 291-5507

Business Profile: Buys, processes, and markets tobacco and wool.

Plan Specifics:
- Partial dividend reinvestment is available.
- No Discount.
- OCP: $25 to $3000 per quarter.
- Selling costs are brokerage fees and transfer tax.
- Company purchases stock monthly with OCPs.
- Approximately 248 shareholders are in the plan.
- Dividends are paid March, June, September, and December.

Performance Rating: **

DRIP Rating: 👍

Standard Federal Bank
(NYSE:SFB)
2600 W. Big Beaver Rd.
PO Box 3703
Troy, MI 48007-3703
(810) 643-9600   (800) 643-9600

Business Profile: Largest thrift headquartered in the Midwest, with operations in Michigan, northern Indiana, and northwestern Ohio.

Plan Specifics:
- Partial dividend reinvestment is not available.
- No Discount.
- OCP: $25 to $3000 per quarter.
- Selling cost is a $2.50 termination fee.
- Company purchases stock quarterly with OCPs.

- Dividends are paid March, June, September, and December.

Performance Rating: ***

DRIP Rating: 👍

Standard Products Co.
(NYSE:SPD)
2130 W. 110th St.
Cleveland, OH 44102-3590
(216) 281-8300   (216) 575-2532

Business Profile: Manufactures rubber and plastic components for the automotive and home appliance industries and is a producer of tread rubber for truck tire retreading.

Plan Specifics:
- Partial dividend reinvestment is not available.
- No Discount.
- OCP: $50 to $3000 per quarter.
- Stock is purchased monthly with OCPs.
- Selling costs include brokerage fees.
- Dividends are paid January, April, July, and October.

Performance Rating: **

DRIP Rating: 👍

Stanhome, Inc. (NYSE:STH)
333 Western Ave.
Westfield, MA 01085
(413) 562-3631 Ext. 377

Business Profile: Produces and markets household items and distributes giftware.

Plan Specifics:
- Partial dividend reinvestment is not available.
- No Discount.
- OCP: $10 to $5000 per quarter.

- Selling costs are brokerage commissions.
- Company purchases stock quarterly with OCPs.
- Dividends are paid January, April, July, and October.

Performance Rating: ***

DRIP Rating: 👍

Stanley Works (NYSE:SWK)
1000 Stanley Dr.
New Britain, CT 06053
(203) 225-5111

Business Profile: Manufactures professional and do-it-yourself home-improvement items such as hand tools and hardware. Operations in industrial tools, fasteners, and power operated doors.

Plan Specifics:

- Need 10 shares in order to enroll in the plan.
- Partial dividend reinvestment is not available.
- No Discount.
- OCP: $25 to $5000 per month.
- Stock is purchased monthly with OCPs.
- Selling costs include brokerage fees and $10 exit fee.
- $2 service fee for reinvestment of dividends ($8 per year).
- Dividends are paid March, June, September, and December.

Performance Rating: ***

DRIP Rating: 👍

Star Banc Corp. (NYSE:STB)
PO Box 1038
Cincinnati, OH 45201
(513) 632-4000

Business Profile: Ohio-based multibank holding company with offices in Ohio, Indiana, and Kentucky.

Plan Specifics:

- Partial dividend reinvestment is not available.
- No Discount.
- OCP: $50 to $5000 per quarter.
- Selling costs are minimal.
- Company purchases stock quarterly with OCPs.
- Approximately 2000 shareholders are in the plan.
- Dividends are paid January, April, July, and October.

Performance Rating: ****

DRIP Rating: 👍

State Street Boston Corp.
 (NYSE:STT)
State Street Bank and Trust Co.
c/o Boston Financial Data
2 Heritage Dr.
North Quincy, MA 02171
(800) 426-5523

Business Profile: Massachusetts bank holding company and a leading mutual fund custodian.

Plan Specifics:

- Partial dividend reinvestment is not available.
- No Discount.
- OCP: $10 to $1000 per month.
- Selling costs are approximately 15 cents per share.
- Purchasing fees are brokerage and service charges.
- Company purchases stock once a month with OCPs.
- Dividends are paid January, April, July, and October.

Performance Rating: ****

DRIP Rating: 👍

Stone & Webster, Inc. (NYSE:SW)
c/o Chemical Bank
Dividend Reinvestment Dept.
PO Box 24935, Church St. Sta.
New York, NY 10249
(800) 851-9677   (212) 290-7500

Business Profile: Provides engineering, construction, and management services to companies in the industrial, chemical, and energy-based industries.

Plan Specifics:

- Partial dividend reinvestment is not available.
- No Discount.
- OCP: $50 to $1500 per month.
- Selling costs are brokerage commissions and $5 termination charge.
- Company purchases stock monthly with OCPs.
- Dividends are paid February, May, August, and November.

Performance Rating: **

DRIP Rating: 👍

Strawbridge & Clothier
(NASDAQ:STRWA)
801 Market St.
Philadelphia, PA 19107-3199
(215) 629-6000   (800) 526-0801

Business Profile: Operates department and discount stores primarily in Philadelphia and surrounding areas.

Plan Specifics:

- Partial dividend reinvestment is available.
- No Discount.
- OCP: $25 to $5000 per quarter.
- OCP is invested quarterly.
- Selling fees are brokerage commissions.

- Dividends are paid February, May, August, and November.

Performance Rating: ***

DRIP Rating: 👍

Stride Rite Corp. (NYSE:SRR)
5 Cambridge Center
Cambridge, MA 02142
(617) 491-8800

Business Profile: Major supplier of athletic and casual footwear for children and adults.

Plan Specifics:

- Partial dividend reinvestment is not available.
- No Discount.
- OCP: $10 to $1000 per month.
- Purchasing fees are brokerage commissions and a 5 percent service charge (maximum $2.50) for each dividend and/or cash investment.
- Selling costs are brokerage commissions and a 5 percent service charge (maximum $2.50).
- Company purchases stock monthly with OCPs.
- Dividends are paid March, June, September, and December.

Performance Rating: **

DRIP Rating: 👍

Suffolk Bancorp
(NASDAQ:SUBK)
6 W. 2nd St.
Riverhead, NY 11901
(516) 727-2700   (212) 936-5100

Business Profile: Bank holding company in New York.

Plan Specifics:

- Partial dividend reinvestment is available.

- 3 percent discount on reinvested dividends (does not apply when purchasing on the open market).
- OCP: $300 to $5000 per quarter.
- Selling fees are $15 termination fee, brokerage fees, and any other costs of sale.
- Stock is purchased at least quarterly with OCPs.
- Dividends are paid January, April, July, and October.

Performance Rating: NR
DRIP Rating: ☜

Sumitomo Bank of California
(NASDAQ:SUMI)
Attn: Corporate Secretary
320 California St.
San Francisco, CA 94104
(415) 445-8000

Business Profile: Conducts commercial banking and trust services throughout California.

Plan Specifics:

- Partial dividend reinvestment is available.
- No Discount.
- OCP: not available.
- Must go through own broker to sell shares.
- Approximately 450 shareholders are in plan.
- Dividends are paid January, April, July, and October.

Performance Rating: NR
DRIP Rating: ☜

Summit Bancorporation (NJ)
(NASDAQ:SUBN)
One Main St.
Chatham, NJ 07928
(201) 701-2666   (800) 851-9677

Business Profile: Multibank holding company headquartered in New Jersey.

Plan Specifics:

- Partial dividend reinvestment is available.
- 3½ percent discount on reinvested dividends and OCPs.
- OCP: $50 to $5000 per month.
- Selling costs are brokerage commissions, transfer taxes, and a sales fee of $15.
- Stock is purchased on the 15th of each month with OCPs.
- Safekeeping services are available.
- Dividends are paid March, June, September, and December.

*Performance Rating: ****
DRIP Rating: 👍

Summit Properties, Inc.
(NYSE: SMT)
212 S. Tryon St., Ste. 500
Charlotte, NC 28281
(704) 334-9905

Business Profile: Real estate investment trust which invests primarily in multifamily apartment communities in southeastern U.S.

Plan Specifics:

- Partial dividend reinvestment is available.
- 5 percent discount on reinvested dividends.
- OCP: $100 to $10,000 per month.
- OCP is invested monthly.
- Selling costs are brokerage commissions.
- Dividends are paid February, May, August, and November.

*Performance Rating: ***
DRIP Rating: 👍

Sun Bancorp, Inc.
(NASDAQ: SUBI)
2-16 S. Market St.
PO Box 57
Selinsgrove, PA 17870
(717) 374-1131

Business Profile: Pennsylvania-based banking concern.

Plan Specifics:

- Partial dividend reinvestment is not available.
- No Discount.
- OCP: $50 to $10,000 per quarter.
- OCP is invested quarterly.
- Purchasing fees include service charge of 5 percent of amount invested (maximum $2.50).
- $3 termination fee.
- Must sell shares through own broker.
- Dividends are paid March, June, September, and December.

Performance Rating: NR
DRIP Rating: 👍

Sun Co., Inc. (NYSE:SUN)
Ten Penn Center
1801 Market St.
Philadelphia, PA 19103-1699
(215) 888-8494

Business Profile: Refines, produces, and markets petroleum, serving portions of the Northeast and Midwest.

Plan Specifics:

- Partial dividend reinvestment is not available.
- No Discount.
- OCP: up to $10,000 per quarter.
- Selling costs are approximately 17 cents per share.
- Company purchases stock twice per quarter with OCPs.

- Dividends are paid March, June, September, and December.

Performance Rating: **
DRIP Rating: 👍

Sundstrand Corp. (NYSE:SNS)
PO Box 7003
4949 Harrison Ave.
Rockford, IL 61125-7003
(815) 226-2136

Business Profile: Produces aircraft components and systems and industrial equipment.

Plan Specifics:

- Partial dividend reinvestment is not available.
- No Discount.
- OCP: $25 to $3000 per month.
- Selling costs, if any, are minimal.
- Company purchases stock monthly with OCPs.
- Dividends are paid March, June, September, and December.

Performance Rating: **
DRIP Rating: 👍

SunTrust Banks, Inc. (NYSE:STI)
PO Box 4625
Atlanta, GA 30302
(404) 588-7822

Business Profile: Holding company for banks in Florida, Georgia, and Tennessee.

Plan Specifics:

- Partial dividend reinvestment is not available.
- No Discount.
- OCP: $10 to $60,000 per year.
- Selling costs are 9 cents per share brokerage fee.
- Company purchases stock monthly with OCPs.

- Dividends are paid March, June, September, and December.

Performance Rating: ****

DRIP Rating: 👍

Supervalu, Inc. (NYSE:SVU)
c/o Norwest Bank Minnesota
PO Box 738
South St. Paul, MN 55075-0738
(612) 450-4064

Business Profile: Food wholesaler and manager of retail supermarkets and general merchandise stores.

Plan Specifics:

- Partial dividend reinvestment is not available.
- No Discount.
- OCP: $10 to $3000 per quarter.
- Selling costs are brokerage commissions and any other fees.
- Company purchases stock around the 15th of each month if there are enough funds to purchase at least 100 shares.
- Dividends are paid March, June, September, and December.

Performance Rating: ***

DRIP Rating: 👍

Susquehanna Bancshares, Inc.
(NASDAQ:SUSQ)
26 N. Cedar St.
Lititz, PA 17543-7000
(717) 626-4721

Business Profile: Offers banking services in Pennsylvania and in northern Maryland.

Plan Specifics:

- Partial dividend reinvestment is not available.
- No Discount.

- OCP: $100 to $2500 per quarter.
- Purchasing fees for OCPs are $5 per investment.
- Selling costs are brokerage fees and a service charge.
- Company purchases stock around the 20th of the month with OCPs.
- Dividends are paid February, May, August, and November.

Performance Rating: NR

DRIP Rating: 👍

Synovus Financial Corp.
(NYSE:SNV)
Corporate Trust Dept.
PO Box 120
Columbus, GA 31902
(706) 649-2387

Business Profile: Southeast interstate bank holding company. Nonbanking operations in credit card processing.

Plan Specifics:

- Partial dividend reinvestment is available.
- No Discount.
- OCP: up to $2500 per month.
- Investors can sell shares through the plan weekly. Brokerage fees will be charged.
- Company purchases stock monthly with OCPs.
- Over 6820 shareholders are in plan.
- Dividends are paid January, April, July, and October.

Performance Rating: ****

DRIP Rating: 👍

Sysco Corp. (NYSE:SYY)
1390 Enclave Parkway
Houston, TX 77077-2099
(713) 584-1390

Business Profile: Distributor of food and related products to restaurants, fast-food chains, hotels, schools, hospitals, and other providers of food service.

Plan Specifics:
- Partial dividend reinvestment is not available.
- No Discount.
- OCP: not available.
- Dividends are paid February, May, August, and November.

Performance Rating: *****
DRIP Rating: ☞

Talley Industries, Inc.
(NYSE:TAL)
2702 N. 44th St., Ste. 100A
Phoenix, AZ 85008
(602) 957-7711

Business Profile: Supplies solid propellant products for government use and manufactures industrial products.

Plan Specifics:
- Partial dividend reinvestment is not available.
- No Discount.
- OCP: $10 to $1000 per month.
- Selling costs are service charge of $1 and brokerage commissions.
- Company purchases stock monthly with OCPs.
- Preferred dividends are eligible for reinvestment for additional common shares under the plan.
- The company is not currently paying a dividend.

Performance Rating: *
DRIP Rating: 👍

Tambrands, Inc. (NYSE:TMB)
c/o First Chicago Trust-NY
PO Box 2533
Jersey City, NJ 07303-2533
(914) 696-6000   (800) 446-2617

Business Profile: Nation's leading producer of tampons.

Plan Specifics:
- Partial dividend reinvestment is available.
- No Discount.
- OCP: $25 to $60,000 per year.
- Selling costs are brokerage commissions and a service fee.
- Company purchases stock monthly with OCPs.
- Automatic investment services are available.
- Dividends are paid March, June, September, and December.

Performance Rating: ****
DRIP Rating: 👍

Taubman Centers, Inc.
(NYSE:TCO)
200 E. Long Lake Rd.
Bloomfield Hills, MI 48304
(810) 258-7519

Business Profile: Owns and operates shopping centers.

Plan Specifics:
- Partial dividend reinvestment is available.
- No Discount.
- OCP: not available.
- Selling costs are brokerage fees.
- Dividends are paid January, April, July, and October.

Performance Rating: **

DRIP Rating: ℘

TCF Financial Corp. (NYSE:TCB)
801 Marquette Ave.
Minneapolis, MN 55402
(612) 661-8859 (800) 730-4001

Business Profile: Minnesota-based savings bank holding company.

Plan Specifics:

- Partial dividend reinvestment is available.
- No Discount.
- OCP: $25 to $5000 per quarter.
- Selling costs are $15 service fee and commissions.
- Company purchases stock quarterly with OCPs.
- Approximately 4950 shareholders are in the plan.
- Dividends are paid February, May, August, and November.

Performance Rating: ***

DRIP Rating: ⚒

TECO Energy, Inc. (NYSE:TE)
TECO Plaza
702 N. Franklin St.
Tampa, FL 33602
(813) 228-4111

Business Profile: Holding company which operates Tampa Electric Co. Derives a major portion of its profits from coal mining, barging, and gas production.

Plan Specifics:

- Partial dividend reinvestment is available.
- No Discount.
- OCP: $25 to $100,000 per year.
- Selling costs are brokerage commissions and any transfer tax.
- Company purchases stock monthly with OCPs.
- Dividends are paid February, May, August, and November.

Performance Rating: *****

DRIP Rating: ⚒

Telephone & Data Systems, Inc. (ASE:TDS)
c/o Harris Trust and Savings
PO Box 755
Chicago, IL 60690
(312) 461-3310 (312) 630-1900

Business Profile: Telephone holding company with operations in local telephone service, cellular telephones, and radio paging.

Plan Specifics:

- At least 10 shares needed to enroll in the plan.
- Partial dividend reinvestment is available.
- 5 percent discount on reinvested dividends.
- OCP: $10 to $5000 per quarter.
- Must sell shares through own broker.
- Company purchases stock monthly with OCPs.
- Preferred dividends are eligible for reinvestment for additional common shares under the plan.
- Dividends are paid March, June, September, and December.

Performance Rating: ***

DRIP Rating: ⚒

Temple-Inland, Inc. (NYSE:TIN)
c/o NCNB Texas National Bank
PO Box 830345
Dallas, TX 75283-0345
(409) 829-2211

Business Profile: Manufactures containers, paperboard,

containerboard, market pulp, and building materials.

Plan Specifics:

- Partial dividend reinvestment is available.
- No Discount.
- OCP: $25 to $1000 per quarter.
- Stock is purchased at least quarterly with OCPs.
- Selling costs are $1 service fee plus pro rata share of brokerage commissions.
- Dividends are paid March, June, September, and December.

Performance Rating: ***

DRIP Rating: 👍

Tenet Healthcare Corp. (NYSE:THC)
c/o Bank of New York
PO Box 11258, Church St. Stat.
New York, NY 10286
(800) 524-4458   (310) 998-8000

Business Profile: Major hospital management company with general and specialty hospitals.

Plan Specifics:

- Partial dividend reinvestment is not available.
- No Discount.
- OCP: $10 to $1000 per month.
- Selling costs are brokerage fees.
- Stock is purchased monthly with OCPs.
- Company is currently not paying a dividend.

Performance Rating: ***

DRIP Rating: 👍

Tenneco, Inc. (NYSE:TEN)
c/o First Chicago Trust-NY
PO Box 2533
Jersey City, NJ 07303-2533
(800) 446-2617   (713) 757-2131

Business Profile: Holding company with interests in natural gas pipelines, construction, and farm equipment.

Plan Specifics:

- Initial purchases may be made directly from the company (minimum $500).
- Partial dividend reinvestment is available.
- No Discount.
- OCP: $50 to $60,000 per year.
- Stock is purchased weekly with OCPs.
- Purchasing fees are brokerage commissions and a service charge of 5 percent of the amount invested ($3 maximum).
- Selling costs are brokerage commissions and service fee.
- Automatic investment services are available.
- Preferred dividends are eligible for reinvestment in additional common shares under the plan.
- Stock may be sold via the telephone.
- Dividends are paid March, June, September, and December.

Performance Rating: ***

DRIP Rating: 👍

Texaco, Inc. (NYSE:TX)
2000 Westchester Ave.
White Plains, NY 10650
(800) 283-9785

Business Profile: Fully integrated oil company.

Plan Specifics:
- Initial purchases of stock may be made directly through the company (minimum $250).
- Partial dividend reinvestment is not available.
- No Discount.
- OCP: $50 to $120,000 per year.
- Commission of 5 cents per share for both purchasing and selling.
- Company purchases stock three times each month with OCPs.
- Participants may purchase shares of stock for others by making an initial cash investment in that person's name.
- Dividends are paid March, June, September, and December.

Performance Rating: ****

DRIP Rating: 👍

Texas Instruments, Inc. (NYSE:TXN)
PO Box 655474
13500 N. Central Expressway
Dallas, TX 75265
(214) 995-2011   (312) 461-3930

Business Profile: Produces a variety of electrical and electronics products.

Plan Specifics:
- Partial dividend reinvestment is available.
- No Discount.
- OCP: not available.
- $3 for termination of an account.
- Dividends are paid January, April, July, and October.

Performance Rating: ****

DRIP Rating: 👍

Texas Utilities Co. (NYSE:TXU)
2001 Bryan Tower
Dallas, TX 75201
(214) 742-4000   (800) 828-0812

Business Profile: Texas electric utility holding company.

Plan Specifics:
- Need at least 10 shares to enroll in plan.
- Partial dividend reinvestment is not available.
- No Discount.
- OCP: $25 to $4000 per month.
- Selling costs are brokerage commissions.
- Company purchases stock monthly with OCPs.
- Approximately 50,000 shareholders are in the plan.
- Dividends are paid January, April, July, and October.

Performance Rating: **

DRIP Rating: 👍

Textron, Inc. (NYSE:TXT)
c/o First Chicago Trust-NY
PO Box 2533
Jersey City, NJ 07303-2533
(800) 446-2617   (401) 421-2800

Business Profile: Manufactures aerospace equipment for government defense market. Also has operations in automotive parts, outdoor products, and financial services.

Plan Specifics:
- Partial dividend reinvestment is available.
- No Discount.
- OCP: $25 to $1000 per month.
- Stock is purchased around the 1st business day of the month with OCPs.

- Selling costs are brokerage commissions and related expenses.
- Dividends are paid January, April, July, and October.

Performance Rating: ****

DRIP Rating: 👍

Thermo Remediation, Inc.
(ASE: THN)
1964 S. Orange Blossom Trail
Apopka, FL 32703
(617) 575-3120   (617) 622-1000

Business Profile: Operates soil-remediation centers which treat soil to remove petroleum contamination.

Plan Specifics:

- Partial dividend reinvestment is not available.
- No Discount.
- OCP: not available.
- Dividends are paid March and September.

Performance Rating: ***

DRIP Rating: 👎

Thomas & Betts Corp.
(NYSE:TNB)
1555 Lynnfield Rd.
Memphis, TN 38119
(901) 682-7766   (800) 446-2617

Business Profile: Leading supplier of electronic connectors, accessories, and systems.

Plan Specifics:

- Partial dividend reinvestment is not available.
- No Discount.
- OCP: $10 to $3000 per quarter.
- Stock is purchased monthly with OCPs.

- Selling costs are $5 handling fee and brokerage commissions.
- Stock may be sold via the telephone.
- Dividends are paid January, April, July, and October.

Performance Rating: *****

DRIP Rating: 👍

Thomas Industries, Inc.
(NYSE:TII)
c/o Wachovia Bank of North Carolina, N.A.
PO Box 3001
Winston-Salem, NC 27102
(502) 893-4600

Business Profile: Manufacturer of lighting products and precision built fractional horsepower compressors and vacuum pumps.

Plan Specifics:

- Partial dividend reinvestment is not available.
- No Discount.
- OCP: $25 to $3000 per month.
- Selling costs are brokerage commissions.
- Company purchases stock monthly with OCPs.
- Dividends are paid January, April, July, and October.

Performance Rating: **

DRIP Rating: 👍

Thornburg Mortgage Asset Corp.
(NYSE:TMA)
119 E. Marcy St., Ste. 201
Santa Fe, NM 87501
(505) 989-1900   (800) 426-5523

Business Profile: Real estate investment trust which invests primarily in adjustable-rate mortgage-backed securities.

Plan Specifics:
- Partial dividend reinvestment is available.
- 3 percent discount on OCPs and reinvested dividends.
- OCP: $50 to $15,000 per quarter.
- OCP is invested quarterly.
- Selling costs are brokerage fees.
- Dividends are paid January, April, July, and October.

Performance Rating: **

DRIP Rating: 👍

Tidewater, Inc. (NYSE:TDW)
1440 Canal St.
New Orleans, LA 70112
(504) 568-1010

Business Profile: Energy concern providing support services for offshore drilling activities.

Plan Specifics:
- Partial dividend reinvestment is not available.
- No Discount.
- OCP: $25 to $5000 per quarter.
- Purchasing fees are brokerage costs and 5 percent service charge (maximum $2.50).
- Selling costs include brokerage fees and a service charge.
- Stock is purchased quarterly, and more often if enough funds accumulate, with OCPs.
- Dividends are paid February, May, August, and November.

Performance Rating: **

DRIP Rating: 👍

Time Warner, Inc. (NYSE:TWX)
75 Rockefeller Plaza
New York, NY 10019
(800) 279-1238   (212) 484-8000

Business Profile: Operations in magazines, filmed entertainment, cable television, music recording, and book publishing.

Plan Specifics:
- Partial dividend reinvestment is available.
- 5 percent discount on reinvested dividends.
- OCP: $25 to $10,000 per quarter.
- Stock is purchased monthly with OCPs.
- Selling costs are brokerage commissions and a $5 service charge.
- Dividends are paid March, June, September, and December.

Performance Rating: ****

DRIP Rating: 👍

Times Mirror Company
  (NYSE:TMC)
Times Mirror Square
Los Angeles, CA 90053
(213) 237-3700   (800) 522-6645

Business Profile: Publishes newspapers, books, and magazines. Publisher of the *Los Angeles Times*, *Newsday*, *The Baltimore Sun*, and *The Hartford Courant*.

Plan Specifics:
- Partial dividend reinvestment is available.
- No Discount.
- OCP: $250 to $10,000 per quarter.
- $2.50 charge for each withdrawal of full-share certificates from the plan.
- Company purchases stock quarterly with OCPs.
- Dividends are paid March, June, September, and December.

Performance Rating: ***
DRIP Rating: ⑨

Timken Co. (NYSE:TKR)
1835 Dueber Ave. SW
Canton, OH 44706-2798
(216) 471-3376

Business Profile: Manufacturer of tapered roller bearings and alloy steel.

Plan Specifics:

- Partial dividend reinvestment is available.
- 5 percent discount on reinvested dividends.
- OCP: not available.
- Must sell shares through own broker.
- Approximately 3000 shareholders are in the plan.
- Direct deposit of dividends is available.
- Dividends are paid March, June, September, and December.

Performance Rating: ***
DRIP Rating: ⑨

TNP Enterprises, Inc.
(NYSE:TNP)
PO Box 2943
Fort Worth, TX 76113
(817) 731-0099   (800) 527-7844

Business Profile: Texas-based electric utility holding firm serving clients in Texas and New Mexico.

Plan Specifics:

- Partial dividend reinvestment is available.
- No Discount.
- OCP: $25 to $5000 per quarter.
- Must sell shares through own broker.

- Company purchases stock monthly with OCPs.
- Dividends are paid March, June, September, and December.

Performance Rating: **
DRIP Rating: 👍

Torchmark Corp. (NYSE:TMK)
2001 Third Ave., S.
Birmingham, AL 35233
(205) 325-4200   (800) 446-2617

Business Profile: Insurance and financial services holding company.

Plan Specifics:

- Partial dividend reinvestment is available.
- No Discount.
- OCP: $100 to $3000 per quarter.
- Company purchases stock 8 times a year with OCPs.
- Purchasing costs include a service charge ($2.50 max.) per dividend reinvestment and a $2.50 max. service charge per OCP investment plus brokerage commissions.
- Selling costs include a service charge ($2.50 max.) plus brokerage commissions.
- Dividends are paid February, May, August, and November.

Performance Rating: ****
DRIP Rating: 👍

Toro Co. (NYSE:TTC)
c/o Norwest Bank Minnesota
PO Box 738
South St. Paul, MN 55075-0738
(612) 887-8526   (612) 888-8801

Business Profile: Important supplier of commercial and consumer lawn equipment, snow throwers, and irrigation systems.

Plan Specifics:

- Partial dividend reinvestment is not available.
- No Discount.
- OCP: $10 to $1000 per month.
- Selling costs are brokerage commissions and other costs of sale.
- Company purchases stock around the 12th of each month if enough funds accumulate to purchase at least 100 shares.
- Dividends are paid January, April, July, and October.

Performance Rating: **

DRIP Rating: 👍

Total Petroleum (North America) Ltd. (ASE:TPN)
PO Box 500
Denver, CO 80202
(303) 291-2000

Business Profile: Refines, transports, and sells petroleum and petroleum products.

Plan Specifics:

- Partial dividend reinvestment is available.
- 5 percent discount on reinvested dividends.
- Purchasing fees are brokerage commissions for open market purchases.
- OCP: not available.
- Must go through own broker to sell shares.
- Approximately 62 percent of common stockholders are in the plan.
- Dividends are paid January, April, July, and October.

Performance Rating: **

DRIP Rating: 👍

Total System Services, Inc. (NYSE:TSS)
PO Box 120
Columbus, GA 31902
(800) 503-8903   (706) 649-2310

Business Profile: Provides credit-card data processing services for financial institutions. Synovus Financial Corp. owns 82 percent.

Plan Specifics:

- Partial dividend reinvestment is not available.
- No Discount.
- OCP: up to $6000 per quarter.
- Must sell stock through own broker.
- Purchasing costs include brokerage fees.
- Stock is purchased quarterly with OCPs.
- Dividends are paid January, April, July, and October.

Performance Rating: ***

DRIP Rating: 👍

Transamerica Corp. (NYSE:TA)
c/o First Interstate Bank - CA
PO Box 60975
Los Angeles, CA 90060
(800) 522-6645   (213) 742-4969

Business Profile: Financial service institution engaged in lending, leasing, and real estate finance and property-casualty insurance.

Plan Specifics:

- Partial dividend reinvestment is available.
- No Discount.
- OCP: $10 to $5000 per month.

- Selling costs are brokerage commissions and a small handling fee.
- Company purchases stock monthly with OCPs.
- Dividends are paid January, April, July, and October.

Performance Rating: ***

DRIP Rating: 👍

TransCanada Pipelines Ltd. (NYSE:TRP)
c/o Montreal Trust
Western Gas Tower
530 8th Ave., SW
Calgary, Alberta T2P 358 Canada
(403) 267-6800

Business Profile: Owns Canada's major pipeline system used to transport natural gas from western to eastern markets.

Plan Specifics:

- Partial dividend reinvestment is not available.
- 5 percent discount on reinvested dividends.
- OCP: $50 to $5000 (Canadian) per quarter.
- Must sell shares through own broker.
- Company purchases stock quarterly with OCPs.
- Preferred dividends are eligible for reinvestment for additional common shares under the plan.
- Dividends are paid January, April, July, and October.

Performance Rating: **

DRIP Rating: 👍

Tribune Company (NYSE:TRB)
c/o First Chicago Trust-NY
PO Box 2533
Jersey City, NJ 07303-2533
(312) 222-9100   (800) 446-2617

Business Profile: Communications company involved in newspaper publishing, broadcasting, and entertainment.

Plan Specifics:

- Partial dividend reinvestment is available.
- No Discount.
- OCP: $50 to $2000 per month.
- Selling costs are brokerage commissions, $5 handling charge, and any other costs of sale.
- Company purchases stock monthly with OCPs.
- Stock can be sold via the telephone.
- Dividends are paid March, June, September, and December.

Performance Rating: *****

DRIP Rating: 👍

Trinova Corp. (NYSE:TNV)
3000 Strayer
PO Box 50
Maumee, OH 43537-0050
(419) 867-2200

Business Profile: Manufacturer and distributor of engineered components and systems for the industrial, aerospace, defense, and automotive markets.

Plan Specifics:

- Partial dividend reinvestment is not available.
- No Discount.
- OCP: $10 to $20,000 per year.

- Stock is purchased monthly with OCPs.
- Selling costs are 10 cents per share brokerage fees and $5 per transaction.
- Approximately 3300 shareholders are in the plan.
- Dividends are paid March, June, September, and December.

Performance Rating: **

DRIP Rating: 👍

True North Communications, Inc. (NYSE:TNO)
101 E. Erie
Chicago, IL 60611-2897
(312) 751-7000   (800) 446-2617

Business Profile: Provides advertising, direct marketing, and sales promotion.

Plan Specifics:

- Partial dividend reinvestment is not available.
- No Discount.
- OCP: $25 to $1000 per month.
- OCP is invested monthly.
- Must go through own broker to sell stock.
- Dividends are paid January, April, July, and October.

Performance Rating: ***

DRIP Rating: 👍

TRW, Inc. (NYSE:TRW)
1900 Richmond Rd.
Cleveland, OH 44124
(216) 291-7000

Business Profile: Leading provider of space and defense products, car and truck components, and information systems.

Plan Specifics:

- Partial dividend reinvestment is not available.
- No Discount.
- OCP: $10 to $1000 per quarter.
- Stock is purchased quarterly with OCPs.
- Purchasing fees are brokerage commissions.
- Selling costs are brokerage commissions.
- Preferred dividends are eligible for reinvestment for additional common shares under the plan.
- Dividends are paid March, June, September, and December.

Performance Rating: ****

DRIP Rating: 👍

Twin Disc, Inc. (NYSE:TDI)
1328 Racine St.
Racine, WI 53403
(414) 634-1981

Business Profile: Manufactures heavy-duty transmission equipment.

Plan Specifics:

- Partial dividend reinvestment is not available.
- No Discount.
- OCP: $10 to $2000 per month.
- Stock is purchased quarterly, and possibly more frequently, with OCPs.
- Selling costs are nominal brokerage commissions.
- Dividends are paid March, June, September, and December.

Performance Rating: **

DRIP Rating: 👍

Tyco International Ltd.
(NYSE:TYC)
One Tyco Park
Exeter, NH 03833
(603) 778-9700

Business Profile: Leading worldwide provider of fire protection systems, flow-control products, electronic components, and packaging materials.

Plan Specifics:

- Partial dividend reinvestment is not available.
- No Discount.
- OCP: $25 to $1000 per month.
- Selling costs are service charge of $2.50 and brokerage commissions.
- Company purchases stock monthly with OCPs.
- Dividends are paid February, May, August, and November.

Performance Rating: ***
DRIP Rating: 👍

UGI Corp. (NYSE:UGI)
PO Box 858
Valley Forge, PA 19482
(800) 756-3353

Business Profile: Supplies natural gas and electric service to customers in Pennsylvania. Largest propane distributor in the country.

Plan Specifics:

- Partial dividend reinvestment is available.
- 3 percent discount on reinvested dividends.
- OCP: $25 to $3000 per quarter.
- Selling costs are brokerage fees.
- Company purchases stock monthly with OCPs.

- Preferred dividends are eligible for reinvestment for additional common shares under the plan.
- Dividends are paid January, April, July, and October.

Performance Rating: ***
DRIP Rating: 👍

UJB Financial Corp. (NYSE:UJB)
301 Carnegie Center
PO Box 2066
Princeton, NJ 08543-2066
(609) 987-3452   (800) 446-2617

Business Profile: New Jersey-based bank holding firm.

Plan Specifics:

- Partial dividend reinvestment is not available.
- No Discount.
- OCP: $10 to $10,000 per quarter.
- Purchasing fees are brokerage commissions.
- Selling costs are a service fee and any brokerage commissions.
- Company purchases stock the 1st trading day of each month with OCPs.
- Dividends are paid February, May, August, and November.

Performance Rating: ***
DRIP Rating: 👍

Unicom Corp. (NYSE: UCM)
PO Box 767
Chicago, IL 60690-0767
(800) 950-2377

Business Profile: Provides electricity in Chicago and northern Illinois areas. Owns largest network of nuclear plants.

Plan Specifics:

- Partial dividend reinvestment is available.

- No Discount.
- OCP: $25 to $60,000 per year.
- Purchasing and selling costs include brokerage commissions.
- Company purchases stock monthly with OCPs.
- Approximately 72,000 shareholders are in the plan.
- Dividends are paid February, May, August, and November.

Performance Rating: **

DRIP Rating: 👍

Union Bank (NASDAQ:UBNK)
c/o Harris Trust Co. of California
707 Wilshire Blvd., Ste. 4800
Los Angeles, CA 90017
(213) 239-0672

Business Profile: Banking institution in California.

Plan Specifics:

- Partial dividend reinvestment is available.
- 5 percent discount on reinvested dividends.
- OCP: $25 to $3000 per quarter.
- Stock is purchased quarterly with OCPs.
- Costs include $2.50 charge for each withdrawal of full-share certificates from plan and $2.50 charge for transfer of shares to plan account.
- Must sell shares through own broker.
- Dividends are paid January, April, July, and October.

Performance Rating: ***

DRIP Rating: 👍

Union Camp Corp. (NYSE:UCC)
c/o Bank of New York
PO Box 11002, Church St. Sta.
New York, NY 10277-0702
(201) 628-2000

Business Profile: Manufactures paper, paperboard, and wood-based chemicals.

Plan Specifics:

- Partial dividend reinvestment is not available.
- No Discount.
- OCP: $25 to $15,000 per year.
- Must go through own broker to sell shares.
- Company purchases stock around the 1st business day of the month with OCPs.
- Dividends are paid March, June, September, and December.

Performance Rating: ***

DRIP Rating: 👍

Union Carbide Corp. (NYSE:UK)
Shareholder Services
39 Old Ridgebury Rd.
Danbury, CT 06817-0001
(203) 794-2212

Business Profile: Supplies petro-chemicals and specialty chemicals.

Plan Specifics:

- Partial dividend reinvestment is not available.
- No Discount.
- OCP: $25 to $1000 per month.
- Selling costs are brokerage commissions.
- Company purchases stock monthly with OCPs.
- Approximately 24,000 shareholders are in the plan.
- Dividends are paid March, June, September, and December.

Performance Rating: ***
DRIP Rating: 👍

Union Electric Co. (NYSE:UEP)
PO Box 149
St. Louis, MO 63166
(800) 255-2237

Business Profile: Electric utility serving customers in Missouri and Illinois.

Plan Specifics:
- Partial dividend reinvestment is available.
- No Discount.
- OCP: up to $60,000 per year.
- Selling costs are approximately 5 cents per share brokerage commissions.
- Company purchases stock monthly with OCPs.
- Preferred dividends are eligible for reinvestment for additional shares under the plan.
- Customers may make initial purchase of stock directly through the company (no minimum).
- Automatic investment services are available.
- Direct deposit of dividends is available.
- Approximately 50,000 shareholders are in the plan.
- Dividends are paid March, June, September, and December.

Performance Rating: ****
DRIP Rating: 👍

Union Pacific Corp. (NYSE:UNP)
c/o First Chicago Trust-NY
PO Box 2533
Jersey City, NJ 07303-2533
(800) 446-2617   (610) 861-3200

Business Profile: Owns major railroad and motor carrier operations. Also has oil and gas interests.

Plan Specifics:
- Partial dividend reinvestment is available.
- No Discount.
- OCP: $10 to $60,000 per year.
- Stock is purchased monthly with OCPs.
- Selling costs are brokerage commissions, handling charges, and any other costs of sale.
- Stock may be sold via the telephone.
- Dividends are paid January, April, July, and October.

Performance Rating: ****
DRIP Rating: 👍

Union Planters Corp.
 (NYSE:UPC)
PO Box 387
Memphis, TN 38147
(901) 523-6656

Business Profile: Interstate bank holding company with operations in Tennessee, Alabama, Arkansas, Mississippi, and Kentucky.

Plan Specifics:
- Partial dividend reinvestment is available.
- 5 percent discount on reinvested dividends.
- OCP: $100 to $2000 per quarter.
- Must go through own broker to sell shares.
- Company purchases stock monthly with OCPs.
- Dividends are paid February, May, August, and November.

Performance Rating: ***
DRIP Rating: 👍

United Bankshares, Inc.
(NASDAQ:UBSI)
United Square
Fifth and Avery Streets
Parkersburg, WV 26102
(304) 424-8800

Business Profile: Multibank holding company.

Plan Specifics:

- Partial dividend reinvestment is not available.
- No Discount.
- OCP: $25 to $3000 per quarter.
- Selling costs are brokerage commissions.
- Company purchases stock quarterly with OCPs.
- Dividends are paid January, April, July, and October.

Performance Rating: ***
DRIP Rating: 👍

United Carolina Bancshares Corp.
(NASDAQ:UCAR)
PO Box 632
127 W. Webster St.
Whiteville, NC 28472
(910) 642-5131

Business Profile: North Carolina-based bank holding organization.

Plan Specifics:

- Partial dividend reinvestment is not available.
- No Discount.
- OCP: $25 to $5000 per month.
- Company purchases stock monthly with OCPs.
- Purchasing costs include brokerage fees.

- Must go through own broker to sell shares.
- Automatic investment services are available.
- Approximately 3400 shareholders are in the plan.
- Dividends are paid February, May, August, and November.

Performance Rating: ***
DRIP Rating: 👍

United Cities Gas Co.
(NASDAQ:UCIT)
5300 Maryland Way
Brentwood, TN 37027
(615) 373-0104

Business Profile: Provides residents in 10 states with natural gas.

Plan Specifics:

- Partial dividend reinvestment is available.
- 5 percent discount on reinvested dividends.
- OCP: $25 to $10,000 per quarter.
- Company purchases stock monthly with OCPs.
- Must sell shares through own broker.
- Customers of the utility may make initial purchases directly from the firm (minimum $250).
- Preferred dividends are eligible for reinvestment for additional common shares under the plan.
- Dividends are paid March, June, September, and December.

Performance Rating: ***
DRIP Rating: 👍

United Dominion Realty Trust, Inc. (NYSE:UDR)
10 S. Sixth St.
Richmond, VA 23219-3802
(804) 780-2691

Business Profile: Real estate investment trust which invests primarily in apartments in the Southeast.

Plan Specifics:

- Partial dividend reinvestment is available.
- No Discount.
- OCP: $50 to $5000 per quarter.
- OCP is invested quarterly.
- Selling costs are brokerage fees and a $5 termination fee.
- Dividends are paid January, April, July, and October.

Performance Rating: ***
DRIP Rating: 👍

United Illuminating Co. (NYSE:UIL)
PO Box 1948
New Haven, CT 06509-1948
(800) 524-4458

Business Profile: Public electric utility servicing Connecticut communities.

Plan Specifics:

- Partial dividend reinvestment is available.
- No Discount.
- OCP: $10 to $40,000 per year.
- Company purchases stock monthly with OCPs.
- If company purchases stock in open market, participants will be charged brokerage fees.
- Selling fees are brokerage fees and any handling charges.
- Dividends are paid January, April, July, and October.

Performance Rating: **
DRIP Rating: 👍

United Mobile Homes, Inc. (ASE: UMH)
125 Wyckoff Rd.
Eatontown, NJ 07724
(908) 389-3890

Business Profile: Owns and operates 20 mobile home parks in New York, New Jersey, Pennsylvania, Ohio, and Tennessee.

Plan Specifics:

- Partial dividend reinvestment is available.
- 5 percent discount on reinvested dividends and OCPs.
- OCP: $500 to $40,000 per quarter.
- Company purchases stock quarterly with OCPs.
- Dividends are paid March, June, September, and December.

Performance Rating: ****
DRIP Rating: 👍

U.S. Bancorp (NASDAQ:USBC)
PO Box 8837
Portland, OR 97208
(503) 275-6472

Business Profile: Holding company for banks in Oregon, Washington, California, Nevada, and Idaho.

Plan Specifics:

- Partial dividend reinvestment is available.
- No Discount.
- OCP: $25 to $6000 per quarter.
- Company purchases stock monthly with OCPs.
- Investors must sell shares through broker.
- Dividends are paid January, April, July, and October.

Performance Rating: ***
DRIP Rating: 👍

U S West, Inc. (NYSE:USW)
c/o Boston Financial Data
PO Box 8936
Boston, MA 02266-8936
(800) 537-0222

Business Profile: Telecommunications company serving the Great Plains, Rocky Mountain, and Pacific Northwest states.

Plan Specifics:
- Initial purchases may be made directly from the company (minimum $300).
- Need 4 shares to participate in the plan.
- Partial dividend reinvestment is available.
- No Discount.
- OCP: $25 to $100,000 per year.
- Company purchases stock weekly with OCPs.
- DRIP administrative fees are $4 per year.
- Selling costs are approximately 6 cents per share.
- Automatic investment services are available.
- Dividends are paid February, May, August, and November.

Performance Rating: ****
DRIP Rating: 👍

United Water Resources, Inc.
(NYSE:UWR)
200 Old Hook Rd.
Harrington Park, NJ 07640
(201) 767-2811

Business Profile: Public utility holding company supplying water to portions of New Jersey and New York.

Plan Specifics:
- Partial dividend reinvestment is available.
- 5 percent discount on reinvested dividends and 3 percent discount on OCPs.
- OCP: $25 to $3000 per quarter.
- Selling costs are brokerage commissions.
- Company purchases stock monthly with OCPs.
- Customers of certain utility subsidiaries may make initial purchase of stock directly through the plan ($25 minimum).
- Approximately 11,000 shareholders are in the plan.
- Dividends are paid March, June, September, and December.

Performance Rating: ***
DRIP Rating: 👍

UNITIL Corp. (ASE:UTL)
216 Epping Rd.
Exeter, NH 03833-4571
(603) 772-0775   (800) 999-6501

Business Profile: Public utility holding company operating in New Hampshire and Massachusetts.

Plan Specifics:
- Partial dividend reinvestment is available.
- 5 percent discount on reinvested dividends.
- OCP: $25 to $5000 per quarter.
- Selling costs are brokerage commissions and transfer taxes.
- Company purchases stock quarterly with OCPs.

- Dividends are paid February, May, August, and November.

Performance Rating: ***

DRIP Rating: 👍

Universal Corp. (NYSE:UVV)
PO Box 25099
Richmond, VA 23260
(804) 359-9311   (804) 254-1303

Business Profile: Major factor in leaf tobacco market with operations in agriproducts.

Plan Specifics:

- Partial dividend reinvestment is available.
- No Discount.
- OCP: $10 to $1000 per month.
- No selling costs.
- Company purchases stock monthly with OCPs.
- Dividends are paid February, May, August, and November.

Performance Rating: ***

DRIP Rating: 👍

Universal Foods Corp.
(NYSE:UFC)
433 E. Michigan St.
Milwaukee, WI 53202
(414) 271-6755

Business Profile: Produces yeast products, food flavorings and colors, and dehydrated seasonings.

Plan Specifics:

- Partial dividend reinvestment is available.
- No Discount.
- OCP: $25 to $1500 per month.
- Selling costs include fees, commissions, and other expenses.
- Company purchases stock monthly with OCPs.

- Dividends are paid March, June, September, and December.

Performance Rating: ****

DRIP Rating: 👍

Universal Health Realty Income
Trust (NYSE:UHT)
367 S. Gulph Rd.
King of Prussia, PA 19406
(610) 265-0688

Business Profile: Real estate investment trust investing in income-producing health-care facilities.

Plan Specifics:

- Partial dividend reinvestment is available.
- No Discount.
- OCP: $25 to $5000 per month.
- Purchasing fees may include brokerage commissions and 5 percent charge on each investment (maximum $3).
- Stock is purchased monthly with OCPs.
- Selling costs are brokerage commissions and a service charge of 5 percent on each sale (maximum $10).
- Dividends are paid March, June, September, and December.

Performance Rating: ***

DRIP Rating: 👍

Unocal Corp. (NYSE:UCL)
c/o Chemical Bank
PO Box 24935
New York, NY 10242-4935
(800) 279-1249   (800) 252-2233

Business Profile: Integrated crude oil and natural gas producer.

Plan Specifics:
- Need 25 or more shares to enroll.
- Partial dividend reinvestment is available.
- 3 percent discount on reinvested dividends.
- OCP: $50 to $10,000 per month.
- Stock is purchased monthly with OCPs.
- Fees include a 5 percent service charge on OCPs (max. $3), a $5 safekeeping fee (one time), a $5 withdrawal fee (per withdrawal), and a $15 sales administrative fee (per sale).
- Preferred dividends are eligible for reinvestment for additional common shares under the plan.
- Dividends are paid February, May, August, and November.

Performance Rating: ***
DRIP Rating: 👍

UNUM Corp. (NYSE:UNM)
c/o First Chicago Trust-NY
PO Box 2533
Jersey City, NJ 07303-2533
(800) 446-2617

Business Profile: Provider of a wide range of disability, health, life insurance, and group pension products.

Plan Specifics:
- Partial dividend reinvestment is available.
- No Discount.
- OCP: $100 to $60,000 per year.
- Selling costs are brokerage commissions and any other costs of sale.
- Company purchases stock monthly with OCPs.

- Dividends are paid February, May, August, and November.

Performance Rating: ***
DRIP Rating: 👍

Upjohn Co. (NYSE:UPJ)
7000 Portage Rd.
Kalamazoo, MI 49001
(800) 253-8600   (800) 323-1849

Business Profile: Major provider of prescription pharmaceuticals, including steroids and antibiotics.

Plan Specifics:
- Partial dividend reinvestment is available.
- No Discount.
- OCP: $25 to $6000 per quarter.
- Selling costs are brokerage fees.
- Company purchases stock monthly with OCPs.
- Approximately 20,000 shareholders are in the plan.
- Dividends are paid February, May, August, and November.

Performance Rating: ****
DRIP Rating: 👍

Upper Peninsula Energy Corp.
(NASDAQ:UPEN)
600 Lakeshore Dr.
PO Box 130
Houghton, MI 49931-0130
(906) 487-5000

Business Profile: Holding company whose main subsidiary provides electric service to northern Michigan (Upper Peninsula) customers.

Plan Specifics:
- Partial dividend reinvestment is not available.
- No Discount.
- OCP: $50 to $5000 per quarter.

- Selling costs are brokerage fees and a handling charge of $3.
- Company purchases stock quarterly with OCPs.
- Dividends are paid February, May, August, and November.

Performance Rating: ***

DRIP Rating: 👍

US BANCORP, Inc.
(NASDAQ:UBAN)
Main and Franklin Streets
Johnstown, PA 15901
(814) 533-5319   (617) 575-3170

Business Profile: Bank holding company.
Plan Specifics:
- Partial dividend reinvestment is not available.
- 3 percent discount on reinvested dividends and OCPs.
- OCP: $10 to $2000 per month.
- OCPs are invested monthly.
- Shareholder assumes all liquidation costs.
- Dividends are paid January, April, July, and October.

Performance Rating: NR
DRIP Rating: 👍

USF&G Corp. (NYSE:FG)
c/o Bank of New York
PO Box 11258, Church St. Sta.
New York, NY 10286
(800) 524-4458

Business Profile: Leading property-casualty insurance company.
Plan Specifics:
- Partial dividend reinvestment is available.
- No Discount.
- OCP: $50 to $5000 per quarter.

- Selling costs are minimal brokerage fees.
- Company purchases stock monthly with OCPs.
- Dividends are paid January, April, July, and October.

Performance Rating: **

DRIP Rating: 👍

USLIFE Corp. (NYSE:USH)
c/o Chemical Bank
PO Box 3069, JAF Bldg.
New York, NY 10116-3069
(800) 851-9677

Business Profile: Holding company with major operations in life insurance.
Plan Specifics:
- Partial dividend reinvestment is available.
- No Discount.
- OCP: $25 to $4000 per quarter.
- Selling costs include brokerage and handling charges.
- Stock is purchased monthly with OCPs.
- Dividends are paid March, June, September, and December.

Performance Rating: ****
DRIP Rating: 👍

UST Corp. (NASDAQ:USTB)
40 Court St.
Boston, MA 02108
(617) 726-7000

Business Profile: Bank holding company with operations in Massachusetts and Connecticut.
Plan Specifics:
- Partial dividend reinvestment is available.

- 10 percent discount on reinvested dividends and OCPs.
- OCP: $3 multiplied by number of shares held in account ($100 minimum). Must have at least 34 shares to participate in OCP part of plan.
- OCPs are invested quarterly.
- Must sell shares through own broker.
- The company is currently not paying a dividend.

Performance Rating: **

DRIP Rating: ☞

UST, Inc. (NYSE:UST)
100 W. Putnam Ave.
Greenwich, CT 06830
(203) 622-3656

Business Profile: Leading producer of smokeless tobacco, cigars, pipes, and wine.

Plan Specifics:

- Partial dividend reinvestment is available.
- No Discount.
- OCP: $10 to $10,000 per month.
- Selling costs are brokerage fees and a bank service fee (maximum $5).
- Company purchases stock around the 15th and the last business day of each month with OCPs.
- Dividends are paid March, June, September, and December.

Performance Rating: ****

DRIP Rating: 👍

USX Corp.-Marathon (NYSE:MRO)
600 Grant St., Room 611
Pittsburgh, PA 15219-4776
(412) 433-4801   (412) 433-1121

Business Profile: Operations in gas and oil production.

Plan Specifics:

- Partial dividend reinvestment is available.
- Discount on reinvested dividends and OCPs can range from 0-3 percent.
- OCP: $50 to $5000 per month. Waiver required for amounts over $5000.
- Selling costs are brokerage commissions and any transfer tax.
- Company purchases stock monthly with OCPs.
- Dividends are paid March, June, September, and December.

Performance Rating: **

DRIP Rating: 👍

USX Corp.-U.S. Steel Group (NYSE:X)
600 Grant St., Room 611
Pittsburgh, PA 15219-4776
(412) 433-4801   (412) 433-1121

Business Profile: Nation's largest integrated steel maker.

Plan Specifics:

- Partial dividend reinvestment is not available.
- Discount on reinvested dividends and OCPs can range from 0-3 percent.
- OCP: $50 to $5000 per month. Waiver required for amounts over $5000.

- Selling costs are brokerage commissions and any transfer tax.
- Company purchases stock monthly with OCPs.
- Dividends are paid March, June, September, and December.

Performance Rating: **

DRIP Rating: ◆

UtiliCorp United, Inc.
  (NYSE:UCU)
Shareholder Relations
PO Box 13287
Kansas City, MO 64199-3287
(816) 421-6600   (800) 487-6661

Business Profile: Provides electric power and natural gas to eight states and a Canadian province.

Plan Specifics:

- Initial purchase of stock may be made directly from the company ($250 minimum).
- Partial dividend reinvestment is available.
- 5 percent discount on reinvested dividends.
- OCP: $50 to $10,000 per month.
- Selling costs are approximately $20 plus 12 cents per share.
- Company purchases stock monthly with OCPs.
- IRA option is available.
- Automatic investment services are available.
- Approximately 22,300 share-holders are in the plan.
- Dividends are paid March, June, September, and December.

Performance Rating: ****

DRIP Rating: ◆

Valley National Bancorp (NJ)
  (NYSE:VLY)
1445 Valley Rd.
Wayne, NJ 07470
(201) 773-6662

Business Profile: New Jersey bank holding company.

Plan Specifics:

- Firm prefers that a minimum of 25 shares are held to enroll.
- Partial dividend reinvestment is not available.
- No Discount.
- OCP: $50 to $2000 per month.
- No selling costs.
- Company purchases stock at least monthly with OCPs or more frequently if enough funds accumulate to purchase 100 shares.
- Dividends are paid January, April, July, and October.

Performance Rating: ***

DRIP Rating: ◆

Valley Resources, Inc. (ASE:VR)
PO Box 7900
Cumberland, RI 02864-0700
(401) 334-1188   (800) 524-4458

Business Profile: Diversified energy company providing natural gas utility service in northern Rhode Island, with subsidiaries providing retail propane service, sales, and rental of gas-fired appliances.

Plan Specifics:

- Partial dividend reinvestment is available.
- 5 percent discount on reinvested dividends.
- OCP: $25 to $5000 per month.

- Participants incur brokerage fees and a service charge when selling.
- Company purchases stock monthly with OCPs.
- Dividends are paid January, April, July, and October.

Performance Rating: ***

DRIP Rating: 👍

Varian Associates, Inc.
(NYSE:VAR)
PO Box 10800
Palo Alto, CA 94303-0883
(415) 424-5314   (800) 730-4001

Business Profile: Manufactures electronic devices, semiconductor equipment, and analytical instruments.

Plan Specifics:

- Partial dividend reinvestment is not available.
- No Discount.
- OCP: $100 to $2500 per month.
- Company purchases stock every month with OCPs.
- Purchasing fees are brokerage commission and a service charge of 5 percent (maximum $5) for each dividend and/or OCP.
- Selling costs include brokerage fees and service charges ($5 maximum).
- Dividends are paid February, May, August, and November.

Performance Rating: ***

DRIP Rating: 👍

Venture Stores, Inc. (NYSE:VEN)
c/o Mellon Transfer Services
PO Box 750
Pittsburgh, PA 15230-9624
(800) 426-5754   (314) 281-5500

Business Profile: Operates a regional chain of retail discount stores in the Midwest.

Plan Specifics:

- Must own at least 50 shares to participate.
- Partial dividend reinvestment is not available.
- No Discount.
- OCP: $25 to no maximum.
- Purchasing fees are brokerage commissions and a service charge of $1.50 per statement.
- Company purchases stock every month with OCPs.
- Selling costs include brokerage fees and a $3 service charge per transaction.
- Safekeeping services are available ($5 fee per deposit).
- The company is not currently paying a dividend.

Performance Rating: *

DRIP Rating: 👎

Vermont Financial Services Corp.
(NASDAQ:VFSC)
100 Main St.
Brattleboro, VT 05301
(802) 257-7151

Business Profile: Commercial banking organization in Vermont.

Plan Specifics:

- Partial dividend reinvestment is not available.
- No Discount.
- OCP: up to $3000 per quarter.
- Must go through own broker to sell shares.
- Company purchases stock quarterly with OCPs.
- Dividends are paid February, May, August, and November.

Performance Rating: NR
DRIP Rating: 👎

Versa Technologies, Inc.
 (NASDAQ:VRSA)
9301 Washington Ave.
PO Box 085012
Racine, WI 53408
(414) 886-1174

Business Profile: Produces silicone rubber products, fluid power products, and parts and devices for the medical and food-processing markets.

Plan Specifics:
- Partial dividend reinvestment is available.
- No Discount.
- OCP: $50 to $6000 per quarter.
- Company purchases stock twice a month with OCPs.
- Selling costs are brokerage commissions and taxes.
- Dividends are paid February, May, August, and November.

Performance Rating: ***
DRIP Rating: 👍

VF Corp. (NYSE:VFC)
c/o First Chicago Trust-NY
PO Box 2533
Jersey City, NJ 07303-2533
(800) 446-2617

Business Profile: Manufactures jeans, sportswear, intimate apparel, and occupational clothing.

Plan Specifics:
- Partial dividend reinvestment is not available.
- No Discount.
- OCP: $10 to $3000 per quarter.
- Company purchases stock quarterly with OCPs.

- Purchasing fees are brokerage commissions and a service charge of 5 percent of the amount invested (maximum $2.50).
- Selling costs are brokerage fees.
- Dividends are paid March, June, September, and December.

Performance Rating: ****
DRIP Rating: 👍

Vulcan Materials Co.
 (NYSE:VMC)
c/o First Chicago Trust-NY
PO Box 2533
Jersey City, NJ 07303-2533
(201) 324-0498   (205) 877-3202
(800) 446-2617

Business Profile: Major supplier of construction material and industrial chemicals.

Plan Specifics:
- Partial dividend reinvestment is not available.
- No Discount.
- OCP: $10 to $3000 per quarter.
- Purchasing fees are brokerage commissions and a service charge of 5 percent (maximum $2.50) for each investment of a dividend or OCP.
- Selling costs are brokerage commissions and other costs of sale.
- Company purchases stock quarterly with OCPs.
- Dividends are paid March, June, September, and December.

Performance Rating: ***
DRIP Rating: 👍

Wachovia Corp. (NYSE:WB)
301 N. Main St.
Winston-Salem, NC 27150
(910) 770-5000

Business Profile: Holding company for banks in North Carolina, South Carolina, and Georgia.

Plan Specifics:

- Partial dividend reinvestment is available.
- No Discount.
- OCP: $20 to $2000 per month.
- Selling costs are brokerage fees.
- Company purchases stock once a month with OCPs.
- Over 13,000 shareholders are in the plan.
- Dividends are paid March, June, September, and December.

Performance Rating: ****
DRIP Rating: 👍

Walden Residential Properties, Inc. (NYSE:WDN)
c/o First Nat'l Bank of Boston
Dividend Reinvestment and
 Stock Purchase Plan
PO Box 1681
Mail Stop 45-01-06
Boston, MA 02105-1681
(617) 575-3120   (214) 788-0510

Business Profile: Real estate investment trust which invests in properties located primarily in southwestern U.S. and Florida.

Plan Specifics:

- Partial dividend reinvestment is available.
- 5 percent discount on reinvested dividends and OCPs.
- OCP: $100 to $10,000 per month.
- OCP is invested monthly.
- Selling costs are brokerage fees.
- Dividends are paid March, June, September, and December.

Performance Rating: **
DRIP Rating: 👍

Walgreen Co. (NYSE:WAG)
200 Wilmot Rd.
Deerfield, IL 60015
(312) 461-5535   (312) 461-3885

Business Profile: Largest United States retail drugstore chain.

Plan Specifics:

- Partial dividend reinvestment is not available.
- No Discount.
- OCP: $10 to $5000 per quarter.
- Selling costs are brokerage commissions.
- Stock is purchased approximately 8 times a year with OCPs.
- Dividends are paid March, June, September, and December.

Performance Rating: *****
DRIP Rating: 👍

Warner-Lambert Co. (NYSE:WLA)
201 Tabor Rd.
Morris Plains, NJ 07950
(201) 540-2000   (800) 446-2617

Business Profile: Leading provider of pharmaceuticals, over-the-counter drugs, and gum.

Plan Specifics:

- Partial dividend reinvestment is available.
- No Discount.
- OCP: $10 to $60,000 per year.
- Selling costs are brokerage commissions and a handling charge.

- Stock is purchased monthly with OCPs.
- Stock may be sold via the telephone.
- Dividends are paid March, June, September, and December.

Performance Rating: *****

DRIP Rating: 👍

Washington Energy Co.
(NYSE:WEG)
Attn: Treasury Dept.
PO Box 1869
Seattle, WA 98111
(800) 320-4597   (206) 622-6767

Business Profile: Washington-based gas utility holding company.

Plan Specifics:
- Partial dividend reinvestment is available.
- No Discount.
- OCP: $25 to $5000 per quarter.
- Company issues stock to the plan quarterly for OCPs.
- Selling costs are brokerage fees.
- Approximately one-half of direct shareholders are enrolled in the plan.
- Dividends are paid March, June, September, and December.

Performance Rating: **

DRIP Rating: 👍

Washington Gas Light Co.
(NYSE:WGL)
1100 H St. NW
Washington, DC 20080
(800) 221-9427   (703) 750-4440

Business Profile: Supplies natural gas to areas of Washington, D.C., Virginia, and Maryland.

Plan Specifics:
- Partial dividend reinvestment is available.
- No Discount.
- OCP: $25 to $20,000 per quarter.
- Company purchases stock on the 1st trading day of the month with OCPs.
- Selling costs are approximately 3-5 cents per share.
- Preferred dividends are eligible for reinvestment for additional common shares under the plan.
- Approximately 12,000 shareholders are in the plan.
- Dividends are paid February, May, August, and November.

Performance Rating: ***

DRIP Rating: 👍

Washington Mutual, Inc.
(NASDAQ:WAMU)
Dividend Reinvestment and
Stock Purchase Plan
PO Box 750
Pittsburgh, PA 15230-0750
(800) 522-6645   (206) 461-8856

Business Profile: Washington-based financial institution.

Plan Specifics:
- Partial dividend reinvestment is available.
- No Discount.
- OCP: $50 to $10,000 per quarter.
- Company purchases stock monthly with OCPs.
- Selling fees may include brokerage costs.
- Automatic investment services are available.
- Dividends are paid February, May, August, and November.

Performance Rating: ***
DRIP Rating: 👍

Washington National Corp.
(NYSE:WNT)
300 Tower Parkway
Lincolnshire, IL 60069
(708) 793-3000

Business Profile: Financial services holding organization. Writes and sells life, annuity, and health insurance.

Plan Specifics:

- Partial dividend reinvestment is available.
- 5 percent discount on reinvested dividends.
- OCP: $25 to $5000 per quarter.
- Selling costs include brokerage fees.
- Company purchases stock quarterly with OCPs.
- Preferred dividends are eligible for reinvestment for additional common shares under the plan.
- Approximately 800 shareholders are in the plan.
- Dividends are paid January, April, July, and October.

Performance Rating: ***
DRIP Rating: 👍

Washington Real Estate
Investment Trust (ASE:WRE)
10400 Connecticut Ave.
Kensington, MD 20895
(301) 929-5900   (800) 937-5449

Business Profile: Real estate investment trust investing in income-producing properties in Baltimore-Washington region.

Plan Specifics:

- Partial dividend reinvestment is available.
- No Discount.
- OCP: $100 to $25,000 per year.
- Selling costs are brokerage expenses.
- Company purchases stock monthly with OCPs.
- Dividends are paid March, June, September, and December.

Performance Rating: ****
DRIP Rating: 👍

Washington Trust Bancorp, Inc.
(NASDAQ:WASH)
23 Broad St.
PO Box 512
Westerly, RI 02891-0512
(401) 348-1200

Business Profile: Bank holding company serving most of southern Rhode Island and a portion of southeastern Connecticut.

Plan Specifics:

- Partial dividend reinvestment is not available.
- No Discount.
- OCP: $25 to $1000 per quarter.
- Company purchases stock quarterly with OCPs.
- Must go through a broker to sell shares from the plan.
- Automatic investment services are available.
- Dividends are paid January, April, July, and October.

Performance Rating: NR
DRIP Rating: 👍

Washington Water Power Co. (NYSE:WWP)
PO Box 3647
Spokane, WA 99220
(800) 727-9170   (509) 489-0500

Business Profile: Supplies electricity and gas service to customers in Washington and Idaho.

Plan Specifics:
- Partial dividend reinvestment is not available.
- No Discount.
- OCP: up to $100,000 per year.
- Purchasing and selling fees may include brokerage commissions.
- Company purchases stock around the 15th of month with OCPs.
- Dividends are paid March, June, September, and December.

Performance Rating: **

DRIP Rating: 👍

Weingarten Realty Investors (NYSE:WRI)
c/o Ameritrust Co.
PO Box 6477
Cleveland, OH 44101
(216) 737-5745

Business Profile: Real estate investment trust developing shopping centers primarily in southern states.

Plan Specifics:
- Partial dividend reinvestment is available.
- No Discount.
- OCP: $10 to $15,000 per quarter.
- Company purchases stock at least quarterly with OCPs.
- Purchasing fees are 5 percent of amount invested (maximum $3) and brokerage fee.

- Selling costs are brokerage commission and $5 service charge.
- $5 termination fee.
- Dividends are paid March, June, September, and December.

Performance Rating: ***

DRIP Rating: 👍

Weis Markets, Inc. (NYSE:WMK)
1000 S. Second St.
Sunbury, PA 17801
(717) 286-4571

Business Profile: Manages retail food stores in Pennsylvania.

Plan Specifics:
- Partial dividend reinvestment is not available.
- No Discount.
- OCP: $10 to $3000 per quarter.
- Selling costs are brokerage commissions.
- Company purchases stock quarterly with OCPs.
- Dividends are paid February, May, August, and November.

Performance Rating: ****

DRIP Rating: 👍

Wells Fargo & Co. (NYSE:WFC)
c/o First Chicago Trust Co.-NY
PO Box 2598
Jersey City, NJ 07303-2598
(800) 446-2617

Business Profile: Bank holding company based in California.

Plan Specifics:
- Partial dividend reinvestment is available.
- 3 percent discount on reinvested dividends.
- OCP: $150 to $2000 per month.

- Selling fees include $15 handling charge and brokerage fees.
- Stock is purchased monthly with OCPs.
- Dividends are paid February, May, August, and November.

Performance Rating: ***

DRIP Rating: ℘

Wendy's International, Inc. (NYSE:WEN)
4288 W. Dublin-Granville Rd.
Dublin, OH 43017
(614) 764-3100   (212) 936-5100

Business Profile: Owns and operates Wendy's quick-service restaurants.

Plan Specifics:

- Partial dividend reinvestment is available.
- No Discount.
- OCP: $20 to $20,000 annually.
- Selling costs are brokerage charges and a $2 service fee.
- Company purchases stock monthly with OCPs.
- Dividends are paid March, May, August, and November.

Performance Rating: ****

DRIP Rating: 👍

Wesbanco, Inc. (NASDAQ:WSBC)
1 Bank Plaza
Wheeling, WV 26003
(304) 234-9208

Business Profile: Bank holding company conducting a general banking, commercial, and trust business.

Plan Specifics:

- Partial dividend reinvestment is available.

- No Discount.
- OCP: $10 to $5000 per quarter.
- Selling costs are brokerage commissions.
- Company purchases stock quarterly with OCPs.
- Dividends are paid January, April, July, and October.

Performance Rating: NR

DRIP Rating: 👍

West (The) Company (NYSE:WST)
101 Gordon Dr.
PO Box 645
Lionville, PA 19341-0645
(800) 937-5449

Business Profile: Leading maker of specialized packaging components for the pharmaceutical and medical device industries.

Plan Specifics:

- Partial dividend reinvestment is not available.
- No Discount.
- OCP: $50 to $5000 per month.
- Company purchases stock monthly with OCPs.
- No selling fees.
- Dividends are paid February, May, August, and November.

Performance Rating: ***

DRIP Rating: 👍

Westamerica Bancorp (NASDAQ:WABC)
c/o Bank of America
PO Box 37002
San Francisco, CA 94137
(415) 257-8000

Business Profile: California-based bank holding company.

Plan Specifics:
- Partial dividend reinvestment is not available.
- No Discount.
- OCP: $25 to $400 per month.
- Selling costs are brokerage fees.
- Company purchases stock monthly with OCPs.
- Dividends are paid February, May, August, and November.

Performance Rating: ***

DRIP Rating: 👍

Westcoast Energy Inc. (NYSE:WE)
Ste. 3400, Park Pl.
666 Burrard St.
Vancouver, BC V6C 3M8
Canada
(604) 488-8000

Business Profile: Canadian corporation in the natural gas industry. Holds core assets in gas pipelines, processing, and distribution.

Plan Specifics:
- Partial dividend reinvestment is available.
- 5 percent discount on reinvested dividends.
- OCP: $50 to $5000 (Canadian) per quarter.
- Stock is purchased quarterly with OCPs.
- Must sell shares through own broker.
- Preferred dividends are eligible for reinvestment for additional common shares under the plan.
- Dividends are paid March, June, September, and December.

Performance Rating: **

DRIP Rating: 👍

Western Investment Real Estate Trust (ASE: WIR)
3450 California St.
San Francisco, CA 94118-1837
(415) 929-0211

Business Profile: Real estate investment trust which invests primarily in community shopping centers.

Plan Specifics:
- Partial dividend reinvestment is available.
- No Discount.
- OCP: $500 to $5000 per quarter.
- OCPs are invested quarterly.
- Investors may have to sell shares through broker.
- Dividends are paid March, June, September, and December.

Performance Rating: **

DRIP Rating: 👎

Western Resources, Inc.
(NYSE:WR)
818 Kansas Ave.
PO Box 889
Topeka, KS 66601-0889
(800) 527-2495

Business Profile: Natural gas and electric utility serving customers in Kansas and Oklahoma.

Plan Specifics:
- Initial purchases may be made directly through the plan ($250 minimum).
- Partial dividend reinvestment is available.
- No Discount.
- OCP: $20 to $60,000 per year.
- Purchasing fees are brokerage commissions and any other fees.
- Selling costs are brokerage commissions and any transfer tax.

- Company purchases stock monthly with OCPs.
- Safekeeping services are available.
- Dividends are paid January, April, July, and October.

Performance Rating: ***

DRIP Rating: 👍

Westinghouse Electric Corp. (NYSE:WX)
Westinghouse Building
Gateway Center
Pittsburgh, PA 15222
(412) 244-2000   (800) 507-7799

Business Profile: Engaged in five core businesses: broadcasting, electronic systems, environmental, industries, and power systems.

Plan Specifics:
- Partial dividend reinvestment is available.
- No Discount.
- OCP: $100 to $5000 per month.
- Selling costs are brokerage commissions and any applicable transfer taxes.
- Company purchases stock monthly with OCPs.
- Dividends are paid March, June, September, and December.

Performance Rating: ***

DRIP Rating: 👍

Westport Bancorp, Inc. (NASDAQ:WBAT)
87 Post Rd., E.
Westport, CT 06880
(203) 222-6911

Business Profile: Bank holding company offering commercial banking, consumer banking, and trust services.

Plan Specifics:
- Partial dividend reinvestment is not available.
- 5 percent discount on reinvested dividends and OCPs.
- OCP: $25 to $3000 per quarter.
- Company purchases stock quarterly with OCPs.
- Dividends are paid February, May, August, and November.

Performance Rating: NR

DRIP Rating: 👍

Westvaco Corp. (NYSE:W)
299 Park Ave.
New York, NY 10171
(212) 688-5000

Business Profile: Manufactures bleached board and printing paper.

Plan Specifics:
- Partial dividend reinvestment is available.
- No Discount.
- OCP: up to $5000 per quarter.
- Selling costs are brokerage charges.
- Company purchases stock monthly with OCPs.
- Dividends are paid January, April, July, and October.

Performance Rating: ***

DRIP Rating: 👍

Weyerhaeuser Co. (NYSE:WY)
c/o Chemical Bank
PO Box 3069, JAF Bldg.
New York, NY 10116-3069
(800) 561-4405

Business Profile: Timber and forest-products concern.

Plan Specifics:
- Partial dividend reinvestment is available.
- No Discount.
- OCP: $100 to $5000 per quarter.
- Stock is purchased monthly with OCPs.
- Purchasing fees are brokerage commissions and 4 percent service charge (maximum $1.50) on reinvested dividends and $5 charge for investments of OCPs.
- Selling costs are brokerage fees.
- $3 charge for safekeeping of certificates.
- $5 fee for issuance of certificates.
- Dividends are paid February, May, August, and November.

Performance Rating: ****
DRIP Rating: 👍

Whirlpool Corp. (NYSE:WHR)
c/o Harris Trust & Savings
PO Box A3309
Chicago, IL 60690
(800) 526-8762

Business Profile: Leading manufacturer and marketer of household appliances.

Plan Specifics:
- Partial dividend reinvestment is available.
- No Discount.
- OCP: $10 to $50,000 per year.
- Stock is purchased monthly with OCPs.
- No selling costs.
- Dividends are paid March, June, September, and December.

Performance Rating: ****
DRIP Rating: 👍

Whitman Corp. (NYSE:WH)
3501 Algonquin Rd.
Rolling Meadows, IL 60008
(708) 818-5000

Business Profile: Consumer goods and beverage company.

Plan Specifics:
- Partial dividend reinvestment is available.
- No Discount.
- OCP: $10 to $60,000 per year.
- Selling costs include brokerage fees and a handling charge.
- Company purchases stock monthly with OCPs.
- Dividends are paid January, April, July, and October.

Performance Rating: ***
DRIP Rating: 👍

WICOR, Inc. (NYSE:WIC)
PO Box 334
Milwaukee, WI 53201
(800) 236-3453   (414) 291-6550

Business Profile: Natural gas utility holding company serving customers in Wisconsin.

Plan Specifics:
- Partial dividend reinvestment is not available.
- No Discount.
- OCP: $100 to $10,000 per month.
- Selling costs are brokerage fees.
- Company purchases stock monthly with OCPs.
- Residents of Wisconsin may make initial purchase of stock directly from the company ($100 minimum).
- Approximately 8000 shareholders are in the plan.
- Dividends are paid February, May, August, and November.

Performance Rating: ****
DRIP Rating: 👍

Wilmington Trust Co.
(NASDAQ:WILM)
Rodney Square North
Wilmington, DE 19890
(302) 651-1000   (302) 651-1448

Business Profile: Conducts commercial banking, investment management, and savings operations.

Plan Specifics:
- Partial dividend reinvestment is available.
- No Discount.
- OCP: $10 to $5000 a quarter.
- Company purchases stock monthly with OCPs.
- Selling costs include brokerage fees.
- Automatic investment services are available.
- Dividends are paid February, May, August, and November.

Performance Rating: ****
DRIP Rating: 👍

Winn-Dixie Stores, Inc.
(NYSE:WIN)
PO Box B
5050 Edgewood Ct.
Jacksonville, FL 32203-0297
(904) 783-5000

Business Profile: Owns and manages supermarkets in southern states.

Plan Specifics:
- Must have 10 shares to enroll or remain in the plan.
- Partial dividend reinvestment is not available.
- No Discount.

- OCP: $10 to $10,000 per month.
- Must go through own broker to sell shares.
- Company purchases stock monthly with OCPs.
- Dividends are paid every month.

Performance Rating: *****
DRIP Rating: 👍

Wisconsin Energy Corp.
(NYSE:WEC)
PO Box 2949
231 W. Michigan St.
Milwaukee, WI 53201
(800) 558-9663

Business Profile: Provides electric power, gas, and steam to portions of Wisconsin and Michigan.

Plan Specifics:
- Initial purchases may be made directly from the company ($50 minimum).
- Partial dividend reinvestment is available.
- No Discount.
- OCP: $25 to $50,000 per quarter.
- Selling costs are approximately 5-10 cents per share.
- Company purchases stock twice a month with OCPs.
- Automatic investment services are available.
- Preferred dividends are eligible for reinvestment for additional common shares under the plan.
- Telephone redemption is available.
- Automatic deposit of dividends is available.
- Approximately 60,000 shareholders are in the plan.
- Dividends are paid March, June, September, and December.

Performance Rating: *****
DRIP Rating: 👍

Witco Corp. (NYSE:WIT)
520 Madison Ave.
New York, NY 10022-4236
(203) 552-2000

Business Profile: Manufactures specialty chemicals and petroleum products.
Plan Specifics:
- Partial dividend reinvestment is not available.
- No Discount.
- OCP: $10 to $20,000 per year.
- Selling costs include brokerage fees.
- Company purchases stock monthly with OCPs.
- Dividends are paid January, April, July, and October.

Performance Rating: ***
DRIP Rating: 👍

WLR Foods, Inc.
(NASDAQ:WLRF)
PO Box 7000
Broadway, VA 22815
(703) 896-7001

Business Profile: Fully integrated provider of turkey and chicken products with operations in Virginia, West Virginia, and Pennsylvania.
Plan Specifics:
- Partial dividend reinvestment is available.
- No Discount.
- OCP: $100 to $20,000 per year.
- Stock is purchased quarterly with OCPs.
- There are no fees associated with the plan.

- Certificate safekeeping is available.
- Dividends are paid January, April, July, and October.

Performance Rating: **
DRIP Rating: 👍

WMX Technologies, Inc.
(NYSE:WMX)
3003 Butterfield Rd.
Oak Brook, IL 60521
(708) 572-8800

Business Profile: Largest operator of waste collection and disposal services.
Plan Specifics:
- Partial dividend reinvestment is not available.
- No Discount.
- OCP: $25 to $2000 per month.
- Company purchases stock monthly with OCPs.
- Selling costs are approximately 5 cents per share.
- Dividends are paid January, April, July, and October.

Performance Rating: *****
DRIP Rating: 👍

Woolworth Corp. (NYSE:Z)
Woolworth Bldg.
233 Broadway
New York, NY 10279
(212) 553-2000   (800) 446-2617

Business Profile: Owns and operates general merchandise, specialty, and shoe stores.
Plan Specifics:
- Partial dividend reinvestment is available.
- No Discount.
- OCP: $20 to $60,000 per year.

- Selling costs are brokerage commissions and other costs of sale.
- Company purchases stock monthly with OCPs.
- Dividends are paid March, June, September, and December.

Performance Rating: **

DRIP Rating: 👍

Worthington Industries, Inc. (NASDAQ:WTHG)
1205 Dearborn Dr.
Columbus, OH 43085
(614) 438-3210   (800) 442-2001

Business Profile: Manufactures processed steel products, injection-molded plastic parts, and steel castings.

Plan Specifics:

- Partial dividend reinvestment is available.
- No Discount.
- OCP: $50 to $5000 per quarter.
- Selling costs are brokerage fees.
- Company purchases stock quarterly with OCPs.
- Dividends are paid March, June, September, and December.

Performance Rating: ***

DRIP Rating: 👍

WPL Holdings, Inc. (NYSE:WPH)
PO Box 2568
Madison, WI 53701-2568
(800) 356-5343   (608) 252-3407

Business Profile: Provides electric energy, natural gas, and water in south-central Wisconsin. Also has businesses in energy services, environmental services, and affordable housing.

Plan Specifics:

- Partial dividend reinvestment is available.
- No Discount.
- OCP: $20 to $25,000 per month.
- Company purchases stock monthly with OCPs.
- Selling costs include brokerage fees.
- Automatic investment services are available.
- Direct deposit of dividends into a checking or savings account is available.
- Preferred dividends are eligible for reinvestment for additional common shares under the plan.
- Approximately 15,700 shareholders are in the plan.
- Dividends are paid February, May, August, and November.

Performance Rating: *****

DRIP Rating: 👍

WPS Resource Corp. (NYSE:WPS)
700 N. Adams St.
PO Box 19001
Green Bay, WI 54307
(414) 433-1050   (800) 236-1551

Business Profile: Utility company supplying electricity and natural gas to customers in northern Wisconsin and an adjacent part of Michigan.

Plan Specifics:

- Initial purchases may be made directly from the company ($100).
- Partial dividend reinvestment is available.
- No Discount.
- OCP: $25 to $100,000 per year.

- Selling costs are brokerage commissions.
- Company purchases stock monthly with OCPs.
- Safekeeping services are available.
- Dividends are paid March, June, September, and December.

Performance Rating: *****

DRIP Rating: 👍

Wrigley (Wm.) Jr. Co. (NYSE:WWY)
410 N. Michigan Ave.
Chicago, IL 60611-4287
(312) 644-2121   (800) 824-9681

Business Profile: World's largest producer of chewing gum.

Plan Specifics:
- Partial dividend reinvestment is not available.
- No Discount.
- OCP: $50 to $5000 per month.
- No selling costs.
- Company purchases stock monthly with OCPs.
- Safekeeping services are available.
- Dividends are paid February, May, August, and November.

Performance Rating: *****

DRIP Rating: 👍

Xerox Corp. (NYSE:XRX)
Dividend Reinvestment Services
PO Box 23228
Rochester, NY 14603
(800) 828-6396

Business Profile: Leading producer of copiers and duplicators.

Plan Specifics:
- Partial dividend reinvestment is available.
- No Discount.
- OCP: $10 to $5000 per month.
- Stock is purchased monthly with OCPs.
- Selling costs include broker fees.
- Preferred dividends are eligible for reinvestment for additional common shares under the plan.
- Dividends are paid January, April, July, and October.

Performance Rating: ****

DRIP Rating: 👍

Yankee Energy System, Inc. (NYSE: YES)
599 Research Parkway
Meriden, CT 06450-1030
(203) 639-4465   (800) 288-9541

Business Profile: Owner of Yankee Gas Services Co., the largest natural gas distribution company in Connecticut.

Plan Specifics:
- Must own at least 50 shares to enroll.
- Partial dividend reinvestment is not available.
- No Discount.
- OCP: $100 to $10,000 per month.
- Company purchases stock monthly with OCPs.
- A $1.50 service charge will be charged each quarter for dividend reinvestment participants and each month an OCP is made.
- Selling costs include brokerage fees and a $5 service fee.

- Shareholders holding fewer than 100 shares may sell all of their shares without paying any brokerage or service charge.
- Family members of existing shareholders may make initial purchases of stock directly from the company ($500 minimum).
- Certificate safekeeping is available.
- Dividends are paid March, June, September, and December.

Performance Rating: ***

DRIP Rating: 👎

York Financial Corp. (NASDAQ:YFED)
PO Box 15068
101 S. George St.
York, PA 17405-7068
(717) 846-8777   (800) 278-4353

Business Profile: Pennsylvania-based savings and loan holding company.

Plan Specifics:
- Partial dividend reinvestment is available.
- 10 percent discount on reinvested dividends.
- OCP: $25 to $2500 per quarter.
- Company purchases stock quarterly with OCPs.
- Selling costs are brokerage commissions and a $1.50 termination fee.
- Dividends are paid February, May, August, and November.

Performance Rating: ***

DRIP Rating: 👍

Zero Corp. (NYSE:ZRO)
444 S. Flower St., Ste. 2100
Los Angeles, CA 90071-2922
(213) 629-7000

Business Profile: Manufactures enclosures and cooling equipment and provides packaging services for electronics industry. Produces enclosures for airline industry.

Plan Specifics:
- Partial dividend reinvestment is not available.
- No Discount.
- OCP: $25 to $8000 per month.
- Purchasing and selling costs are brokerage commissions.
- Company purchases stock monthly with OCPs.
- Approximately 2400 shareholders are in the plan.
- Dividends are paid March, June, September, and December.

Performance Rating: ***

DRIP Rating: 👍

Zions Bancorporation (NASDAQ:ZION)
1380 Kennecott Bldg.
Salt Lake City, UT 84133
(801) 524-4787   (801) 524-4849

Business Profile: Bank holding company with operations in Utah, Nevada, and Arizona.

Plan Specifics:
- Partial dividend reinvestment is available.
- No Discount.
- OCP: $10 to $5000 per quarter.
- Stock is purchased quarterly with OCPs.
- Must go through own broker to sell shares.

- Preferred dividends are eligible for reinvestment for additional common shares under the plan.
- Dividends are paid January, April, July, and October.

Performance Rating: ***

DRIP Rating: 👍

Zurn Industries, Inc. (NYSE:ZRN)
One Zurn Pl.
Erie, PA 16514-2000
(814) 452-2111

Business Profile: Supplies services and products for waste-to-energy plants and water quality control systems.

Plan Specifics:

- Partial dividend reinvestment is available.
- No Discount.
- OCP: $30 to $3000 per quarter.
- Selling costs are $5 termination charge and brokerage fees.
- Company purchases stock quarterly with OCPs.
- Approximately 1500 shareholders are in the plan.
- Dividends are paid January, April, July, and October.

Performance Rating: ***

DRIP Rating: 👍

DRIPs by Performance Ratings

Five Stars (*****)

Abbott Laboratories

Air Products & Chemicals, Inc.

Albertson's, Inc.

American Brands, Inc.

American Home Products Corp.

Ameritech Corp.

Amoco Corp.

AMP, Inc.

Anheuser-Busch Cos., Inc.

AT&T Corp.

Bard (C. R.), Inc.

Becton, Dickinson and Company

Bell Atlantic Corp.

BellSouth Corp.

Block (H & R), Inc.

Bristol-Myers Squibb Co.

Brooklyn Union Gas Co.

Browning-Ferris Industries, Inc.

Campbell Soup Co.

Chevron Corp.

Clorox Co.

Coca-Cola Company

Colgate-Palmolive Co.

CPC International, Inc.

Dauphin Deposit Corp.

Dial Corp.

Diebold, Inc.

Donnelley (R. R.) & Sons Co.

Du Pont (E. I.) de Nemours & Co.

Duke Power Co.

Emerson Electric Co.

Energen Corp.

Equifax, Inc.

Exxon Corp.

Fifth Third Bancorp

Gannett Co., Inc.

General Electric Co.
General Re Corp.
Genuine Parts Co.
Gillette Co.
Heinz (H. J.) Co.
Hershey Foods Corp.
Hubbell, Inc.
Indiana Energy, Inc.
International Flavors & Fragrances,
 Inc.
Johnson & Johnson
Kellogg Co.
Kimberly-Clark Corp.
Laclede Gas Co.
Lilly (Eli) & Co.
Marriott International
Marsh & McLennan Companies,
 Inc.
McDonald's Corp.
MCN Corp.
Medtronic, Inc.
Merck & Co., Inc.
Minnesota Mining & Mfg. Co.
Morgan (J. P.) & Co., Inc.
Morton International, Inc.
Motorola, Inc.
Norfolk Southern Corp.
Northern States Power Co.
NYNEX Corp.
Paychex, Inc.
PepsiCo, Inc.
Pfizer, Inc.
Philip Morris Companies, Inc.
Procter & Gamble Co.
Raytheon Co.
Regions Financial Corp.
Rollins, Inc.

RPM, Inc.
Rubbermaid, Inc.
Sara Lee Corp.
SBC Communications, Inc.
Schering-Plough Corp.
Scientific-Atlanta, Inc.
Sherwin-Williams Company
Southern Co.
Southern Indiana Gas & Electric Co.
Sysco Corp.
TECO Energy, Inc.
Thomas & Betts Corp.
Tribune Company
Walgreen Co.
Warner-Lambert Co.
Winn-Dixie Stores, Inc.
Wisconsin Energy Corp.
WMX Technologies, Inc.
WPL Holdings, Inc.
WPS Resources Corporation
Wrigley (Wm.) Jr. Co.

Four Stars (****)

AFLAC, Inc.
Alco Standard Corp.
Allegheny Power System, Inc.
AlliedSignal, Inc.
American Business Products, Inc.
American Express Co.
American Greetings Corp.
American Heritage Life Investment
 Corp.
American Water Works Co., Inc.
Aon Corp.
Armstrong World Industries, Inc.
Arnold Industries, Inc.
Associated Banc-Corp.

Atlanta Gas Light Co.
Atlantic Richfield Co.
Atmos Energy Corp.
Avery Dennison Corp.
Avnet, Inc.
Baker Hughes, Inc.
Baltimore Gas and Electric Co.
Banc One Corp.
Bancorp Hawaii, Inc.
BancorpSouth, Inc.
Bandag, Inc.
BanPonce Corp.
Banta Corp.
Barnett Banks, Inc.
Bausch & Lomb, Inc.
Baxter International, Inc.
Bay State Gas Co.
Bemis Co., Inc.
Beneficial Corp.
Black Hills Corp.
Boatmen's Bancshares, Inc.
Bob Evans Farms, Inc.
Brady (W. H.) Co.
Briggs & Stratton Corp.
British Petroleum Co. PLC
Brown-Forman Corp.
California Water Service Co.
Carlisle Companies, Inc.
Carolina Power & Light Co.
CCB Financial Corp.
Central & South West Corp.
Central Fidelity Banks, Inc.
Central Louisiana Electric Co., Inc.
Centura Banks, Inc.
Century Telephone Enterprises, Inc.
Chubb Corp.
CIGNA Corp.

Cincinnati Bell, Inc.
Cincinnati Financial Corp.
Citicorp
Citizens Banking Corp.
Citizens Utilities Co.
Clarcor, Inc.
Clayton Homes, Inc.
CNB Bancshares, Inc.
Comerica, Inc.
Computer Associates Int'l, Inc.
COMSAT Corp.
ConAgra, Inc.
Connecticut Energy Corp.
Connecticut Natural Gas Corp.
Conrail, Inc.
Consolidated Edison Co. of New York
Consolidated Natural Gas Co.
CoreStates Financial Corp.
Corning, Inc.
Cracker Barrel Old Country Store, Inc.
Crane Co.
Crompton & Knowles Corp.
CSX Corp.
Dayton Hudson Corp.
Dean Foods Co.
Deposit Guaranty Corp.
Dominion Resources, Inc.
Donaldson Co., Inc.
Dow Chemical Co.
Dow Jones & Co., Inc.
DPL, Inc.
DQE
Duracell International, Inc.
Eastman Kodak Co.
Eaton Corp.

Equitable Resources, Inc.

Federal National Mortgage Association

Federal Signal Corp.

First Commercial Corp.

First Empire State Corp.

First Michigan Bank Corp.

First Security Corp.

First Tennessee National Corp.

First Union Corp.

First Virginia Banks, Inc.

Firstbank of Illinois Co.

Florida Progress Corp.

Fluor Corporation

FPL Group, Inc.

Franklin Resources, Inc.

Frontier Corp.

General Mills, Inc.

Giant Food, Inc.

GoodMark Foods, Inc.

Grand Metropolitan PLC

GTE Corp.

Hannaford Brothers Co.

Hanson PLC

Harcourt General, Inc.

Harland (John H.) Company

Harley-Davidson, Inc.

Harsco Corp.

Home Depot, Inc.

Honeywell, Inc.

Hormel Foods Corp.

Household International, Inc.

HUBCO, Inc.

Illinois Tool Works, Inc.

Imperial Oil Ltd.

Independent Bank Corp. (MI)

Intel Corp.

International Business Machines Corp.

International Paper Co.

Interpublic Group of Companies, Inc.

IPALCO Enterprises, Inc.

Jefferson-Pilot Corp.

Johnson Controls, Inc.

Kennametal, Inc.

Kerr-McGee Corp.

KeyCorp

Knight-Ridder, Inc.

KU Energy Corp.

Lancaster Colony Corp.

LG&E Energy Corp.

Limited (The), Inc.

Lincoln National Corp.

Lincoln Telecommunications Co.

Lockheed Martin Corp.

Loctite Corp.

Lowe's Companies, Inc.

Lubrizol Corp.

Luby's Cafeterias, Inc.

MacDermid, Inc.

Madison Gas & Electric Co.

Manpower, Inc.

Mark Twain Bancshares, Inc.

Marshall & Ilsley Corp.

Mattel, Inc.

May Department Stores Company

McCormick & Co., Inc.

McGraw-Hill Cos., Inc.

MDU Resources Group, Inc.

Mercantile Bankshares Corp.

Mercury Finance Company

Merrill Lynch & Co., Inc.

Millipore Corp.

Mobil Corp.

Monsanto Co.

Moore Corp.

Nalco Chemical Co.

National City Corp.

National Data Corp.

National Fuel Gas Co.

National Service Industries, Inc.

NationsBank Corp.

NBD Bancorp, Inc.

Nestle S.A.

New Jersey Resources Corp.

New York Times Co.

Newell Co.

NICOR, Inc.

NIPSCO Industries, Inc.

Nordson Corp.

Northwest Natural Gas Co.

Northwestern Public Service Co.

Norwest Corp.

Novo-Nordisk A/S

Nucor Corp.

Old Kent Financial Corp.

Omnicare, Inc.

Otter Tail Power Co.

Pacific Telesis Group

PacifiCorp

Pall Corp.

Penney (J. C.) Co., Inc.

Pentair, Inc.

Pep Boys—Manny, Moe & Jack

Phelps Dodge Corp.

Piedmont Natural Gas Co.

Pioneer-Standard Electronics, Inc.

Pitney Bowes, Inc.

PPG Industries, Inc.

Premier Industrial Corp.

Quaker Oats Co.

Questar Corp.

Ralston—Ralston Purina Group

Rhone-Poulenc Rorer, Inc.

Rite Aid Corp.

Roadway Services, Inc.

Rockwell International Corp.

Rollins Truck Leasing Corp.

Russell Corp.

Safety-Kleen Corp.

St. Joseph Light & Power Co.

St. Paul Companies, Inc.

SCANA Corp.

SCEcorp

Schwab (Charles) Corp.

Second Bancorp, Inc.

ServiceMaster Limited Partnership

Smucker (J. M.) Co.

Sonoco Products Co.

South Jersey Industries, Inc.

Southern National Corp.

SouthTrust Corp.

Sprint Corp.

Star Banc Corp.

State Street Boston Corp.

SunTrust Banks, Inc.

Synovus Financial Corp.

Tambrands, Inc.

Texaco, Inc.

Texas Instruments, Inc.

Textron, Inc.

Time Warner, Inc.

Torchmark Corp.

TRW, Inc.

Union Electric Co.

Union Pacific Corp.

United Mobile Homes, Inc.

Universal Foods Corp.
Upjohn Co.
USLIFE Corp.
UST, Inc.
U S West, Inc.
UtiliCorp United, Inc.
VF Corp.
Wachovia Corp.
Washington Real Estate Investment
  Trust
Weis Markets, Inc.
Wendy's International, Inc.
Weyerhaeuser Co.
Whirlpool Corp.
WICOR, Inc.
Wilmington Trust Co.
Xerox Corp.

Three Stars (***)

AAR Corp.
Acme-Cleveland Corp.
Aetna Life and Casualty Co.
Albany International Corp.
Albemarle Corp.
Alcan Aluminium Ltd.
Allergan, Inc.
Allied Group, Inc.
Allstate Corp.
ALLTEL Corporation
Aluminum Company of America
AMCOL International Corp.
AMCORE Financial, Inc.
Amerada Hess Corp.
American Electric Power Co., Inc.
American Filtrona Corp.
American General Corp.
AmSouth Bancorp.

Angelica Corp.
Aquarion Co.
ARCO Chemical Co.
Arrow Financial Corp.
Arvin Industries, Inc.
ASARCO, Inc.
Ashland, Inc.
Ashland Coal, Inc.
Atlantic Energy, Inc.
Avon Products, Inc.
Ball Corp.
Bando McGlocklin Capital Corp.
Bank of Boston Corp.
Bank of Granite Corp.
Bank of New York Co., Inc.
Bank South Corp.
BankAmerica Corp.
Bankers First Corp.
Bankers Trust New York Corp.
Banknorth Group, Inc.
Barnes Group, Inc.
BayBanks, Inc.
BCE, Inc.
Beckman Instruments, Inc.
Bindley Western Industries, Inc.
Birmingham Steel Corp.
Black & Decker Corp.
Blount, Inc.
Boise Cascade Corp.
Boston Bancorp
Boston Edison Co.
Bowater, Inc.
British Airways PLC
Brunswick Corp.
Brush Wellman, Inc.
BSB Bancorp, Inc.
BT Financial Corp.

Cabot Corp.

Cadmus Communications Corp.

California Bancshares, Inc.

Callaway Golf Co.

Canadian Pacific Ltd.

Carpenter Technology Corp.

Cascade Natural Gas Corp.

Caterpillar, Inc.

Cedar Fair LP

Central Vermont Public Service Corp.

Champion International Corp.

Charter One Financial, Inc.

Chase Manhattan Corp.

Chemed Corp.

Chemical Banking Corp.

Chesapeake Corp.

Chittenden Corp.

Chrysler Corp.

Church & Dwight Co., Inc.

CILCORP, Inc.

Cincinnati Milacron, Inc.

CINergy Corp.

CIPSCO, Inc.

Cleveland-Cliffs, Inc.

Coca-Cola Bottling Co. Consolidated

Coca-Cola Enterprises, Inc.

Colonial BancGroup, Inc.

Colonial Gas Co.

Commerce Bancorp, Inc.

Commercial Intertech Corp.

Commonwealth Savings Bank

Community Bank System, Inc.

Connecticut Water Service, Inc.

Consolidated Papers, Inc.

Cooper Industries, Inc.

Countrywide Credit Industries, Inc.

CPI Corp.

Crestar Financial Corp.

Cummins Engine Co., Inc.

Dana Corp.

Dean Witter, Discover & Co.

Deere & Company

Delmarva Power & Light Co.

Delta Air Lines, Inc.

Delta Natural Gas Co., Inc.

Detroit Edison Co.

Dexter Corp.

Dresser Industries, Inc.

Duriron Co., Inc.

Eastern Enterprises

Eastman Chemical Company

Ecolab, Inc.

EG&G, Inc.

EnergyNorth, Inc.

Engelhard Corp.

Enron Corp.

Equitable Companies, Inc.

Equitable of Iowa Companies

Essex County Gas Company

Ethyl Corp.

F&M National Corp.

Federal-Mogul Corp.

Federal Paper Board Co., Inc.

Federal Realty Investment Trust

Ferro Corp.

FINA, Inc.

Financial Trust Corp.

First American Corp. (TN)

First Bank System, Inc.

First Chicago Corp.

First Citizens BancShares, Inc.

First Commerce Corp.

First Fidelity Bancorp.
First Interstate Bancorp
First Midwest Bancorp, Inc.
First Mississippi Corp.
First Northern Savings Bank
First of America Bank Corp.
Firstar Corp.
FirstMerit Corp.
Fleet Financial Group, Inc.
Fleming Companies, Inc.
Florida Public Utilities Co.
Flowers Industries, Inc.
Ford Motor Co.
Foster Wheeler Corp.
Fuller (H. B.) Co.
GATX Corp.
General Motors Corp.
General Public Utilities Corp.
General Signal Corp.
Georgia-Pacific Corp.
Goodrich (B. F.) Co.
Goodyear Tire & Rubber Co.
Gorman-Rupp Co.
Goulds Pumps, Inc.
Grace (W. R.) & Co.
Graco, Inc.
Guardsman Products, Inc.
Hanna (M. A.) Co.
Harleysville Group, Inc.
Harris Corp.
Hartford Steam Boiler Inspection & Insurance Co.
Hawaiian Electric Industries, Inc.
Heilig-Meyers Company
Hercules, Inc.
Houghton Mifflin Company
Houston Industries, Inc.

Huntington Bancshares, Inc.
Idaho Power Co.
Ingersoll-Rand Co.
Inland Steel Industries, Inc.
Interchange Financial Services Corp.
International Multifoods Corp.
ITT Corp.
IWC Resources Corp.
James River Corp.
Jefferson Bankshares, Inc.
Jostens, Inc.
Justin Industries, Inc.
K N Energy, Inc.
Kaman Corp.
Kansas City Power & Light Co.
Keithley Instruments, Inc.
Kellwood Company
Keystone Financial, Inc.
Keystone Heritage Group, Inc.
Keystone International, Inc.
Kmart Corp.
Knape & Vogt Manufacturing Company
Kysor Industrial Corp.
La-Z-Boy Chair Co.
Lance, Inc.
Lilly Industries, Inc.
Liz Claiborne, Inc.
Louisiana-Pacific Corp.
Lukens, Inc.
Mallinckrodt Group, Inc.
MAPCO, Inc.
Marsh Supermarkets, Inc.
MASSBANK Corp.
McKesson Corp.
Mead Corp.

Media General, Inc.

Meditrust

Medusa Corp.

Mellon Bank Corp.

Mercantile Bancorp., Inc.

Meridian Bancorp, Inc.

Meridian Diagnostics, Inc.

Merry Land & Investment Co., Inc.

Mid Am, Inc.

MidAmerican Energy Co.

Middlesex Water Co.

Midlantic Corp.

Minnesota Power & Light Co.

Mobile Gas Service Corp.

Modine Manufacturing Co.

Montana Power Co.

Nash-Finch Co.

National Health Investors, Inc.

Nationwide Health Properties, Inc.

Neiman-Marcus Group, Inc.

Nevada Power Co.

New England Electric System

New Plan Realty Trust

North Carolina Natural Gas Corp.

Northern Telecom Ltd.

Northrop Grumman Corp.

Ohio Casualty Corp.

Oklahoma Gas & Electric Co.

Old National Bancorp (IN)

Old Republic International Corp.

Olin Corp.

OM Group, Inc.

Oneok, Inc.

Orange & Rockland Utilities, Inc.

Outboard Marine Corp.

Owens & Minor, Inc.

Pacific Enterprises

Panhandle Eastern Corp.

Parker Hannifin Corp.

Pennzoil Co.

Peoples Energy Corp.

Perkin-Elmer Corp.

Petroleum Heat and Power Co., Inc.

Philadelphia Suburban Corp.

Pioneer Hi-Bred International, Inc.

Ply Gem Industries, Inc.

PMC Capital, Inc.

PNC Bank Corp.

Polaroid Corp.

Portland General Corp.

Potlatch Corp.

Potomac Electric Power Co.

Praxair, Inc.

Providian Corp.

Public Service Co. of North Carolina

Quaker State Corp.

Raymond Corp.

ReliaStar Financial Corp.

Reynolds & Reynolds Co.

Reynolds Metals Co.

RLI Corp.

Roanoke Electric Steel Corp.

Rouse Co.

Ryder System, Inc.

Rykoff-Sexton, Inc.

St. Paul Bancorp, Inc.

Salomon, Inc.

San Diego Gas & Electric Company

Santa Fe Pacific Pipeline Partners, LP

Seafield Capital Corp.

Sears, Roebuck & Co.

Selective Insurance Group, Inc.

Sierra Pacific Resources

Signet Banking Corp.

Simpson Industries, Inc.

Snap-on, Inc.

Southeastern Michigan Gas Enterprises

Southern California Water Co.

Southern New England Telecommunications Corp.

Southwestern Public Service Co.

Standard Federal Bank

Stanhome, Inc.

Stanley Works

Strawbridge & Clothier

Summit Bancorporation (NJ)

Supervalu, Inc.

TCF Financial Corp.

Telephone & Data Systems, Inc.

Temple-Inland, Inc.

Tenet Healthcare Corp.

Tenneco, Inc.

Thermo Remediation, Inc.

Times Mirror Company

Timken Co.

Total System Services, Inc.

Transamerica Corp.

True North Communications, Inc.

Tyco International Ltd.

UGI Corp.

UJB Financial Corp.

Union Bank

Union Camp Corp.

Union Carbide Corp.

Union Planters Corp.

United Bankshares, Inc.

United Carolina Bancshares Corp.

United Cities Gas Co.

United Dominion Realty Trust, Inc.

United Water Resources, Inc.

UNITIL Corp.

Universal Corp.

Universal Health Realty Income Trust

Unocal Corp.

UNUM Corp.

Upper Peninsula Energy Corp.

U.S. Bancorp

Valley National Bancorp (NJ)

Valley Resources, Inc.

Varian Associates, Inc.

Versa Technologies, Inc.

Vulcan Materials Co.

Washington Gas Light Co.

Washington Mutual, Inc.

Washington National Corp.

Weingarten Realty Investors

Wells Fargo & Co.

West (The) Company

Westamerica Bancorp

Western Resources, Inc.

Westinghouse Electric Corp.

Westvaco Corp.

Whitman Corp.

Witco Corp.

Worthington Industries, Inc.

Yankee Energy System, Inc.

York Financial Corp.

Zero Corp.

Zions Bancorporation

Zurn Industries, Inc.

Two Stars (**)

ADAC Laboratories

Allegheny Ludlum Corp.

Amcast Industrial Corp.
American Health Properties, Inc.
American Recreation Centers, Inc.
AmVestors Financial Corp.
Apache Corp.
ASR Investments Corp.
Baldwin Technology Company, Inc.
Bangor Hydro-Electric Co.
Bay View Capital Corp.
Berkshire Gas Co.
Berkshire Realty Company, Inc.
Bethlehem Steel Corp.
BMJ Financial Corp.
Boddie-Noell Properties
Bradley Real Estate, Inc.
Braintree Savings Bank
Brown Group, Inc.
Burnham Pacific Properties, Inc.
California Financial Holding
  Company
Capstead Mortgage Corp.
CBI Industries, Inc.
Centerior Energy Corp.
Central Hudson Gas & Electric
  Corp.
Central Maine Power Co.
Chesapeake Utilities Corp.
Chiquita Brands International, Inc.
CML Group, Inc.
CMS Energy Corp.
Columbia Gas System, Inc.
Columbus Realty Trust
Commonwealth Energy System
Consumers Water Co.
Copley Properties, Inc.
Cousins Properties, Inc.
Cyprus Amax Minerals Co.

D & N Financial Corp.
DeBartolo Realty Corp.
Duke Realty Investments, Inc.
E'Town Corp.
Eastern Co.
Eastern Utilities Associates
Elco Industries, Inc.
EMC Insurance Group, Inc.
Empire District Electric Co.
Enserch Corp.
Entergy Corp.
Evergreen Bancorp, Inc.
Fay's, Inc.
First Colony Corporation
First Federal Capital Corp.
First Financial Holdings, Inc.
Food Lion, Inc.
GenCorp, Inc.
General Housewares Corp.
Giddings & Lewis, Inc.
Great Western Financial Corp.
Green Mountain Power Corp.
Handleman Co.
Handy & Harman
Haverfield Corp.
Health & Retirement Properties
  Trust
Health Care REIT, Inc.
Hibernia Corp.
Homestake Mining Co.
HRE Properties
Huffy Corp.
IES Industries, Inc.
Illinova Corp.
Imo Industries, Inc.
Imperial Holly Corp.
Inco Ltd.

Insteel Industries, Inc.

Interstate Power Co.

IRT Property Co.

Jacobson Stores, Inc.

Kollmorgen Corp.

Kranzco Realty Trust

Kuhlman Corp.

Lafarge Corp.

Long Island Lighting Company

Louisiana Land & Exploration Company

LTC Properties, Inc.

Lyondell Petrochemical Co.

Magna Group, Inc.

Manitowoc Company, Inc.

Maytag Corp.

McDermott International, Inc.

Monmouth Real Estate Investment Corp.

Nashua Corp.

New York State Electric & Gas Corp.

Niagara Mohawk Power Corp.

NorAm Energy Corp.

North Fork Bancorporation, Inc.

Northeast Utilities Service Co.

NOVA Corporation

NUI Corp.

Occidental Petroleum Corp.

Ohio Edison Co.

Oneida Ltd.

Pacific Gas & Electric Co.

PaineWebber Group, Inc.

PECO Energy Co.

Pennsylvania Enterprises, Inc.

Phillips Petroleum Co.

Piccadilly Cafeterias, Inc.

Pinnacle West Capital Corp.

PMC Commercial Trust

PP&L Resources, Inc.

Presidential Realty Corp.

Providence Energy Corp.

Public Service Co. of Colorado

Public Service Enterprise Group, Inc.

Puget Sound Power & Light Co.

Quanex Corp.

Real Estate Investment Trust of CA

Rochester Gas & Electric Corp.

Rollins Environmental Services, Inc.

Savannah Foods & Industries, Inc.

SIFCO Industries, Inc.

Sizeler Property Investors, Inc.

Smith (A. O.) Corp.

Sonat, Inc.

Sotheby's Holdings, Inc.

South West Property Trust, Inc.

Southwest Gas Corp.

Southwest Water Co.

Southwestern Energy Co.

SPX Corp.

Standard Commercial Corp.

Standard Products Co.

Stone & Webster, Inc.

Stride Rite Corp.

Summit Properties, Inc.

Sun Co., Inc.

Sundstrand Corp.

Taubman Centers, Inc.

Texas Utilities Co.

Thomas Industries, Inc.

Thornburg Mortgage Asset Corp.

Tidewater, Inc.

TNP Enterprises, Inc.

Toro Co.

Total Petroleum (North America) Ltd.
TransCanada Pipelines Ltd.
Trinova Corp.
Twin Disc, Inc.
Unicom Corp.
United Illuminating Co.
USF&G Corp.
UST Corp.
USX Corp.—Marathon
USX Corp.—U.S. Steel Group
Walden Residential Properties, Inc.
Washington Energy Co.
Washington Water Power Co.
Westcoast Energy Inc.
Western Investment Real Estate Trust
WLR Foods, Inc.
Woolworth Corp.

One Star (*)

Amax Gold, Inc.
American Industrial Properties REIT
American Real Estate Partners, LP
Angeles Mortgage Investment Trust
Angeles Participating Mortgage Trust
Asset Investors Corp.
Bedford Property Investors, Inc.
Figgie International, Inc.
First Union Real Estate Investments
Mid-America Realty Investments
Morrison Knudsen Corp.
National-Standard Co.
RYMAC Mortgage Investment Corp.
Talley Industries, Inc.
Venture Stores, Inc.

Top-Rated DRIPs by Industry Groups

The following top-rated DRIPs are among the leaders in their industry groups:

Advertising

Interpublic Group of Companies, Inc.

Aerospace and Defense

Lockheed Martin Corp.
Raytheon Co.
Rockwell International Corp.
TRW, Inc.

Agribusiness

ConAgra, Inc.
Ralston—Ralston Purina Group

Apparel Manufacturers

Russell Corp.
VF Corp.

Appliances

Whirlpool Corp.

Auto Equipment

Bandag, Inc.
Briggs & Stratton Corp.
Eaton Corp.

Genuine Parts Co.

Pep Boys—Manny, Moe & Jack

Banking

Associated Banc-Corp.
Banc One Corp.
Bancorp Hawaii, Inc.
Barnett Banks, Inc.
Boatmen's Bancshares, Inc.
CCB Financial Corp.
Central Fidelity Banks, Inc.
Citicorp
Comerica, Inc.
Dauphin Deposit Corp.
Fifth Third Bancorp
First Michigan Bank Corp.
First Security Corp.
First Union Corp.
First Virginia Banks, Inc.
KeyCorp
Mark Twain Bancshares, Inc.
Marshall & Ilsley Corp.
Mercantile Bankshares Corp.
Morgan (J. P.) & Co., Inc.
National City Corp.
Norwest Corp.
Regions Financial Corp.
SouthTrust Corp.
Star Banc Corp.
State Street Boston Corp.
SunTrust Banks, Inc.
Synovus Financial Corp.
Wachovia Corp.
Wilmington Trust Co.

Brewing

Anheuser-Busch Cos., Inc.

Building Supplies

Armstrong World Industries, Inc.
PPG Industries, Inc.
RPM, Inc.
Sherwin-Williams Co.
Weyerhaueser Co.

Chemicals

Air Products & Chemicals, Inc.
Brady (W. H.) Co.
Crompton & Knowles Corp.
Dow Chemical
Du Pont (E. I.) de Nemours & Co.
Loctite Corp.
Lubrizol Corp.
MacDermid, Inc.
Monsanto Co.
Nalco Chemical Co.

Communications

Ameritech Corp.
AT&T Corp.
Bell Atlantic Corp.
BellSouth Corp.
Century Telephone Enterprises, Inc.
Cincinnati Bell, Inc.
COMSAT Corp.
Frontier Corp.
GTE Corp.
Lincoln Telecommunications Co.
NYNEX Corp.
Pacific Telesis Group
SBC Communications, Inc.
Scientific-Atlanta, Inc.
Sprint Corp.
U S West, Inc.

Computer Manufacturers/ Software

Computer Associates Int'l, Inc.
Diebold, Inc.
International Business Machines
  Corp.

Consumer Products

Clorox Co.
Colgate-Palmolive Co.
Duracell International, Inc.
Procter & Gamble Co.

Containers and Packaging

Bemis Co., Inc.
Clarcor, Inc.
Sonoco Products Co.

Cosmetics and Toiletries

Gillette Co.
Tambrands, Inc.

Discount and Variety

Home Depot, Inc.
Lowe's Companies, Inc.

Drug

Abbott Laboratories
American Home Products Corp.
Bristol-Myers Squibb Co.
Lilly (Eli) & Co.
Merck & Co., Inc.
Novo-Nordisk A/S
Pfizer, Inc.
Rhone-Poulenc Rorer, Inc.
Schering-Plough Corp.

Warner-Lambert Co.

Drug Chains

Rite Aid Corp.
Walgreen Co.

Electric Utilities

Allegheny Power System, Inc.
Baltimore Gas and Electric Co.
Black Hills Corp.
Carolina Power & Light Co.
Central & South West Corp.
Central Louisiana Electric Co., Inc.
Citizens Utilities Co.
Consolidated Edison Co. of New
  York
Dominion Resources, Inc.
DPL, Inc.
DQE
Duke Power Co.
Florida Progress Corp.
FPL Group, Inc.
IPALCO Enterprises, Inc.
KU Energy Corp.
LG&E Energy Corp.
Madison Gas & Electric Co.
MDU Resources Group, Inc.
NIPSCO Industries, Inc.
Northern States Power Co.
Northwestern Public Service Co.
Otter Tail Power Co.
PacifiCorp
St. Joseph Light & Power Co.
SCANA Corp.
SCEcorp
Southern Co.

Southern Indiana Gas & Electric Co.
TECO Energy, Inc.
Union Electric Co.
UtiliCorp United, Inc.
Wisconsin Energy Corp.
WPL Holdings, Inc.
WPS Resources Corp.

Electrical Equipment

Emerson Electric Co.
Federal Signal Corp.
Hubbell, Inc.
Thomas & Betts Corp.

Electronics, Components

AMP, Inc.
Avnet, Inc.
Intel Corp.
Motorola, Inc.
Pioneer-Standard Electronics, Inc.

Electronic Instruments

Texas Instruments, Inc.

Filter Products

Millipore Corp.
Pall Corp.

Financial Services/Broker

American Express Co.
Beneficial Corp.
Federal National Mortgage
  Association
Franklin Resources, Inc.
Household International, Inc.
Mercury Finance Company

Merrill Lynch & Co., Inc.
National Data Corp.
Schwab (Charles) Corp.

Food

Campbell Soup Co.
CPC International, Inc.
Dean Foods Co.
General Mills, Inc.
GoodMark Foods, Inc.
Grand Metropolitan PLC
Heinz (H. J.) Co.
Hershey Foods Corp.
Hormel Foods Corp.
International Flavors & Fragrances,
  Inc.
Kellogg Co.
McCormick & Co., Inc.
Nestle S.A.
Quaker Oats Co.
Sara Lee Corp.
Smucker (J. M.) Co.
Sysco Corp.
Wrigley (Wm.) Jr. Co.

Food Chain

Albertson's, Inc.
Giant Food, Inc.
Hannaford Brothers Co.
Universal Foods Corp.
Weis Markets, Inc.
Winn-Dixie Stores, Inc.

Health Care

Bard (C. R.) Inc.
Bausch & Lomb, Inc.

Baxter International, Inc.
Becton, Dickinson and Company
Johnson & Johnson
Medtronic, Inc.
Omnicare, Inc.

Hotel

Marriott International

Household Furnishings

Lancaster Colony Corp.
Newell Co.
Rubbermaid, Inc.

Housing

Clayton Homes, Inc.

Industrial Components

Illinois Tool Works, Inc.
Kennametal, Inc.
Pentair, Inc.
Premier Industrial Corp.

Industrial Machinery

Crane Co.
Donaldson Co., Inc.
Fluor Corp.

Life Insurance

AFLAC, Inc.
American Heritage Life Investment
  Corp.
Aon Corp.
CIGNA Corp.
Jefferson-Pilot Corp.
Lincoln National Corp.

Torchmark Corp.
USLIFE Corp.

Liquor

Brown-Forman Corp.

Metal and Mining

Phelps Dodge Corp.

Multi-industry

AlliedSignal, Inc.
Carlisle Companies, Inc.
Corning, Inc.
Dial Corp.
General Electric Co.
Hanson PLC
Harcourt General, Inc.
Harley-Davidson, Inc.
Harsco Corp.
Honeywell, Inc.
Johnson Controls, Inc.
Minnesota Mining &
  Manufacturing Co.
Morton International, Inc.
National Service Industries, Inc.
Nordson Corp.
Textron, Inc.

Natural Gas

Atlanta Gas Light Co.
Atmos Energy Corp.
Bay State Gas Co.
Brooklyn Union Gas Co.
Connecticut Energy Corp.
Connecticut Natural Gas Corp.
Consolidated Natural Gas Co.

Energen Corp.
Equitable Resources, Inc.
Indiana Energy, Inc.
Laclede Gas Co.
MCN Corp.
National Fuel Gas Co.
New Jersey Resources Corp.
NICOR, Inc.
Northwest Natural Gas Co.
Piedmont Natural Gas Co.
Questar Corp.
South Jersey Industries, Inc.
WICOR, Inc.

Office Supplies

American Business Products, Inc.
Avery Dennison Corp.
Moore Corp.
Pitney Bowes, Inc.

Oil/Oil Services

Amoco Corp.
Atlantic Richfield Co.
Baker Hughes, Inc.
British Petroleum Co. PLC
Chevron Corp.
Exxon Corp.
Imperial Oil Ltd.
Kerr-McGee Corp.
Mobil Corp.
Texaco, Inc.

Paper

Alco Standard Corp.
International Paper Co.
Kimberly-Clark Corp.

Photo Equipment

Eastman Kodak Co.

Pollution Control

Browning-Ferris Industries, Inc.
WMX Technologies, Inc.

Printing

American Greetings Corp.
Banta Corp.
Donnelley (R. R.) & Sons Co.
Harland (John H.) Co.

Property Liability

Chubb Corp.
Cincinnati Financial Corp.
General Re Corp.
Marsh & McLennan Companies, Inc.
St. Paul Companies, Inc.

Publishing

Dow Jones & Co., Inc.
Gannett Co., Inc.
Knight-Ridder, Inc.
McGraw-Hill Cos., Inc.
New York Times Co.
Time Warner, Inc.
Tribune Company
Xerox Corp.

Rails

Conrail, Inc.
CSX Corp.
Norfolk Southern Corp.
Union Pacific Corp.

Real Estate Investment Trust

United Mobile Homes, Inc.
Washington Real Estate Investment
  Trust

Restaurants

Bob Evans Farms, Inc.
Cracker Barrel Old Country Store,
  Inc.
Luby's Cafeterias, Inc.
McDonald's Corp.
Wendy's International, Inc.

Retail Department Stores

Dayton Hudson Corp.
Limited (The) Inc.
May Department Stores Company
Penney (J. C.) Co., Inc.

Services

Block (H & R), Inc.
Equifax, Inc.
Manpower, Inc.
Paychex, Inc.
Rollins, Inc.
Safety-Kleen Corp.

ServiceMaster Limited Partnership

Soft Drink

Coca-Cola Company
PepsiCo, Inc.

Steel

Nucor Corp.

Tobacco

American Brands, Inc.
Philip Morris Companies, Inc.
UST, Inc.

Toys

Mattel, Inc.

Trucking

Arnold Industries, Inc.
Roadway Services, Inc.
Rollins Truck Leasing Corp.

Water Utilities

American Water Works Co., Inc.
California Water Service Co.

Appendix C

Closed-End Funds with DRIPs

I'm sure most of you are familiar with mutual funds. These are investment companies that take in funds from many individuals, commingle the money, and buy a portfolio of stocks which they manage. There are two types of mutual funds, open-end and closed-end funds.

Open-end mutual funds have surged in popularity in the last two decades. These funds provide a way for investors with limited dollars—many mutual funds have minimum investments of just $100 to $1000—to have portfolio diversification as well as professional money management. Some of the big open-end fund families are Fidelity, Vanguard, T. Rowe Price, Scudder, Dreyfus, and Twentieth Century.

Closed-end funds are similar to open-end funds in that the funds permit investment in a basket of stocks selected and managed by an investment company. However, there are a few major differences. Open-end funds continually sell new shares to the public and redeem shares at the fund's net asset value—the market value of the firm's portfolio of stocks minus short-term liabilities. Closed-end funds, however, sell only a certain number of shares at the initial public offering, just like a stock. Once the shares are sold, the fund is "closed," and new money is not accepted.

Another major difference is that closed-end funds trade on the stock exchanges, while open-end funds do not. Because closed-end funds are publicly traded, their prices are set by supply and demand among various investors, just like common stocks. Thus, unlike open-end funds which always redeem shares at the net asset value, it is not unusual to see a closed-end mutual fund trade above or below its net asset value, and sometimes these premiums or discounts are quite large.

Analysts and academicians have explored several possible explanations for the disparity between the trading price of a closed-end fund and its net asset value. One reason is that closed-end funds have large potential tax liabilities in the form of unrealized capital gains. Therefore, this tax liability is factored into the price of the closed-end fund and thus reduces the price. Other reasons given for the disparity between a closed-end fund's price and net asset value include the potential pricing problems for fund investments that may not trade frequently (and where current prices to establish net asset value are, at best, estimates of the true value of the investment); poor diversification, as in the case of closed-end funds that invest in the stocks of a single country; and the lack of flexibility on the part of the managers because of the fixed capitalization of closed-end funds.

Regardless of the reasons, the fact is that in many instances, closed-end funds allow investors to buy a basket of stocks more cheaply than if the stocks in that basket were purchased separately.

Great, you're thinking, but what does all this have to do with DRIPs? Well, many closed-end funds offer DRIPs for their shareholders, and investing in a closed-end fund through a DRIP presents some interesting possibilities.

First, if the closed-end fund is trading at a discount to net asset value, reinvesting your dividends received from the stocks held in the closed-end fund, in effect, lets you purchase a basket of stocks at a discount. Also, keep in mind that those dividends are being earned on the full value of the assets of the fund.

For example, let's say you purchase a closed-end fund with a net asset value of $35 per share that is trading for $25 per share—a 28 percent discount. (Discounts, especially during bear markets, may reach or even exceed this level.) Now, the dividends on the investments in the fund come to a total of $2 per share, giving the fund a yield of 5.7 percent ($2 in dividends divided by the net asset value of $35). But remember, you only paid $25 per share for this basket of stocks that are worth $35 per share. Thus, the yield on your investment is even higher—8 percent.

Now, you reinvest the dividend via the fund's DRIP. That $2 per share in dividends is invested to purchase additional shares of the closed-end fund at a discount to the net asset value. Now, over time the closed-end fund closes the gap to a price which is a 10 percent discount to the net asset value ($31.50). You now have a gain of 26 percent on all shares purchased at $25 per share.

In addition to reinvested dividends, several closed-end funds permit optional cash payments (OCPs). If the fund is trading at a discount, these voluntary funds will, in some cases, be invested at a price that is lower than the net asset value of the fund.

How do you know if a closed-end fund is trading at discount or premium? Such information is given regularly in *The Wall Street Journal* and *Barron's*.

What are some factors to consider when investing in a closed-end fund?

- Merely because a closed-end fund is trading at a discount doesn't make it a good investment. It is important to evaluate if the fund meets your investment objective, abides by an investment strategy that makes sense to you, and fits in with the rest of your portfolio. This latter factor is crucial. For example, if your only investment is going to be a closed-end fund, it probably isn't a good idea to buy a single-country, closed-end fund.

- Never buy a closed-end fund at the initial public offering. Most closed-end funds perform poorly immediately following the initial public offering. Of course, there are exceptions. Still, you'll probably dodge a bullet or two by waiting and taking a fresh look at the fund six months or so after it is issued.

- Avoid investing in closed-end funds that are trading at premiums to their net asset values. Remember, since closed-end funds trade on the exchanges, their prices are governed by supply and demand. If a particular sector gets hot and investors flock to the group, these funds can trade at steep premiums. However, you wouldn't pay $25 for a $20 shirt. Why should you pay $25 per share for a basket of stocks worth $20 per share?

The following closed-end funds offer DRIPs. The closed-end funds which permit optional cash payments (OCPs) are highlighted. Investors should obtain prospectuses on plans of interest before investing.

ACM Government Income Fund,
  Inc. (NYSE:ACG)
(800) 426-5523
OCP: Yes

ACM Government Opportunity
  Fund, Inc. (NYSE:AOF)
(800) 331-1710
OCP: No

ACM Government Securities Fund,
Inc. (NYSE:GSF)
(800) 426-5523
OCP: Yes

ACM Government Spectrum Fund,
Inc. (NYSE:SI)
(800) 426-5523
OCP: Yes

Adams Express Co. (NYSE:ADX)
(800) 432-8224
OCP: Yes

Allied Capital Corp.
(NASDAQ:ALLC)
Allied Capital Corp. II
(NASDAQ:ALII)
(800) 937-5449
OCP: No

Allmon (Charles) Trust, Inc.
(NYSE:GSO)
(800) 542-3863
OCP: Yes

ASA Limited (NYSE:ASA)
(800) 446-2617
OCP: Yes

Austria Fund (The) (NYSE:OST)
(800) 426-5523
OCP: Yes

Baker, Fentress & Co. (NYSE:BKF)
(312) 461-6834
OCP: Yes

Bancroft Convertible Fund, Inc.
(ASE:BCV)
(201) 631-1177
OCP: Yes

Blue Chip Value Fund (NYSE:BLU)
(800) 288-9541
OCP: Yes

Brazil Fund, Inc. (NYSE:BZF)
(800) 225-2470
OCP: Yes

Capital Southwest Corp.
(NASDAQ:CSWC)
(214) 233-8242
OCP: Yes

Castle Convertible Fund, Inc.
(ASE:CVF)
(212) 806-8800
OCP: No

Chile Fund (The) (NYSE:CH)
(800) 852-4750
OCP: Yes

Circle Income Shares, Inc.
(NASDAQ:CINS)
(317) 321-8180
OCP: No

CNA Income Shares, Inc.
(NYSE:CNN)
(800) 432-8224
OCP: Yes

Colonial High Income Municipal
Trust (NYSE:CXE)
(800) 442-2001
OCP: No

Colonial Investment Grade
Municipal Trust (NYSE:CXH)
(800) 442-2001
OCP: No

Current Income Shares, Inc.
(NYSE:CUR)
(800) 554-3406
OCP: Yes

Dean Witter Government Income
Trust (NYSE:GVT)
(800) 869-3863
OCP: No

Dreyfus Strategic Municipal Bond
Fund, Inc. (NYSE:DSM)
(800) 331-1710
OCP: No

Dreyfus Strategic Municipals, Inc.
(NYSE:LEO)
(800) 432-8224
OCP: Yes

Duff & Phelps Selected Utilities
(NYSE:DNP)
(800) 432-8224
OCP: Yes

Ellsworth Convertible Growth &
Income Fund (ASE:ECF)
(201) 631-1177
OCP: Yes

Excelsior Income Shares, Inc.
(NYSE:EIS)
(212) 852-3732, (800) 257-2356
OCP: No

First Australia Prime Income Fund,
Inc. (ASE:FAX)
(800) 451-6788
OCP: Yes

First Financial Fund, Inc. (NYSE:FF)
(800) 451-6788
OCP: No

Fort Dearborn Income Securities,
Inc. (NYSE:FTD)
(800) 446-2617
OCP: Yes

Fortis Securities, Inc. (NYSE:FOR)
(800) 800-2638
OCP: No

Gabelli Equity Trust, Inc.
(NYSE:GAB)
(914) 921-5070, (800) 426-5523
OCP: Yes

General American Investors Co.,
Inc. (NYSE:GAM)
(212) 916-8416
OCP: No

Germany Fund, Inc. (NYSE:GER)
(800) 437-6269
OCP: No

Germany (New) Fund, Inc. (The)
(NYSE:GF)
(212) 474-7052, (800) 342-8756
OCP: No

Hancock (John) Investors Trust
(NYSE:JHI)
(800) 426-5523
OCP: No

Hatteras Income Securities, Inc.
(NYSE:HAT)
(800) 851-9677
OCP: No

High Income Advantage Trust
(NYSE:YLD)
(800) 869-3863
OCP: No

INA Investment Securities, Inc.
(NYSE:IIS)
(800) 426-5523
OCP: No

India Fund (The), Inc. (NYSE:IFN)
(800) 421-4777
OCP: Yes

InterCapital Income Securities, Inc.
(NYSE:ICB)
(800) 869-3863
OCP: No

Italy Fund, Inc. (The) (NYSE:ITA)
(800) 331-1710
OCP: Yes

Kleinwort Benson Australian
Income Fund, Inc. (NYSE:KBA)
(800) 442-2001, (800) 237-4218
OCP: Yes

Korea Fund, Inc. (NYSE:KF)
(800) 451-6788
OCP: Yes

Liberty All-Star Equity Fund
(NYSE:USA)
(800) 542-3863
OCP: Yes

Lincoln National Convertible
Securities (NYSE:LNV)
(800) 442-2001
OCP: Yes

Lincoln National Income Fund
(NYSE:LND)
(800) 442-2001
OCP: Yes

Malaysia Fund, Inc. (NYSE:MF)
(800) 442-2001
OCP: Yes

MassMutual Corporate Investors
(NYSE:MCI)
(800) 647-7374
OCP: Yes

MassMutual Participation Investors
(NYSE:MPV)
(800) 647-7374
OCP: Yes

Mentor Income Fund, Inc.
(NYSE:MRF)
(800) 825-5353
OCP: No

Mexico Fund, Inc. (NYSE:MXF)
(212) 936-5100
OCP: No

MFS Multimarket Income Trust
(NYSE:MMT)
(800) 637-2304
OCP: Yes

MFS Municipal Income Trust
(NYSE:MFM)
(800) 637-2304
OCP: Yes

Montgomery Street Income
Securities, Inc. (NYSE:MTS)
(800) 442-2001
OCP: Yes

Morgan Grenfell Smallcap Fund,
Inc. (NYSE:MGC)
(212) 230-2600
OCP: No

New America High Income Fund,
Inc. (NYSE:HYB)
(800) 426-5523
OCP: Yes

Oppenheimer Multi-Sector Income
Trust (NYSE:OMS)
(800) 647-7374
OCP: Yes

Petroleum & Resources Corp.
(NYSE:PEO)
(410) 752-5900
OCP: Yes

Portugal Fund (The) (NYSE:PGF)
(800) 852-4750
OCP: Yes

Salomon Brothers Fund, Inc.
(NYSE:SBF)
(800) 432-8224
OCP: Yes

Scudder New Asia Fund, Inc.
(NYSE:SAF)
(800) 426-5523
OCP: Yes

Scudder New Europe Fund, Inc.
(NYSE:NEF)
(800) 442-2001
OCP: Yes

Seligman Quality Municipal Fund
(NYSE:SQF)
Seligman Select Municipal Fund
(NYSE:SEL)
(800) 221-2450
OCP: No

Source Capital, Inc. (NYSE:SOR)
(800) 851-9677
OCP: Yes

Spain Fund (The) (NYSE:SNF)
(800) 426-5523
OCP: Yes

Taiwan Fund, Inc. (NYSE:TWN)
(800) 426-5523
OCP: Yes

TCW Convertible Securities Fund,
Inc. (NYSE:CVT)
(800) 432-8224
OCP: No

Templeton Global Income Fund,
Inc. (NYSE:GIM)
(813) 823-8712
OCP: Yes

Thai Fund, Inc. (NYSE:TTF)
(800) 442-2001
OCP: Yes

Transamerica Income Shares
 (NYSE:TAI)
(800) 288-9541
OCP: Yes

Tri-Continental Corp. (NYSE:TY)
(800) 874-1092
OCP: Yes

USLIFE Income Fund, Inc.
 (NYSE:UIF)
(800) 851-9677
OCP: Yes

Van Kampen Merritt Municipal
 Income Trust (NYSE:VMT)
(800) 341-2929
OCP: No

Worldwide Value Fund, Inc.
 (NYSE:VLU)
(800) 577-8589
OCP: Yes

Zweig Fund, Inc. (NYSE:ZF)
(800) 432-8224
OCP: Yes

Zweig Total Return Fund, Inc.
 (NYSE:ZTR)
(800) 331-1710
OCP: No

Appendix D
DRIP Record Book

Company Name	$ Investment W/OCP	$ Investment W/Rein. Div.	Date	Purchase Price	Shares	Fees	Date Sold	Selling Price	Capital Gain/Loss

Bibliography

Currier, Chet, and Smyth, David, *No Cost/Low Cost Investing*, Franklin Watts, New York, 1987.

Dreman, David, "Crisis Investing," *Forbes*, October 22, 1990, p. 386.

Evergreen Enterprises, Laurel, MD, *Directory of Companies Offering Dividend Reinvestment Plans*, 1994.

Institute of Econometric Research, *Market Logic* newsletter, pp. 6–7, October 12, 1990.

Scholes, Myron S., and Wolfson, Mark A., "Decentralized Investment Banking: The Case of Discount Dividend-Reinvestment and Stock-Purchase Plans," *Journal of Financial Economics*, pp. 7–35, 1989.

Standard & Poor's Directory of Dividend Reinvestment Plans, 1995 Edition, McGraw-Hill, New York.

Thompson, Rex, "The Information Content of Discounts and Premiums on Closed-End Fund Shares," *Journal of Financial Economics*, pp. 151–186, 1978.

(Certain statistics courtesy of Ibbotson Associates and Lipper Analytical Services, Inc.)

Index

414   Index

419

About the Author

Charles B. Carlson has been providing profitable investment advice to individual investors for more than a decade. He is the editor of the well-respected *DRIP Investor*, a newsletter devoted exclusively to dividend reinvestment plans (DRIPs). Mr. Carlson is also the market strategist of *Dow Theory Forecasts*, one of the nation's oldest and most widely read newsletters for individual investors. Mr. Carlson, who is a Chartered Financial Analyst (CFA) and holds an MBA degree from the University of Chicago, is a frequent guest expert on numerous radio and television programs such as *The Today Show*. His work has also been quoted and recommended in *Business Week, Money, The New York Times, USA Today, The Washington Post, Kiplinger's Magazine*, and hundreds of other publications nationwide. Mr. Carlson is also the author of *No-Load Stocks* and *Free Lunch on Wall Street*, both published by McGraw-Hill.

Your Monthly Guide To Buying Stocks Without A Broker

DRIP Investor covers all aspects of no-load stocks and dividend reinvestment plans (DRIPs) — how to buy stocks without a broker, how to buy stocks at a discount, and how to buy blue-chips on the "installment plan" for as little as $10 a month.

This authoritative monthly service is written by Charles Carlson, CFA, author of *No-Load Stocks*, *Free Lunch on Wall Street*, *The 60 Second Investor*, the best-selling *Buying Stocks Without A Broker* and market strategist for the highly respected *Dow Theory Forecasts*. As a reader of *Buying Stocks Without A Broker*, you may receive the Charter Rate of only $59 for a full year — a 25% savings. <u>Money-back guarantee.</u> You may cancel any time for a pro rata refund.

With your subscription you will receive a *DRIP Investor* custom 3-ring storage binder plus your FREE 32-page DRIP Starter Kit, a step-by-step blueprint to success in dividend reinvestment plans.

To take advantage of this generous offer, fill out the coupon below and mail today.

DETACH HERE

- -

DRIP *Investor* Charter Rate Offer

❑ **YES,** start my subscription to *DRIP Investor* immediately at the Charter Rate of $59 for one year, a $20 savings. I may cancel any time for a pro rata refund.

Payment Method
❑ Check or money order
❑ Please charge my ❑ VISA ❑ MC ❑ American Express

_ _ _ _ - _ _ _ _ - _ _ _ _ - _ _ _ _

Name (Please Print)	Credit Card Number
Address	Expiration Date
City State Zip	Signature

❑ **MAYBE.** Please send two pre-subscription issues for my inspection. Then I'll decide later whether or not to subscribe. Mail today to:

BSW

DRIP *Investor* • 7412 Calumet Ave., Ste. 200 • Hammond, IN 46324-2692

Not valid until accepted by DRIP Investor, Hammond, Indiana